AF361463

Brilliant Modernism

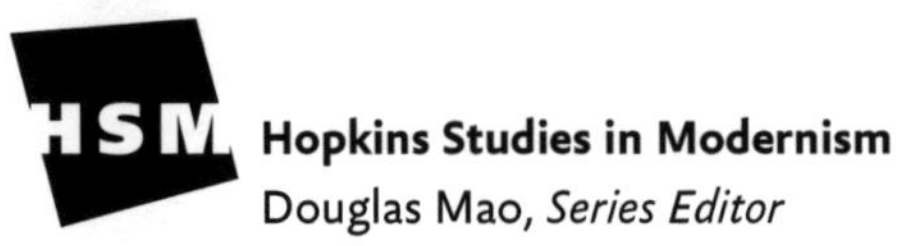

Hopkins Studies in Modernism

Douglas Mao, *Series Editor*

Brilliant Modernism

Cultures of Light and
Modernist Poetry

Nicoletta Asciuto

Johns Hopkins University Press
Baltimore

Johns Hopkins University Press
2715 North Charles Street
Baltimore, Maryland 21218
www.press.jhu.edu

Library of Congress Cataloging-in-Publication Data

Names: Asciuto, Nicoletta, author.
Title: Brilliant modernism : cultures of light and modernist poetry /
    Nicoletta Asciuto.
Description: Baltimore : Johns Hopkins University Press, 2025. |
    Series: Hopkins studies in modernism | Includes bibliographical
    references and index.
Identifiers: LCCN 2024026578 | ISBN 9781421450629 (hardcover) |
    ISBN 9781421450636 (paperback) | ISBN 9781421450643 (ebook)
Subjects: LCSH: Modernism (Literature) | Poetry, Modern—20th
    Century—History and criticism. | Electric lighting—Influence. |
    LCGFT: Literary criticism.
Classification: LCC PN56.M54 A75 2024 | DDC 809.1/04—dc23/
    eng/20240723
LC record available at https://lccn.loc.gov/2024026578

A catalog record for this book is available from the British Library.

*Special discounts are available for bulk purchases of this book.
For more information, please contact Special Sales at
specialsales@jh.edu.*

To
Gašper and Leone,
also lovers of lights

Contents

Brilliant Modernism

Introduction

Modernist Brilliance, Brilliant Modernism

Here is our poetry, for we have pulled down the stars to
our will.

Ezra Pound, "PATRIA MIA" (1912)[1]

London, the late 1920s. In his studio, an up-and-coming photographer stages
the transformation of a young woman into a bright star. Her costume and
the scenery certainly contribute, in part, to this metamorphosis. But what
captures the photographer's vision is neither the star-shaped pins adorning
her hair *à la mode du jour* nor the odd sparkly staff she is made to hold during
the sitting, which she may have agreed awkwardly to do. It is neither her
vaguely enigmatic expression nor the clouds of cellophane she sits amid,
which give her body an evanescent glow. It is, rather, the dazzlingly power-
ful thousand-watt light bulb, placed behind the young woman's face, that
transforms her into a living star and the embodiment of the modern age.[2]
This is the photographer's touch of genius, the sine qua non of his compo-
sition. The electric light breaks into the image, marking out the contours of
the young woman's face in a masterful feat of backlighting. But the more we
look at the photograph, the more our eyes are drawn to the light. We lose
sight of the woman's body starkly contrasted against the white-hot back-
ground. We can only see the light; we can only see the woman *as* light. It is
the electric light, and not her star-shaped pins, that ultimately morphs her
into modern starlight.

This sparkling young woman is Nancy Beaton, sister of British photogra-
pher Cecil Beaton, who loved to photograph his sisters in extravagant cre-
ations he would craft especially for them.[3] The famous shot is titled *Miss
Nancy Beaton as a Shooting Star* (1929; fig. I.1). It is well known that Beaton's
indoor and studio portraits of women frequently featured such dramatic

Fig. I.1. Cecil Beaton, *Miss Nancy Beaton as a Shooting Star*, 1929. Gelatin silver print mounted on card, 49 × 38.8 cm (19 × 15 in.). Cecil Beaton Archive. Digital image © Condé Nast.

black-and-white contrasts. Less attention is paid to the fact that this crucial element of his style depended on his skillful and daring use of artificial light.

Early in his career, Beaton mastered the use of electricity to illuminate his subjects, giving new expression to their bodies.[4] Such emblematic images of the Bright Young Things as *Baba Beaton as "Heloise" in Great Lovers*

Pageant (1927), *Anna May Wong* (1929), or *The Silver Soap Suds* (1930) exemplify an explosive, dazzling artistic use of electric light—a manufactured brilliance verging on a mannerism.[5] In *The Book of Beauty* (1930), he describes observing his sisters under different lights: "I see new unsuspected qualities in Baba as she sits against the lamp or by the light of the fire, and surreptitiously from the corner of my eye I notice Nancy looking quite different in a luminous effect of reflected light at the theatre."[6] Baba and Nancy are not empty canvases painted by light—what Beaton sees is how their bodies, their features and idiosyncrasies, change (for the better!) when exposed to different lights. His early experimental photographs burst so much with electrical brilliance that one is left wondering what the artist intended the subject of these photographs to be: the rich glow of these charming women or that sensation of the age, electric light? Beaton was a practitioner of "the art of artifice," which allowed him to transform others, as well as himself, into new visions, and modern artifice was best expressed through electric light.[7]

As a modern photographer, Beaton understood the larger implications of electric light in art as well as society. His use of electric light is not purely pragmatic, as a way to enhance the beauty of his subjects, nor is his application of electric light limited to this elite group of young socialites, the so-called Bright Young Things. His portrayal of his sister as a sidereal figure draws liberally on the time-honored stereotype of the woman as a beautiful star, but the electrified glow erupting behind her head points to a different conception of femininity. In her shooting-star costume, Nancy is not simply a beautiful young woman with star-shaped hairpins; she holds her luminous staff as a modern female Prometheus bringing fire to earth—though in her case, it is starlight she showers over the earth. By the late 1920s, at the time this photograph was taken, the artificially illuminated skyline had already replaced the antiquated natural lights of the sky at night. Quite literally, electricity had plucked down the starry sky and offered it to humans to maneuver and control. How do we begin, then, to understand the exact purpose of electric light in representations of femininity such as Beaton's photograph? What different story does it tell us not just about old and new lights, but about early twentieth-century representations of gender and of the self?

To understand this photograph of Nancy-as-an-electrical-star is to witness an artist coming to terms with societal transitions to new mores, new understandings of gender, and new aesthetics. The implementation at the turn of the twentieth century of electric light in the various layers of every-day life, and its superimposition onto other sources of light, both natural (moon, stars) and artificial (candles, gaslight, arc lamps), disrupted bound-aries of time and place, transforming the night into a new environment that people at the time could barely recognize. This technological disruption actively *shaped* modern life, not only producing an altered atmosphere, a difference in night visibility, and an improved provision of light in most places but bringing about transformations in human existence. Hence *Shooting Star* raises questions that are central to this book. To what extent did early twentieth-century cultures of light enable and promote transforma-tions in modern society, especially shifts in gender roles and representation? How did modern poets and artists register, influence, and amplify such changes? What happens in the process to the stars and especially to the moon, queen of the night sky, poetic muse, and age-old symbol of feminin-ity? What might knowledge of a world lit up by competing technologies of light tell us about the formation of modernist aesthetics?

The lights punctuating the early twentieth-century night meant some-thing specific to the people of the period. Writers—and poets in particular—in the folds of modernism and the avant-gardes were particularly suscepti-ble to these changes. The intense scientific scrutiny of the moon carried out at the end of the nineteenth century, along with the dimming of its bril-liance by electric lights, spurred modernist poets to produce works that transformed the cultural and aesthetic value of the moon. For young poets honing modern verse, the moon was no longer a congenial poetic muse; it became instead an irrelevant antique. Because this book focuses on the early days of electrification, it is concerned not only with electrical brilliance but with the different modes of brilliance available. It untangles the intricate network of symbolic codes associated with the panoply of lights that illumi-nated the early twentieth-century night, and assesses their impact on mod-ernist poetry. This synergy of old and new light forms, old and new visions of gender, old and new aesthetics, is at the heart of the work of the group of poets and artists I call Brilliant Modernists. In this book, I focus our atten-tion onto early twentieth-century cultural meanings of light and illumina-tion, and their implications for modernist poetry as a self-referential and programmatic art. In so doing, I single out a number of individual poets and artists, as well as larger configurations of authors, who harnessed lived ex-periences of the changing lightscape to modulate their own concerns about poetry, art, and the newly altered society around them. To track this history of changing lights at the turn of the twentieth century, we must first understand something of modernism's relationship to its recent past. No story of modernism can begin without tapping deep into its nineteenth-century roots, and this is exactly where we begin.

Light of Change

On the dark—and quite possibly stormy—night between October 21 and 22, 1879, artificial light changed forever. Historians of illumination technologies concur: the mythical evening when Thomas Alva Edison and his team made their first successful experiment with incandescent electricity is the watershed moment in the global history of light.[8] This date is undoubtedly useful in pinpointing the juncture at which electric light began to be an important commodity and consequently the most widespread form of artificial illumination. But it is also the turning point at which people in the West started to understand, consume, and appreciate artificial illumination and the urban nightscape in radically new ways. A central scene in the recent film on the early electric-light trade, *The Current War* (2017), suggestively reimagines this moment, with Benedict Cumberbatch as Edison appearing in a sea of naked pear-shaped light bulbs, all lighting up at once.

Up to this point in history, lighting had always been linked to fire: think candles, torches, oil lanterns, and even gaslight, which also functioned as an effective source of heating and looked much like actual fire. Illumination technologies belonged less to the conceptual realm of the artificial and much more to that of the natural. Now, with the flipping of a switch, it became possible instantly to light up a whole city with thousands of light bulbs in one go. This simple act erased the gradual illumination of cities (think of the lamplighter, whose strenuous work every night was no longer needed) and consequently flattened the passing of time. Before incandescent electricity, arc lights had been changing the outlook of cities at night and changed perceptions of illumination. Based on the exchange of carbon electrodes, arc lighting would generate a strong arc of light of a power comparable to some two thousand candles.[9] It was the most common early form of electrical illumination in urban and large public spaces in the last decades of the nineteenth century, but it did not enjoy lasting glory owing to its perceived negative effect on people and to its light being too ghastly, too noisy, and ultimately unreliable.[10] The new incandescent electric light, by contrast, with its lack of heat and noise, its new forms of glass and wires, and its unnaturally intense brightness, precipitated novel conceptions of artificial lighting, transforming its meaning for good.

Changes in sources of light bring with them changes in cultural practice, attitude, and meaning.[11] While the physical act of lighting a candle in 1900 may seem fundamentally the same as it does today, a thick description of both acts reveals a world of difference.[12] Today, in the Global North especially, candles endure in limited contexts, on graves and birthday cakes, in churches, at Christmas, for Diwali, as companions to Valentine's Day dinners, and in contemporary cultures of self-care. It is in these moments and their web of social norms and symbolic codes that we can grasp the contemporary meanings of a candle and candlelight.[13] As a result of technological change, lighting a candle, observing the moon, or flipping an electric switch are all cultural acts that have taken on different significance over time. While a particular culture of light cannot be reduced to a material change in artificial means, as this book shows, the new shapes and forms of light fundamentally shaped modern society and modernist culture.

Today it is easy to assume that a brighter world is a safer world: one in which you can walk and drive with ease. But a more brilliantly lit world is not a better one by default. At the same time that we find the safety and convenience of modern illumination hard to relinquish, we are increasingly aware of the existence and consequences of light pollution. At the end of the 1870s, when the intensity of electricity began to change the appearance of the urban night, electricity's brightness brought about concerns and preoccupations of a new order. A song by acclaimed music hall and pantomime authors Frank W. Green and Alfred Lee, entitled "The New Electric Light" (1879), fastidiously enumerates the things that electricity is now able to show at night.[14] In one of the stanzas, we read:

> 'Twill show who calls when we are out and then oh! fearful sell,
> 'Twill show whenever we go out, where we make calls as well.
> 'Twill let us know who are our friends and give us clear insight,
> To all that's right and all that's wrong will this electric light.[15]

A glowingly illuminated world meant less privacy and secrecy and increased opportunity for surveillance and control.[16] Caledoniensis, the mysterious author of the satirical pamphlet *Gas and the Electric Light* (simultaneously published in Edinburgh, London, and Dublin in 1879), agreed that electric light brought "into view much that requires to be hidden; thrusting back, by contrast, that which should necessarily be prominent; and, placing in front what were better invisible, for all practical and utile purposes."[17] But a world in which we can better look at one another and at our surroundings is also one that invites a new sense of introspection, an activity embraced by many of the Brilliant Modernists of this book. After all, a new sense of seeing demands a new sense of looking and a new sense of searching. Even though, as the song says, it is the electric light that shows so conspicuously "all that's right and all that's wrong," it was effectively the coexistence of numerous lights of varying intensity that at the turn of the century initiated an obsessive compulsion to surveil others as well as oneself.

What the modern lightscape might have meant to modernist authors was determined by the various sources of illumination that coexisted, and even competed, with one another. At the turn of the century, most Europeans and North Americans were competent users of a number of different lighting technologies, to which they were exposed on a daily basis. As Chris Otter reminds us,

> New technologies never fully or immediately replace old ones: there is never a point of rupture dividing, say, the "age of electricity" from "the age of gas" or "the age of tallow." Instead, technologies, as they become embedded and integrated into everyday practice, become superimposed over, and slightly displace, older artifacts. Illumination is a splendid illustration of this process. The nineteenth century is the history, not of the rise of electricity or even of gaslight, but of the proliferation, concatenation, and spatial juxtaposition of multiple light forms. In 1900, one might routinely have encountered electric, gas, and oil lamps as well as candles over the course of a day.[18]

What Otter says of the nineteenth century holds true today for our own technological transitions in the new millennium. Technologies, even those we deem life-changing or groundbreaking, never entirely supersede one another from one day to the next. As I sit in my room writing this introduction, I can think of at least four different types of illumination in my flat, including candles and a dimmable lamp mimicking the warm radiance of an oil lantern. But what does it mean to be constantly living in a space with different light forms present at once, lights of different intensity and carrying different cultural meanings? What I attempt in this book is to tease out some of the complex cultural meanings that became newly associated with different forms of illumination (moonlight, candlelight, gaslight, and electric and arc lighting) at a time of significant technological transition, and to identify their relevance for modernist poetry and poetics. What did it mean for poets to inhabit a world that was witnessing the gradual displacement of the moon, against gaslight first and subsequently against electricity? What might it mean to experience a reality simultaneously lit by fuzzy gas lamps and sharp arc lights? These juxtapositions clearly have important bearings not just on the levels of illumination present in modern cities but also on the creation of concurrent cultural shifts. Moonlight, technically the major nocturnal illuminant for most of human history, inspired and nourished the poetry of many for centuries in its role as muse and symbol of a romanticized femininity. Gaslight, Otter's claim notwithstanding, remains strongly of the nineteenth century in our collective imagination as in literary imagination today. Gaslight is remembered as a technology of huge social impact, the trademark of Jack the Ripper crime scenes, the initiator of night rhapsodies and the culture of flâneurs.[19] Arc lighting and early electric light, by contrast, were the bright flags of a new modernity, making cities appear sharp, contrasting, geometrical, and instantly more masculine. *Brilliant Modernism* takes its bearings from this historical and cultural moment in which the moon effectively loses its status as city light and is replaced by the more brilliant lights of gas and electricity—in poetry as well as in the lived experiences of the time.

As the art world fluttered between old and new aesthetics, it also began to steer from a preference for natural brightness to a love of manufactured lights. The nineteenth century's predisposition for darkness and low lights, too, was no longer felt relevant. In his groundbreaking *New York Nocturne: The City After Dark in Literature, Painting, and Photography, 1850-1950*, William Chapman Sharpe claims "one could argue that at first, modernists preferred natural darkness to manufactured light, until about 1910, when they had to accept the larger cultural changeover to bright nights."[20] The tantalizing coincidence of modernist interest switching from natural darkness to artificial lights with the approximate date at which Virginia Woolf felt "human character changed" invites a strong reading of historical change that I partly resist and partly complicate in this book.[21] The change from an aesthetic preference for (generally moonlit) natural darkness over one of artificial lighting certainly did not occur as quickly as flipping an electrical switch. Rather than simply accepting a new aesthetic mode, modernist poets actively and variously responded to the socio-technological and cultural changes they witnessed, harnessing this transitional technological moment to address wider questions of gender, race, and modernity. And as we shall see, the transition from a modern poetry and art of natural darkness to a culture of electricity was further complicated by the aesthetic endurance of moonlight.

Lunar into Electric

The moon: a satellite, a reflector, a mystery, a woman, a mood. Historically queen of the night sky, the moon cannot produce any light of its own, and yet it acts as the nocturnal rival to gaslight and electricity. There can be no comprehensive understanding of the modern, artificially illuminated nightscape without an attempt to understand, in turn, the moon's shifting cultural role. Within the narrative proposed in this book, the moon occupies a distinctive place, as its fading brilliance alternately appears in, and disappears from, the modernists' line of sight. With the arrival of gaslight in the 1830s, and even more so after Edison's famed October night of 1879, the moon gradually loses its status as stand-in for feminine beauty and eternal poetic muse. Urban electrification brings about a deep change to the canvas of the modern night, with the moon quite literally pushed away into the corners of the sky and electric lamps moved to the foreground. Georgia O'Keeffe imagines this major historical and aesthetic change in her famous painting *New York Street with Moon* (1925), which I discuss more at length in Chapter Four. Poets and artists of the new century walk around cities at night alert and awake, not to monitor the phases of the moon, as older generations might have done, but to check out electrification and its disruption of urban aesthetics. Streetlamps, illuminated windows, and lit-up advertisements and signs all take center stage at night. The moon has, by the early decades of the twentieth century, lost most, though not all, of its poetic relevance and developed into a relic, a curiosity—an afterthought even. As imagist T. E. Hulme puts it in his epigrammatic poem "Above the Dock" (1912), it is "but a child's balloon, forgotten after play."[22] Hulme's poem captures the fading glory of the moon at the turn of the century, reduced to a neglected toy and an image of vanishing childhood memories. The moon has changed meaning for modernists. Or rather, as I show throughout this book, the modernists turn to the moon with different eyes, changing its meaning and relevance for modern poetry, art, and society. As it becomes superseded by electricity in everyday life, the moon becomes the embodied reminder of a recent past in which it was indeed its light that would dictate nocturnal rhythms. Perceived as the ghost of a bygone era, the moon comes to represent the lunar art and poetry of the nineteenth century, urging modernists—to borrow Ezra Pound's notorious slogan—to make it new.[23] A new kind of poetry called for a new type of moon.

The poems and artworks routinely associated with Symbolism, Decadence, and Crepuscularism are lunar. The writers who most clearly influenced the poets and artists in this book (though sometimes this influence took the shape of outrage or even literary vendetta) were devotees of *le clair de lune* (moonlight). French poets Jules Laforgue, Tristan Corbière, and Paul Verlaine, in spite of writing in brilliantly gaslit Paris, embraced moonlight as a distinctive trait of their poetry, to the extent that we can call them "lunar dandies." The phrase is Laforgue's own invention; in "Pierrots" (II) he jokingly writes of "Ces dandys de la Lune/S'imposent, en effet,/De chanter 'S'il vous plaît?'/De la blonde à la brune." (These lunar dandies set/Themselves to sing this measure/In fact: "What is your pleasure?"/From blond through to brunette, lines 13-16).[24] I borrow the phrase only half in jest to refer to the mode of masculinity presented in their poetry, a masculinity at once corroborated and challenged by the figure of the moon-woman. Laforgue acted as a master of this lunar temple in poetry, writing both obsessively and irreverently about the moon. In *L'Imitation de Notre-Dame la Lune* (*The Imitation of Our Lady the Moon*, 1886), a cycle of poems dedicated to the moon, moonlight is the only relevant illumination for his nocturnes and is the illuminated embodiment of the unattainable woman of his desires. Laforgue's speaker would do anything for the moon: "Ah! tout pour toi, Lune, quand tu t'avances/Aux soirs d'août par les féeries du silence!" (Ah! Anything for you, Moon, when you move/Across the silent fairylands on August evenings, "Clair de lune").[25] Ten years later, English Decadent Ernest Dowson would reprise Laforgue's lunar cycle in *The Pierrot of the Minute: A Dramatic Phantasy in One Act* (1896), in which we encounter a Pierrot unsuccessfully wooing a Moon-Maiden in a dreamy, romantic tête-à-tête under *le clair de lune*. In the limited edition published by Leonard Smithers, Aubrey Beardsley's illustrations first introduce us to a Pierrot drawn according to the French tradition, with exaggeratedly loose white clothes (fig. I.2), going on to present us with a caricature of the dandy poet, Dowson, as Pierrot, but with a thin dark mustache and unruly hair (fig. I.3). The late nineteenth-century poet identifies with Pierrot, and wants to be Pierrot, in part because his muse is the lunar woman: aesthetically attractive yet as intangible as the moonbeams of which she is made and as unsatisfying as any worshipped idol.

Fig. I.2. Aubrey Beardsley, frontispiece, from Ernest Dowson's *The Pierrot of the Minute: A Dramatic Phantasy in One Act* (London: Leonard Smithers, 1896).

Fig. I.3. Aubrey Beardsley, vignette, from Ernest Dowson's *The Pierrot of the Minute: A Dramatic Phantasy in One Act* (London: Leonard Smithers, 1896).

But lunar was also modernist work affected by the aesthetics of these movements. Lunar, too, was the poetry of women who felt the need to engage with, rather than reverting, tradition in their verse. Nancy Cunard's early verse comes across as profoundly lunar, still fluctuating much between nineteenth-century taste and modernist form. Unlike Loy in "Lunar Baedeker" (1923), who sees the moon as no longer fit for purpose, as a hindrance to women's emancipation, and as the constant reminder of an unwieldy past (epitomized by "the museums of the moon"), Cunard does not find renewed strength in electric light but sees the moon in the same way as the lunar dandies of Symbolism and Decadence, as the "puissant unattainable" ("Moon").[26] Her fittingly titled *Sublunary* (1923) inhabits a world caressed by dim lights and governed by the moon. Cunard's Paris is, by comparison, far from the one described by contemporary Hope Mirrlees in *Paris: A Poem*

(1920) in the same years, in which Sigmund Freud "waves his garbage in a glare of electricity" (1920).[27] In this Paris, electrification promotes a sense of scrutiny and lack of privacy, of which Freud's psychoanalysis appears to be both symptom and cause. Rather, Cunard's Paris is one of moonlight smoothing out the rough edges of the modern city, the "light half-sinister of Paris moons."[28] In much of Cunard's poetry, which is dominantly both nocturnal and urban, the absence of electricity results in an outdated picture of Paris, and what we might call a "retro-modernist" and seemingly anachronistic aesthetic. In spite of her adventurous personality in life, in her poetry Cunard prefers to tread in the footsteps of her predecessors and to eschew revolutionary gestures.

William Butler Yeats, considered by some a modernist champion for his role in the Irish Literary Revival, did not care for electric light either, as to him the new technology spoiled the familiarity of O'Connell Bridge at dusk and embodied what he called "modern heterogeneity," or the irruption of the technological and the unfamiliar modern.[29] He was, in fact, unabashedly lunar. His love of moons and hatred of electricity brings him closer to the Symbolist and Decadent poets with whom he shared much of his poetic sensibility. To revere the moon means to respect tradition, and to perpetuate gender archetypes, in poetry as well as in society. The changing nightscape, then, raises significant aesthetic questions for the poets of the time: Should the modern poet be writing about the moon? And if so, in what vein? Many of the modernists in this book—as children of the 1890s and of its *clair de lune* traditions—began writing and painting in lunar fashion. But they came to recognize the pale light of the moon as the deep root of nineteenth-century aesthetic taste and gender roles. It became altogether necessary to eradicate this germ and "kill the moonlight" of the previous literary traditions.[30] But doing away with moonlight and its lunar women—if only poetically—was no easy feat. As we shall see, replacements for both were in preparation.

The new designs for electric lampposts in Milan and New York, the introduction of flowery lampshades for the home, as well as the phallic silhouette of a naked light bulb—to name only a few examples—all contributed to a gendering of light that complicates and challenges societal roles of the time. The cultures of light explored in this book encompass both the materiality of various everyday illumination technologies (different types of lamps and their shapes, for example) and the evolving meanings, attitudes, and practices associated with light and its quotidian manifestations (what did it mean to the people of the early twentieth century to be simultaneously exposed to significantly different lights?). As I discuss throughout this book, transformations in urban and domestic lighting at once supported alterations in gender roles, a phenomenon highly visible, I argue, in the art and literature of the early twentieth century. Today, we may not immediately think of light as a gendered entity: intangible, formless, and colorless, we find light gender neutral too. Light is just light: what else? Within the folds of modernism and the avant-garde, however, artificial light was often appropriated as feminine. This would come naturally to writers whose first language understood most terminology of light as grammatically gendered feminine. Much like the Italian Futurists (Chapter Two), and William Carlos Williams or Jean Toomer (Chapter Four), the Czech avant-garde poet Jaroslav Seifert sees streetlights as tantalizingly feminine in "Ulice" ("Street," 1925): "z paprsků světel každá lampa dlouhé vlasy má/které bys marně potom uviděti chtěl" (each lamp for hair has long beams of light/which you would in vain try to see then, lines 3-4).[31] After all, the Czech word for lamp, *lampa*, as the French *lampe*, is feminine. Domestic lamps are, too, reimagined as feminine by Pedro Salinas, Spanish poet of the *Generación del 1927*, who in "35 bujías" ("35 Candlepower," 1925) superimposes the image of his lover against that of an electric lamp, which become "artificial princesa,/amada eléctrica" (artificial princess,/electrical beloved, lines 22-23).[32] But electric light was strongly presented to the general public as feminine in advertisements across Europe and North America, not always under the influence of linguistic gendering but rather as a result of the popular trope of *la fée électricité* (the electricity fairy) in France and its romanticizing variations in other Western countries.[33] Electricity made its debut onto the world's stage as a charming young woman, holding or standing near electric lamps (fig. I.4), or even embodying the form and colors of the new light bulbs (plate 1). These images, though originating in France, became available transnationally and gave way to a number of variations in other countries.[34] Electrical journals, too, contributed to an identification of "women with technological objects, both of them properly under male control."[35] The story of feminized electric light is both empowering and objectifying of women: a trope picked up by the modernists in this book. The ways in which the designs and forms of lamps changed and were proposed in the early twentieth century dovetailed with modernist efforts to negotiate the cultural and iconographic transition from lunar to electric, from natural to artificial, and ultimately from the aesthetics of the previous century to those of the current one.

Fig. I.4. Lucien Lefèvre, *Electricine: Eclairage de Luxe* (Electricine: Luxury Lighting). Color lithography, 27.9 × 38.1 cm (11 × 15 in.). Plate 55, in *Les Maîtres de l'affiche: publication mensuelle contenant la reproduction des plus belles affiches illustrées des grands artistes, français et étrangers*, edited by Jules Chéret (Paris: Chaix, 1897). Digital image © Alamy.

A Modern Prometheus

The experience of widespread electricity magnified the sense of technological empowerment. The issue was no longer that stars were suddenly "quite put out" by lamps, as Emma Hardy wrote in 1874, lamenting the absence of starlight over Paris.[36] Rather, it was that lamps had turned into modern stars. As early as 1878, Robert Louis Stevenson had taken wry exception to the way electricity was changing the appearance of the world at night, calling gas lamps the "biddable, domesticated stars" of "city-folk."[37] For Stevenson, gas lighting was advancement enough in the "stride" of this modern Prometheus; electricity seemed an unnecessary exacerbation.[38] If gaslight united hearts, electricity was divisive:

> [In Paris] a new sort of urban star now shines out nightly, horrible, unearthly, obnoxious to the human eye; a lamp for a nightmare! Such a light as this should shine only on murders and public crime, or along the corridors of lunatic asylums, a horror to heighten horror. To look at it only once is to fall in love with gas, which gives a warm domestic radiance fit to eat by. Mankind, you would have thought, might have remained content with what Prometheus stole for them and not gone fishing the profound heaven with kites to catch and domesticate the wildfire of the storm.[39]

For Stevenson, as for many Victorians, electric light was far from magical. In this essay, the Scottish writer captures the practical challenge of acclimatizing to life under electric light.[40] Early prototypes of incandescent electricity and arc light emanated a glare quite different in shade and color to gas lighting, which was distasteful to many.[41] The brighter, the more instant, and the more mechanical electric light proved itself to be, the more gas came to appear natural, intimate, warm, and human. For such commentators, gas illumination, not electric light, was effectively the "natural" successor to the fire stolen by Prometheus. Far from inspiring optimism about human progress, the electric "lamp for a nightmare," a manifestation of humanity's degeneracy, updated and modernized Promethean pride. "Star-rise by electricity" would be, as Stevenson imagined, the result of a debased society and a monstrous modernity.[42] Taming and exploiting electricity—fishing for lightning—is, then, an act of self-destructive hubris.

Stevenson's—or rather, what we might want to call a cautious Victorian's—vision of electric lighting as an unnecessary technological ostentation and symptom of modern audacity reverted in the 1910s as writers began to appropriate electricity for its in-your-face brilliance and its disassociation from the natural. Modernists were acutely aware of the anxieties stimulated by the seemingly otherworldly electricity. But they were aware, too, that electric light challenged nineteenth-century bourgeois notions of privacy, propriety, and sobriety, and they were eager to celebrate its subversive power and make it their own. To write about the lights changing the face of the city at night was not a simple documentary act of recording human experience. It involved capturing and appreciating the potential of this light to inspire and sustain a new kind of writing. As electric light disrupted the norms of the world around them, modernist poets aimed to unsettle poetic conventions and culture.

In the hands of Filippo Tommaso Marinetti and the Italian Futurists, electric light became a powerful revolutionary tool, an open invitation to embrace modernity and abandon tradition. As Marinetti and company were visiting Venice in July 1910, the Futurist leader cried out to a crowd of reluctant Venetians:

> Io pure amai, o Venezia, la sontuosa penombra del tuo Canal Grande, impregnata di lussurie rare, e il pallore febbrile delle tue belle, che scivolano giù dai balconi per scale intrecciate di lampi, di fili di pioggia e di raggi di luna, fra i tintinni di spade incrociate. . . .
>
> Ma basta! Tutta questa roba assurda, abbominevole e irritante ci dà la nausea! E vogliamo ormai che le lampade elettriche dalle mille punte di luce taglino e strappino brutalmente le tue tenebre misteriose, ammalianti e persuasive!
>
> ---
>
> (O Venice, I too once loved the sumptuous half-shadows of the Grand Canal steeped in exotic voluptuousness, the feverish pallor of your beautiful women who glide down from their balconies on stairways illuminated by lamplight, amid a slanting rain and rays of moonlight, to the tinkling of crossed swords. . . .
>
> But enough! All this absurd, abominable, and irritating stuff makes us sick. And now instead we want electric lamps with a thousand rays of light that can brutally stab and strangle the mysterious shadows—pestiferous, alluring shadows.)[43]

Here, in *Discorso futurista ai Veneziani* ("Marinetti's Futurist Speech to the Venetians," 1910), as in the manifesto *Contro Venezia Passatista* ("Against Passéist Venice," April 1910), which precedes this speech by just a couple of months, Marinetti's words are not a complaint against Venice's poorly lit streets and canals. Rather, for the enterprising Futurist, Venetian moonlight was shorthand for nostalgia, passéism, romantic love, repressed femininity, and for the literary movements of Symbolism and Decadence: everything that needed to be changed in society, relationships, and writing. And the quick fix to all things moonlight, and therefore to salvage the quintessentially passéist city of Venice from sure destruction, must be its antagonist, electric light: "Venga finalmente il regno della divina Luce Elettrica, a liberare Venezia dal suo venale chiaro di luna da camera ammobigliata" (Let the reign of divine Electric Light finally come to liberate Venice from its venal moonlight for furnished rooms to let).[44] The eternal Northern Italian city had been consistently "an anachronism in the cultural imagination," to borrow Jennifer Scappettone's words—always out of step with history, always behind, and yet always present.[45] To think of Venice as modern was—and remains—paradoxical; to imagine a brightly electrified Venice, a city of lights like Paris or New York, impossible. Venice embodied the natural and the sensual, the slow and the exotic, the sickly and the pale—exactly the opposite of what modernism and the avant-gardes were striving for. Electric light, on the other hand, represents for Marinetti the artificial and the cerebral, the fast and the ordinary, the wholesome and the bright. In this sense, electric light principally signifies an aesthetic insurgence against the previous literary and artistic tastes, and a cultural attack on the mores of the previous century: modern writing and modern art had to work against the pallor, lamplight, and moonlight of Symbolism and Decadence, just as modern men and women had to rise against limiting gender roles. Siding with the artificial brilliance of electric light meant siding with the change promised by a faster and brighter world.

In the same year as Marinetti's Venetian manifesto, Ezra Pound returned to New York after a long stretch in Europe.[46] Perhaps this protracted absence spurred him to appreciate the American city through eyes veiled with nostalgia; or rather, his eyes, now used to the dimmer lights of Europe, needed time to acclimatize again to the brilliance of nighttime New York.[47] Two years later, he would remember the experience of illuminated New York in "Patria Mia," a series of articles on America for the *New Age*:

And New York is the most beautiful city in the world?

It is not far from it. No urban nights are like the nights there. I have looked down across the city from high windows. It is then that the great buildings lose reality and take on their magical powers. They are immaterial; that is to say, one sees but the lighted windows.

Squares after squares of flame, set and cut into the ether. Here is our poetry, for we have pulled down the stars to our will.[48]

"Pull[ing] down the stars to our will" is for Pound a Promethean act intrinsically connected to the making of poetry. As Prometheus stole fire from the gods, so human progress appropriated starlight for the modern city, by way of electricity. Unlike Stevenson's despair over human degeneracy, Pound equates New York's urban electrification to what he would like him and his fellows to do in poetry—as electric light turns the city into a powerful vision, modernist poetry should embrace the sense of empowerment offered by electrification. This equation empowered both male and female poets to rewrite the night and reshape its significance. In the illuminated evening, New York yields its heavy industrial modernity to the enchanted brightness of the early twentieth-century electrified night. Seen in this way, Pound's electrified vision of New York has much in common with Marinetti's Venice: electric light reshapes and transforms cities, as they become new barely recognizable entities. For this craftsman of Anglophone avant-gardes, modern poetry is the urban night, and its aesthetics those of the night's artificial beauty. Nocturnal illumination's exceptional allure for modernist poets fueled their desire to become, themselves, brilliant lights suspended in the sky over New York, London, Paris, Florence, or Milan.

In English, we ordinarily employ the words *brilliance* and *brilliant* to denote intense brightness, both in its relation to actual light and, figuratively, to someone's intelligence. In our common understanding of brilliance, then, we instinctively draw a connection between light and intellect, between radiating light and being human. Yet brilliance is not just light. It is light *against* dark. Brilliance does not, and cannot, exist by itself: even when not made explicit, brilliance—both of lights and of people—can only present itself by way of contrasts. Its nature is to obscure everything else. Brilliance always needs a dark foil against which to shine and dazzle; a candle's intense light is lost on a sunny day. As electric light swept through cities, illuminating them against the night, its brilliance also directly competed with, and obscured, the moon. As we have seen, much in the same way, modernism and the avant-gardes adopted the brilliance of artificial illumination to position themselves against what they saw as the literature of darkness and low lights of the preceding century. The lights of the modernist poetry and art in this book show lines of both continuation and antagonism with nineteenth-century authors and movements, and especially with Symbolism and Decadence, which thrived on the pale glimmer of the moon and the fuzzy glow of gas as key features of their otherwise dark style and aesthetics. But for modernist writers and artists, the brilliance of lighting technologies was more than an interesting recurring image or trope, more than the atmospheric backdrop of their nocturnal rendezvous. Modernists interpreted and appropriated artificial lights as an intrinsic part of their creative process, and one that distinctively set them apart from, and against, their predecessors.

Natural Artificial

Just as electric light energized writers with the possibility of a new kind of writing, modernists were especially fascinated by electricity because of the tension between the natural and the artificial it so vividly encapsulated. Ever present in human society and interaction since a differentiation between *technē* (art and technology) and *physis* (nature) was first felt and theorized, the antithesis between the natural and the artificial—or, to use the terms popularized by American historian Lewis Mumford and that still resonate with us today, between the "organic" and the "mechanical"—has become a distinctive mark of industrialized modernity.[49] Electricity was, for many modernist writers, the very embodiment of that tension. A natural phenomenon in itself, electricity looked and felt everything but organic and natural. Although gas lighting was technically also an artificial source of illumination, electricity surpassed it. Electric light was perceived to be *more* artificial than gas lamps, or oil lamps, or candles—its brilliance, therefore, a fabrication, an invention, an artifice.

As a result, poets and artists alike went in search of the right kind of language to define, and to talk about, electric light and the modern juxtaposition of the natural and the artificial. In his notes for the monumental unfinished *Passagenwerk* (*Arcades Project*, written 1927-40), in the section "Modes of Lighting," Walter Benjamin recorded the following passage from a short story by Guy de Maupassant. To the first observers of early electrification, the new light would have looked much like this:

> Et les globes électriques, pareils à des lunes éclatantes et pâles, à des œufs de lune tombés du ciel, à des perles monstrueuses, vivantes, faisaient pâlir sous leur clarté nacrée, mystérieuse et royale, les filets de gaz, de vilain gaz sale, et les guirlandes de verres de couleur.
>
> ———
>
> (And the electric globes—like shimmering, pale moons, like moon eggs fallen from the sky, like monstruous, living pearls—dimmed, with their nacreous glow, mysterious and regal, the flaring jets of gas, of ugly, dirty gas, and the garlands of colored glass.)[50]

To the eyes of the perceptive, night-obsessed flâneur from "La nuit (cauche-mar)" ("The Night [Nightmare]," 1887), these perfectly round lamps pop-ping up all around the city could only remind him of the other major night illuminant: the moon. The only simile at the narrator's disposal to describe the experience of early electric lighting, as well as the inadequacy of gas-lights, was to repropose the artificial as an out-of-the-ordinary natural. The artificial could only be appreciated and understood in relation to the natural.

But if for the fin de siècle writer the "electric globes" are *like* moons, al-beit not quite *the* moon, for Filippo Tommaso Marinetti some twenty years later the moon would be directly replaced by an impressive number of its artificially controlled counterparts. In his 1909 text "Tuons le clair de lune!!" ("Let's Murder the Moonlight!!"), which I discuss in depth in Chapter Two, the Futurist leader plans a visionary attack on moonlight, as the *clair de lune* of the French nineteenth-century tradition, in these terms:

— Tuons le clair de lune!

Les uns coururent aux prochaines cascades; des roues géantes furent dressées et des turbines transformèrent la vitesse des eaux en des spasmes magnétiques qui, par des fils, grimpèrent sur des poteaux jusqu'à des globes lumineux et bruissants.

C'est ainsi que trois cents lunes électriques biffèrent de leurs rayons de craie éblouissante l'antique reine verte des amours.

——————

("Let's murder the moonlight!"

Some of us ran to nearby waterfalls; gigantic wheels were hoisted, and turbines transformed the velocity of the waters into electromagnetic spasms that climbed up wires suspended on high poles, until they reached luminous, humming globes.

So it was that three hundred electric moons, with rays of blinding chalky white-ness, canceled the old green queen of love affairs.)[51]

If, for Maupassant, Parisian arc lamps looked like moons, for Marinetti they do not resemble but *are* electric moons—moons that have been electrified: conquered, as it were, by electricity. The natural becomes invested with qualities of the artificial, while the artificial aims to conquer, and reproduce, natural qualities. This process of adjustment and intersection was taking place in everyday lighting culture as well. In *Lighting the Home* (1920), Mat-thew Luckiesh, director of General Electric's Lighting Research Laboratory and the American authority on light and color through the first half of the twentieth century, would write, for example, about the use of tinted lights indoors to recreate the effects of the early lights of the morning or the deeper lights of twilight or even moonlight (see fig. I.5).[52] Though Luckiesh concedes that few people would be able to afford a skylight with controllable rheostats and dimmers over their dining table, his study attests to the possibilities of electric lighting to replace and supersede natural light, and to accommodate even the most demanding taste for interior lighting fixtures.[53] As another example of modern Promethean hubris inspired and promoted by electricity, Luckiesh's advice on how to use colored lights in order to recreate specific light effects indoors effectively works as a complement to Marinetti's obsession with replacing the real moon with electrified versions.

While Mumford in *Technics and Civilization* (1934) would reflect, much later, that "machines [. . .] are lame counterfeits of living organisms" and that indeed "our best electric lamps cannot compare in efficiency with the light of the firefly," modernist writers urged us to contemplate what the effects of this act of "counterfeiting" of the natural operated by the artificial might be.[54] Indeed, modernism's fascination with electricity directly relates to the centuries-old debate on the relationship between nature and art. Theodor Adorno interpreted the natural and the artwork-artifact (the "artifactual") not as sheer oppositions to each other but rather as oppositions that are necessarily mutually referential.[55] Nature must always refer "to the experience of a mediated and objectified world, [while] the artwork to nature as the mediated plenipotentiary of immediacy."[56] For Adorno, reflecting on natural beauty is an essential part of aesthetic theory; the natural and the artifactual, or what is not natural, therefore fully rely on one another.[57] In his memoir "Earth-Being," Jean Toomer acknowledges the following: "If, like other children, I was an unconscious natural poet of Nature, finding beauty and delight in trees, flowers, rain, snow, sky and clouds, moon, stars, so also was I a natural poet of man's artifices. Copper sheets were as marvelous to me as the petals of flowers; the smell of electricity was as thrilling as the smell of earth after a spring shower."[58] Toomer is at once a poet of the natural world and "naturally" drawn to the artificial. The natural and the artificial are necessary worlds for the modern poet; while they are not necessarily in opposition and can happily coexist, they also generate a tension that poets have tried to express, replicate, and resolve for centuries. Toomer was treading in the footsteps of fellow American Ralph Waldo Emerson, who in his essay "The Poet" (1844) notably wrote that the factory village and the railway disrupting the American landscape were "works of art [. . .] not yet

Above the glass ceiling are red, green, and blue lamps controlled by rheostats. By varying the intensities of the three colored lights a vast variety of color effects may be obtained such as dawn, sunlight, sunset, twilight's afterglow, and moonlight.

Fig. I.5. "Above the glass ceiling are red, green, and blue lamps controlled by rheostats. By varying the intensities of the three colored lights a vast variety of color effects may be obtained such as dawn, sunlight, sunset, twilight's afterglow, and moonlight." Plate I, frontispiece, in Matthew Luckiesh, *Lighting the Home* (New York: The Century Co., 1920).

consecrated" to poetry, adding, however, that "the poet sees them fall within the great Order not less than the beehive or the spider's geometrical web."[59] For Emerson, the poet was able to capture the essence of all things—whether natural or not, whether previously considered material for poetry or not. But Toomer's interest in both nature and artifice also points to an essentialist strategy striving to unify oppositional ideas and contrast set associations of race and gender (see Chapter Four). Toomer, like other modernists in this book, engaged with the variously illuminated world around him to conceptualize, on the one hand, his creative process and, on the other, the changing world around him.

The artificial brilliance of electric light enabled modernists to articulate changes in perception and subjectivity. In the lavishly detailed description of "one's luncheon" in *A Room of One's Own* (1929), Virginia Woolf dismissed electric light as superficial, seeing it as a mark of disingenuousness: "And thus by degrees was lit, half-way down the spine, which is the seat of the soul, not that hard little electric light which we call brilliance, as it pops in and out upon our lips, but the more profound, subtle and subterranean glow which is the rich yellow flame of rational intercourse. No need to hurry. No need to sparkle."[60] For Woolf the glitz of table-talk and the switchable brilliance of electric light are interchangeable: both are flashy, trivial, inconsistent; both may sparkle, but they hardly illuminate a complex mind or the world around it. Electric light is too immediate to represent any thought worth having, while flames more aptly symbolize deep-seated rationality, the pondered logos shining through an individual. What Woolf's words also appear to imply is the realization that an utterly modern electrical subjectivity, in its artificiality, ought to be subordinate to the glow and richness of flames, whose depth would better suit human nature and disposition.

Thirty years later, Gaston Bachelard could concur with Woolf, arguing that the flames of fire, candles, and oil lamps stimulated reveries and introspection; observing a flame urges us to dream, to imagine, to meditate.[61] The static light of an electric lightbulb, operated by a simple switch, cannot stir the same reveries as the flames of an oil lamp and marks the beginning of what Bachelard calls the "age of administered light": the modern age, and the age of modern lighting.[62] While Bachelard was liable, even more than Woolf, to a deep-rooted nostalgia for those technologies of light being phased out by the time he was writing *La flame d'une chandelle* (*The Flame of a Candle*, 1961), his anthropologically astute insights about lamps and flames tell us something about the hold of particular lighting technologies on the imagination. For Bachelard, regaining that sensitivity to light, which he thought humanity had lost, was crucial, because he understood that cultures of light shaped subjectivity. Experiencing and observing light becomes an act of observing oneself as well as others. But, if we stop to think about it, it was precisely the advent of electricity and the coexistence of different cultures of light that reasserted the primacy of natural flame of a fire or a candle as an appropriate medium for introspection. With the rise of electrification, the symbolic codes pertaining to candlelight, gaslight, and moonlight were radically reassessed. Many modernist poets perceived electric light as a dynamic force corresponding to their own internal creativity and to the process of invention. Electricity empowered them to reshape themselves as explosive poetic agents for a new age.

Of Lights and Modernisms

Until now, scholars have paid little attention to the pivotal role played by illumination technologies in the early days of modernism. Since at least the 1960s historians of modernism and the avant-gardes have explored the importance for this new writing and its aesthetics of early twentieth-century technological progress more generally. Notable among them were Marshall McLuhan, founder of the Centre for Culture and Technology (1968) at the University of Toronto; Leo Marx, the American historian who authored the influential *The Machine in the Garden: Technology and the Pastoral Ideal in America* (1964); and Raymond Williams, one of the first major proponents of cultural approaches to literature. This cultural-historicist tradition continued with Hugh Kenner, whose *The Mechanic Muse* (1987) sees modernist writing as a direct refraction of the new experiences of urban modernity, though the Canadian scholar regrettably stops at the work of the usual suspects of High Modernism: T. S. Eliot, Ezra Pound, James Joyce, and Samuel Beckett.[63]

More recently, the cultural-historicist work of Tim Armstrong, David Trotter, and Alex Goody has demonstrated how modernist texts made processes of technological change more intelligible.[64] Trotter's *Literature in the First Media Age: Britain between the Wars* (2013) and Goody's *Technology, Literature and Culture* (2013) both point to the way modernist writers (especially novelists) engaged with media technologies as a means to reflect on, and reimagine, modern urban experiences. In stressing the lingering late nineteenth-century cultural legacy of early modernist poetry, I take my cue from Goody's claim that a certain Victorian techno-culture was handed down to the subsequent generation of writers.[65] With its focus on poetry, this book joins the current revitalizing of contextual readings of modernist poetry, exemplified in the recent books of Susan McCabe, Seth Perlow, Goody, and Edward Allen, who offer compelling cultural and historicist readings of modernist poetry, emphasizing the relevance of cinema, information technologies, leisure technologies, and media technologies respectively.[66] By taking early twentieth-century cultures of lights as an important—and so far invisible—context for modernism, I aim to restore the visual and imaginative elements of modernist poetry in ways that are distinct from previous scholarly work on technology and modernism. Looking at lesser-known modernist poems alongside well-known ones, I propose a different story of modernism—one in which poets consciously harnessed contemporary cultures of light to interrogate, discuss, and represent issues and concerns about modernity and changing society.

While in *Artificial Darkness: An Obscure History of Art and Media*, Noam Elcott redirects our attention to manufactured darkness as a discourse that is often neglected in favor of technologies of light, in the opening to *Dark Nights, Bright Lights: Night, Darkness, and Illumination in Literature*, a volume of essays exploring the historical impact of artificial illumination on literature from the 1890s to the present, Susanne Bach and Folkert Degenring lament that research on light and illumination remains "a marginal area of interest in most disciplines," and especially in literary studies.[67] This lack of interest may be due to the fact that light and lighting are, on the one hand, ubiquitous and, on the other, intangible aspects of the everyday: unless we are physicists, electricians, or scenographers, we might find it hard to quantify, measure, and ultimately understand light. Hence, with very few exceptions, light and illumination technologies have been conspicuously absent from historicist examinations of modernist culture. William Brevda writes on electrical advertisement signs in American fiction of the period, and Richard Leahy offers a survey of the symbolism of various lighting technologies for nineteenth-century authors, tantalizingly stopping at the early twentieth century with the claim that "the nineteenth-century chapter of artificial light's story essentially closed in 1914."[68] As *Brilliant Modernism* illustrates, this assertion oversimplifies a network of aesthetic affiliations identified and perpetuated by modernist poets. What Brevda, Leahy, and the authors in Bach and Degenring's edited volume have in common is a reliance on seeing light and illumination as symbols, and electrification—when discussed at all—as a motif, a repetitive pattern, an atmosphere, a background. But to relegate illumination technologies to the role of interesting symbols in literature is to misrepresent their active power in fashioning and mediating not only aesthetic sensibilities but also culture—especially evolving understandings of the self and self-representations of masculinity and femininity, race, and modernity.

A multidisciplinary methodology, taking into full consideration the artistic and visual elements of light cultures, is the best way to demonstrate the impact of changes in illumination: an approach exemplified in the work of Lynda Nead, Kate Flint, and William Chapman Sharpe. By looking at artwork and literary texts together, Nead is able to theorize the gaslight aesthetics of the nineteenth century in her famous *Victorian Babylon: People, Street, and Images in Nineteenth-Century London* (2000) and later to unravel the turn-of-the-century fascination with astronomy in *The Haunted Gallery: Painting, Photography, and Film, c. 1900* (2007).[69] More recently, Flint, already the author of the discipline-defining *The Victorians and the Visual Imagination* (2000), gave a detailed and inspiring account of the twentieth-century cultural and aesthetic changes brought about by flash technology.[70] But it was Sharpe who first proposed an ambitiously wide-ranging and visually appealing account of how technological changes in the illumination of New York shaped painters', photographers', and writers' perception of the city and determined a new kind of modern self-understanding based on altering perceptions of the night.[71] With the intensification of gas lighting and the introduction of arc lighting, followed by incandescent electricity, the night was no longer a reign of terrors but rather an empowering space for most men and women. In *Brilliant Modernism*, I embrace a similar multidisciplinarity, weaving a complex pattern that takes in modernist poetry, visual arts, and technologies of light. This web of relations makes manifest novel and previously uncharted connections between the beginnings of modernism and early twentieth-century cultures of light. Light is not perception in and of itself, in that it is effectively invisible without backgrounds, surfaces, or textures; it only becomes visible against matter, as it bounces off it, reverberates, reflects. Light manifests itself through refractions, shades of colors, glossy surfaces, mirrors, and multiple illuminations. My analysis therefore juxtaposes poetry with contemporary visual culture, including illustrations, advertisements, photographs, and paintings. Understanding, and visualizing, the multiple facets of light culture at the early stages of modernism's emergence is a crucial aspect of this book. Every chapter in *Brilliant Modernism* consists of a series of thick descriptions, in which the meanings of individual poems are probed through wide-ranging contextualization of the acts of poetry-making.[72] While the poems and the poets always stay at the fore-front of this research, the borders between text and context blur and slip away, making vivid the ways in which early twentieth-century cultures of light shaped modernist poetry and vice versa.

Mapping my research onto a plurality of key modernist cultures and geographies (Paris, Florence, Milan, New York), I embrace a permeable notion of modernism, in line with historicist approaches that have, over the past decade or so, fostered a widening of the discipline of modernist studies.[73] This book aligns itself with New Modernist Studies, which, as Douglas Mao and Rebecca L. Walkowitz observe, has, since the founding of the Modern-ist Studies Association in 1998, favored new "temporal, spatial, and vertical directions" for the expansion of modernism as a field of study.[74] In *Brilliant Modernism*, I engage with modernism in all of the three extensions identified by Mao and Walkowitz. While my time frame is relatively narrow, consider-ing just over twenty years of poetry, the material it engages with points back to modernism's nineteenth-century beginnings, thus extending the book's temporal scope back to the middle of the preceding century. By including texts in other European languages, I firmly participate in the "transnational turn"—though we might just as well call it a "comparative turn"—in modern-ist studies, which allows me to cross geographical borders and the national-istic constraints of language-specific research, and to initiate a new dialogue between Eliot's Paris, Marinetti's Milan, Loy's Florence, and Lola Ridge's New York.[75]

This book thus endorses Paul K. Saint-Amour's claim that "in the house of modernist studies, *modernism* has left off playing bouncer and started playing host" (emphasis in original).[76] The term "modernism," as employed throughout this volume, is a generous one, attached to poets well estab-lished in the canon (T. S. Eliot, William Carlos Williams, and Langston Hughes) as well as to authors who have haunted its peripheries, sometimes because of their limited output but more frequently owing to scholarly bias. Bring-ing these figures together reinstates texts clearly modernist in form and con-tent that have slipped through the critical net of modernist studies, and places them in profitable conversation with the mandarins of their time.[77] Loy and Ridge, whose poetry I discuss in Chapters Three and Four respec-tively, were at the center of efforts to disrupt and reconfigure traditional conceptualizations of literature and art. They were affiliated with and gravitated toward Futurism, Dadaism, Surrealism (Loy), and important modernist editorial ventures such as *Others: A Magazine of the New Verse*, and *Broom: An International Magazine of the Arts* (Ridge especially). My two author-specific chapters, Chapters One and Three (on Eliot and Loy respectively), rebalance the importance of these two poets: Loy, la belle of European and American avant-gardes, neglected or misunderstood by scholars for decades, and Eliot, the big gun of modernism and the subject of scholarly attention for most of the twentieth century, are equals in the overarching narrative of this book. Chapter Two further demonstrates how women played a key role in the shaping and gendering of Futurism's engagement with illumination technologies, while Chapter Four realigns canonical US modernists such as Williams, E. E. Cummings, Alfred Stieglitz, Georgia O'Keeffe, Hughes, and Claude McKay, with Ridge, and Gwendolyn B. Bennett, seeing them for the first time as a single artistic formation. By way of this historicist and cultural approach, I recover many modernist women poets and artists who, for a good portion of the twentieth century, were partially or entirely lost to literary history. Drawing on an extensive selection of primary materials to complement the poetry analyzed here allows me to contribute to the rethinking of modernism as a wider, less exclusively literary, cultural project. These materials include archival resources as well as numerous published documents pertaining to cultures of light, made more accessible in recent years as a result of the digital revolution in modernist studies.[78] Over the pages of this book, the cultures of light shaping and shaped by modernist poetry and arts come to life, becoming more intelligible thanks to the inclusion of these newly available intertexts and resources.

Outline

The book is organized into four chapters, with two focusing on an individual author and two on a larger formation of poets and artists. Much like the exhibition rooms of an art gallery or museum, the chapters are arranged chronologically and with some temporal overlap, so each chapter cascades into the subsequent one. The book thus builds a temporal arc beginning with material that feels, and is, closer to the nineteenth century and its gaslit sensibilities, and ending with more electrically driven poetry and artwork. I begin *Brilliant Modernism* with the towering figure of T. S. Eliot but rewrite him as the tentative young writer Tom. Chapter One, "Observing Light: T. S. Eliot," takes its cue from Kenner's question of what Eliot observed as a young poet, providing the first detailed account of the cultures of light that shaped Eliot's poetic observations of the illuminated city in his early Parisian poems.[79] On the back of his Symbolist readings at Harvard, Eliot crafted poetry glowing with moons and gaslit lamps, which he derived from Charles Baudelaire and Jules Laforgue. Imagining himself as a modern lunar dandy, Eliot caricatured the poets of the preceding century. Taking in documentary photography, popular science textbooks, George Augustus Sala's personification of gaslight, and Aubrey Beardsley's illustrations, this chapter provides an explanation for Tom Eliot's decision, immersed though he was in electrified and electrifying cities, to write of talking streetlamps, gaslit interiors, and old moons. Eliot's poetic observations of the modern lit-up city reveal a young poet's preoccupations with masculinity, modernity, and the creation of a new verse: preoccupations that reveal an imperative to exorcise his relationship with his poetic forebears.

Chapter Two, "Killing the Moonlight: F. T. Marinetti and the Futurist Avant-Garde," continues the topic of the lunar dandy through the figure of Filippo Tommaso Marinetti, the serial killer of moons. His "lunicides" are deployed as poetic escamotages allowing Marinetti and his Futurist crowd to reposition their literary affiliations against Symbolist moonlight aesthetics. More significantly, the chapter uncovers how the murdering of moonlight, epitome of passéism and outdated femininity, was a trope used by Futurists not only to modernize their verse but also to destabilize traditional gender dynamics. Examining poems by Marinetti alongside poetry by both men and women gravitating around this light-driven avant-garde, including Libero Altomare, Paolo Buzzi, Ada Negri, Maria Ginanni, Fanny Dini, Mario Carli, Emilio Mario Dolfi, Escodamé, Fillia, and Enzo Mainardi, and artwork by Giacomo Balla, Natalia Goncharova, Rosa Rosà, and Růžena Zátková, this chapter offers the first account of how Futurists reacted and responded to Marinetti's call to arms against moonlight in their poetry and art. In particular, I reevaluate Futurist women's role and agency in the aesthetic appropriation of electric light as a tool for artistic emancipation.

Chapters Three and Four further complicate the question of gender. Chapter Three is wholly dedicated to Mina Loy as the poet and maker of lamps. It tells the story of her poetic, technological, artistic, and personal engagement with electric light. Loy is the icon of *Brilliant Modernism*, quick to grasp the importance of electric light for modern life. Appropriating and domesticating the new artificial light, Loy harnessed its potential as a suitable language for poetry, an illumination technology fit for domestic space, a compelling object for the art world, and—most importantly—a powerful medium for her own, and other women's, emancipation. By looking at the strongly gendered beginnings of electric light, as well as Loy's flirtations with Decadence and Futurism, her lamp designs, and other artworks by artists from the time such as Constantin Brancusi, Georgia O'Keeffe, Tina Modotti, and Joseph Cornell, this chapter unravels the ways in which the domestic, the artistic, and the feminist overlap and coalesce in Loy.

My final chapter, "Bringing Down the Stars: American Modernists," examines a selection of American poets and artists to demonstrate how electric brilliance was embraced as a central feature of the new poetry and art they were creating, harnessed to different ends by different individuals within the larger formation of American modernists. Starting with Ezra Pound's reflections on the distant landscape of illuminated New York and modern poetry, and Vladimir Mayakovsky's poem "Бруклинский мост" ("Brooklyn Bridge," 1925), the chapter theorizes the concept of a modernist electrical imagination, as emerging from the self-reflective prose and poetry of William Carlos Williams, E. E. Cummings, and artwork by Francis Picabia. It then moves on to propose that the electrified nightscape observed from afar acts as a dark screen onto which male artists and poets could project one's own visions and desires, as in the photography of Alfred Stieglitz, and the poetry of William Carlos Williams and Jean Toomer. By contrast, Lola Ridge and Georgia O'Keeffe, who were deeply attracted to the city of New York in spite of its aggressively masculine connotations, found it necessary to reappropriate the illuminated cityscape, adopting electric light as a symbol of women's resistance against gender-normative categories, and as a manifesto for political empowerment, and the deconstruction of the male gaze. Finally, the chapter turns to African American modernists, showing how, for photographer James Van Der Zee and poets Langston Hughes and Gwendolyn B. Bennett, electric light enables a new understanding of blackness as intrinsically luminous.

For poets across Britain, Europe, and America, the illuminated nightscape was not simply a recurring theme, a forest of symbols, or an interesting diversion. It heralded a bright new aesthetic, started a long-awaited impetus to a new writing, and sparked revolutionary ideas about gender. It was, too, a form of exorcism of the outdated lights and luminaries of the past. The advent of electrical illumination permitted a coexistence of light and dark by unifying day and night, old and new, natural and artificial. The supersession of previously considered irreconcilable opposites now enabled a single all-embracing vision, significantly adding to the period of momentous change that was the early twentieth century. To study the natural and artificial brilliance of the nocturne is to reconsider modernist poets' radical engagement with the changing world. Out of the modernist poetry and the artificial illumination of the 1910s and 1920s emerged a new poetic idiom that invented as much as mediated the experience of twentieth-century modernity.

1 Observing Light

T. S. Eliot

J'ai conservé depuis lors une affection particulière pour le
paysage normand, que j'ai vu d'abord au clair de lune . . .
(I have since retained a particular affection for the Norman
landscape, which I first saw in the moonlight . . .)

T. S. Eliot, "WHAT FRANCE MEANS TO YOU" (1944)[1]

October 1910. A transatlantic ship from New England is about to land at the
harbor in Cherbourg, Normandy.[2] It is a night as soft as only October nights
in continental Europe can be, enveloping everything in its warm embrace.
Thrilled American tourists and melancholic European returners crowd the
decks and bridges of the ocean liner, filled with the anticipation of treading
on French soil—the mark of a new adventure for the former, perhaps the end
of one for the latter. In the midst of this cacophonously multilingual group,
a young man, alert and curious about his fellow travelers during the cross-
ing, is now exclusively interested in the landscape emerging before him, as
if the moonlight had started etching against the backdrop of the night. His
black parted hair dances in a disorderly way in the ocean breeze as his eyes
fix on the glimmering contours of moonlit Normandy. This graduate of Har-
vard University, a poet in the making, has recently turned twenty-two and
is headed to Paris to study for a year.

Study was the only excuse that might have persuaded T. S. Eliot's parents
to finance his year in Paris. To them, France was foreign, scandalous, differ-
ent, remote.[3] For Tom Eliot, on the other hand, France meant poetry. But
not just any poetry. The French writers who inspired Eliot to make his trans-
atlantic journey wrote a poetry of moonlight: think of Charles Baudelaire's
"Tristesses de la lune" ("Sorrows of the Moon," 1857), Paul Verlaine's "Clair
de lune" ("Moonlight," 1869), Tristan Corbière's "Décourageux" ("Disenthu-

siast," 1873), or Jules Laforgue's *L'imitation de Notre-Dame la Lune* (*The Imitation of Our Lady the Moon*, 1886).[4] Although the *clair de lune* tradition in poetry had been around since at least the seventeenth century, it was in the decades 1860–1910 that the moonlit nocturne matured into a flexible form through which painters and poets probed the boundaries of their own art.[5] For many nineteenth-century poets, in particular those affiliated with Symbolism and Decadence, the moon and its shine were the creative force behind their sickly pale verse: moonlight was a quintessential element of their aesthetics.[6] But what did moonlight mean to young Eliot? Does his early poetry, as is often thought, simply reproduce the conventional lyrical tropes Eliot found ubiquitous in the writings of his poetic heroes? Eliot's arrival in Normandy, which in his later recollections he remembered as kissed by the light of the moon, seems to emblematize his sentiments about French poetry (Symbolism in particular) and his idea of France in general. But beyond tracing poetic influences on his early poetry, this chapter shows that Eliot was far from a passive receiver of Symbolist lore. Focusing on his early poetry written between 1909 and 1914, I explore how Eliot accommodated Symbolist and Decadent imagery of natural and artificial light for his own aesthetic purposes. Homing in on Eliot's creative process and exploring contemporary cultures of light, I demonstrate how Eliot's moon- and gaslit nocturnes began to express recognizably modernist concerns. The self in Eliot's early poetry becomes detached from the natural moonlight adored by Symbolists and finds its suitable reflection in the artificial streetlighting of the modern metropolis.

Well before reading anything in French, in the magazine Eliot edited for his family when he was only ten years old, little Tom was already fantasizing about "the busy streets of Paris" and its "motly [*sic*] crowd," which he even attempted to reproduce in a charming, albeit basic, drawing in which an imaginary bird's-eye view of a Parisian street is dotted with circles, each one representing a person and, perhaps, an odd street lamp.[7] Eliot went on to study French at Smith Academy, which was perhaps not quite the first manifestation of Eliot's Francophile interests but more, I say, the continuation of his childhood dreams of Paris.[8] While at Harvard, Eliot learned to appreciate the poetry of the French Symbolists through Arthur Symons's second US edition of *The Symbolist Movement in Literature* (1908; first edition 1899).[9] On the back of that reading, he hunted out Laforgue and other poets in "a foreign bookshop somewhere in Boston."[10] Indeed, "ce n'est pas un accident qui m'avait conduit à Paris," Eliot would recall thirty-four years later for *La*

France libre; "depuis plusieurs années, la France représentait surtout, à mes yeux, la *poésie*" (it was not a coincidence that had led me to Paris. For many years France had represented above all, in my eyes, *poetry*; emphasis in original).[11] In 1959, Donald Hall, interviewing Eliot for the first instalment of the now-acclaimed series "The Art of Poetry," asked him whether he considered "becoming a French Symbolist poet like the two Americans of the last century," Stuart Merrill and Francis Vielé-Griffin.[12] Replying affirmatively, Eliot confessed: "I only did that during the romantic year I spent in Paris after Harvard. I had at that time the idea of giving up English and trying to settle down and scrape along in Paris and gradually write French."[13] In the interview, Eliot dismisses this as a youthful dream—as unattainable as it was naive; and, we might add, anachronistic. By the time Eliot arrived in Paris, Symbolism had largely been relegated to the past.[14] And yet, Eliot was determined to tread the same boulevards that Baudelaire and his gang had roamed, to experience the same *clair de lune*, and to make a poet of himself as they had done themselves.

Eliot's appreciation of Symbolist poetry partly accounts for the reason he played a rather passive role in Parisian literary and artistic circles during his first sojourn there.[15] Eliot was uninterested in the "post-Symbolist buzz" of the city at the end of la belle époque.[16] Rather, he wanted to observe, read, and imagine, as per his maxim on how to experience the French capital, recalled by Robert McAlmon: "[Eliot] said of Paris that the right way to take it is as a place and a tradition, rather than as a congeries of people who are mostly futile and timewasting, except when you want to pass an evening agreeably in a café. When he was living there years ago he had only the genuine stimulus of the place, for he had not known any of the writers or painters as companions—knew them rather as spectacles, listened to, on rare occasions, but never spoken to."[17] We ought not to be surprised to read that for the author of "Tradition and the Individual Talent" (1919), Paris is first and foremost "a place and a tradition," rather than any number of living people. Yet we should not be tricked into believing that Eliot's year in Paris lacked in friendships or human contact, as he was sustained by the companionship of two Frenchmen: Alain-Fournier and Jean Verdenal. Fournier tutored Eliot in French language and literature, introducing him to the works of Charles-Louis Philippe; Verdenal shared with Eliot and Fournier a passion for French Symbolist poetry (as well as Richard Wagner).[18] The latter friend stayed imprinted in Eliot's memory in Symbolist strokes, "touched by a sentimental sunset, the memory of a friend coming across the Luxembourg

Gardens in the late afternoon, waving a branch of lilac."[19] Eliot's immersion in the city as a place and as a tradition was largely free from nostalgia but deeply affected his early poetry and, as we shall see, is visible in his poems written in the US before leaving for Paris, those of his Parisian stay, and the ones composed immediately after Paris. Over the years 1909-14, Eliot favors a poetry of night walking, interiority, and scrutiny: a contemplative act directed at once toward the city space and toward himself as a becoming poet *and* man. The different kinds of light constellating Eliot's nocturnal walks urge him to fold inward to get to the essence of his own art. The two brilliant moments of Normandy's "clair de lune," as observed at his first landing, and the "sentimental sunset" of his friend Verdenal's lasting memory mark Eliot's early poetic phase. This phase, however, is characterized not by the pure distillation of French Symbolism that Donald Hall may have had in mind in his interview with Eliot but by a unique accommodation of Symbolist elements within a synthesis of his own. In these early poetic experimentations, Eliot's treatment of turn-of-the-century cultures of light updates, modernizes, and helps him exorcise his Symbolist affiliations.

The first part of this chapter argues that the way Eliot writes about city lights, a key element in Symbolist literature, in his early poetry displays a certain anachronism—we might call it a nineteenth-century filter or patina— that invites a particular scrutiny of the self and of the poet's work through the city. The city of Paris in particular, for Eliot, contained all times and all experiences—"tantôt Paris était tout le passé; tantôt tout l'avenir: et ces deux aspects se combinaient en un présent parfait" (sometimes Paris was all past; sometimes it was all future: and these two aspects combined to form a perfect present)—and thus encouraged the act of observing the wider society, as well as a form of retrospective lyrical scrutiny.[20] For Eliot, whose first visit to Paris was stimulated by the reading of Symbolist poetry, the City of Lights retained its nineteenth-century air and appearance, despite presenting itself as an exciting hub for new artistic movements. In Eliot's French year, the experience of Paris and that of the French poetry he loved become one: when he walks in Paris, he tries to see the city of Baudelaire, Laforgue, and company, as they would have seen it.

Paris in 1910 was a refulgent, illuminated spectacle. At the end of the nineteenth century, Paris had been quick to adopt arc lighting and then incandescent electricity, with its first electrical company already operating in 1878, and the city was at the forefront of electrical illumination displays with the major international exhibitions of 1881 (*Exposition internationale d'Élec-*

tricité, the first International Electrical Exposition), 1889, and 1900 (*Exposition Universelle*, or Paris Exposition).[21] Apart from being *la Ville Lumière* (the City of Lights), at this time Paris also gained the title of *la Capitale Électrique* (the Electric Capital).[22] Guillaume Apollinaire, in a contemporary poem from *Alcools* (1913), depicts *"Soirs de Paris ivres du gin / Flambant de l'électricité"* (*Paris evenings drunk with gin / Radiant with electricity*; italics in the original).[23] At least two Eliot scholars have maintained that the electrification of Paris had a strong visual impact on Eliot's poetic imagination during his stay there. Nancy Hargrove, in her chapter dedicated to Parisian daily life the year of Eliot's visit, briefly mentions the replacing of gas lamps with electric ones by 1900, and an exhibition of the electrified house of the future, *La Maison Électrique*, which Eliot might "have been drawn to see for himself," as it coincided with his arrival in Paris in October 1910.[24] But Hargrove leaves readers to make any connections with Eliot's poetry for themselves. More recently, Andrew Thacker has suggested that electrification, together with the plurality of different lighting technologies, is a relevant context for Eliot's conceptualization of a "spatial modernity," especially in the poem "Rhapsody on a Windy Night," which, as we shall see, features Parisian lampposts.[25] Indeed, although most Parisian streetlamps were electrified by the 1890s, in the early 1900s and into the 1910s different lighting technologies overlapped in the streets of Paris; the ordinary evening stroller could routinely encounter gas, arc, and incandescent (electric) light in the same outing.[26] It is, therefore, remarkable that Eliot, who was very sensitive to nuances of light and whose poems are constellated with both natural and artificial lights, should never mention the word "electric" in his early poems or letters from this period.[27] Given that Apollinaire was writing about electrified Paris in 1913, and, as we shall see in Chapter Two, Futurist Marinetti was excited about electric moons in 1909, it is striking that Eliot, a poet historically associated with the modern city, should seem so uninterested in electric light.

Writing about Eliot and American technological progress in "Eliot Observing" (*The Mechanic Muse*, 1987), Hugh Kenner comments:

> We never ask what it's routine to ask about Wordsworth or even Keats: what Thomas Eliot may have observed when he opened his eyes, and what he made of it.
>
> Yet he called his first book *Prufrock and Other Observations*, and in its earliest poems, the first two Preludes, an alert man in an American city is taking note of the new century's novelties.[28]

What did Eliot see when he opened his eyes? Kenner's question sounds like a call for poetry scholars to take up the historians' tools, while also suggesting that contemporaneity had to be of interest to Eliot the modernist poet. But what if Eliot cared less about the material realities of the 1910s, or at least what we deem to have been new at that time, than about the final decades of the nineteenth century? What if materiality, the furniture of Eliot's early poetry, is more dependent on what Eliot read than what he saw in everyday life? In his early poems, Eliot examines the city in order to look *back* at how the city was for his nineteenth-century idols and to look *within* himself. Living in the electrified city, Eliot nevertheless decided to fill his poems with gas lamps and ancient moons. This chapter offers an interpretation of Eliot's brightly illuminated poetry of 1909-14 against the backdrop of his engagement with the Symbolists and nineteenth-century cultures of light.

Réverbères

For Eliot, who believed letters were photographs of the moments in which they were written—"a different hour would produce a different light, a different letter"—the choice of precise shades of light and natural or artificial light sources was a pivotal node of all his writing.[29] His early poetry in particular glows with light, from the moth-destroying flames of "The Burnt Dancer" (1914) to the autumn sunlight of "La Figlia Che Piange" (1911-12), the lamp of "The Love Song of St. Sebastian" (1914), and the bright lines of "The Little Passion" (1915). For Eliot, different lights evoke different moods and atmospheres (night, twilight, or a foggy evening); yet, while essential to the scenery of a poem, they often remain in the background. On occasions, however, artificial lighting takes center stage, emerging from the poetic landscape as the voice of the poem: light is no longer a backdrop, a temporal factor, or an externalized sentiment—it takes on subjectivity and becomes a focal point of Eliot's poetic experimentation.

In a much later correspondence with his friend John Hayward, who was the effective editor of "Little Gidding" (1942), Eliot would note the importance of discerning between shades of light. Eliot, who had been "persistent[ly] worrying over the characterisation of the half-light setting" for the "compound ghost" passage in "Little Gidding," considers the possibility of including a direct reference to a lighting technology—"after lantern-end"—to indicate the exact shade of light before morning, when street lighting goes out.[30] The word "lantern," much like the word "street-lamp" in "Rhapsody," signals at once a specificity of time and object:[31] "I am still however wrestling with the demon of that precise degree of light at that precise time of day. I want something more *universal* than black-out (for even if the blackout goes on forever, I want something holding good for the past also—something as universal as Dante's old tailor threading his needle. On the other hand, any reference to the reverberes [*sic*; French for streetlamps, lampposts] wd. take the mind directly to *pre-war* London, which would be unfortunate. It must therefore be a country image or a general one" (emphasis in original).[32] Eliot had been looking for a term that would convey the universality of that moment between artificial lighting fading out and natural daylight rising, but making use of the technologically specific word "lantern" in the poem would have made the passage temporally and historically explicit. In the end, Eliot opted for the phrase "waning dusk," which is not bound or limited by language suggestive of a precise cultural moment and is universally understandable, without any prerequisite of a set experience. Eliot thought of streetlighting as redirecting the reader's mind to prewar times perhaps because of World War II's blackout. Throughout their private correspondence, Eliot and Hayward often boasted of their Frenchism by casually dropping untranslated French terms in their letters; here the French *réverbère* is thrown in to talk, counterintuitively, about London streetlamps.[33] It is not unlikely that lampposts in Eliot's imagination spoke French, tied to his memories of Paris; but the village of Little Gidding in Cambridgeshire was a long way from Paris. The point Eliot is making, however, is really about the fundamental tension between the particular and the universal. Different poetic effects call for different poetic means, and specific objects have a specific poetic impact. Understood in this sense, light and lighting in Eliot's poetry betray a conscious use of the culturally and historically particular, rather than the universal. "Rhapsody on a Windy Night," one of Eliot's Paris poems from this period, is an excellent example of how the lights in Eliot's poetry, instead of reflecting Eliot's contemporary experience of the city, hark back to a previous historical period—in this case, the late nineteenth century.

In "Rhapsody on a Windy Night," written in Paris under the spell of the French metropolis in 1910-11, the speaker roams through the night, his walk marked by hourly clock chimes, the mutterings of a talking streetlamp, and the sight of a scant number of other creatures.[34] While the form of "Rhapsody" is, as Eliot said himself, "freer" than that of other poems of this phase, its furnishings are distinctly nineteenth century.[35] The poem opens on a part-sentimental, part-magical note, with the street "Held in a lunar synthesis,/Whispering lunar incantations" (*P* 18, lines 3-4). In this scenario, a streetlamp takes the floor and addresses the poet directly:

> Half-past one,
> The street-lamp sputtered,
> The street-lamp muttered,
> The street-lamp said, "Regard that woman
> Who hesitates toward you in the light of the door
> Which opens on her like a grin.   (*P* 18, lines 13-18)

Much like in Oscar Wilde's "Impression du Matin" (1881), where "one pale woman all alone/[. . .]/loitered beneath the gas lamps' flare,/with lips of flame and heart of stone," gaslight enhances and distorts the features of the women—often prostitutes—it illuminates.[36] Eliot's streetlamp begins to speak at half-past one a.m. with a little difficulty, as if clearing its throat (if it had one!) to get the right tone of voice to deliver its advice to this young flâneur, clearly a version of Baudelaire's "passionate observer."[37] In fact, the lamppost's speech, Frenchified by the peculiarity of the English "regard," urges the poet to look at the woman appearing in the light projecting from the entrance of a house onto the street. The French word for lamppost—*réverbère*—encourages this act of observation: from the verb *réverbérer* (to reverberate), a synonym of *refléter* (to reflect), its literal translation into English would be "reverberator," now an obsolete word that indicates a reflector or a reflecting lamp.[38] If the lamppost is Parisian, as Eliot is inducing us to think, he is also emphasizing the act of reflection prompted by this streetlight.

An hour later, the streetlamp speaks more clearly, but then returns to its sputtering, muttering, and humming as it directs attention to the moon (*P* 19, lines 46-51). We might be led to think that the streetlamp's voice and its inarticulate sounds are figments of the poet's imagination: when do lamps speak otherwise? For Andrew Thacker, "the regular pronouncements of the lamps act as the spatial equivalent to the clock marking time"; in turn, the clocks are for Jewel Spears Brooker in dialogue with Bergson's own ideas of time.[39] Certainly, these ideas may be at play in "Rhapsody," but the lamps here are not just a manifestation of Bergsonian intellect or "practical memory," their humming "one continuous duration," or simply the result of the flâneur's manipulation of the space around him.[40] Rather, the lamps' coherent utterance speaks to the poem's roots in the nineteenth century.[41] Why does Eliot imagine French urban space as so fundamentally linked with a nineteenth-century lighting technology? What does the fact that the street-lamp in "Rhapsody" is lit by gas rather than electricity mean for Eliot and for our understanding of the poem and Eliot's poetic practice? To this end, a brief explanation and contextualization of that historical period in urban culture, in Paris and elsewhere, is needed to understand what gaslight and street-lighting signified for the Symbolists and late nineteenth-century culture.

Between 1853 and 1870, Paris had undergone several transformations that substantially altered its appearance, under the punctilious work of prefect Georges-Eugène Haussmann, employed by Napoleon III to put the emperor's new vision of the French capital into effect. Much of what we associate with Paris today, such as the width of its elegant boulevards or the uniformity of its spatial perspectives, was born in the nineteenth century.[42] If Parisian streetlamps automatically bring us back to this period in Paris's modernization, it is because their singular design, together with that of the characteristic kiosks and *vespasiennes* (street urinals), was a direct result of Haussmannization.[43] Their abundant presence along the streets of Paris responded to Haussmann's motto of "Light before all else," which celebrated modern gaslight throughout the city and gained Paris the title of *la Ville Lumière*.[44] Gas lamps for Haussmann were not simply decorative illumination technologies; their position and distance one from the other had to convey order and symmetry.[45] This new enhanced system of gas lighting, apart from improving urban safety, simultaneously invited, in the words of David Harvey, "scrutiny in a way that had not been possible before" and resulted in closer inspection of the city as well as its social and cultural renovations by the Parisians.[46] Charles Baudelaire's prose poem "Les yeux des pauvres" ("The Eyes of the Poor," written 1864) encapsulates this historical change, exuberantly portraying the dazzlingly bright gaslight of the new cafés: "Le café étincelait. Le gaz lui-même y déployait toute l'ardeur d'un début, et éclairait de toutes ses forces les murs aveuglants de blancheur, les nappes éblouissantes des miroirs, les ors des baguettes et des corniches" (The café was dazzling. Even the gas burned with all the ardor of a début, and lighted with all its might the blinding whiteness of the walls, the expanse of mirrors, the gold cornices and moldings).[47] The display of gaslit splendor attracts a poor family of three, who remain at the door, entranced by the luminous luxuriance of the scene. The gas lamps "heighten the joy" of experiencing a new urban reality, one in which looking at the newly lit-up streets plays an important role.[48] Gas illumination blurs the boundaries between outdoors and indoors at night, with the streets as bright as the shops, houses, and cafés. The nearly cinematic crisscrossing of glances in the poem exemplifies the new type of visibility gaslight allows: with its lights, the café attracts rich and poor alike, even though the latter are only allowed to observe it from outside. At this moment in history, the contours of outside and inside become permeable, heightening the work of mutual scrutiny.

Contemporary photography intensified this scrutiny. From 1858 to 1878, Charles Marville (pseudonym of Charles-François Bossu) was entrusted with the important task of photographing first the area of Bois de Boulogne and later various areas of *vieux Paris* and of the Haussmann reconstruction, work that gained him the reputation of "photographe de la ville de Paris" (photographer of the city of Paris).[49] Yet Marville's photographs are more than simple documentary work. Nadar (Gaspard-Félix Tournachon), the more famous French photographer of the nineteenth century, called Marville "un peintre" (a painter), recognizing the artistic value of his photography whose structures often evoke the vanishing point of Renaissance art and architecture (see fig. 1.1).[50] Marville's detailed visual narrative of Paris's Haussmannization charmed the world with its combination of art and historical document. It featured in illustrated magazines throughout the 1870s and covered every corner of the Paris Pavilion at the Universal Exhibition of 1878.[51] Marville's series dedicated to the *réverbères* stands out as a special testimony to the Paris of the 1860s as a city of "luxury, modernity, and, of course, light."[52] These lamps framed Paris as a nineteenth-century city: the city of la belle époque and Art Nouveau, in daylight as at night.[53]

Marville's photographs celebrate Paris's streetlamps above everything else. Thanks to the low angle in these images, the lampposts come to life in all their uncanny, unreal sharpness.[54] The lamppost, standing at the center of the photograph, creates "dynamic ricochet effect[s]" between buildings and sculptures, trees, signposts, and monuments, rising as "a proud sentinel of the street."[55] Marville's *réverbères* have more in common with portraiture than with landscape or documentarian photography.[56] In *Arts et Métiers* (1864), for example, Marville immortalizes a lamppost guarding a ghostly crowd on boulevard de Sébastopol (fig. 1.2), while in *Jardin du Luxembourg* (1878), the lamppost is in open dialogue with the line of streetlamps, statues, and monuments (fig. 1.3). Marville's lampposts are much more than items of street furniture or pure illumination technologies: in his unreal city, emptied of all Parisians but those who could stand still for long enough to be captured

Fig. 1.1. Charles Marville, *Rue de la Bûcherie, du cul de sac Saint-Ambrose* (Street rue de la Bûcherie, from the Saint-Ambrose cul de sac), 1866–1868. Albumen print, 32 × 27.1 cm (12 5/8 × 10 11/16 in.). Robert B. Menschel Fund, National Gallery of Art, Washington. Digital image courtesy of the National Gallery of Art.

in his long exposure times, the streetlamps come to life, populating the urban space and contributing to Paris's signature style.[57]

By contrast, in the documentary photography of a contemporary of Eliot's, Eugène Atget, Parisian lampposts vanish in the misty air of his photographs, flatten out to merge with the background, or hide behind Morris columns

Fig. 1.2. Charles Marville, *Arts et Métiers (Ancien Modèle)*, 1864. Albumen silver print from glass negative, 36.6 × 24.1 cm (14 7/16 × 9 1/2 in.). Alfred Stieglitz Society Gifts 2007, The Metropolitan Museum of Art, New York. Digital image courtesy of the Metropolitan Museum of Art.

Fig. 1.3. Charles Marville, *Jardin du Luxembourg*, 1878. Albumen silver print mounted on carboard, 35.5 × 26.5 cm (14 1/8 × 10 1/2 in.). Digital image courtesy of State Library of Victoria, Melbourne.

Fig. 1.4. Eugène Atget, *Nymphe, sculpture par Louis Auguste Edmond Lévêque, jardin des Tuileries, 1er arrondissement, Paris* (Nymph, by the sculptor Louis Auguste Edmond Lévêque, Tuileries gardens, 1st arrondissement), 1907. Albumen silver print, 21.3 × 17.9 cm (9 1/4 × 6 7/8 in.). Digital image courtesy of Musée Carnavalet, Paris.

and other monuments (fig. 1.4), showing how, while Atget may have been a conscious disciple of Charles Marville, Marville's interest in the centrality of Haussmann's lamps in the street remains unique.[58] Yet some of Atget's photographs, such as *Rue Boutebrie* (fig. 1.5), clearly put the younger photographer in direct dialogue with Marville: the lamppost, much like in many of Marville's photographs, stands in for the living traffic of the otherwise empty

Fig. 1.5. Eugène Atget, *Rue Boutebrie, de l'angle des rues de la Parcheminerie et des Prêtres-Saint-Séverin vers le musée de Cluny, 5ème arrondissement, Paris* (Corner of Rue de la Parcheminerie and rue Boutebrie, looking towards Saint-Germain boulevard and Musée de Cluny, 5th arrondissement), 1922. Albumen silver print, 18 × 21.7 cm (6 7/8 × 9 1/4 in.). Digital image courtesy of Musée Carnavalet, Paris.

street. Atget's photographs reveal a similar anachronism to that expressed in Eliot's poetry from this period: immortalizing old Paris in the 1920s, his pictures have little in common with contemporary modernist and avant-garde photography from the same time, and hold a visual power that, in Geoff Dyer's words, "urge[s] us and themselves back in time"—to the nineteenth century.[59] That in the 1910s Atget should not be quite so interested in photographing streetlamps as a subject for his documentarian work was an aesthetic choice that distinguishes him from Marville but also from Haussmann's obsession with symmetry. Looking at Marville's photographs allows us to understand the aesthetic and cultural role of streetlamps in post-Haussmann Paris. Haussmann's streetlamps *are* Paris: its gaslight renovation and the setting-up of a new public lighting system constitute the social and aesthetic texture of modern Paris. The central position of the streetlamp in

Marville's photographs emphasized the idea that streetlights were the watchmen of the modern street, a popular trope at the time.

Because gas lamps were such prominent protagonists of the late nineteenth-century streets, they acquired particular cultural significance. Indeed, with no gas illumination, no fin de siècle.[60] As Eliot's gas lamp speaks and moralizes by replicating the cracking sounds of actual gas, in the nineteenth century gas lighting was thought to have a voice and even a say in social matters. George Augustus Sala, one of the "young men" in Charles Dickens's circle and a Victorian journalist famous for his nocturnal excursions in London and Paris, exploited the imaginative potential of his name's initials (GAS), which he used to sign off his articles, and effectively gave the new technology a voice and a persona.[61] Sala's identification with gas was so well known that toward the end of the Victorian journalist's career, *Punch* humorously recognized that "electric light was rendered almost unnecessary by the presence of GAS whose brilliant reflections will make memorable the brightest days of the *Daily Telegraph* as the George Augustan Era of Journalism."[62]

In an essay entitled "The Secrets of the Gas" (1854, first published in Dickens's magazine *Household Words*, subsequently collected in *Gaslight and Daylight*, 1859), Sala adopts "gaslight" as a term to supplant nighttime, the time in which lamps come alive.[63] In this essay, not only does Sala see and admire gaslight, but he is also able to hear it:[64] "The Gas has its secrets, and I happen to know them. The Gas has a voice, and I can hear it—a voice beyond the rushing whistle in the pipe, and the dull buzzing flare in the burner. It speaks, actively, to men and women of what is, and what is done and suffered by night and by day; and though it often crieth like Wisdom in the streets and no man regardeth it, there are and shall be some to listen to its experiences, hearken to its counsels, and profit by its lessons."[65] By virtue of his initials, Sala is initiated to the secrets of the gas, the exact content of which he unravels for four full double-column pages in *Household Words*. Gas is, for Sala, a voice that "often crieth like Wisdom in the streets and no man regardeth it," unintelligible to most, and reminiscent of Biblical language. Sala, the seasoned journalist and nocturnal flâneur, goes on to add:

> As I walk about the streets by night, endless and always suggestive intercommunings take place between me and the trusty, silent, ever-watchful gas, whose secrets I know. In broad long streets where the vista of lamps stretches far far away into almost endless perspective; in courts and alleys, dark by day but lighted

up at night by this incorruptible tell-tale; on the bridges; in the deserted parks; on wharfs and quays; in dreary suburban roads; in the halls of public buildings; in the windows of late-hour-keeping houses and offices, there is my gas—bright, silent, and secret. Gas to teach me; gas to counsel me; gas to guide my footsteps [. . .] through the crooked ways of unseen life and death [. . .]. He who will bend himself to listen to, and avail himself, of the secrets of the gas, may walk through London streets proud in the consciousness of being an Inspector—in the great police force of philosophy—and of carrying a perpetual bull's-eye in his belt. [. . .] Not a bolt or bar, not a lock or fastening, not a houseless night-wanderer, not a homeless dog, shall escape that searching ray of light which the gas shall lend him, to see and to know.[66]

Sala's gas does not quite speak here, but lets him see the world through its eyes by virtue of its being virtually everywhere—certainly, a string to a journalist's bow. But what Sala's fantasy lets us see is how gaslight was associated with forms of control and surveillance. Authorities in major cities harnessed light as a way to control the night, which, in the words of Joachim Schlör, was felt to be "unstructured, less ordered and therefore potentially threatening."[67] Streetlamps, consequently, came to symbolize the order and control of those who watch the streets, symbols of order in "la lutte contre la nuit" (the battle against the night) as argued by historian Simone Delattre.[68] More and more lamps were erected in areas considered dangerous to reinstate urban safety, which effectively brought out an even starker chiaroscuro contrast between brightly illuminated places and those left in the dark.[69] As Lynda Nead says, street lighting meant that "daytime order" could intrude into the urban night.[70] Sala's gaslight urges him to turn to the corners of the city that were previously less visible: improved illumination brings about better vision; better vision brings about knowledge of one's surroundings and therefore wisdom. Sala's gaslight, by controlling and seeing everything, acts almost as an extension of a Society for the Suppression of Vice: if you can see your surroundings when walking in the uncontrolled darkness of the night, you should be able to avoid depravity. But the observers of the exposed corruption will not necessarily avoid it. Much like any moralistic literature that minutely represents vice to condemn it, the gaslit pageant of the seedy urban nightlife does not guarantee a desired moral response from its spectators. In fact, being able to behold and observe vice might make it easier to yield to it.

The visibility of city nightlife was tantalizing for young Eliot, as is evident from a letter written on the last day of 1914. Writing from Oxford, Eliot confides some intimate reflections to his friend Conrad Aiken:

> How much more self-conscious one is in a big city! Have you noticed it? Just at present this is an inconvenience, for I have been going through one of those nervous sexual attacks which I suffer from when alone in a city. Why I had almost none last fall I don't know—this is the worst since Paris. [. . .] I feel the deprivation [of female society] at Oxford [. . .] but there, with the exercise and routine, the deprivation takes the form of numbness only; while in the city it is more lively and acute. One walks about the street with one's desires, and one's refinement rises up like a wall whenever opportunity approaches. I should be better off, I sometimes think, if I had disposed of my virginity and shyness several years ago: and indeed I still think sometimes that it would be well to do so before marriage.[71]

Eliot's self-consciousness and ambivalent feelings when alone in a big city are integral to "Rhapsody on a Windy Night." In the poem, a young man's lonely excursions in a big city prompt him to consider and reconsider his own condition, to let his desires—both sexual and literary—loose while at the same time experiencing the necessity to check himself.[72] As is well known to Eliot scholars, Eliot said he learned from Baudelaire "the poetical possibilities [. . .] of the more sordid aspects of the modern metropolis."[73] As in "Les yeux des pauvres" mentioned earlier, for example, for this *poète maudit* the lamps illuminated the areas and inhabitants that had previously remained virtually invisible in the city. In "Le Crépuscule du soir" ("Dusk"), Baudelaire picturesquely describes how the shadier creatures of the night creep out of their holes to take over the city, swapping places with the "honest" day workers. In this poem, the most interesting nocturnal vice for Baudelaire—prostitution—does not spread, move, threaten, or attract but rather *is lighted*: "A travers les lueurs que tourmente le vent / La Prostitution s'allume dans les rues" (Against the glimmering teased by the breeze / Old Prostitution blazes in the streets, lines 14-15).[74] As Gaston Bachelard points out in *La flamme d'une chandelle* (*The Flame of a Candle*, 1961), the reflexive French verb *s'allumer* puts the emphasis back on the light-shining subject.[75] Joachim Schlör, reporting documents from the Parisian police, further explains how earlier in the nineteenth century, lamp lighting directly regulated the prostitutes' hours of activity.[76] For Baudelaire and his contemporaries, there was a direct correlation between prostitution and illumination: prostitution lights up the city streets, coming on at dusk together with the gas

lamps. Ironically, at a time of improved urban illumination, the police's ef-
forts to make prostitution invisible, by limiting it to brothels and dark alleys,
and pushing it into the later hours of the day and into the night, only suc-
ceeded in making it more visible.[77]

The gradual lighting up of the gas lamps marks the beginning of Eliot's
urban peregrinations. The first section of his "Preludes" (1909-11), a poem
written between Cambridge and Paris (*P* 412), suggestively evokes—in the
visual singling out of its last line—the moment when our flâneur can begin
his explorations of the city and of himself: "And then the lighting of the
lamps" (*P* 15, line 13). As Tom Eliot walks about the city at night, his desires
are projected onto the backdrop of the urban night, showing them for what
they really are. In "Prufrock's Pervigilium" (1911-12), a section originally be-
longing to "The Love Song of J. Alfred Prufrock," gas allows the speaker to
see urban nightlife:

> And when the evening woke and stared into its blindness
> I heard the children whimpering in corners
> Where women took the air, standing in entries—
> Women, spilling out of corsets, stood in entries
> Where the draughty gas-jet flickered
> And the oil cloth curled up stairs.   (lines 4-9)[78]

With only a few but definite brushstrokes, Eliot paints a picture of the cause
and the effect of the speaker's nervous breakdown: prostitutes, a long-stand-
ing object of fascination for Eliot.[79] As in "Rhapsody," where the woman
hesitates in the lamplit doorway, the prostitutes stand on the liminal space
of the doorstep, doubly illuminated by the light from indoors and from the
street, inviting the passerby to cross the threshold. Instead of bringing order
and security, artificial illumination projects and amplifies the poet's desires.
As we have seen, flickering gaslight was an inescapable element of the
"dangerous night" in the nineteenth-century imagination, and it persists in
the way later generations envisaged the nineteenth-century metropolis; in
"Prufrock's Pervigilium," it contributes to the unsavoriness of the scene.[80] By
emphasizing the distasteful elements illuminated in front of the poet's eyes,
gaslight gives him the knowledge and wisdom necessary to avoid the situa-
tion that Eliot's "refinement" would surely not approve of.

It is no wonder that this light should give a voice and a body to Eliot's
frustrations. In "Portrait of a Lady" (1910-11), Eliot dramatizes a composite
rendezvous with Adeleine Moffatt, a Boston lady known for her tea parties

for select Harvard undergraduates (*P* 400). Adeleine makes numerous propositions to the speaker, which never seem to be engaged with, let alone reciprocated. In the poem, we never see or hear the speaker answer her directly, until Part III, where the speaker's thoughts manifest themselves by way of the silent language of light:

> "Perhaps you can write to me."
> My self-possession flares up for a second;
> *This* is as I had reckoned.
> "I have been wondering frequently of late
> (But our beginnings never know our ends!)
> Why we have not developed into friends."
> I feel like one who smiles, and turning shall remark
> Suddenly, his expression in a glass.
> My self-possession gutters; we are really in the dark.   (*P* 13, lines 10-18)

The speaker's "self-possession" communicates its state by way of visual verbs associated with candles and oil lamps ("flares" and "gutters"). The lamp is, after all, as Bachelard remarks, a "disciplined" flame: it represents man's conquest over fire—it is a humanized technology that can be controlled and regulated by man.[81] In this excerpt from Eliot's poem, the lamp coincides with the speaker's self-possession: it will not allow his emotions or feelings to overcome it; it will keep them at bay. In a similar way to the lantern of Mina Loy's opening to *Songs to Joannes*, which I discuss in Chapter Three, the speaker sees their interiority as a lamp whose manufactured light can be regulated by reason. In Eliot's case, however, the speaker's self-possession abandons him, guttering and trickling down the wick of the lamp, eventually extinguishing, and leaving the room and the speaker in the dark. We are left to ponder on what happens when one's self-possession leaves one in the dark.

By contrast, in "Rhapsody on a Windy Night," the personified light of reason never abandons the poet. By virtue of the lighting now focusing on the woman in the doorway, the speaker can see her and notice all the faults of her appearance, from her dress right up to her eyes. When the streetlamp turns its light to a street cat, the first-person voice claims to "have seen eyes in the street / Trying to peer through lighted shutters" (*P* 19, lines 41-42). Imagining the life behind the invitingly illuminated spaces was presumably one of the reasons for these nocturnal walks in the first place: the lit-up interiors entice the eyes of the flâneur to search more and understand more deeply. For Joachim Schlör, the new lights turn the street into a space that is simultaneously external and internal.[82] This concept is also sketched in Walter Benjamin's essay "The Paris of the Second Empire in Baudelaire," in which he famously discusses the vogue for night walking under gaslight. Benjamin proposes the development of a new understanding of the street: "The appearance of the street as an *intérieur* in which the phantasmagoria of the *flâneur* is concentrated is hard to separate from the gaslight" (italics in original).[83] The talking streetlamps of Eliot's imagination are an integral part of this phantasmagoria; the city becomes his private space, the space of his frustrations and of his desires—the space of his interiority. To paraphrase what Alfred Döblin said in 1913 in a different context—"ich bin nicht ich, sondern die Straße, die Laternen"—the mind of Eliot's speaker in "Rhapsody" is also the street, as well as the streetlamps.[84] The light from Eliot's streetlamp creates a ricochet effect between the lamp, the illuminated creatures (woman, cat, moon), and the speaker. Much as the streetlamps in Marville's pictures and Sala's essay form a dynamic relationship between the elements of the street, the poet's mind becomes the street, his thoughts zigzagging between reason and vice.

At the end of the poem, the speaker ends his nocturnal meanderings by finally crossing over into the internal space of his house, accompanied, once more, by the lamp, which this time peers into his own indoor space, his private room, from the staircase:

> The lamp said,
> "Four o'clock,
> Here is the number on the door.
> Memory!
> You have the key,
> The little lamp spreads a ring on the stair.
> Mount.
> The bed is open; the tooth-brush hangs on the wall,
> Put your shoes at the door, sleep, prepare for life."
> The last twist of the knife.   (*P* 20, lines 69-78)

His phantasmagoria is over; he is no longer the street, the streetlamps, the cat, the moon, the prostitute. The speaker comments on the lamp's last speech simply as "the last twist of the knife," a phrase that has left—and still leaves—many Eliot scholars in the dark; Brooker calls it "an image of violent severance," while for Rebecca Beasley it is the embodiment of the lamp's trivial and mechanized pronouncements.[85] But the lamp is far from making trivial statements: it has prepared, and continues to prepare, the speaker for life. Bachelard wrote that "when the evening is come the lamp is lighted, a poet of lamps lives more than a mechanical moment."[86] This is true of Eliot's "Rhapsody": the lamps do not simply mark a mechanical passing of time; they stir, fuel, urge his writing because, by staging his states of mind on the street, they prompt him to scrutinize himself.[87] Even when the speaker enters his house, the lamp continues its role as moral guide, except that this feels for him like "the last twist of the knife": the unwanted suppression of all desires, and a confirmation of the fears and apprehensions associated with late-night street walking, in what becomes a metaphorical murder scene.

In his early poetry, Eliot harnesses artificial illumination to better articulate the thoughts and desires of the lyrical I. Lamps and lampposts are the luminous expression of the speaker's rationality: they speak the wisdom he already knows but is reluctant to accept. These manufactured lights voice the psychological and moral dilemmas of the speaker's interiority; they make serious pronouncements about his life, and his present condition, urging him to investigate himself and check his desires. Eliot is uninterested in his electrical everyday; rather, it is the street lighting from nineteenth-century cultures of light that allows him to experiment with the poetic self in poems written "under the sign of Laforgue," which recreate an anachronistic, pseudo-Symbolist effect. Pseudo-Symbolist indeed, as gaslight is rarely the voice of lyrical subjectivity for the French Symbolists, for whom moonlight more fittingly reflects their sense of poetic self. But for Eliot, as we shall see in the next section, the moon is a passé aesthetic mode.

Lunar Dandy

Eliot's anachronistic poetics was not really apparent to his contemporaries, except for one alert American critic and poet. In a mordant review of Eliot's poetry in 1936 for the *Yale Review*, Louis Untermeyer made a long lunge to define the core of Eliot's poetics: "T. S. Eliot has become a symbol of all that is advanced in poetry, and yet he is an anachronism in the sense that he is both futurist and *fin de siècle*. No one, as far as I know, has compared him to the aesthetes of the Nineties; yet his course and theirs are curiously similar" (italics in original).[88] It is striking that Eliot's belatedness was apparent to a contemporary such as Untermeyer. Today scholars recognize Eliot's debt to the literature of the 1890s.[89] But what scholars have not picked up on is how Eliot's poetics is articulated through his specific choices of light imagery. The natural light of the moon and the artificial illumination of oil lamps and gas lighting allows Eliot to manifest his poetics as it oscillates between Symbolism and Decadence on one side, and the avant-gardes and modernism on the other. In this section, the moons of Eliot's early poetry make for a crucial point of contact and divergence with the Symbolists, helping him shift closer to more avant-gardist positions, such as that of Futurism, the subject of my next chapter.

The moon does not bear a grudge ("La lune ne garde aucune rancune," *P* 19, line 51), writes Eliot in French, alluding, as Christopher Ricks points out (and Grover Smith before him), to a couplet in Jules Laforgue's "Complainte de cette bonne lune" (Ballad of the Dear Old Moon): "—Là, voyons, mam'zell' la Lune,/ Ne gardons pas ainsi rancune" (Come now, Miss Moon, don't cherish a grudge like that, *P* 422). Certainly, most moons in Eliot's very early poetry are cognates of Laforgue's and Corbière's Symbolist moons, as earlier critics have established. But, whenever Eliot calls the moon in, it is never quite in the style of an infinitely solitary *clair de lune* à la Debussy or, rather, à la Verlaine. Eliot's personae are always, or imagine themselves to be, in the company of a woman: effectively, the moon always supervises a man's interactions with the other sex, in a poetry that, to borrow Stephen Romer's metaphor, has its "taproot" in "sexual unease."[90] As a self-conscious young man and poet apprentice, Eliot learns from the French masters how to metamorphose into the decadent "dandy of the moon" of which Laforgue speaks: "Ces dandys de la Lune/ S'imposent, en effet,/ De chanter 'S'il vous plaît'/ De la blonde à la brune." (These lunar dandies set/ Themselves to sing this measure/ In fact: "What is your pleasure?"/ From blond through to brunette, "Pierrots II," lines 13-16).[91] For Laforgue, despite being irreverent and, at times, a little cynical, the moon was a cult, a worship, a love, however strange: he was "one of those who come into the world with a ray of moonlight in their brains."[92] A contemporary review of Laforgue's collection *L'imitation de Notre-Dame la Lune* (1885) comments on the meaning of the moon for the French poet:

> M. Jules Laforgue vient d'apporter sa contribution à ce culte nocturne. Ce n'est ni Séléné ni Tanit, ni Celle qui dit: "Tu subiras éternellement l'influence de mon baiser. Tu seras belle à ma manière", mais une Lune jolie et qui le sait, aux contingences philosophiques. Elle s'avance dans une nuit pleine de silencieuse infinité

claire; pas le moindre écho des gens de la terre. C'est la "Dame très lasse / De nos terrasses."

(M. Jules Laforgue has just made his contribution to this nocturnal cult. It is neither Selene nor Tanit, nor the One who says, "You will forever be under the influence of my kiss. You will be beautiful in my way," but a pretty Moon who knows it, with philosophical contingencies. She walks into a night full of silent clear infinity; not the slightest echo from the people of the earth. This is the "very bored Lady / Of our terraces.")[93]

Laforgue is an adherent of a distinctively fin de siècle cult of the moon and to the decadent sensibilities of the 1880s, following which the melancholic, "truth-seeking lunar dandies" must naturally "scorn the sun" and the glaring reality of daylight.[94] For Laforgue, as for Corbière in *Les amours jaunes* (*These Jaundiced Loves*, 1873), or Ernest Dowson in *The Pierrot of the Minute* (1897), the moon is the quintessential poetic Muse, a natural companion to nocturnal romances, and, often, a demanding rival of the affairs of the flesh, as Corbière's lines ironically remind us: "Il adorait la lune; / Mais il n'aima jamais—Il n'avait pas le temps" (To the moon he was devoted; / But he never loved—He didn't have time, lines 9–10).[95] Eliot, rather, throws lunar sentimentalism back at Laforgue and the other dandies of the moon.[96] By contrast, William Butler Yeats, a generation older than Eliot, remained unabashedly lunar throughout his career.[97] Even in a poem such as "Adam's Curse" (1903), where the presence of the moon signals a fraught relationship between the speaker and his lover—"That it had all seemed happy, and yet we'd grown / As weary-hearted as that hollow moon" (lines 37–38)—Yeats still sees the moon as the driving force of his poetic inspiration.[98] Eliot sees the moon with more critical eyes, as an awkward and passé presence that juxtaposes itself between his masculinity and women, exacerbating his ill-at-ease relationship with the other sex. Yet, Eliot still feels the need to engage with the moon's luminous presence in semi-futurist terms in order to claim his spot in this male-dominated genealogy of moonlight poetry and art.

The sonnet "Nocturne" (1909), one of Eliot's first poems to be published, marks the beginning of Eliot's experimental phase with lunar dandyism. Directly mocking a "moonstruck hero," Eliot plays with the characters of Romeo and Juliet, creating a darkly humorous representation of the star-crossed lovers, under the effect of Jules Laforgue's own retelling of Shakespeare's *Hamlet*.[99] After Romeo serenades under Juliet's balcony, "beneath a bored and courteous moon" (*P* 234, line 4), the speaker decides to cut their romance short as their conversation becomes a little trite. Juliet is then hastily killed:

> Blood looks effective on the moonlit ground—
> The hero smiles; in my best mode oblique
> Rolls toward the moon a frenzied eye profound,
> (No need of "Love forever?"—"Love next week?")
> While female readers all in tears are drowned:—
> "The perfect climax all true lovers seek!"   (*P* 235, lines 9-14)

Eliot's nocturne is devoid of sentimentality: it is ruthless, fierce in its heartless separation of the two lovers on account of boredom. In Laforgue's "Hamlet, ou les suites de la piété filiale" ("Hamlet, or the Consequences of Filial Piety," 1887), Laertes kills Hamlet to spare him from a trivial life, and "la lune inonde tout d'un silence polaire" (the moon bathes everything in a polar silence).[100] Indeed, the "frenzied eye" of "Nocturne" may signal that the speaker is affected by some Hamletic madness; perhaps it is Shakespeare himself, imagined by Eliot as he experiments with different dramatic modes.[101] The moon, for Eliot, challenges the speaker's masculinity: the "frenzied" looks back to the moon imply that the Hamlet-like speaker subscribes to the idea that it is better not to love at all, if it means the end of fun, the end of play.

In a poem from the same year, however, Eliot dismisses the cult of the moon as a malady. In this work, which most explicitly draws on Laforgue, because Eliot tells us so in the title—"Humoresque (After J. Laforgue)" (1909; 1910 in the *Harvard Advocate*, *P* 1080)—he openly teases and mocks the moon, which is at the receiving end of another stern look: "His who-the-devil-are-you stare; / Translated, maybe, to the moon" (*P* 237, lines 11-12). "His" refers to one of the dead marionettes that Eliot draws, according to the recollection of his friend John Hayward, directly from "Locutions de Pierrot XII": "Encore un de mes pierrots mort; / Mort d'un chronique orphelinisme; / C'était un cœur plein de dandysme / Lunaire, en un drôle de corps" (Another of my pierrots dead. Dead of chronic orphanism; his was a heart full of lunar dandyism, in a freakish body, *P* 1081). The voice interjecting in the poem addresses the marionette directly, to throw the accusation of lunar dandyism back at the dead Pierrot: "Your damned thin moonlight, worse than gas—" (*P* 237, line 19). The moon is only a weak ray of light, cursed as the result of Pierrot's moon-mania. It is aesthetically passé, discarded as worse than gaslight, the brighter nocturnal illumination. But for Laforgue, and the Symbolists more generally, the moon was an object of fascination, even when ridiculed, and even when the cities illuminated by gaslight began to eclipse the pale glow of the moon: "Ah! la Lune, la Lune m'obsède . . ./Croyez-vous qu'il y ait un remède?" (The Moon! The Moon is my obsession . . ./ Is there a cure for this confession? lines 1-2), the voice of Laforgue's "Jeux" ("Games") cries.[102] Eliot's speakers, on the contrary, repudiate the moon, mocking its cult. This Symbolist lunar cult was, however, part of a more general nineteenth-century enthrallment with the moon, spurred by popular scientific discourse, with which Eliot, as a child of the 1880s, was also familiar. In the paragraphs that follow, I chart the ways in which the moon in popular culture shaped Symbolist aesthetics and how this lunaphilia would have impacted young Eliot.

At the end of the nineteenth century, lunar aesthetics developed under new impulses: the moon was no longer queen of the night skies, but started to be demystified as a sentimental, romanticized icon and popularized as entertainment. Although the moon had been an object of scientific study and popular attention for centuries, in the 1890s the improvement of printing and photographic technologies meant the moon could be easily observed and scrutinized from the comfort of one's home.[103] While the first daguerreotypes of the moon had appeared as early as the 1840s, by the end of the century lunar photography had advanced to such a level that it allowed, and invited, the general public, now familiar with these lunar images, "to inspect the lights and shades of the lunar surface, to touch its cool expanse, to wonder at the detail and speculate about what lies hidden by the lunar night."[104] Many scientific and nonscientific journals and periodicals published photographic reproductions as well as drawings based on photographs to accompany the words of scientists and scientific popularizers of the time. In this respect, the moon felt considerably more familiar to the general public, who could scrutinize its craters, its white sandy-looking surfaces, its darkness as well as its luminosity. Lunar photography was, for the time, and perhaps for us still today, full of imaginative possibilities.[105] Camille Flammarion, a French nineteenth-century astronomer, capitalized on the imaginative potential of astronomy and the human desire for knowledge, writing dozens of books over seventy years on all aspects of astronomy.[106] Equally popular around Europe and North America at this time was the lecture "A Trip to the Moon," which, thanks to a competent use of optical tricks, electric light, and lantern slides, enabled its audience to undertake a fantastical journey from the earth to the moon and back again.[107] Over the decade from 1899-1909, the French photographer Charles Le Morvan took analytical photogravures of the various sides of the moon, which eventually culminated in the publication of *Carte photographique et systématique de la lune* (Photographic and systematic Chart of the Moon, 1914), a portfolio of forty-eight photogravures and twenty-four ink-on-tissue paper overlays, and the first exhaustive lunar atlas.[108] These images (such as fig. 1.6), if removed from the atlas and arrayed in a grid, come to form two enormous complete views of the waning moon and of the waxing moon—creating a formidable domestic observation of the moon without the need for a telescope or even to put one's nose out of the window.[109]

This abundance of images, photographs, drawings, photogravures, and lantern slides, paired with scientific and pseudoscientific texts and lectures, had a substantial impact, drawing people closer to the night sky than ever before. Paradoxically, if urban lighting made it more difficult to admire the starry sky at night, and to take much notice of the moon, this disenchantment went hand in hand with a widespread desire to observe and comprehend the night sky from one's desk or armchair. Some nineteenth-century scientific popularizers even went as far as to give the night sky a new type of relevance, just as it was fading from cities, obfuscated by gaslight pollution. In *Le ciel: notions elementaires d'astronomie physique* (The sky: elementary notions of physical astronomy, 1864), Amédée Guillemin drew wonderfully organized, precise maps of the night sky, set against the modern skyline of Paris as by magical illusion and complete with details of constellations (such as plate 2):[110] four landscapes, one portrait. If we remove the four landscape plates from Guillemin's book, and place them side by side, we get a 360-degree view of the sky over Paris, which might have worked as an imaginative entertainment or distraction, scientific divulgation, and even home decoration. In other words, by the end of the nineteenth century, contemplating the stars, the moon, and the sky had become an indoor affair.

Eliot, coming of age in the first decade of the twentieth century, was very aware of late nineteenth-century popular astronomy, which he experienced as a child. As Katherine Ebury tells us, Eliot had been interested in cosmology for a long time.[111] In fact, one of the short narratives he penned for his *Fireside* magazine (1898) was a "voyage to the Great Bear," the constellation visible in the summer from the Northern Hemisphere.[112] It is no accident, then, that for his early poem "Inside the gloom" (1910), Eliot should imagine the stars and constellations viewable in the August night sky in the Northern Hemisphere (the poem includes "Scorpion," "Cassiopea," the "Major Bear," "Pegasus," "Cetus," the "Pole Star," and "Bootes"; *P* 255) come to life.[113]

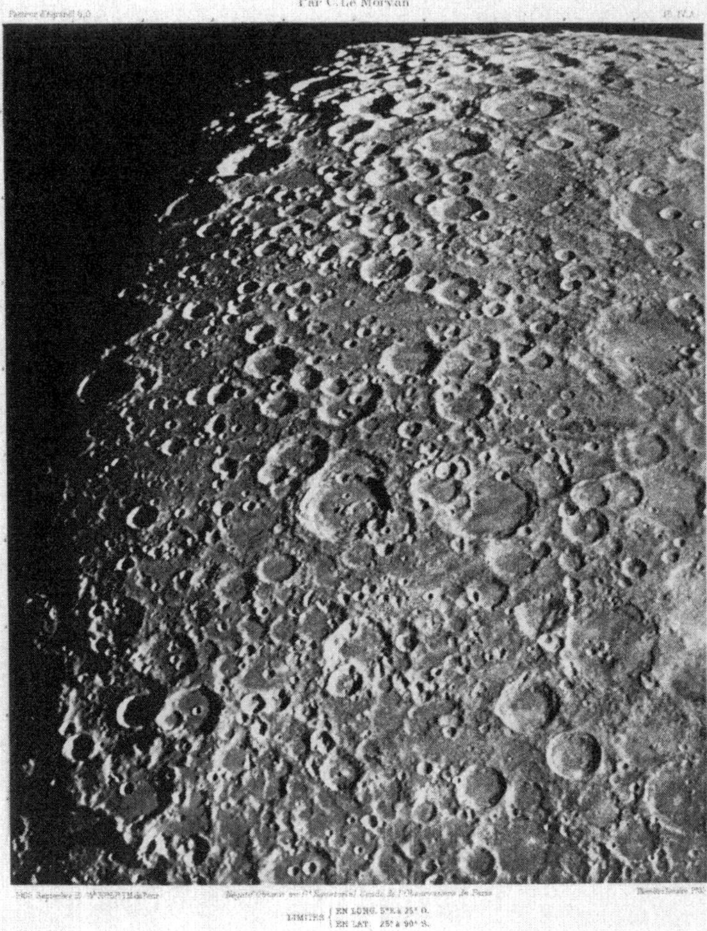

Fig. 1.6. Charles Le Morvan, *Carte photographique de la lune, planche IV.A* (Photographic Chart of the Moon, plate IV.A), September 13, 1900, from Charles Le Morvan, *Carte photographique et systématique de la lune* (Paris: L'Académie des Sciences, 1914). Photogravure, 31.1 × 25.5 cm (12 1/4 × 10 1/16 in.). Pepita Milmore Fund, National Gallery of Art, Washington. Digital image courtesy of National Gallery of Art.

Christopher Ricks flattens this poem to a case of Eliot mimicking Laforgue's "Litanies des premiers quartiers de la lune" ("Litanies for the First Quarters of the Moon," *P* 1117). It is true that Eliot follows a similar rhyme scheme to that in Laforgue's poem (for example: "Lune bénie / Des insomnies, // Blanc médaillon / Des Endymions," lines 1-4); but if Laforgue's poem is a manifesto of his lunar obsessions, Eliot's "Inside the gloom" certainly is not.[114] Eliot here displays a superior sensibility for astronomic nomenclature compared to the French poem, which is exclusively about the moon. In "Inside the gloom," the personified constellations enact a debate on the cosmos, and the meaning of everything, spurred by Bergson's philosophy.[115] Instead of contemplating the stars from the window of his garret room, Eliot's persona might be imagining them come to life from popular cosmology books, such as those of Guillemin or Flammarion. Even with the aid of a telescope, it would have been very difficult to observe and identify all of them from a single room in a city. We might never know for certain, but this poem tells us something crucial about Eliot's poetics. One of the English translators of Laforgue, Peter Dale, suggests that "Eliot took the role of Laforgue as Laforgue took the role of the clown."[116] But, I argue, after openly imitating Laforgue in a few poems, Eliot's poetic goal becomes to outdo Laforgue. In order to achieve this, he returns to the visual and popular culture of the preceding decades, with which his early poetry is so deeply engaged. Eliot, while closely observing the work of Laforgue and other Symbolist and Decadent authors, attempts to supersede them by overturning their lunar values and symbolism. By mocking and repudiating the moon, as he does, he is also mocking them, exorcising his recognizable debt to nineteenth-century French poetry.

Man in the Moon

The quasi-ubiquitous representation of the moon made it easier to be enamored with it but also to caricature, mock, or make fun of others' fascination. In Flammarion's *Astronomie des dames* (*Astronomy for Amateurs*, 1903), for example, he discusses our general propensity to view a human figure in the face of the moon, explaining the different shapes people see there, including a man's head, or a woman's (fig. 1.7).[117] Anthropomorphizing the moon was a popularizing effort to get a step closer to understanding it conceptually and was also a mode that permeated the arts at the turn of the twentieth century. In Aubrey Beardsley's illustrations for the English edition of Oscar Wilde's *Salomé* (1894), he depicted a strange anthropomorphic moon

Fig. 1.7. Plate 67, "The Woman's Head in the Moon," from Camille Flammarion, *Astronomy for Amateurs*, trans. Frances A. Welby (New York: D. Appleton and Company, 1908), 238.

presiding over the apparently homosexual couple of Narraboth and the Page of Herodias.[118] It is a strange moon indeed, as it bears the facial features of Oscar Wilde: plump, round, and with sad, melancholic eyes. In "The Woman in the Moon" (top of fig. 1.8), it even comes accompanied by a flower, possibly a rose, with so many petals that it almost calls to mind the faceting of a diamond; while in "A Platonic Lament" (top right of fig. 1.9), the moon drops the flower over the dead body of Narraboth.[119] The whole of *Salomé* takes place in moonlight, prefiguring the deaths of Narraboth, Jokanaan, and eventually Salomé herself, as epitomized by the play's second line (and the page's first speech): "Regardez la lune. La lune a l'air très étrange. On dirait une femme qui sort d'un tombeau. Elle ressemble à une femme morte. On dirait qu'elle cherche des morts" (Look at the moon. How strange the moon seems! She is like a woman rising from a tomb. She is like a dead woman. One might fancy she was looking for dead things).[120] Moonlight in *Salomé* symbolizes unrequited love, decay, death, and perversion. In Beardsley's illustration, the moon only appears as a caricature of Wilde, highlighting his feminine

Fig. 1.8. Aubrey Beardsley, *The Woman in the Moon* (plate 1), from *Salomé: A Tragedy in One Act: Translated from the French of Oscar Wilde, with Sixteen Drawings by Aubrey Beardsley* (London: John Lane, The Bodley Head, 1907).

Fig. 1.9. Aubrey Beardsley, *A Platonic Lament* (plate 7), from *Salomé: A Tragedy in One Act: Translated from the French of Oscar Wilde, with Sixteen Drawings by Aubrey Beardsley* (London: John Lane, The Bodley Head, 1907).

Fig. 1.10. Frame from Georges Méliès's *Le voyage dans la lune* (*A Trip to the Moon*, 1902). Digital image courtesy of Wikimedia Commons.

traits and his queerness. Beardsley's caricature of the moon signals an important aesthetic change in the way artists and people were thinking about all things lunar at the turn of the twentieth century. The moon has lost its status of virgin goddess, and its relevance to modernity veers toward the ridiculous. In 1902, Georges Méliès, in his internationally successful film *Le voyage dans la lune* (*A Trip to the Moon*), fantasizes about incredible landings on a moon that has turned into the laughing stock of the new century:[121] an airship packed with thrilled moon explorers, aiming for one of the moon's craters, eventually lands directly in the moon's eye, disfiguring its face into a bizarre Polyphemus (fig. 1.10). The moon's beauty and femininity are under attack, but risibly so. Eliot's moons are an integral part of this modern fascination with the moon as an outdated relic. His own lunar discourse sits familiarly within this turn-of-the-century culture of the moon, a culture crucially shaped by popular science, Decadent art and literature, and visionary cinema.

For the Decadents, the moon is—fittingly—a decaying image. But what does the moon mean to Eliot? If we return to "Rhapsody on a Windy Night," it is in the streetlamp's third speech that Eliot anthropomorphizes the moon

in a way that is in direct dialogue with late nineteenth-century and Deca-
dent sensibilities:

> "Regard the moon,
> La lune ne garde aucune rancune,
> She winks a feeble eye,
> She smiles into corners.
> She smooths the hair of the grass.
> The moon has lost her memory.
> A washed-out smallpox cracks her face,
> Her hand twists a paper rose,
> That smells of dust and eau de Cologne,
> She is alone
> With all the old nocturnal smells
> That cross and cross across her brain."   (*P* 19, lines 50–61)

Adopting the same words as the page in *Salomé* ("Regardez la lune"), the
streetlamp exhorts the poet's persona—a variation on the lunar dandy—to
look closely at the moon, which appears much like the turn-of-the-century
moons we have just observed: its craters are visible like smallpox scars, and
this moon, like Beardsley's portrayal of Wilde-as-Moon, bestows an enig-
matic smile on the scene below, hiding in the corner (as in *A Platonic Lament*),
with half-opened eyes, and holding a rose. Eliot shares much of his aesthet-
ics with Beardsley, as well as some of Beardsley's satirical agenda.[122] Much
as Beardsley caricatures Wilde, Eliot mocks the moon by throwing it back
at the Decadents, who cherished it so much and made it such a driving part
of their poetics. Eliot's imitation of the Symbolists and the Decadents may
have allowed him to find his voice in his early poetic experiments, but he
does so by part mocking, part imitating the Symbolists and Decadents in
order to craft a new poetics that distinguish his works from theirs.[123] The
moon holds no grudge against its loss of status as a poetic guide, just as it
holds none against the street lighting that has replaced its nocturnal shine:
for Eliot, as for Marinetti and Loy (as we shall see in the next two chapters),
the moon makes for a muse "in reverse." The moon still urges them to write,
but they do so out of a need to state its outdatedness and irrelevance rather
than anything else. The Decadents and the Symbolists find the moon relat-
able—the drive to their poetry; for the modernists discussed in this book,
artificial lighting of various kinds proves to be a more sympathetic and un-
derstandable trope.

Seen from this angle, Eliot's "Conversation Galante" (1909), where the moon is suddenly transformed into an outdated illumination technology, works as a manifesto of his early poetics. In this poem, a young man walks in the company of a lady in the moonlight, psyching himself up perhaps a little too much for this romantic encounter, which, as a result, goes awry. Our parodied lunar dandy clearly thinks it is a good idea to start things off by apostrophizing the moon directly:

> I observe: "Our sentimental friend the moon!
> Or possibly (fantastic, I confess)
> It may be Prester John's balloon
> Or an old battered lantern hung aloft
> To light poor travellers to their distress."   (*P* 27, lines 1-5)

In 1912, T. E. Hulme published "Above the Dock," a four-line poem about yet another moon that "is but a child's balloon, forgotten after play" (line 4), often discussed in conjunction with Eliot's "Conversation Galante" (*P* 447-448).[124] But if Hulme's poem summons up a surreal, humorous association close to that in Eliot's poem, it lacks the gendered tension that Eliot typically associates with the moon. While the speaker's remark about the moon as the "sentimental friend" seemingly positions him as a Pierrot or lunar dandy, it soon enough becomes clear that the Symbolist and Decadent setup of lunar lady and dandy is no longer relevant. She finds his words just babble, distracting them from what should be the real focus of their conversation—her beauty and, presumably, some romantic action. This lady of more modern and practical manners appears ill at ease with her companion's old-fashioned discussion of the moon. Instead of making love to her, he decides to begin theorizing the moon, dismissing it as an old lantern. The moon cannot offer help or inspiration, as it might have to poets of earlier generations.

According to Eliot's memory and the annotations in his notebook, "Conversation Galante" was written in November 1909 (*P* 447), thus following quite closely on the publication date of Filippo Tommaso Marinetti's first two Futurist manifestos (February 20 and April 11).[125] As we shall see in Chapter Two, in the latter, "Tuons le clair de lune!!" ("Let's Murder the Moonlight!!"), Marinetti incites readers to "murder" the moonlight, which for him represents the passéist literary tradition as well as an antiquated perpetuation of cultural gender tropes. I am not suggesting that Eliot had necessarily read Marinetti in the summer of 1909. But what I do want to suggest is that both Eliot and Marinetti share very particular aesthetic and cultural horizons.[126]

Both, at this point, see the moon as an obstacle preventing men from out-flanking the gendered poetic archetypes of the previous century. Both have a great appreciation of the Symbolist masters and an even greater desire to supersede them. For both, becoming a modern artist necessarily means overturning the moon and the influence of lunar aesthetics.

When we talk about Eliot, we often speak of influence, debt, and friend-ship—even when the latter involves dead authors.[127] I have gone beyond this usual framework here and instead focused on observing what he might have *actually* been "observing"—to borrow Kenner's term from *The Mechanic Muse*—and reflecting on what this might tell us about his early poetry. Ob-serving his poetic images of lights and moons has allowed me to unravel his poetics as a creative reaction to his Symbolist and Decadent readings. By paying close attention to Eliot's poetic language of light against the backdrop of late nineteenth-century cultures of light, I have shown how Eliot went about forging a new brilliant poetics, in which the scrutinizing gaze of gas-light collides with that of a mock-Symbolist, self-ironizing moon.

Killing the Moonlight

F. T. Marinetti and the Futurist Avant-Garde

Venga finalmente il regno della divina Luce Elettrica
(Let the reign of divine Electric Light finally come)

F. T. Marinetti, *CONTRO VENEZIA PASSATISTA* ("Against
Passéist Venice," April 1910)[1]

Avant-gardes are often preoccupied with births, origins, and beginnings. In a widely mythologized version of the early hours of February 20, 1909, Filippo Tommaso Marinetti—Egyptian-born, French-educated, Milan-based, a truly transnational writer—walks up and down the streets of Paris, waiting for the newsboys to bring that day's issue of *Le Figaro*. He has been awake all night in anticipation of the moment he can hold this illustrious French newspaper with his name printed alongside an unusual piece entitled "Le Futurisme," the manifesto of his newly founded cultural movement. Once Marinetti returns to his room—or perhaps even on his way home to his haunt—he records his feverish impressions of that moment: "con mani tremanti aprii e lessi come se non fosse mio ma piovuto da quell'alba piovosa raggio di solida luce l'amato fecondo *Manifesto*" (I opened it with trembling hands and I read it as if it was not my thing but rather poured down of that rainy dawn—a ray of solid light—the beloved fertile *Manifesto*; emphasis in the original).[2] The "solid light" irradiating from the pages of the freshly printed *Figaro* bathes him in the glory of the moment, overturning even the weather of that stereotypically gray and wet Parisian morning. Light, both natural and artificial, is at the very core of the new movement's aesthetics and of its manifesto.

This luminous text comprised two distinct, yet richly interconnected, sections: a narration of the movement's semi-mythical origins, followed by a highly precise endecalogue of Futurism's aesthetics.[3] In the former, Marinetti deliberately associates the founding of his movement, and the character of his Futurist friends, with artificial light:

> Nous avions veillé toute la nuit, mes amis et moi, sous des lampes de mosquée dont les coupoles de cuivre aussi ajourées que notre âme avaient pourtant des cœurs électriques. Et tout en piétinant notre native paresse sur d'opulents tapis persans, nous avions discuté aux frontières extrêmes de la logique et griffé le papier de démentes écritures.
>
> ———
>
> (We had stayed up all night—my friends and I—beneath mosque lamps hanging from the ceiling. Their brass domes were filigreed like our souls; just as, again like our souls, they had electric hearts. Trampling our ancestral lethargy into the opulent oriental rugs, we argued all the way to the final frontiers of logic and blackening reams of paper with delirious writings.)[4]

In a verdict typical of scholarly readings of this passage, Arndt Niebisch notes the "ubiquitous presence of the electric light" at the opening of Marinetti's introduction, with the mosque lamp first and the trams afterward. For Niebisch this detail encapsulates the "instantaneous character of the scene," whose "light stimuli" stir the Futurists to action as if by "electric shocks."[5] This contention, however, oversimplifies the scene. The room where the Futurists exercise their subversive creativity is Marinetti's salon in his family house on via Senato in Milan, luxuriously furnished with Middle Eastern decor and saturated with his father's memorabilia from Egypt, the country of Marinetti's childhood.[6] The sensual atmosphere of the room, suggested by the presence of the "lampes de mosquée" and "opulents tapis persans"—which Vincent d'Orlando ironically calls "décadentisme de pacotille" (tat decadence)—is sharply at odds with the spirit of the artistic movement in the making.[7] Futurism, as the name of the movement itself suggests, wants to break away with the past: it wants society, art, and literature to leap into the future; in a way, we might say, Futurism wants to be *the* avant-garde in the strictest sense of the French word, whereby the avant-gardist should always think, work, and imagine ahead of his or her time—anticipating and sometimes even setting future trends.[8] But, curiously, the exotic character of the objects in Marinetti's Milanese flat is reminiscent of the very French and Italian literary traditions (i.e., *Symbolisme/simbolismo, décadence/decadentismo, crepuscolarismo*) from which Marinetti so ardently wished to detach himself and the Futurist movement.[9]

The "lampe de mosque," or mosque lamp (see fig. 2.1), is in fact a central

Fig. 2.1. Photograph of the filigreed brass mosque lamp owned by Marinetti, in Claudia Salaris, *Marinetti* (Florence: La Nuova Italia, 1988), 86. Photograph originally from Luce Marinetti Collection, courtesy of Francesca Barbi Marinetti.

object in this narrative. It suggests the presence of a special relationship between the character of the new movement (and its members), lighting, and late nineteenth-century fascination with the East. This lamp is an ancient type of oil light made of glass, primarily employed for the interior lighting of mosques, where it would generally be hung.[10] In Muslim countries at the turn of the twentieth century, as naked light bulbs on wire were not very aesthetically pleasing, mosque lamps were adapted to the new technology to serve as lampshades, producing a most evocative "hide and veil" effect, with light bulbs "hanging inside them from sockets attached to dish-shaped tops."[11] Through a process of aestheticization and normalization, the glass shades of mosque lamps enclose and decorate the bare light bulbs. In Marinetti's manifesto, the mosque lamp epitomizes the past—both Marinetti's own personal past and antiquity more generally—making his poetics apparent right from its inception.

Yet Marinetti's mosque lamp is a modern one, containing an electric heart. For Christine Poggi, the domestic boundaries of Marinetti's flat imprison the Futurists like the mosque lamps do the light bulbs.[12] For Marjorie Perloff, though, the "electric heart" refers to the actual electrified machines that feature later in the manifesto.[13] And yet, in the original French syntax, the connecting "dont" (meaning "whose") reveals that the electric heart is effectively encased both within the filigreed domes of the mosque lamps and within the Futurists themselves: "sous des lampes de mosquée dont les coupoles de cuivre aussi ajourées que notre âme avaient pourtant des cœurs électriques." Marinetti's simile moves from the literal image of his own mosque lamp, which might have well been electrified and could have contained an actual light bulb, to the transcendental one of the Futurists containing a brilliant, technologically sophisticated electric heart. The Futurist soul is no moon in the night sky, no river running wild high up in the mountains, no waves in the ocean, no strong wind blowing over Italy: the soul of Futurism—its essence—is an electric heart.

It certainly helped that the city hosting most of these first Futurist get-togethers was Milan, at the time Italy's "electric city," home from 1882 to the first electrical power station of continental Europe, forcefully illuminated by over a hundred arc lamps by 1886, and served by an electrified tramway system from 1895.[14] Saying that this scene is clearly the result of early twentieth-century "electrification of cities," then, is not wrong, but it does oversimplify things.[15] Certainly, the electricity in Marinetti's home is what enables the Futurists' "fierce wakefulness," to borrow Poggi's phrase: no electricity, no restlessness, no Futurist manifesto.[16] But this scene, the opening of this primal manifesto, often overlooked in favor of the manifesto's endecalogue, bears a deeper symbolical significance. The electric heart beats at the center of Futurism, breaking into the scene with its typical vitality, luminosity, and modern feeling, but it also recognizes its debt to the past literary tradition, the mosque lamp: Marinetti's electric light is not a straightforward naked bulb, however displeasing to the eye, but is rather trapped in an ancient, religiously connoted, and intricately decorated artefact, from which it wants to burst out. This chapter looks closely at the emergence of new artificial lights against older "natural" ones to reveal Futurism's complex relationship with the late nineteenth-century sensibilities from which it develops, as well as the movement's contribution to the process of appropriating electric light as matter for cultural work in the twentieth century.

Futurists claimed that the characteristic that distinguished their movement from other avant-gardes of the early twentieth century was their special relationship with technology. Right from their first manifesto, the Futurists had been establishing science and technology as cardinal points of their aesthetics. Although the date of Futurism's birth in 1909 may feel "convenient but artificial," it is no coincidence it should imbricate with those of new technological developments, given that Italy, the movement's birthplace, experienced its own economic, industrial, and technological boom over the years 1896-1908, considerably later than other Western countries.[17] A teenage Filippo Tommaso would subsequently remember, in his memoir *La grande Milano tradizionale e futurista* (Milan: Great, Traditional, Futurist; 1969), the moment when, one May evening in the 1890s, he saw for the first time Galleria Vittorio Emanuele gorgeously radiant with gaslight, creating a "piacevole esempio di una imperiosa estetica della macchina che delicatamente metteva in moto i nervi dei miei polpastrelli" (pleasing example of a haughty machine aesthetic, which delicately made the nerves in my fingertips twitch).[18] From the start, then, Marinetti had been programmatically investing Futurism with the emboldening possibilities of new technologies.[19] In the endecalogue of his trendsetting first manifesto (1909), Marinetti famously praised the "automobile rugissante, qui [. . .] est plus belle que la *Victoire de Samothrace*" (roaring automobile, that [. . .] is more beautiful than the *Victory of Samothrace*, *F* 51), clearly inspired by the writings of Italian techno-theorist Mario Morasso, especially his essay "L'artigliere meccanico" (The mechanic artilleryman, 1906).[20] His eleventh and final doctrine spells out the effect of technological development on the literature and art of the future:

> Nous chanterons [. . .] les ressacs multicolores et polyphoniques des révolutions dans les capitales modernes; la vibration nocturne des arsenaux et des chantiers sous leurs violentes lunes électriques; les gares gloutonnes avaleuses de serpents qui fument; les usines suspendues aux nuages par les ficelles de leurs fumées; les ponts aux bonds de gymnastes lancés sur la coutellerie diabolique des fleuves ensoleillés; les paquebots aventureux flairant l'horizon; les locomotives au grand poitrail qui piaffent sur les rails, tels d'énormes chevaux d'acier bridés de long tuyaux et le vol glissant des aéroplanes dont l'hélice a des claquements de drapeaux et des applaudissements de foule enthousiaste.[21]

> (We shall sing [. . .] the multicolored and polyphonic tidal waves of revolution in the modern metropolis; shall sing the vibrating nocturnal fervor of factories and shipyards burning under violent electrical moons; bloated railroad stations that devour smoking serpents; factories hanging from the sky by the twisting threads of spiraling smoke; bridges like gigantic gymnasts who span rivers, flashing at the sun with the gleam of a knife; adventurous steamships that scent the horizon, locomotives with their swollen chest, pawing the tracks like massive steel horses bridled with pipes, and the oscillating flight of airplanes, whose propeller flaps at the wind like a flag and seems to applaud like a delirious crowd. [*F* 51])

This final Futurist resolution is the longest, most detailed, and most convoluted in the manifesto. Marinetti accumulates, rather than simply enumerates; he stirs and excites the readers' imagination by invoking images of present and future technologies, coalesced together, such as "aéroplanes" (airplanes), "énormes chevaux d'acier" (massive steel horses), and "violentes lunes électriques" (violent electrical moons). The accumulation of new and future technologies is extremely specific and at the same time intensely suggestive in both its selection of terms and images: the readers can immediately visualize this extraordinary ultramodern scene generated by Marinetti's words. Indeed, as Domenico Pietropaolo explains, "technology provides [the Futurist imagination] with the instruments it needs in order to visualize" its conceptualizations.[22] In this sense, the Futurists understand technology as a powerful tool of aesthetic creativity, giving substance and precision to their artistic revolution.[23] For Günter Berghaus, technology also offers Futurists a new "cult of the machine" that allows them to exorcise the "shadow side of modernity," which would subsequently see its most extreme realization in Fascist Italy.[24] The Futurists' imaginative appropriation of new technologies creates a "mythopoeia," which in turn understands, glosses, and influences the cultural changes occurring around the Futurists at the turn of the twentieth century.[25]

The endecalogue's intriguing version of electric light—the "violent electrical moons"—seems, at first, to be there just to enhance the evocation of a hyper-technological atmosphere for the Futurists' artistic upheaval. In fact, Marinetti and other poets and artists associated with the early phase of Futurism (1909-25) harness the symbolical antagonism between moonlight and electric light as a powerful way of handling the recent past, developing the trope of murdering the moonlight. The first half of this chapter is dedicated to unraveling Marinetti's close poetic links to Symbolism, showing how murdering the moonlight becomes a potent poetic metaphor for exorcising his relationship with the French poetic tradition. I will analyze this trope in Marinetti's work before exploring its ramifications in poems by Ada Negri, Paolo Buzzi, and Libero Altomare, and in artwork by Giacomo Balla. In the second half of this chapter, I push toward an interpretation of the Futurist attack on moonlight as part of Marinetti's battle against traditional gender roles, showing how the act of killing the moonlight becomes a powerful rhetorical tool in Marinetti's struggle for reimagining femininity and liberating women from the stifling male gaze of the Decadent and Symbolist poets. In this section, I discuss poetry and artwork by both Futurist men and women—Natalia Goncharova, Maria Ginanni, Fanny Dini, Mario Carli, Rosa Rosà, Emilio Mario Dolfi, Escodamé, Fillia, Enzo Mainardi, and Růžena Zátková. This twofold reading of the Futurist victory of arc lighting and electric light over *le clair de lune* plays a crucial role in the overarching narrative of this book, showing how many modernist poets came to see representations of moonlight and electric light as an essential articulation of larger cultural and aesthetic concerns.

A Lunicidal Project

In Marinetti's second Futurist proclamation, "Tuons le clair de lune!!" ("Let's Murder the Moonlight!!," published April 11, 1909), our Futurist troublemaker makes a public attack on the moon as a passé, gendered trope.[26] Marinetti spurs five poet friends and Futurists (Paolo Buzzi, Federico de Maria, Enrico Cavacchioli, Corrado Govoni, and Libero Altomare) to fight against "la Lune charnelle, la Lune aux belles cuisses chaudes" (the carnal

Moon, the Moon of warm beautiful thighs [*F* 59]) so as to rescue themselves from romantic love, melancholy, and desire.[27] In the third section of this text, the moon arrives on the scene, with her "sourire brillant et chaud" (luminous and warm smile) and "toute ruisselante du lait grisant des acacias" (dripping with the intoxicating milk of acacias), immediately stirring the action of a group of "fous" (madmen) enthralled with the moon and its luminous appearance (*LF* 168-169; *F* 58, edited by the author). The Futurists, too, are somewhat susceptible to the charm of the moon (who would not be?), and momentarily abandon themselves to it, before becoming obsessed with the rather portentous (but also comic) idea of murdering the moonlight. The appearance of three hundred electric moons immediately puts this strange idea into effect:

> — Tuons le clair de lune!
>
> Les uns coururent aux prochaines cascades; des roues géantes furent dressées et des turbines transformèrent la vitesse des eaux en des spasmes magnétiques qui, par des fils, grimpèrent sur des poteaux jusqu'à des globes lumineux et bruissants.
>
> C'est ainsi que trois cents lunes électriques biffèrent de leurs rayons de craie éblouissante l'antique reine verte des amours. (*LF* 170)
>
> ---
>
> ("Let's murder the moonlight!"
>
> Some of us ran to nearby waterfalls; gigantic wheels were hoisted, and turbines transformed the velocity of the waters into electromagnetic spasms that climbed up wires suspended on high poles, until they reached luminous, humming globes.
>
> So it was that three hundred electric moons, with rays of blinding chalky whiteness, canceled the old green queen of love affairs. [*F* 59])[28]

Marinetti's imagined electrical moons are, by implication, arc lamps of high luminosity, which cancel and destroy moonlight by substituting it with a new man-controlled type of nocturnal illumination.[29] An unnatural chalklike whiteness surrounds the new electric moons, which replace the old moon grown green with envy and decay, perhaps of Shakespearean memory ("Her [i.e., the moon's] vestal livery is but sick and green," Romeo proclaims upon Juliet's appearance on the balcony in the famous scene).[30] In those early days of arc-light illumination, the presence of these new street moons considerably weakened the illuminating power of the moon in urban spaces: a phenomenon frequently portrayed in illustrations produced globally (see,

Fig. 2.2. Francesco Paolo Michetti, "MILANO—Esperienze d'illuminazione elettrica, in piazza del Duomo, la sera del 18 marzo" (Milan: Experiencing electrical illumination on Piazza del Duomo, the evening of March 18), in *L'Illustrazione italiana*, no. 12 (1877), 181. Digital image courtesy of Biblioteca Storia Moderna e Contemporanea, Rome.

for example, fig. 2.2 showing the first successful experiment with public electrical illumination in Milan in 1877, for *L'Illustrazione italiana* [Italian Illustrated News]). In this sense, Marinetti's text elaborates on the techno-cultural process of the moon's actual disappearance from the urban night sky and its replacement with the electric light. But the moon's almost exaggerated, stereotyped portrayal as feminine adds a gender-political dimension to the scene: like the passive moon in the sky, which we can only observe and admire from below, so have women been perceived—sometimes by themselves but most especially by men. To the Futurist, therefore, electric light must be what moonlight used to be for the Symbolist: an idol to worship. In "Tuons le clair de lune!!" this intuition becomes the essence of Marinetti's newly founded poetics.[31] Marinetti takes on aesthetic agency in this technological revolution by claiming this moment as crucial for the foundation of Futurism, but he also deploys it so as to change and disrupt the literary, artistic, and cultural landscape of the time. As we shall see later in this chapter and more extensively in Chapter Three, these changes instigated by Marinetti are especially evident in the way gender relations play out in Futurism. Marinetti propounds a phenomenon of substitution, by which Futurist aesthetics replace old ones, and Futurist men and women replace Symbolist men and women, just as the electric light has been replacing the moon at night. The old moon is at once the former technology, superseded by the implementation of electric light, and the obsolete aesthetics and morals outflanked by the new Futurist movement. In the sections that follow, I first turn to the aesthetic implications of murdering the moonlight before suggesting its implications for Futurism's own gendering and ungendering of the moon and electric light, and its relevance for the role and agency of women within the movement.

Lunes électriques

Marinetti and Futurism had long, deep roots in the poetics of Symbolism and Decadence, and had been nurturing an ambiguous relationship with the literary forerunners they sought to annihilate on paper. Initially, Marinetti wrote poetry in French: "Les vieux marins" ("The Old Sailors," 1898); *La conquête des étoiles* (*The Conquest of the Stars*, 1902); *Destruction* (1904); *La momie sanglante* (*The Bloody Mummy*, 1904); *La ville charnelle* (*The Sensual City*, 1908).[32] These collections are all, in varying degrees, Symbolist in form and content. On the very eve of the launch of Futurism, Tullio Panteo, the author of the 1908 "booklet" *Il poeta Marinetti* (Marinetti the Poet), frames our young writer as a Symbolist: "pallido e biondo, con lo sguardo sempre lontano, *troublant* come una carezza, [. . .] l'eterno innamorato delle stelle e della luna, il sublime cantore del mare" (pale and blonde, with a far-away gaze, troublant like a caress, [. . .] the eternal lover of the stars and the moon, the sublime singer of the sea).[33] As Luca Somigli points out, this delicate Laforguean lunar dandy makes him a surprising candidate as the aggressive founder of Futurism! While scholarship has tended to focus on Marinetti's Symbolist stars (especially in *La conquête des étoiles*), I turn here to the moon, so characteristic of his immediate poetic forebears and at the center of the poetry Marinetti is writing at this time, suggesting elements of continuity between the dandy of the moon and the serial killer of moonlight.[34]

A line in a dithyramb dedicated to the French Symbolist Henri de Régnier (from *La ville charnelle*) indicates what Marinetti saw as the intellectual nourishment of Symbolist poetics: "La vierge Poésie s'avance à pas de lune" (The virgin Poetry walks with a lunar stride, line 29).[35] Feminine poetry is "virginal," pure, and blessed by the moon. In *Destruction*, he takes a more Laforguean turn, likening the moon to a coconut and then to a spider, before starting to play with electricity and the moon in a way that directly prefigures his first Futurist manifesto.[36] In "Dans les cafés de nuit" ("In the Cafés at Night"), a long piece which starts off as a poem in a semi-Baudelairean key and then mutates into dramatic prose, Marinetti writes:

> Et voilà que soudain sur nos pâleurs,
> les lampes électriques brandissaient leurs cœurs blancs
> qu'elles serraient entre leurs doigts de fer,
> jusqu'à les faire crier expumant de laits bleus.
> O pauvres cœurs blessés des lampes électriques . . .
> [. . .]
> Parfois les lampes électriques versaient dans nos cœurs
> d'aveuglants clairs de lune acides et corrosifs,
> où nos profils, nos luxures et nos désirs métallisés
> parurent tout à coup ciselés dans la nacre
> et l'acier rutilant.[37]   (lines 85-89, 98-102)

(There, suddenly on our pale selves,/the electric lamps wavered their white hearts/which they clutched in their iron fingers,/until they scream oozing blue milk./O poor wounded hearts of the electric lamps . . ./[. . .]/At times the electric lamps poured into our hearts/some blinding moonlight, harsh and caustic,/where our profiles, our lusts and our desires, metallized,/appeared all of a sudden chiseled on the mother of pearl/and the glistening steel.)

Today, it is hard not to read these two stanzas as a dress rehearsal for Marinetti's first manifesto: electric hearts, moonlight, and shiny metal. In this earlier poem, as in the later manifesto, the hearts the speaker conjures are withheld; the electric light is waiting to burst out. This harsh light reveals the speaker's soul against a backdrop at once suggestive of decadent indulgence (the lunar mother of pearl) and Futurist mechanic imagination (the glistening steel). More importantly, however, it uncovers Marinetti's uncertain position between respect for Symbolism and his new avant-gardist instincts, waiting to burst out like the electric light imprisoned within the lamps.

It is, however, in *La ville charnelle*, published only a year before Marinetti's manifesto, and still drenched in that Symbolist lunar dandyism to

which T. S. Eliot was also partial (see Chapter One), that Marinetti gives full
wing to his lunicidal project with a whole poem on the subject, unimagina-
tively titled "La mort de la lune" ("The Death of the Moon"). His tone, lan-
guage, and form are reminiscent of Symbolism, filtering this French style in
much the same way as Eliot did in his Laforguean poems. In this "petit drame
de lumières" (little tragedy of lights), as Marinetti himself describes it, the
Moon dies in ridiculous circumstances:[38]

> Mais, tout à coup, la Lune, comme un enfant,
> trébucha sur les drisses,
> et tomba de très haut, la tête la première,
> blessant et déchirant sa chair sur les cordages.
> Son corps s'est écrasé sur la proue noire,
> et son sang ruissela, rose, dans la pénombre
> tout le long du beaupré, éclaboussant les vagues.   (lines 42-48)[39]
>
> ————
>
> (But, all of a sudden, the Moon, like a child,/trips over the halyards,/and falls
> from high up, head first,/hurting and tearing her flesh on the cordage./Her body
> crashes on the black prow,/and her blood drips, pink, in the darkness/all along
> the bowsprit, tarnishing the waves.)

As we can see, Marinetti's first lyrical lunge at the moon is less bombastic,
less exciting, than what he devised in "Tuons le clair de lune!!," with its death
seemingly accidental and caused by the moon's own goofy clumsiness. What
is here only an ironic, neo-Symbolist poet's passive observation of the moon's
death would later transmute into an avant-garde writer's active offensive
against the moon. Here there is no mention of electric light as the culprit of
the moon's demise: the moon, for Marinetti, is simply an outdated presence
that no longer fits the type of poetry he aims to write. One senses a poet
using the moon as a testing ground to exorcise his debt to Symbolism, push-
ing the boundaries of modern poetry.

Fast forward to the early days of Futurism, a few years later, and we find
Marinetti in *Le Futurisme* (1911) officially abjuring his literary predecessors
(the Symbolists) as "derniers amants de la lune" (last lovers of the moon).[40]
He openly situates himself and his Futurist brothers-in-arms against their
"glorieux pères intellectuels" (glorious intellectual fathers), whom they now
despise, after loving them in the extreme—Edgar Allan Poe, Charles Baude-
laire, Stéphane Mallarmé, and Paul Verlaine (*LF* 82; *F* 93)—as well as their
Italian literary forefathers, Antonio Fogazzaro, Giovanni Pascoli, and Gabriele

D'Annunzio (*LF* 88-89; *F* 94-95). Things take a more ambiguous turn when he goes on to claim Émile Zola, Walt Whitman, Rosny aîné, Paul Adam, Octave Mirbeau, Gustave Kahn, and Emile Verhaeren as "grands précurseurs du futurisme" (great precursors of Futurism), as at least four of them (Adam, Mirbeau, Kahn, and Verhaeren) were closely associated with French and Belgian Symbolism (*LF* 88-89; *F* 94-95). Zola, Verhaeren, and Adam were at least identifiably "technophile," albeit in varying degrees, and Whitman may have appealed to Marinetti for lyrics such as "I Sing the Body Electric" (1855).[41] Nevertheless, given that he himself as a poet underwent a Symbolist phase, Marinetti must have felt it necessary publicly to reject key French and Italian literary predecessors. In this text of poetic self-positioning, however, it is Marinetti's repudiation of D'Annunzio that is most mystifying. D'Annunzio is hailed as the principal enemy of Futurism:

> [Notre Italie] a subi trop longtemps l'influence exténuante de Gabriele d'Annunzio, frère cadet des grands symbolistes français, nostalgique comme eux, et comme eux penché sur le corps nu de la femme.
>
> Il faut à tout prix combattre Gabriele d'Annunzio, parce qu'il a raffiné de tout son talent les quatre poisons intellectuels que nous voulons détruire à tout prix:
>
> 1° La poésie maladive et nostalgique de la distance et de souvenir; 2° le sentimentalisme romantique ruisselant de clair de lune, qui monte vers la femme-Beauté, idéale et fatale; 3° l'obsession de la luxure, avec le triangle de l'adultère, le poivre de l'inceste et l'assaisonnement excitateur du péché chrétien; 4° la passion profonde du passé, double d'une manie d'antiquaire et de collectionneur. (*LF* 88)
>
> ――――――
>
> (For too long Italy has submitted to the enfeebling influence of Gabriele D'Annunzio, the lesser brother of the great French Symbolists, nostalgic like them, and like them hovering above the naked female body.
>
> One must at all costs combat Gabriele D'Annunzio, because with all his great skill he has distilled the four intellectual poisons that we want to abolish forever: 1) the sickly, nostalgic poetry of distance and memory; 2) romantic sentimentality dripping with moonlight that is ascending toward an ideal and fatal Woman-Beauty; 3) obsession with lechery, with the adulterous triangle, the spice of incest and the seasoning of Christian sin; 4) the profound passion for the past and the mania for antiquity and collecting. [*F* 94])

D'Annunzio's work is responsible, in Marinetti's view, for producing a generation of degenerate poets writing in a style that is perceived as derivative of French Symbolism and of D'Annunzio's own Italianized Decadent version. In this Symbolist-derived poetry, Marinetti identifies the root of the problem in the adoration of a passive, idolized female body, brought about by a poetry of moonlight, constituted of introspective moments of memory and nostalgia. Woman herself is not the issue for Marinetti; rather, it is what decades of Symbolist literature (and what went before it) have made of her. This conception—and literary-artistic representation—of woman is perverse, outdated, and must be stopped. Breaking the implicit aesthetic connection between sentimentality, romance, women, and moonlight is what Marinetti proposes to do so as to be able fruitfully to renew Italian culture.

Marinetti's relationship with D'Annunzio had always been oblique. According to his biographer Gino Agnese, he once claimed to be the son of a turbine and of Gabriele D'Annunzio; certainly, as editor of the magazine *Poesia: rassegna internazionale* (Poetry: International Review, 1905-09), he had been actively seeking contributions from D'Annunzio as well as from Pascoli; he had also authored the ironic and highly ambivalent texts *D'Annunzio intime* (Intimate D'Annunzio, 1903) and *Les dieux s'en vont, D'Annunzio reste* (The Gods Leave, But D'Annunzio Stays, 1908).[42] Marinetti had also translated into French the "big guns" of late nineteenth-century Italian poetry (Giosué Carducci, Pascoli, and D'Annunzio), acting as a mediator of Italian poetry in France.[43] Translating clearly helped Marinetti ponder his poetic and literary allegiances, while offering him an opportunity to reflect on issues of form, language, and modernity. His translation of "Le città terribili" (The Terrible Cities) from D'Annunzio's long poem *Maia: Laus Vitae* (Maia: Praise of Life, 1903) certainly shows how translating Italian Symbolist-inflected poetry worked for him as a testing ground to experiment with early Futurist ideas and, as Eleonora Conti suggests, "proto-futurist metaphors."[44] Where D'Annunzio depicts the turning on of the electric street lamps using an old-fashioned simile, Marinetti strategically condenses it in a new Futurist metaphor:

> s'accendono i bianchi
> globi come pendule lune
> tra le attonite file
> dei platani.
>
> ———
>
> (they light the white/globes like pendulous moons/among the astonished rows/ of plane trees.)

> À l'heure où d'innombrables lunes électriques
> s'allument entre les files spectrales des platanes.
>
> ———————
>
> (At a time when countless electric moons/illuminate the spectral lines of plane trees.)[45]

Marinetti's translation of these verses, which appeared in 1906 in Paul Fort's Mallarmean-inspired magazine *Vers et Prose*, reads more like a creative adaptation than an accurate translation. D'Annunzio's lines clearly register the change of the Italian urban lightscape: his "bianchi/globi come pendula lune" recall the new design of Milanese arc lamps that, right around the time of D'Annunzio's poem, had not just been fitted in old gas lamps, as they had been elsewhere, but boasted a new style of their own. No longer needing to be lit up by a lamplighter's stick, their bright round white globes were either positioned on top of a much taller pole (fig. 2.3) or hanging from a network of electrical wires (fig. 2.4), looking much, when lit up, like a moon actually pendent over the city streets. Indeed, our Symbolist poet can only accommodate electrified streetlamps in his poetry by using an extended simile to compare the shape of the lamps with the globular form of the moon, which enables him to partially contain the aesthetic incongruity of these items of street furniture—are they lamps, or are they moons? Are they natural, or artificial?

Marinetti, a generation younger than D'Annunzio, dispenses with such niceties ("the white globes/like pendulous moons") and calls a spade a spade: for the future Futurist it is rather "lunes électriques" which the Symbolist poet actually has in mind but does not dare to articulate. Marinetti's translation condenses, shortens, accumulates, but replaces D'Annunzio's degenerate aesthetics, which imbue the artificial with natural qualities. Perhaps Stefano Bragato is right in calling Marinetti's relationship with D'Annunzio "Oedipal," as it becomes clear that for Marinetti it is vital to outflank D'Annunzio in order to manufacture his own literary personality.[46] Translating D'Annunzio evidently affected Marinetti's imagination more than he would care to admit, as electric moons would consequently be at the heart of "Tuons le clair de lune!!"

Marinetti's own substitution dynamics work much like substitution theories of metaphors: his "electric moons" is a practical demonstration of the process described, years later, by the French philosopher Paul Ricoeur. For Ricoeur, the relationship between the two parts of a metaphor bases itself

Fig. 2.3. A Siemens arc lamp on a post in Piazza della Scala in Milan (design used there from 1885 to 1917), in *Milano illuminata: storia, immagini, urbanistica ed emozioni dell'illuminazione elettrica pubblica* (Milan: AEM, 1993), 19.

Fig. 2.4. An arc lamp pending from electrical wires, with the Church of Santa Maria delle Grazie in Milan in the background, in *Milano illuminata: storia, immagini, urbanistica ed emozioni dell'illuminazione elettrica pubblica* (Milan: AEM, 1993), 18.

on one of "seeing as," which "defines the resemblance" between them.[47] "Seeing as" marks for Ricoeur the intuition by which the reader of poetry can make sense of the metaphor while at the same time enjoying the pictorial, iconic dimension of the metaphor: it "ensures the joining of verbal meaning with imagistic fullness."[48] Marinetti's metaphor is more than "an abbreviated simile," as it works actively on the reader's imagination, conjuring up a dreadful scene of moons replaced by lamps, rather than merely likening arc lamps to the moon, as D'Annunzio does in the instance above.[49] Marinetti hereby operates a substitution between the tenor and the vehicle in the relationship of resemblance (as they are both sources of light), which justifies the borrowing.[50] At the same time, Marinetti's metaphor comments on the reception of new illumination systems in the first decade of the twentieth century: the new street lamps have both imaginatively and effectively replaced the moon. In this case, however, the substitution occurs in reverse, as linguistically the word "moon" replaces "lamp," but figuratively we understand this metaphor as turning nature into artifice. Electric light is still only relatable in natural terms, as a moon turned electric.

Marinetti's early proto-Futurist metaphor of "lunes électriques" could not have gone unnoticed in the French-Italian poetry scene of the time, with its successful coalescence of modern poetry with contemporary urban experience. It seems likely that it attracted the attention of the august *poetessa* of early twentieth-century Italy, Ada Negri (1870-1945). Negri was a keen supporter of Marinetti's early efforts (especially of his magazine *Poesia*) and was in return warmly supported by the Futurists (and, regrettably, later by the Fascists), while technically keeping herself out of the Futurist movement.[51] Negri followed the Futurists at a distance, from her privileged role as Italy's acclaimed lyrical voice. It is during this time that Negri begins to incorporate Marinetti's Futurist metaphor into her own poems. The earliest example is "Selciato cittadino" ("City Cobblestones"), from her fourth collection *Dal Profondo* (*From the Deep*, 1910), where a woman wanders about the city at dusk as the new lights come on:

> L'ultimo fischio echeggia dalle fabbriche,
> l'ultima rondin stride intorno agli embrici,
> l'ultimo sogno langue sui garofani
> dei davanzali, e van le lune elettriche
> sbocciando in alto, tra una rete ferrea
> di fili.   (lines 3-8)

(The last whistle echoes from the factories, / the last swallow chirps around the tiles, / the last dream fades over the carnations / on the windowsills, and the electric moons / blossom up above, among an iron net / of wires.)[52]

Negri's electric moons blossom like flowers, among carnations and swallows, in the midst of an unspecified, industrialized cityscape. After portraying the spectacle of a twilit city, Negri turns to the description of a tumultuous stream in the crepuscular light taking over the flâneuse's body. The electric moonlight of the opening jars with the rest of the poem, which, with its abundant natural imagery, is formally conventional and lexically unadventurous. For Negri, unlike Marinetti, natural language remains necessary even when referring to new technological elements of everyday life, such as electric lamps. In "Nostalgia" (from her subsequent collection *Esilio*, Exile, 1914), Negri employs the phrase "lune elettriche" again, this time to enhance the alienation felt by her persona in a foreign town at night: "Freddo, pioggia, crepuscolo. Beffarde / sbucan le lune elettriche, fra aloni / di nebbia. Oscure ombre mi radon, suoni / rauchi movendo dalle lingue tarde" (Cold, rain, twilight. Mockingly / the electric moons pop out, in haloes / of fog. Dark shadows brush against me, / with hoarse sounds out of their slow tongues, lines 5-8).[53] The electric moons in this case cast a ghastly light over the city of Zürich, making Negri's persona long even more painfully for "il Sole mio, sì bello e lontano" (my Sun, so beautiful and so distant, line 29).[54] Here, as in the earlier poem, the Futurist electric moon jars with the rest of the text, suggesting Negri's reluctance to use more technologically specific words; in fact, terms such as *lampioni* (streetlamps), *fanali* (also streetlamps), or *lampade* (lamps), are used very sparingly, if at all.[55]

Making a swift comparison with Negri's poetry allows us to establish how some of Marinetti's stylistic features traveled even outside of his movement. Negri's adoption of Marinetti's metaphor adds a touch of modernity to a poetic style otherwise reminiscent of nineteenth-century poetry. On the other hand, however, Negri borrows a phrase which she repurposes to suit her poetry, far from the hyper-use of technology advocated by Marinetti and his fellow Futurists. Marinetti's influence was certainly far-reaching, proving to have an impact on writers well outside the movement who admired the victory of electric light over moonlight not only as a captivating idea but as the signature element of international Futurism.

The Futurist who most significantly embodied Marinetti's mantra was Giacomo Balla. He was a painter who started off as a Divisionist and then achieved success as a Futurist, and he illustrates Marinetti's murder of the moon in a powerful painting that is still famously associated with Futurist art today, *Lampada ad arco* (*Street Light*, 1911).[56] In this painting, an arc lamp overpowers the light of a sickle moon cornered at the top right of the frame (see plate 3). Balla seems to have subsequently revised the date of *Lampada ad arco* back from 1911 to 1909, so as to claim paternity of the idea of murdering the moonlight, affirming it was his painting that inspired Marinetti and not vice versa.[57] Clearly, this lunicidal trope was still regarded, years later, as a revolutionary turning point, one that other artists, too, would have liked to appropriate as their own invention. For Lara Pucci, Balla probably intended the painting to be a bridge between the two styles: while the light emanating from Balla's arc lamp is painted in Divisionist style, the content of the painting clearly announces the "dawn of a new era" for Balla as for modern art.[58] Balla's painting was intended for the Futurists' first exhibition of 1912 in Paris but ended up not being selected, most probably because its debt to Divisionism made it seem, at the time, insufficiently representative of the new avant-garde's aesthetics—quite an irony for a painting that has gone down in popular culture as a paradigmatic Futurist artwork![59]

In 1910, alongside Umberto Boccioni, Carlo Carrà, Luigi Russolo, and Gino Severini, Balla signed the treatise "La pittura futurista: manifesto tecnico" ("Futurist Painting: Technical Manifesto"), in which, as well as declaring their interest in "il dolore [. . .] di una lampada elettrica" (the suffering [. . .] of an electric lamp, *F* 65), they prophesied that people should get ready for a new light in art: "Le ombre che dipingeremo saranno più luminose delle luci dei nostri predecessori, e i nostri quadri, a confronto di quelli immagazzinati nei musei, saranno il giorno più fulgido contrapposto alla notte più cupa" (The shadows that we shall paint will be more luminous than the highlights of our predecessors, and our pictures, next to those of the museums, will shine like blinding daylight compared with deepest night, *F* 66).[60] Light, for the Futurists, is a clear mark of aesthetics: they are keen to advance the proposition that the light of the Futurists will shine brighter than that of their predecessors. Equally, though, they aim to transform the night into a second day by noctambulism and electricity. The impact of new illumination on Futurist art is clear. Hence a number of early Futurist paintings depict the new artificially illuminated night; Balla's is a primary example given that he painted *Lampada ad arco* after observing an early Brunt & C. arc lamp outside Termini Railway Station in Rome.[61] In this sense, *Lampada ad arco* becomes even more conspicuously Balla's own artistic contribution to the articulation of Futurist poetics.

Painting a lamp murdering a cornered moon was, in any case, a natural trajectory for Balla. Having experienced the electrification of Turin in the 1880s and subsequently *la ville lumière* at the Paris exhibition of 1900, he was attracted throughout his career to the ways in which light propagated and manifested itself, from cosmology to lamps and streetlights. At the end of 1900, dazzled, he would write to his fiancée Elisa that in Paris in the evening "tutto è luce" (everything is light).[62] In 1904, he would call his first daughter Luce (Light), a rare name in Italy (as against Lucia).[63] In the artwork Balla created after his return from Paris, it is easy to see how he was interested in representing illumination, culminating with his *Lampada ad arco* in 1911. *Il lavoro* (*Work*, 1902), *Notturno romano con lampione* (*Roman Night Scene with Street Lamp*, c. 1902), *Lampione nel cantiere* (*Lamp on Construction Site*, c. 1904), and *La giornata dell'operaio* (*A Worker's Day*, 1904), all feature a streetlamp as the focal point of the painter's attention, much like the photographs of Charles Marville discussed in Chapter One. *Le torri del Museo Borghese* (*The Towers of the Borghese Museum*, c. 1905, plate 4), on the other hand, shows how moonlight too could take a central position in Balla's paintings, with the orange globe of the moon making the contours of the towers of the Villa Borghese fade out in the darkness.[64] Balla's interest in shades of light and illumination paved the way for his Marinetti-inspired painting of 1911. *Lampada ad arco* merges Balla's own sensibility for light with the Futurist visualization of this transitional moment in aesthetics, where art becomes more invested in the potential of the new technology than with nature.

The first poet to translate this change metapoetically into his own work is Paolo Buzzi, who joined Marinetti's Futurist ranks early, seeing it as an opportunity to make a stylistic transition from a sort of fin de siècle late Romanticism (based on the rediscovery of Giacomo Leopardi) and French-Belgian Symbolism.[65] His poem, "Primi lampioni" (First Streetlamps), from *Versi liberi* (Free Verse, 1913), begins with a metapoetic reflection on what the electric light does to his poetic experience:

> Esco alla notte
> contro gli amici lampioni.
> Son gli occhi dei nuovi mostri terreni. Sfavillano
> la luce ignota a' miei avi. Mi fan l'aria moderna

> onde questo respiro d'uomo semplice
> diventa verso libero di poeta complesso.   (lines 1-6)
>
> ---
>
> (At night I bump/into friendly lampposts./They are the eyes of our new earthly
> monsters. They give/out a glow unknown to my ancestors. The air turns mod-
> ern/transforming the breath of this simple man/into the free verse of a complex
> poet.)[66]

The poet's experience of the Milanese night would have been, historically, one brightly lit with gas, arc, and incandescent lamps (the latter being installed in Milan in 1911).[67] But for Buzzi it is not simply about taking stock of the changing atmosphere around him, of the fact that electric lights have now replaced gas lamps, or the moon. The electric lampposts around him insist that a matter of aesthetic transformation is underway. The electrified streetlamps change the experience of the night around him, while also having a direct impact on his poetry: they make it modern. One might be tempted to think that the mere mention of the word "electric," sprinkled over his verse, makes the poem more modern. What Buzzi actually means is that the experience of electric light turns his writing and, in turn, his experience as a modern man into something much richer, much more "complex." In the lines that follow the quoted excerpt, the electric light turns Buzzi's speaker into an acrobat walking on the "ombre lunghe a sbarra dei lampioni" (long shadow-bars of lampposts, lines 7-9), and the boulevard into a watercolor spectacle (lines 10-12).[68] The new electrical reality around him may be what allows him to break away from his ancestors but in a less parricidal way than Marinetti's: the newly electrically lit world is of interest in itself.

Buzzi's poem is, of course, only one of a range of Futurist poems mentioning electric light, but it is, in my opinion, the only one that so explicitly and so aptly connects modern writing ("l'aria moderna," "verso libero") to the electrically lit night. No electricity, no free verse, no modern poetry, is the message of "Primi lampioni." Libero Altomare (pseudonym of Remo Mannoni, *F* 507) also comes close to creating a poetic manifesto of Futurist light in his poem "Sinfonia luminosa" ("Luminous Symphony," first published in the anthology *I poeti futuristi* [Futurist Poets] of 1912), dedicated to a mysterious friend, perhaps intended as an allegory, called Vittorio Luce (Italian for Victor Light). Altomare's poem is fuller of anguish and violence than Buzzi's and follows Marinetti's murderous footsteps more closely. To continue Altomare's musical analogy, the poem begins fortissimo: "Amo le luci sfrontate/che violentano la morbida Notte/ingemmata" (I love brazen lights/that violate the delicate Night/decked with jewels, that snatch/the dreams' veils fluttering in the air/of the slumbering City, lines 1-5).[69] The poet's love for electric light, much like Marinetti's, is a morbid one, with the poetic voice declaring it is due to the light's violence toward the night. The night, personified as feminine and covered in jewels, is marred by the new lights that spread insomnia over the city—"gli elettrici globuli/[. . .] irradiano l'insonnia/nelle sue vene torride" (the electric bulbs/[. . .] illuminate insomnia's sluggish veins, lines 6-8)—and is consequently likened to a ghastly looking, old-fashioned "cortigiana" (courtesan; lines 8-15) of vaguely Baudelairean pedigree. The electric lights however violate the Night, thus illustrating a gendered relationship of strong, masculine, powerful electricity against the weak, feminine, soft night. The moon, appearing at the end of the poem, is just a poor victim of the sun's light (lines 46-49). Even though the topic of the poem may be considered loosely Futurist, Altomare strays quite far from Marinetti's formal, linguistic, and syntactical innovations: Altomare adopts traditional meter, using a combination of *settenari* and *endecasillabi*; he displays a preference for capitalizing certain nouns, such as *Notte* (Night) and *Città* (City), which thereby appear like personifications; he makes profuse use of adjectives and archaic nouns (*beghina*, sanctimonious; *preci*, prayers; lines 48-49), and does not dare to experiment with, say, Futurist double nouns such as Marinetti's "uomo-torpediniera" (man-torpedo boat) or "donna-golfo" (woman-bay; *F* 120), or his advocacy for destructing syntax.[70] This formal adherence to tradition is popular amongst early Futurists, especially if we look at the 1912 anthology *I poeti futuristi*. Marinetti's call to arms for a new Futurist movement effectively recruits a good number of Neo-Symbolists who are keen for change but seem to lack the tools to pursue it.[71]

Following suit from Marinetti's call to arms against the moonlight, a number of Futurist poems typify electric light as inherently violent.[72] Giovanni Gerbino's "Natura spremuta" ("Squeezed Nature"), from the second anthology of Futurist poetry *I nuovi poeti futuristi* (The New Futurist Poets, 1925), portrays a street fight between the night and the electric light, clearly responding to both Marinetti and Altomare:

> La notte è sopra i tetti:
> ancora un poco
> e scende sulle strade
> per fare a cazzotti
> con la luce elettrica.

> L'ombra cresce in un angolo:
> ancora un poco
> e viene assassinata
> dal raggio vivo
> d'una lampadina.
>
> ———
>
> (Night hovers above the rooftops:/a little longer/and descends to the streets/to pick a fight/with the electric light./A shadow grows in a corner:/a little while/and is assassinated/by a sharp/beam of light. [*IFP* 176-177, lines 1-10])

For Gerbino, the moon falls completely out of his poetic equation, and the fight between the night and the electric light loses the gendering identifiable in Altomare's poem. Human ingenuity triumphs over nature: the electric light is a stronger power, as even a little light bulb is able to "assassinate" the shadow. Yet the night is its equal, coming down the streets looking to pick a fight as a serial *boxeur des rues*. Gerbino's reprise brings a breath of fresh air to this widespread Futurist theme as, in spite of the Italian grammatical gendering of the night and the electric light as feminine, he sees both as masculine entities contesting for dominion of the time after daylight. As we shall see in the next section, the gendering of light was an important step in the formation of Futurist poetics, as it was in the movement's development of more gender-inclusive politics.

Against the Woman-as-Moonlight

For most of the twentieth century, Futurist scholarship was wedded to portraying the movement as an all-male ensemble and as a movement dedicated to promulgating male chauvinism. More recently, both Italian-language and English-language scholarship on Futurism has begun to acknowledge the presence, role, and agency of women within the movement.[73] Yet, little has been said about the way Marinetti and other Futurists represent female beauty and agency as a gendered source of light. As we have seen, the Futurists see moonlight as passé, necessarily outflanked by new aesthetics, new technologies, and a new Futurist way of life. For Marinetti, moonlight also means woman. Insofar as women had been frequently associated with the moon, especially in Symbolist poetry, this is not in itself an innovation.[74] But for Marinetti, the light of the moon made women appear different to the male poetic gaze. At stake in his anti-lunar campaigns was a certain cultural representation of women.

In the first Futurist manifesto of 1909, Marinetti rather inelegantly included, at point 9, that on top of glorifying war, patriotism, and anarchism, glorifying "le mépris de la femme" (contempt for woman) was part of their agenda, and, at point 10, that fighting against feminism was necessary (*F* 51).[75] His misogynism caused a stir, and Marinetti must have felt it necessary to qualify his words, given that they were far from being an "effective slogan" to recruit more women into the movement.[76] A year later, Marinetti adjusted his public position with his notorious 1910 lecture at the Lyceum Club for Women in London. Reporting back from that momentous evening for the *Vote*, Margaret Wynne Nevinson, the famous British suffrage campaigner, was shocked at Marinetti's lack of euphemisms, and eulogy of war against everything antiquated, but she still found that "the Suffragettes and Signor Marinetti are at one in deploring the existence of the serpent-of-old-Nile type of woman" ("Futurism and Woman," *F* 75). What they could not agree on—understandably—was Marinetti's claim that "women [are] responsible for what [the Futurists] consider a degenerate type of man" (*F* 75). As Jamie Wood proposes, the speech Nevinson heard was, in all likelihood, "an amalgamation of all the early Futurist manifestos and many of the key principles set out in *Le futurisme*," a compendium of Futurist propagandistic texts that Marinetti published in French in 1911, shortly after his London tour.[77] *Le futurisme* included a popularly misunderstood text, "Le mépris de la femme" ("Contempt for Woman"), in which Marinetti tried, not very successfully, to clarify his position regarding women and Futurism. He writes:

> C'est cette haine contre l'amour tyrannique que nous avons exprimée par cette phrase laconique: le *mépris de la femme*.
>
> Oui, nous méprisons la femme-réservoir d'amour, engin de volupté, la femme-poison, la femme-bibelot tragique, la femme fragile, obsédante et fatale, dont la voix lourde de destinée et la rêveuse chevelure se prolongent et se continuent dans les frondaisons des forêts baignées de clair de lune.[78]
>
> ———
>
> (It is this hatred for the tyranny of love that we have expressed with the laconic phrase: "contempt for woman."
>
> We feel contempt for a woman conceived as the reservoir of love, engine of lust, woman-poison, woman as a tragic bibelot, fragile woman, obsessing and fatal, whose voice, heavy with destiny, and whose dreamy tresses reach out and mingle with the foliage of forests bathed in moonlight. [*F* 86])

It might have helped Marinetti's argument if he had used the phrase "tyranny of love" in his first manifesto in place of "contempt for woman," but he was clearly aiming for fireworks. In this text, if nothing else, he is able to clarify the fact that Futurism is not against woman but more precisely one specific image of woman: the romanticized, fatal version of woman, constructed through the objectifying male gaze, the "woman-in-the-moonlight" or, we might say, "woman-as-moonlight." As Claudia Salaris maintains, Marinetti's "contempt" ought to be considered as a reflection of his anti-Romantic and anti-Symbolist polemics.[79] The woman-as-moonlight under attack represents the habitual love bonds, with all her Decadent, passéist, Romantic connotations.[80]

Marinetti is articulating a concept that imbricates the cultural with the aesthetic, the poetic with the political. He explains that "L'amour, obsession romantique et volupté, n'est autre chose qu'une invention des poètes, qui en ont doté l'humanité. Ce seront les poètes qui le reprendront à l'humanité!"[81] (Love—romantic, voluptuary obsession—is nothing but an invention of the poets, who gave it to humanity. And it will be the poets who will take it away from humanity! *F* 86). If love was invented by the poets, it is the poets themselves who have the power to dismantle this poetic invention, hence Marinetti's personal investment—as a poet—in this cultural and aesthetic enfranchising of woman. Marinetti's position, however, was not free from paternalism and self-centeredness. In 1916 for example, perhaps influenced by the publication of Otto Weininger's 1903 *Geschlecht und Charakter* (*Sex and Character*; translated as *Sesso e carattere* in Italian in 1912), he published *Come si seducono le donne* (How to Seduce Women), with the aim to instruct men (soldiers, given the publication date during World War I, and his Futurist companions, whose seductive capabilities were certainly inferior to his) in how to make love to women.[82] This is certainly how Bruno Corra and Emilio Settimelli, who wrote the preface to Marinetti's book, understood it: "è un tentativo di liberare la nostra razza latina dalle corrosioni velenose del chiaro di luna e dalla lurida prigione della gelosia" (it is an attempt to free our Latin race from the poisonous corruption of moonlight and from the squalid prison of jealousy).[83] Basically, a sort of sexual revolution well before the Swinging Sixties but with the additional ingredient of being anti-moonlight.

Corra and Settimelli repeat almost verbatim Marinetti's mantra that they are not against women but against a certain type of woman—"il tipo di donna fatale, snob, sognatrice, nostalgica stupidamente e culturalmente complicata che riempie e legge i romanzi di D'Annunzio e contro la donna tira-e-molla, ipocrita, bigotta [. . .] che legge e riempie i romanzi di Fogazzaro" (the femme fatale type, snobbish, dreamy, foolishly nostalgic and culturally complicated who features in and reads D'Annunzio's novels and against the "fast-and-loose" woman, hypocritical, sanctimonious, [. . .] who reads and features in Fogazzaro's novels).[84] Valentine de Saint-Point, the first woman artist to color Marinetti's Futurist stance in gendered terms, publicly amends Marinetti's position. Possibly instigated by Marinetti himself with whom she had a brief flirtation, she produced *Manifesto della donna futurista* (*Manifesto of the Futurist Woman*, 1912) and then *Manifesto futurista della lussuria* (*Futurist Manifesto of Lust*, 1913).[85] As Robin Pickering-Iazzi suggests, de Saint-Point's position is important for the shaping of a "female-gendered positionality" in early Futurism, even if still influenced by "male futurist discourse," such as her emphasis on "virilità" (virility; *F* 110), the bestiality of women's love, and repudiation of feminism.[86] In the latter manifesto, de Saint-Point claims women's right to sex, playing again on Marinetti's now well-established lunar associations:

> **Distruggiamo i sinistri stracci romantici**, margherite sfogliate, duetti sotto la luna, tenerezze pesanti, falsi pudori ipocriti. Che gli esseri, avvicinati da un'attrazione fisica, invece di parlare esclusivamente delle fragilità dei loro cuori, osino esprimere i loro desideri, le preferenze dei loro corpi, e presentire le possibilità di gioia o di delusione della loro futura unione carnale.[87]

> ------

> (**We must destroy the fatal rags and tatters of romanticism**, counting daisy petals, moonlight duets, heavy-handed caresses, a false and hypocritical sense of shame. Let people who have been drawn together by physical attraction dare to express their desires, the allure of their bodies, their presentiments of joy or disappointment at the prospect of fleshly union, instead of talking solely about the delicacy of their hearts. [*F* 131; emphasis in the original; edited by the author])

According to de Saint-Point, woman's freedom as a social subject is intrinsically linked to her sexual freedom: physical attraction between two people should not be envisaged as a performative moonlit duet but rather as a mutual attraction. In her earlier manifesto, de Saint-Point, openly against historical feminism, had questioned the usual dual gender division: "**È assurdo dividere l'umanità in donne e uomini;** essa è composta soltanto di **femminilità** e di **mascolinità**" (**it's absurd to divide humanity into women and men**; it is composed only of **femininity** and **masculinity**, *F* 110; emphasis in original).[88] She emphasizes here the necessity for an equity of roles for both man and woman in sexual attraction. De Saint-Point does not go so far as to associate femininity and sexuality with electricity, but it is clear that she exploits Marinetti's moonlight symbolism as one helpfully evocative of the prevailing social, cultural, and literary construction of women. It becomes increasingly apparent that the Futurists mapped out gender issues against questions of natural and artificial light on one side and modern aesthetics on the other. But how did Futurist men and women of the 1910s and 1920s respond to these aesthetic provocations? What updated articulations of light and femininity did they decide to propose?

In the early 1910s, partly because of the sexist rhetoric we have encountered, Futurism had not attracted many women into its fold, with the exception of de Saint-Point, who, after being programmatically enlisted by Marinetti, had officially abandoned the movement by 1914.[89] Between the publication of de Saint-Point's manifestos in 1912-13 and the gathering of women around the Florence-based magazine *L'Italia futurista* (Futurist Italy) in 1916-18, we cannot count many women artists engaging with Futurism, apart from the British avant-garde poet and artist Mina Loy (whom I discuss in Chapter Three), so it is necessary to look elsewhere. Thanks to Marinetti's internationalizing efforts, Futurism's tentacles were wide reaching, and its manifestos generated a response in the work of the Russian avant-garde artist Natalia Goncharova. Goncharova would have been well aware of Marinetti's Futurist manifestos as they were coming out, given that excerpts had been appearing in translation in the major Russian newspapers and magazines as early as 1909, and selections of the Futurist manifestos were subsequently published in 1914.[90] But Goncharova may have attended Marinetti's lectures and seen Umberto Boccioni's and Gino Severini's artwork when visiting Paris in the early 1910s.[91] What is certain is that in 1914 Marinetti visited Russia upon an invitation from Genrix Èdmundovich Tastevin, the Russian delegate of the Parisian Société des grands conferences as well as the editor of a book on Futurism that included Russian translations of some of the manifestos.[92] In Moscow, Marinetti also met Natalia Goncharova and her partner Mihail Larionov at a vodka-drinking outing that followed one of Marinetti's lectures, where Roman Jakobson acted as "a sort of interpreter."[93] According to Vadim Shershenevich, a Russian poet who also met Marinetti during his 1914 visit, the two Russian painters first showed Marinetti their work in Moscow.[94] Upon viewing Goncharova's paintings, Marinetti recognized her as a Futurist, while he deemed Larionov's work artistically poor.[95] In fact, Goncharova went through a technological phase in her artwork while she was taking an active part in the parallel current of Russian Futurism.[96]

Technology played an important role in Goncharova's quotidian experiences at the turn of the twentieth century, but in her paintings, it bears potent witness to humanity's struggles. This attitude is apparent in her artwork *Ткачиха. Ткацкий станок и женщина* (*The Weaver: Loom and Woman*, 1913, plate 5), in which Goncharova's weaver—a woman—becomes one with her loom underneath an electric bulb whose light glaringly denounces the exploitation of the proletarian weaver. To the left, a further row of electric lamps give an indication of the size of the factory.[97] But, following in the footsteps of Futurism, Goncharova also envisioned technology as a tool enabling humanity to surpass itself, as a necessary extension of the human: her weaver, perpendicularly bent over her loom, becomes one with it because weaving technology is an essential part of her work and of her identity; Goncharova's painting turns this weaver into a silkworm of Marxist memory. Goncharova's *Электрическая лампа* (*The Electric Lamp*, 1913, plate 6) is from the same year.[98] Without having seen Balla's painting, Goncharova signs her own manifesto of the aesthetic shift of the time, surpassing both the Italian Divisionist-Futurist painting and Marinetti's manifesto. The moon is not just passé; it is simply no longer needed as a historical or aesthetic foil. What catches the eye in *Электрическая лампа* is the blinding yellowness of an electric bulb that nearly covers the whole canvas, with several bright circles making up the translucent body of the bulb. But, if we want to be careful observers of this painting, our eyes need to adjust to this painting's light, as when we enter a brightly illuminated room after a spell in darkness. Only then we shall be able to see, just above the bulb, the outline of two heads, pink and white, with sketched eyes and hair, close to one another, as they embrace, or perhaps kiss. The electric bulb, as it switches on, is the bright union of two lovers. It is Goncharova's own response to the aesthetics of Futurism: the brilliance of this embrace between two lovers epitomizes an electrical modernity that sees man and woman as equals irradiating light together. Goncharova's painting offers, therefore, an opportunity: as a woman artist, Goncharova does not harness electric light to create a feminized portrayal of technology but rather imagines it as heterogendered, surpassing Futurism's binary imagination.

It is with the Florentine magazine *L'Italia futurista* in 1916 that we finally see a more consistent number of female signatories among Futurist authors.[99] Women writers feature in most issues and are far from passive: the magazine often acts as an outlet for passionate discussions between Futurist men and women about gender and sexuality, such as the debate following the publication of Marinetti's *Come si seducono le donne*, which, while hailed and publicized as permanently murdering the moonlight, sparked off a debate on what the modern—Futurist—woman should be like.[100] Indeed, gender issues were pivotal to this little Futurist magazine, whose pages often proposed, as Lucia Re observes, "the formation of new gender configurations as well as new genres."[101]

In this final section, I am going to examine the works of a number of prose poets published in *L'Italia futurista*, including Maria Ginanni (born Maria Crisi) and Fanny (Francesca) Dini, as well as the illustrations of visual artist Rosa Rosà (born Edyth von Haynau) for Mario Carli's volume of prose poetry published in association with the magazine, entitled *Notti filtrate* (Filtered Nights, 1918). Integral to the early phase of Futurism, these women responded to the Futurist agenda by harnessing the tension between natural and artificial lights in a typically gendered way. For instance, in a short prose poem by Fanny (Francesca) Dini, "Al futurismo trionfante" (To Triumphant Futurism), the female speaker is empowered by the possibilities of the light as proposed by Futurism: "Sono stanca di notti lunate e di canzoni napoletane [. . .] / Vorrei uccidere la persona che amo—di più—fare del suo teschio una lampada—e andare a conversare di cose meravigliose con tutte le notti del mondo" (I am tired of moonlit nights and Neapolitan songs [. . .] / I would like to kill the person I love—the most—turn their skull into a lamp—and go and talk about wonderful things with all the nights of the world).[102] Dini's speaker is all action and is very far from Marinetti's much-despised "woman-as-moonlight." While her associations are still with the natural and nocturnal world ("tutte le notti del mondo"), this is a world she owns and where she can overturn the usual gender dynamics by making a lamp out of her lover's head.[103]

Maria Ginanni, a frequent contributor to the magazine and wife of count Arnaldo Ginanni (who went under the Futurist name Arnaldo Ginna), eventually took up a prominent role within the editorial team first "as editor-in-chief [. . .] when the male editors were at the front."[104] She also edited the collection of books attached to it, *Edizioni de l'Italia futurista* (Editions of Futurist Italy), which, for Lucia Re, makes her one of the first women in a prominent role in Italian publishing.[105] Across the first few issues of *L'Italia futurista* of 1916, Ginanni published several short prose poems, "poetic fragments" or "poetic prose passages," as critics have sometimes referred to them.[106] These texts overflow with images and are really a testimony to Ginanni's visual creativity and interdisciplinary mode of writing. In her first contribution for the very first issue of *L'Italia futurista*, "Frammento di no-vella colorata" (Fragment of a Colorful Novel), she conjures up the impression of a night spent amid glowworms: "Strappatemi la mia anima di mestizia col vostro incanto di dinamismo lucciola—lasciatemi distendere—sui vostri baci—lucciole./Ballate uno dei vostri waltzer di note di luce arpiolate sui raggi della luna—piccoli Chopin di palpiti elettrici" (Rip up my soul of sadness with your charm of glowworm dynamism—let me lay down—on your kisses—glowworms./Dance one of your waltzes with notes of light harped on moonbeams—little Chopins of electric pulses).[107] While she would never entirely follow the Futurist tenets of words-in-freedom, or of syntax destruction (propounded by Marinetti in his 1912 "Manifesto tecnico della letteratura futurista" [Technical Manifesto of Futurist Literature]), Ginanni crafts a new type of poem, the Futurist poetic fragment, which approaches Marinetti's manifesto in its use of analogies and what Paola Sica defines as "an iconic overload of the language"—her impressive pairing of words with a strong visual component—marking her as an effective member of the avant-garde.[108] Ginanni's glowworms, *lucciole* in Italian, are clearly gendered feminine: the word is grammatically feminine and, when it is not used to indicate the luminous insect, refers to prostitutes—the ladies in the light, or with a light.[109] I am not claiming that Ginanni is imagining her speaker surrounded by prostitutes, as the atmosphere she summons up is clearly natural, but she is actively seeking the glowworms' light as something she is not: her speaker is sad (full of moonlight, we might say), and the intermittent light of the glowworms turns them, for Ginanni, into little electrical nocturnes ("Chopins"). While, for Paola Sica, Ginanni was "less provocative" than other Futurist women writers about questions of gender and often adopted an "androcentric perspective" in her prose, in her poetic passages she endows the intermittent and always dominant light of the glowworms with femininity and with a desire for women to surpass Marinetti.[110] In "Frammenti di novelle colorate" (Fragments of Colorful Novels), she makes the necessary gesturing toward Marinetti's manifesto by way of the (by now) ritualistic Futurist slandering of the moon: "la luna si mostra verdastra in un enorme bozzolo che vomita la sua bava di fosforo" (the moon is greenish in an enormous cocoon, vomiting its phosphorous drool).[111] The fragment ends, however, with an empowered lyrical I, who associates herself with a blasting light destroying everything passéist around her: "Tutto è scoppio di luce formid-abile./*Ho per capelli dei fulmini*" (It all bursts into exceptional light./*I have lightnings in my hair*).[112] As Sica observes, Ginanni's woman is not one "presid[ing] over domestic spaces"; rather "she controls sidereal dimensions":[113] light becomes a way for Ginanni to allow women to transcend bodily, and consequently gender, constraints.

In a longer piece by Ginanni, "Le lucciole" (The Glowworms), published in a later issue of *L'Italia futurista* in the same year, she returns to the theme of the glowworms (again "piccoli Chopin di palpiti elettrici"). Paola Sica reads this poem as a manifestation of Ginanni's occultist interests, which she would have shared with other women of *L'Italia futurista*; Ginanni, however, directly links the glowworms to the act of writing poetry.[114] They are the poet's instrument by which she can kill the night, an action she associates with a new poetic style:

> Perché questo mio Poema è formato così? Perché tutto a sbalzi e luci staccate?
> Eppure brilla di una forza meravigliosa, definitiva! [. . .] Forse ho ucciso la notte
> 　　inutilmente!
> Infatti questo mio Poema è il primo assieme di germi che darà un nuovo tessuto
> 　　vitale, una molteplicità d'immagini staccate parallele. Ogni immagine una
> 　　cellula. [. . .]
>
> Armata di questa nuova forza cerebrale scenderò nel mondo che dovrà pensare
> 　　come io vorrò. Con milioni di dita filiformi mi insinuerò nei cervelli umani
> 　　liberandoli dalle catene logiche e ripeterò il fenomeno che le scie taglienti
> 　　delle lucciole hanno operato in me.
> *Incomincerò domani.*[115]
>
> ———
>
> (Why is my Poem written like this? Why is it all bumps and disconnected
> 　　lights?
> Yet it shines with a definitive, wonderful force! [. . .] Perhaps I have killed the
> 　　night in vain!
> My Poem is effectively the first gathering of germs that shall make a new tissue
> 　　of life, a multiplicity of parallel, disconnected images. Every image is a cell.
> 　　[. . .]
>
> Armed with this new cerebral force I will come down into the world who shall
> 　　now have to think as I want it to. With millions of threadlike fingers I shall
> 　　insinuate myself in all human brains and free them from the chains of logic,
> 　　repeating what the glowworms' sharp trails have done to me.
> *I shall begin tomorrow.*)

Ginanni's glowworms fill the night sky with their dynamic light, rapidly moving everywhere, an impression reinforced by the way the glowworms keep showing up on different parts of the page. Her electrical glowworms embody her new poetics, which is made up of numerous distinct, repeated images. In his introduction to Ginanni, Emilio Settimelli praises her prose poem "Le lucciole" for its ability to render the exact feeling of a night illuminated by the intermittent light of the glowworms.[116] Ginanni, in other words, executes her own metaphorical murdering of moonlight by filling the night with electrified glowworms that represent her creative impulse and by envisioning a new mode of poetry scintillating with many detached, illuminated images.

Light also stimulates the creative imagination of Vienna-born Rosa Rosà, another Futurist satellite and author of the short novel *Una donna con tre anime* (*A Woman with Three Souls*, 1918) and of some witty words-in-freedom published in *L'Italia futurista*, as well as the highly talented illustrator of Bruno Corra's *Sam Dunn è morto* (Sam Dunn Is Dead, 1917) and Mario Carli's *Notti filtrate* (Filtered Nights, 1918).[117] Franca Zoccoli has said of Rosà's illustrations that she "develops a composite style where Expressionist, Secessionist and Art-Nouveau elements, echoes from Klimt and Kubin, and even memories of Beardsley, mix with Futurist dynamic compenetrations and abstract geometric patterns," while also comparing them to early Surrealism.[118] In her work for Carli's collection of prose poems about the night, published for Maria Ginanni's *Edizioni de L'Italia futurista*, Rosà shows real artistic independence. While Carli's poetry comes across as a work still oscillating, both in content and form, between Symbolism and Futurism, Rosà's illustrations go a step further. Her images to accompany Carli's sleepwalker's dreamscapes of an illuminated night center on different shades of blue (possibly a gesture to the writers of *L'Italia futurista*, who liked to associate themselves with the color blue).[119] Rosà's choice certainly emphasizes her attraction to the lights of Carli's prose nocturnes.[120] The color blue adopted by the Futurists and by Rosà also plays up the presence of electrification, which renders these nocturnes colder and crisper.

Rosà depicts natural and artificial lights in ways that effectively contradict Carli's poetry. Let us take Rosà's plates 3 and 4: both illustrations, as per her style in *Notti filtrate*, are framed within irregular geometrical figures, suggesting their importance as recovered shards of a greater whole. They are fragments, offering a particular slanted view of Carli's nocturnes. In Poem 3, for example, Carli's persona resorts to Decadent tropes calling "la Via Lattea [. . .] il principio di un'immensa putrefazione" (the Milky Way [. . .] the start of an immense putrefaction) and asserting that "la luna è un'ipotesi arabescata dai rifiuti dell'ideale" (the moon is a hypothesis, arabesqued with the

dregs of the ideal).[121] Rosà's illustration (see plate 7) sees a luminous, per-
fectly round moon dart off oblique rays of light. Rosà, however, completely
ignores the verse's figure of the man attacking the moon, the stars, and the
night, focusing the image on the intensely luminous moon and its ara-
besqued beams, which, as a result, lack the scummy connotations of the
original. When Carli, in Poem 4, mocks the moon as the initiator of a foolish
cult—"la luna [è] un'ostia da tabernacolo, biascicata e corrosa dai sospiri di
tutti gli amanti" (the moon [is] a tabernacle host, gnawed at and spoiled by
the sighs of all her lovers)—Rosà contrasts it with a powerful, blinding light
and rather gives more visual prominence to "la vaporosa veste a fiorami della
dolce Lucia" (sweet Lucia's voluminous flowery gown) as centerpiece.[122]
Throughout *Notti filtrate*, Rosà's illustrations do much more than silently
accompany the words of her fellow Futurist: hers is artwork in its own right,
and it openly challenges Carli's Futurist pretensions.

Baudelaire, however, the most influential early exponent of the prose
poem, is the demon haunting *Notti filtrate*, revealing Carli's inability to go
beyond the French Symbolist that inspired the poetry of his beginnings.[123]
Carli openly acknowledges Baudelaire in Poem 6, where it becomes appar-
ent that the French poet is an essential part of Carli's poetic texture: "Fra i
suoi più bizzarri poemi, Baudelaire mi ha lasciato in dono questa Notte ver-
dastra, che ha bistrato la città con ogni cura, e ha concesso un'ironia a ogni
fanale, un profumo di vizio ad ogni solitudine pietrosa" (Among his strangest
poems, Baudelaire bequeathed me this greenish Night, carefully coloring
everything with bister, and bestowed irony on every light, and a scent of
vice on every stony solitude).[124] As late as 1918, Carli is struggling to get past
Baudelaire, making Poem 6 a reprise of the typically Baudelairean sordid
street, ending again on an association between the moon and absinthe. Rosà's
illustration emphasizes Carli's lit-up street, with lampposts reminding us
of the nineteenth-century street aesthetics of Paris (Chapter One) or Milan
(above). Yet like the houses in the background, Rosà's lamps twist and crook,
visually expressing the irony (or rather the deviancy?) of the street (see fig.
2.5). As often in her work, she breathes a new "mysterious life" into every-
day objects, making them the focal points of her illustration.[125] *Notti filtrate*
culminates with the lamps in Carli's city being switched off nearly completely:
"Come queste lampade che una mano di paura ha spente sulla mezzanotte
. . . [. . .] Insistenza dei fanali superstiti sul fiume, sgoccianti nell'acqua il loro
ronzio di fusi in cerca di equilibrio!" (Like these lamps, turned off by a hand
of fear over midnight . . . [. . .] The surviving lights by the river insist, dripping

Fig. 2.5. Rosa Rosà (Edyth von Haynau), Plate 6, in Mario Carli, *Notti filtrate: 10 liriche di Mario Carli con 10 disegni di Rosa Rosà* (Florence: Edizioni de *L'Italia futurista*, 1918), 23. Digital image courtesy of Beinecke Rare Book & Manuscript Library, Yale University. Credit © Famiglia Fornari (Heirs of Rosa Rosà).

their droning of fuses in the water, in search for balance!).[126] The city looks even *too* calm—"inverosimile calma" (improbable calm)—to be really Futurist.[127] Rosà again departs from Carli's text to offer the reader a glowing streetlamp at the center of her illustration—this time, not a nineteenth-century gas lamp as in the previous illustration but a brilliantly electrified globe on a tall, straight post (plate 8), domineering over the urban background and the dark waters. By placing a powerful electrical lamppost in the middle of her illustration, with the glowing cityscape in the background, Rosà adds dynamism to the excessive calm of Carli's poem, increasing its Futurist potential. Rosà's insertion of her images into irregular, quasi-sculptural forms generates further movement and dynamism to Carli's words.

Rosà is drawn to the few references to light in Carli's poems and chooses to amplify them, making light and illumination the real protagonist of her illustrations for *Notti filtrate*, rather than the poet flâneur, or the other nocturnal creatures of his imagination—cats, women, mermaids, and so on. Illustrating Carli's book provides Rosà with an opportunity to show her artistic independence while articulating the tenets of a more markedly avant-garde agenda. Futurist women artists and writers harnessed representation of natural and artificial lights to express their poetic and artistic affiliations but were reluctant to deploy electric light casually as a gendered trope.

Ultimately, male Futurists of the 1920s began to compose poetry that detached women from the clichés of Symbolism, creating a more fundamentally Futurist ethos that helps shape how men of this group imagine, represent, and view women. In 1925 Marinetti published a second anthology of Futurist poetry, entitled *I nuovi poeti futuristi* (New Futurist Poets). For the exclusively male Futurist poets in this collection, women come to embody a new technological aesthetics. Propelled in part by the cultural association between *macchina* and *donna* (both feminine terms), these Futurists rewrite woman as electrical, and electrical technologies as feminine, part of a larger cultural trend I will discuss in Chapter Three. In Emilio Mario Dolfi's "Zaija," for example, he describes a woman actually wearing light:

> Creatura di dolore e di piacere
> riflessa nel vetro
> con la maniglia d'ottone in cintura
> e le OSRAM che fan da pendenti
> agli orecchi.
>
> ———
>
> (Creature of grief and pleasure / reflected in the window / a brass handle in your belt / and OSRAM serving as rings / in your ears. [*IFP* 158-159, lines 1-5])

Dolfi's woman is bedecked with light bulbs: OSRAM was the German brand familiar internationally since 1919. This woman is later compared to a tiger "running swifly": the scene shifts abruptly from wondrous technological tableau to jungle environment, only to return to the night, figured this time as a mixture of woman, tiger, and fast car. In the poem "Veloci in pioggia" ("Speeding through the Rain"), Escodamé (pen name of Michele Leskovic) develops this set of tropes by making a more overt connection between woman and his car, a Lancia Lambda (first produced in 1923): "boccuzza rossa tra chiavette nere 'sistema Bosch' profumo acuto di benzina nell'orbita di metallo bianco la lampadina viola allunga languide ciglia nella chiusa intimità femminile di questa calda alcova in viaggio" (red mouth between black switches "System Bosch" pungent gasoline odour within this intimate feminine alcove the white socket's violet bulb extends its languid eyelashes, *IFP* 164-165). Escodamé's poem is a brazen celebration of his new car as vampily feminine. Both Dolfi and Escodamé eroticize their relationship with machines by feminizing them, perhaps also, as Cinzia Sartini Blum believes, as part of Futurism's attempt to embody "new technological realities [. . .] in a familiar object of love and mastery."[128] This is a clear trend in this second anthology, in which male authors frequently and unapologetically figure women as technology and vice versa. For Giovanni Gerbino, for example, the women in the streets appear like "rossissimi papaveri/con gli apparecchi/telefonici/negli occhi" (bright red poppies/with telephones/in their eyes).[129] But it is in the contributions by Fillia (pen name of Luigi Colombo) and Enzo Mainardi that we witness a more direct and specific overlap of women with electric light.

In "Notturno" ("Nocturne"), Fillia writes: "sotto il fanale sporco (sanculotto elettrico che à [*sic*] vinto la nobiltà depravata delle stelle) una prostituta—femmina bionda domina l'arcobaleno artificiale della notte con il colore azzurro—vivo dei suoi vestiti di seta" (beneath the filthy streetlight [electric *sansculotte* conqueror of the stars' depraved nobility] a blond prostitute—female dominates the night's artificial rainbow with her blue—vivid silk garments, *IFP* 170-171). The streetlight illuminates the stereotypical scene of the prostitute standing in the light of the lamp, but Fillia feels the need to pause in his poetic flow with a parenthesis reminding the reader that the electric lamps have replaced the stars by way of an aesthetic and technological revolution (hence the reference to the French revolutionaries, the sansculottes). The colder electric light however turns this Baudelairean setup into a Futurist nocturne: her lit-up dress is blue, and the atmosphere is crisp and sharp; we are a long way away from Baudelaire's (and Eliot's) warmly lit, yellowish and sepia seedy Parisian streets. As noted above, blue was a preferred color of the Futurists, partly because it underlined the way electric light turned the night into a brightly lit, but colder, affair for the eyes. The moral atmosphere of the encounter with a prostitute at night has also vanished under the light of this electric sansculotte: Fillia's persona is enthused by the meeting with this light-emanating woman who dominates the night and commands the rainbow. In "La donna magnetica" ("Magnetic Woman") by Enzo Mainardi, the poet ponders how best to paint his sparkling, velvety lover: "Per ben dipingerla rovescio Baudelaire,/penso ad una gatta nera/dall'elettrico pellame" (To descibe her I rewrite Baudelaire,/I think of a black cat/with electric fur, *IFP* 182-183, lines 3-5).[130] In both instances, Fillia and Mainardi gesture toward the Baudelairean night only to head off in a different direction: for Mainardi it is important to overturn Baudelaire ("rovescio"); the prostitute in Fillia's poem is actually the presence vivifying the night. At the question of how he shall paint (or describe) his magnetic woman, Mainardi's speaker answers:

> Una serra di lampi elettrici
> riscaldata d'abbaglianti profumi?
> L'azzurro che sprigiona
> annega il canto della luna!
> ————————
> (A hothouse with electric lights/warmed by dazzling perfumes?/Its blue fumes/drown the moon's song! [*IFP* 182-183, lines 11-14])

Clearly, murdering the moonlight is still an important frame of reference even in the mid-1920s, but Mainardi's poem sees the new Futurist woman as an electrified and electrifying presence who is able to drown moonlight with her radiance. In this case, electrifying women involves going back again to the gendered battle animated by Marinetti at the start of his Futurist enterprise, while at the same time surpassing it: these later Futurists eventually see women no longer as moonlight but as independent lights conquering the night.

As we have seen, where Futurist women poets and artists employed electric light as site of agency through which they make a distinct contribution to Futurist poetics, by the mid-1920s, male Futurist poets were developing and elaborating the trope of woman as an electrified and electrifying machine, objectifying women into electrically luminous, feminine personae. This trend in the feminization of electricity makes the contemporaneous work of Italy-based Czech painter Růžena Zátková all the more important for this chapter. Especially in the late 1910s and early 1920s, Zátková gravitated around the Rome-based circles of Futurism, and, even though she resisted being labeled a Futurist, she befriended Balla as well as Goncharova and Larionov, and, when she married Beny's (Benedetta Cappa Marinetti's) brother, Arturo Cappa, she effectively became Marinetti's sister-in-law.[131] Though still under the influence of the theories of light developed by both Boccioni and Larionov, Zátková displayed significant artistic independence, developing her own cycle of mixed-media assemblages, *pitture luminose* (luminous paintings).[132]

In 1921-22, Zátková worked on a series of portraits of Marinetti *as* light. According to art historian Alena Pomajzlová, Zátková appears to have produced a total of six paintings of Marinetti's head—three oil paintings, and three watercolor sketches—a unique case of repetition within her works.[133] In the first of these, Marinetti's head is painted in black and white; in those to follow, she paints Marinetti's head as an explosion of color and semi-abstract forms.[134] Far from being timid or feminine, the portrait, to borrow Franca Zoccoli's adjectives, is "fiery," "congested," and "violent."[135] Zátková was particular in distinguishing the portraits as *Marinetti—sluneční světlo* (*Marinetti—Sunlight*; plate 9) and *Elektrický Marinetti* (*Marinetti—Electric Light*, or Electrical Marinetti), even though what remains of the two versions (we only have the watercolor preparatory sketch for *Elektrický Marinetti*) look nearly identical in terms of form and composition. Interestingly, according to Marinetti's wife Benedetta, his personal favorite (which he would purchase from Zátková) was the one representing himself as the sun: ironic, given his bombastically declared love of electrical technologies, though symptomatic of an avant-garde movement that drew its artistic energies and momentum from Marinetti himself.[136] In one of her drawings from approximately 1920, Zátková imagined the human mind "inseminated" ("feccondata" [*sic*]) by God as a round light piercing the darkness with its highly luminous rays (see fig. 2.6). This drawing, which may predate her series of Marinetti's portraits, sees Zátková exploring associations between light and intellect and divine power: all these meanings converge in her representation of Marinetti's head. Marinetti is emanating light like some solar divinity. For her, it would seem, there was virtually no difference between a solar Marinetti and an electrical one. Zátková in fact saw Marinetti as an electric lamp, not unlike Goncharova's. On December 6, 1921, she would write to her sister Zdena, informing her of Marinetti's upcoming visit to Prague and taking the opportunity to describe this extravagant Italian to her sister. Zátková ends her message on a humorous note, which appears in brackets before her signature: "Básník Marinetti vyznačuje se také tím, že nemá dlouhé kadeře, jak se na básníka sluší, ale pleš přes celou hlavu. Ta pleš však—i ta se vyznačuje—ta se jmenuje: <u>elektrická</u> pleš futuristy Marinettiho!" (Marinetti the poet is also distinguished in that he hasn't got long curls as befits a poet, but a completely bald head. That bald head though—even that is distinguished—is called: the <u>electric</u> bald head of the Futurist Marinetti!).[137] For Zátková, Marinetti's physical appearance does not quite fit the Romantic image of the male poet. More importantly though, she likens Marinetti's notoriously bald head to an arc lamp or an electric bulb, its globe completely smooth, round, naked, and luminous. In her portraits of Marinetti, then, her oscillation between the sun's masculine ethos and electricity's more ambivalent gendering points to a conflation of the two: the Futurist poet is, for Zátková ultimately, an electric sun. Moonlight murdered, Marinetti rises as the electrical divinity of a new luminous way of making art and literature.

Turning to the art of Zátková enables us to reflect on how Marinetti came to embody the Futurist poet par excellence. Zátková's painting further complicates the gendering of electric light we have witnessed within Futurism and outside it. For this group, electric light was a fluid trope, appropriated by Futurist men and women alike. Electric light was the essence of the avant-garde artist and writer: it represented their genius, and the ability of that genius to work and think ahead of their times. As we shall see in the next chapter, Mina Loy also associates electric light with Futurist genius but takes a more openly feminist stance with regard to the aesthetic purposes of this new kind of illumination.

The act of murdering the moonlight, I have suggested, was the crucial metapoetic myth that enabled Marinetti to articulate Futurism's distinct aesthetic and social values. Central to the Futurists' narrative of a radical break with the past, poetic attitudes toward moonlight in art and literature became a litmus test of Futurist allegiances. Murdering the moonlight became both an act of artistic exorcism of the Symbolist heritage and a sign of a poetic lineage. Paradoxically, the only way Futurism could break with Symbolism was to construct and represent the nineteenth-century movement as its ideological opposite, available to be attacked, shattered, and reconfigured. Moreover, this iconoclasm was not radically disruptive but aspirational and proleptic. The act of killing the moonlight launched a long, vexed, and often traumatic process of detachment from the poetic language of the fin

Fig. 2.6. Růžena Zátková, *Mente umana fecondata da Dio/Lidská duše zúrodněná Bohem* (Human Mind Inseminated by God), c. 1920. Grease pencil on paper, 21.7 × 17 cm. Private collection. Digital image courtesy of Alena Pomajzlová. Credit © Francesca Barbi Marinetti.

de siècle. Rather than completely disappearing from the Futurist poetic land-scape, the moon continued to inhabit Futurist poetry, only to be periodi-cally scapegoated and exorcised. These struggles were often personal. Mari-netti, much like Eliot, started his writing career as a lunar dandy; his Futurist poetics clearly depends on a specific genealogy of lunar poetry. Ultimately however, electric light takes center stage, changing the texture of the Futurist nocturne, turning it shades of brilliant blue. More importantly, Futurist killing of natural moonlight and celebration of artificial electric light prised open urgent questions about gender. Because Futurist technophilia is still regarded as an expression of the movement's hypermasculinity, representations of women in Futurist poetry and Futurist women themselves tend to be marginalized. As this chapter has shown, the Futurists' killing of moonlight, while initially dramatized as an act of misogyny, actually enabled a deeper and more widespread involvement of women writers and artists in the Futurist movement. If attacking the moon as a symbol of passive femininity was exciting to Futurist men, it was empowering for Futurist women, opening new possibilities for female agency and creativity.

Living with Lanterns

Mina Loy

> One day, during a play rehearsal, a lamp lashed to my waist burst into flame and was barely cut free before it exploded.
>
> Mina Loy, "NOTES ON CHILDHOOD"[1]

Impasse Ronsin, number 11, 15th arrondissement, Paris. The alley does not look particularly charming or picturesque today, with its mix of postwar and contemporary architecture, and the traffic noise coming in from the nearby rue de Vaugirard. But let us time travel, and let our imagination take us to an undefined afternoon or evening in 1921. The French-Romanian sculptor Constantin Brancusi has invited some friends over for an aperitif in his studio, which, since 1916, has been located in this cul-de-sac in Montparnasse.[2] As we cruise around the room, glass in hand, we spot that other French-Romanian, Tristan Tzara, poet and founder of Dadaism, accompanied by the American photographer Berenice Abbott, the *Little Review* couple Margaret Anderson and Jane Heap, and Mina Loy, the "brilliant literary enigma" of modernism.[3] At one point in the soirée, Brancusi presumably, who was taught photography by Man Ray, suggests playing with his camera to immortalize the meeting of these six modernists.[4]

A few photographs survive. In one, we see Brancusi, Abbott, Loy, and Anderson sitting on what must be a couch or a bench with some cushions; Heap is in the background, behind Loy and Anderson; in front of them, we see the tops of seemingly emptied bottles in a row, and a globe-shaped lamp; the notorious "cracked walls" of Brancusi's studio make the backdrop.[5] Tzara, who was present but does not feature in this photograph, might have taken the shot. In a second photograph of the soirée (see fig. 3.1), the camera, perhaps operated by cable release, has clearly been moved so as better to capture people's faces but not their hands.[6] For many, I am sure, the most

Fig. 3.1. Constantin Brancusi, "Brancusi, Tristan Tzara, Berenice Abbott, Mina Loy, Jane Heap et Margaret Anderson dans l'atelier vers 1921-1922" (Brancusi, Tristan Tzara, Berenice Abbott, Mina Loy, Jane Heap and Margaret Anderson at Brancusi's studio c. 1921-1922). Centre Pompidou, MNAM-CCI/Philippe Migeat/Dist. RMN/GP. © Succession Brancusi. All rights reserved. ADAGP, Paris and DACS, London 2023.

interesting difference between the two shots lies in Tzara's spectral appearance, due to the camera's slow shutter speed; for me, however, it is Loy's changed position. In this photograph, Loy looks as though she may be holding the globe lamp previously on Brancusi's coffee table. The light from the lamp now illuminates Loy's, Tzara's, and Anderson's faces from below, forming stark shadows of the six artists, showing the wall's cracks in all their beauty, and conferring a supernatural air on the photograph. Perhaps Abbott, a good friend of Loy and a photographer, proposed that Loy should hold the lamp or rather pull it toward her, or perhaps Loy herself, attracted to the lamp as if it were one of the artifacts she had made herself, decided to sit in front of it.

However the evening proceeded, and whoever decided that Loy should sit in front of the lamp for this photograph, Loy scholars have largely overlooked the relevance of this photographed gesture. For Roger Conover, the photograph is visual proof of her friendship with Constantin Brancusi; for Amy E. Elkins, of Loy's friendship with Berenice Abbott.[7] For Susan Rosenbaum, since Loy sits at the center of the photograph, she is "literally bridg-ing European [. . .] and American avant-gardes"; for Suzanne W. Churchill, Linda Kinnahan, and Rosenbaum again, the Loy of this picture "is a central, animating, illuminating presence," but these authors also lament the fact that this photograph has been largely associated with Brancusi's overshad-owing presence in it rather than Loy's.[8] Yet, this moment, as documented in Brancusi's photographs, has a significance for Loy scholarship that goes be-yond the fascinating historical trouvaille or the cool throwback from the depths of some artist's archive: it defines Loy as a poet, as an artist, and as a woman.

Loy started making lampshades in New York in 1917, and at the time of this picture she might have been contemplating restarting this business en-terprise in Paris, as indeed she did in 1923 (two years after this photograph was probably taken).[9] All the while, she had been writing and publishing her own poetry, as well as making art and looking after her three children. This chapter tells the story of Loy's poetic, technological, artistic, and personal engagement with electric light. When Loy grasps its potential for modern life, she appropriates the new artificial light and domesticates it, harnessing its potential as a new figure for poetry, an illumination technology fit for the domestic space, a compelling object for the art world, and—perhaps most importantly—a powerful tool for her own, and women's, emancipation. The pages that follow will articulate the intersection of these distinct facets of Loy's art and career.

Before examining the qualities of light and brilliance in Loy's early poetry and lamp art (1914-27), I want to dwell a little longer on 1921, the year of this prodigious gathering. In an undated draft of an essay entitled "Brancusi and the Ocean," Loy hailed her friend as "one of the few moderns."[10] Bran-cusi's approach to art clearly worked on Loy as a continuous source of inspi-ration for what a *real* modern artist should be like, and what the modern artist's work should look like and signify. According to Loy's recollection in "Phenomenon in American Art" (1950), in the summer of 1921 our poet-artist paid a visit to the "wonderful" Mariette Mills, where she came "face to face, or rather face to flight" with one of the two copies of Brancusi's *Golden Bird* (*LLB* 199, 1919-20): "a metallic mould of static soaring," Loy recalls, "whose reflection of boughs within Parisian skies beyond her windows, gave to solidity an hallucinatory transparence."[11] A few months after Loy's first "face to flight" encounter with Brancusi's *Bird*, in the autumn of 1921 the *Little Review* would publish their famous "Brancusi Number," with photographs of Brancusi's works intersecting—or rather, interrupting—texts by Ezra Pound, Mina Loy, Francis Picabia, Kenneth Burke, and Jean Cocteau, among others.

Golden Bird features in two plates, number 17 (fig. 3.2) and number 24 (fig. 3.3), and for Loy's biographer, it is the latter photograph that "caught Mina's eye."[12] But it was the other picture, plate 17, that reappeared in the *Dial* a year later (November 1922) alongside Loy's new poem "Brancusi's Golden Bird."[13] Ashley Lazevnick, in her perceptive article on Brancusi's sculpture and Loy's poem, explains how Loy, viewing the artwork in person first and photographed in the *Little Review* afterward, constructs what is "at once a record of experience and an interpretation of experience."[14] As we have seen, Loy's memory of this bird still, quite literally, glowed some thirty years later in her essay "Phenomenon on American Art," and her memory of that first sight of *Golden Bird* at Mariette Mills's house must have been rekindled by the highly luminous photographs in the *Little Review*. In her ekphrastic poem, Loy writes:

> an incandescent curve
> licked by chromatic flames
> in labyrinths of reflections
>
> This gong
> of polished hyperaesthesia
> shrills with brass
> as the aggressive light
> strikes
> its significance   (*LLB* 79-80, lines 22-30)

This poem is as resplendent with bright light as Brancusi's sculpture and its photographic image, stirring the senses in several directions at once in a heightened synesthesia blending sound, vision, and meaning. Tara Prescott is right when she claims that "the hyperbolic shine of *Golden Bird* has importance for its modernist context."[15] If Loy's use of "polished" calls to mind the smooth lines of *Golden Bird*, it also alludes to Ezra Pound's discussion, in his *Little Review* essay introducing the sculptor, of Brancusi's "polish" as "a transient glory" and as an expression of "a desire for greater precision of the form."[16] The polished form of *Golden Bird* is optimal in deflecting light, both in Mariette Mills's house, where it mirrors the skies outside the window, and in Brancusi's own photographs, where it reverberates the glare of full sun in

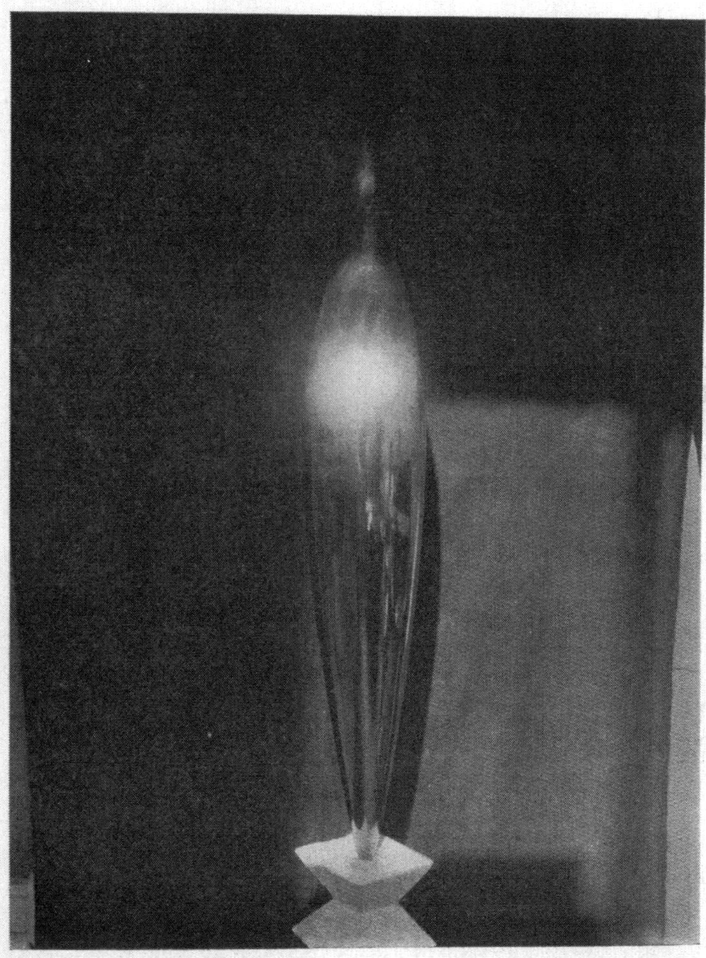

Fig. 3.2. Photograph of plate 17, from *The Little Review: A Quarterly Journal of Arts and Letters*, Autumn 1921 (Brancusi Number), picturing Constantin Brancusi's *Golden Bird* in his studio in Impasse Ronsin.

Fig. 3.3. Photograph of plate 24, from *The Little Review: A Quarterly Journal of Arts and Letters*, Autumn 1921 (Brancusi Number), picturing Constantin Brancusi's *Golden Bird* accompanied by *Mlle. Pogany*.

Brancusi's studio.[17] The phrase "incandescent curve" is Loy's own apprecia-
tion of what Prescott calls the artwork's "flame-like shape," but it is also the
poetic synthesis of *Golden Bird*'s smooth curves with incandescent light in
both plates.[18]

Plate number 17 is, in this respect, an excellent example of Brancusi's
"*photos radieuses* (radiant photos) [. . .] characterized by flashes of light that
explode the sculptural gestalt" as well as the sculptor's own talent for am-
plifying the imperfections of his photographs, which, perversely, he never
attempted to camouflage.[19] The glare in his photograph must be "the ag-
gressive light" that caught Loy's attention: right at the center of the black-
and-white photograph, the blotch of exposed light is more conspicuous
than in any other contemporaneous or subsequent photograph of *Golden
Bird*. Brancusi purposefully uses camera and light source to make his *photo
radieuse* resound and explode with the violence of the reflected light. Loy,
greatly susceptible to nuances of light, is attracted by the boldness of the lit
sculpture, which, she knows, brims with meaning. Indeed, as Laura Scuriatti
argues, what interests Loy is Brancusi's ability "to transcend the materiality
of sculpture."[20] Brancusi's photographs enhance the significance of light for
the original sculpture. In the same way that Brancusi pushes and probes the
boundaries of sculpture with photography, Loy seeks to expand the limits
of poetry by way of a new attention to technological language and lamp art.
When, in his 1982 review of *The Last Lunar Baedeker*, the great critic of mod-
ernism, Hugh Kenner, claimed that "to be the Brancusi of poetry [. . .] may
have been [Mina Loy's] impossible ambition," he was off the mark.[21] Both
artists harnessed the potential of light to transcend the limits of their art in
aggressively significant ways.

Decadent into Modern

When, in their introduction to the groundbreaking *Salt Companion to
Mina Loy*, Suzanne Hobson and Rachel Potter call Loy "a brilliant literary
enigma," they could not have found a more appropriate epithet.[22] Born in
England, Mina Loy lived in Germany, Italy, France, and Mexico before set-
tling down in the United States; she got married twice and gave birth to four
children; she was a poet as well as a writer of plays, a visual artist, a designer
of clothing, a feminist, a Futurist (and then a Surrealist), a maker and de-
signer of lamps and lampshades, and the owner of a shop.[23] This is a woman
artist and poet who, in a way that continues to resist labeling and pigeon-
holing, embodies, genders, and plays in multiple ways on and with the bril-

liance of both natural and artificial light in the construction of her own re-
fulgent persona and kaleidoscopic art.[24] As handed down by Loy herself, the
legend of her poetry's birth was indissolubly linked to her flesh-and-bone
encounter with Italian Futurism in the person of Filippo Tommaso Mari-
netti, father founder of this would-be all-destroying movement. Some time
after encountering Marinetti's charming yet bombastic personality in the
autumn of 1913, Loy confessed to her friend Mabel Dodge Luhan, "I am in
the throes of conversion to Futurism—But I shall never convince myself—
There is no hope in any system that combats 'le mal avec le mal'—& that is
really Marinetti's philosophy—Though he is one of the most satisfying per-
sonalities I ever came in contact with."[25] Although Loy's conversion to Fu-
turism was never really formalized, her meeting with Marinetti did spur Loy
into action, opening up the possibility of a new art and a new type of poetry.
In a letter of 1914, for example, in which Loy updates her husband Stephen
Haweis about their children, she wrote: "Joella has a poor handwriting Giles
does futurist drawings—Do not fear I am not intellectual enough to become
a futurist—But am intelligent enough to have given up everything else."[26] In
another letter to Dodge Luhan from the same year, Loy recognized her debt
to Marinetti "for twenty years added to my life from mere contact with his
exuberant vitality."[27] In another (undated) letter to her friend and agent Carl
Van Vechten, Loy, however, challenged what was presumably being said of
her at the time: "Now dear Carlo—if you like you can say that Marinetti
influenced me—merely by waking me up—I am in no way considered a
Futurist by Futurists—& as for (G. Papini he has in no way influenced—my
work!! So dont say a word about it—& also he wouldn't like it—he's very
passatist—really)."[28] While she did not regard herself as a Futurist, and nei-
ther did the Italians, it was clearly apparent to her family and friends that
Loy had been undergoing a Futurist phase, or at least one tinged by Futur-
ism. Loy must have found Marinetti's syntax-breaking and form-hating po-
etics profoundly appealing and liberating, as her early poetic experiments
demonstrate. In her writings of 1914-15, and even of 1917-19 (the year of
"Lions' Jaws," her parody of Futurist and Decadent writers), Futurist in-
fluence on Loy extends beyond form to include her repositioning within a
feminist context and consequently her appreciation of the conflictual rela-
tionship between nature and technology. The latter issue, in typically Fu-
turist manner, acted as a metaphorical disguise for the war of the sexes on
the one hand and the defeat of passéist literary movements on the other. In
this section, I will first show how a scrutiny of Loy's precise employment of

brilliant lights enhances our understanding of her early engagement with Futurist issues during the years of her "conversion," 1914-15.

As Loy scholars know well, in 1913, while living in Florence, she and her friend Frances Stevens met Giovanni Papini, philosopher and editor of the literary magazine *Lacerba* (1913-15), the hotbed of Florentine avant-gardes in the 1910s, as well as Marinetti himself, with both of whom Loy engaged emotionally.[29] It was, indeed, shortly after her encounter with Marinetti in Florence in the autumn of that year that Loy started writing her own poems.[30] Carl Van Vechten managed to place some of her early work in American magazines: the first of these to be published was "Café du Néant," in the August 1914 issue of *International: A Review of Two Worlds*, later republished the following year in *Rogue* as a set of three poems entitled "Three Moments in Paris."[31] These poems clearly revisit experiences in Loy's previous life in Paris between 1903 and 1907, while "appropriat[ing] Futurist vocabulary in mocking defiance" of her Futurist pals themselves.[32] Yet a closer look at "Café du Néant" shows that the Futurist-inflected form and language of this poem are tainted with content steeped in the Parisian atmospheres of fin de siècle Decadence. The eponymous café was a real venue, the Cabaret du Néant (Cabaret of Nothingness), situated at 34 boulevard de Clichy, in the famous Pigalle red-light district, not far from that extravagant symbol of fin de siècle Paris, the Moulin Rouge.[33] The Cabaret du Néant was such a popular attraction in late nineteenth-century Paris that its productions were exported to the Casino Theatre on Broadway in New York City.[34]

In "Café du Néant," Loy resuscitates a Decadent phantasmagoria through the new language of her Marinettian awakening; the poem, as Andrew Michael Roberts notes, has certain "elements [. . .] of Baudelairean decadence" and, for Burke, is one that bids "farewell to the past," that is Symbolism, Decadence, and Loy's previous life in Paris, "as if already looking back from the future" through the eyes of the Florentine-Futurist Loy.[35] In this, Loy is influenced, I argue, by her attraction to lights, which finds its beginnings here and is evident throughout her later poetry. It is certainly relevant that Loy should have chosen the Cabaret du Néant as the setting of this poem, as it was one of a number of "quaint" taverns and cabarets that were popular in the decades preceding World War I and that, we can presume, Loy visited in the company of Stephen Haweis or her Montparnasse gang.[36] One of a number of "cabarets excentriques," the Cabaret du Néant was in good company on the boulevard de Clichy alongside the Cabaret d'Enfer (the Cabaret of Hell), the Cabaret du Ciel (the Cabaret of Heaven), and many more.[37]

While the illusions in the Cabaret d'Enfer (and, I speculate, the Cabaret du Ciel too) relied on the "skillfully managed" employment of "colored electric lights," especially red, the Cabaret du Néant artfully employed candles, Argand oil burners, magic lanterns, and an optical effect similar to Röntgen, or X-rays.[38] Whereas the visual effects in the Cabaret d'Enfer were—somehow counterintuitively—electrical, given that gas or oil burners would have better simulated the heat and noise of actual fires, the creators of the Cabaret du Néant designed effects that would make its atmosphere even more artificially Decadent than Decadent aesthetics, tout court. The Tavern of the Dead, as its name was often popularly rendered into English, relied on the previously mentioned lighting technologies, which, alongside mirrors and glasses, were harnessed to produce optical illusions of sheeted ghosts, X-rayed skeletons, and even female spirits.[39]

In its brevity, Loy's opening, "Little tapers leaning lighted diagonally / Stuck in coffin tables of the Café du Néant" (*LLB* 16, lines 1-2), perfectly reconstructs the tilted candles and bone-and-skull chandeliers of the Salle d'Intoxication (intoxication room).[40] In *Magic: Stage Illusions and Scientific Diversions, including Trick Photography* (1897), Albert A. Hopkins describes:

> The spectators on entering the Cabaret pass through a long hall hung with black and find themselves in a spectral restaurant. Along the walls coffins are placed for tables, and on the end of each coffin is a burning candle. From the center of the ceiling hangs what is termed "Robert Macaire's chandelier," made to all appearances of bones and skulls. The spectators are here at liberty to seat themselves at the tables and are served with what they desire by a mournful waiter dressed like a French mourner with a long crape streamer hanging from his silk hat. Around the walls of the room are placed pictures to which the spectator's attention is called by the lecturer. Seen by the light of the room these pictures are ordinary scenes, but a new aspect is given to each when lights directly behind it are turned on; the figures in it appear as skeletons, each picture being in fact a transparency giving a different effect as it is lighted from the rear or as seen simply by reflected light.[41]

Hopkins's detailed recollection allows us to travel back to the heyday of the cabaret for a moment and imagine the original position of the illusions and lights, intended to entertain the spectators of the show. In this dark atmosphere, the candles and Argand oil burners were ideal for their weaker intensity and luminosity (especially if compared to the electric lights deployed in the Cabaret of Hell, for example). The feebleness of the candles and the warmth of the Argand, and the additional light radiating from the women, reinforce the room's and the poem's Decadent atmospheres: "Eyes that are full of love/And eyes that are full of kohl/Projecting light across the fulsome ambiente" (*LLB* 16, lines 5-7). In the darkness of the room, kohl, the fashionable eye cosmetic of the time, frames the whites of the women's eyes, which become additional sources of light illuminating the cabaret with their life, love, and sensuality.[42]

Yet the women in the poem are not simply "projecting light" (*LLB* 16, line 7) with their presence and love: they equally receive and absorb the cabaret's lights. With only a few brushstrokes, Loy paints a Decadent rendezvous between a man and a woman in the ghostly and yet romanticized low light of a candle: "Nostalgic youth/Holding your mistress's pricked finger/In the indifferent flame of the taper" (*LLB* 16, lines 17-19). In the final lines of the poem, Loy sketches what at a first glimpse looks like the illusion of an X-rayed skeleton on a woman's body:

> And at a given spot
> There is one
> Who
> Having the concentric lighting focussed precisely upon her
> Prophetically blossoms in perfect putrefaction
> Yet   there are cabs outside the door.   (*LLB* 17, lines 29-36)

Hopkins explains this kind of optical illusion in such detail we could reproduce it ourselves today, should we wish to: the cabaret employed Argand oil burners on the side of each coffin, behind a glass with a skeleton's profile (fig. 3.4). Interestingly, women spectators were also invited to participate in this visual gimmick. John Chancellor, the author of a male-oriented guide to Paris, *How to Be Happy in Paris without Being Ruined!* (1926), describes how the same visual effect was applied to paintings and to mistresses frequenting the cabaret:[43]

> Without any warning her outer garments vanish, and she is made to appear in some very provocative underclothing. She is quite unconscious of this immodest proceeding, and the expression of apprehensive astonishment with which she stares at the audience—who are laughing in simple, child-like delight—is worth the entire ten francs.
>
> Altruistically, no more of this performance will be described, but it is as well to mention that the lady in the chair appears to do all sorts of things that no well-bred lady would ever do in public.[44]

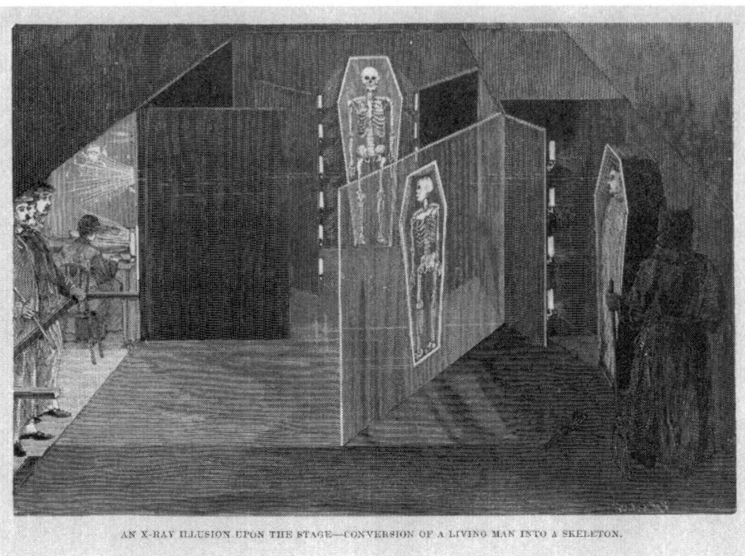

Fig. 3.4. "An X-Ray Illusion Upon the Stage—Conversion of a Living Man into a Skeleton," from Albert A. Hopkins, *Magic: Stage Illusions and Scientific Diversions, including Trick Photography* (London: Sampson Low, Marston and Company Limited, 1897), 58.

Roberts, who is to be credited for sourcing this remarkable historical finding, believes such details account for Loy's interest in Baudelairean decadence and Parisian bohemia.[45] The show, with its extreme exhibition of passé lighting, certainly piqued Loy's imagination at the time of visiting the cabaret. At the Cabaret du Néant some ten years after its first opening, Loy would have perceived it as the physical evidence of an aesthetic sensibility already two decades old, rendered even more antiquated and ridiculous by the "tapers" and oil lamps, especially if compared with other amusements on the boulevard de Clichy. Given the context, then, the "concentric lighting" on the woman may well be the switched-on lights directed at her, which, like stage lights on her body, give an illusion of naughty lingerie while revealing her imperfections and her aging. About ten years after her visit, when Futurism was completely outflanking Decadent aesthetics, she reconsiders her visit in light of the Futurists' proselytizing. While "Café du Néant" echoes Futurist poetry in its anarchic form and revolutionary punctuation-less syntax, its furniture is ten years old, marking the poem as a rite of passage for Loy as an avant-gardist: uncertain as to whether she should mock the Symbolists and Decadents or the Futurists, the pseudo-Futurist Loy decides to combine both currents in one single poem. The show at the Cabaret du Néant proposes a Decadent version of femininity that is at once hypnotic for the crowd and already kitsch and passé: the taxis are waiting outside, ready to take the customers of the cabaret to their next engagement. It also suggests, however, that taste was about to move on. With "Café du Néant," Loy critiques a certain fin de siècle Decadent portrayal of femininity in which women are presented as romantic, passive, and available objects: the lighting is "focussed precisely upon her" but not by or for her.

Across her early writings, lights (light per se as well as different types of light and lighting) are for Loy relevant signals of aesthetics but also of gender; for her, light, literary and artistic sensitivities, and the battle of the sexes are all inextricably linked. In "Pazzarella," a short story based on Loy's relationships with Papini and Marinetti (*SEML* 333), probably written when she was living in Florence, a play of light and dark is associated with her fictional alter ego, the eponymous Pazzarella/Pazzerella.[46] From the overture of her story, the Futurist male voice observing Pazzarella frames her feminine personality as crepuscular, twilight sucking, and overall disturbing:

> Surrounded by fading colours and clouded mirrors, seated before the tarnished gilding of a dilapidated clavichord, she let her idle fingers under their crepuscular jewels crawl over the keys, evoking tired melodies that sobbed and slipped into the silence without defining their complaint.
>
> When she was unoccupied she was just as disturbing. Her eyes resembled two bewildered swallows flown by accident into her face and caught in lines of suffering as yet undefined. Eyes that, being lost, had become fixed in patient expectation of clairvoyance, neglecting the present to search for the unknown. There was something about her of a plant that has matured in a cellar as though she had had to draw her alimentary light from an enduring twilight. (*SEML* 65–66)

The description of the ambience around her evokes the atmosphere of a fin de siècle domestic interior, with low lights, opaque mirrors, "dilapidated" furniture, and obsolete instruments, an aesthetics Futurism at least superficially claimed to abhor, as we have seen in the previous chapter. Throughout the text, Loy has her Futurist narrator (Geronimo) punctuate his narrative with allusions to low or failing lights: the woman of the story is in "the lamplight" (*SEML* 74), her eyes "glowed in the twilight" (*SEML* 81), her soul is illuminated "with a crazy half-light" (*SEML* 96), and finally she "twitter[s] to the dawn" (*SEML* 97). Loy's irony is fierce.[47] Geronimo, a.k.a. the avant-garde man, sees Pazzarella, by extension, as a representative of the female sex as seen by the Futurists and can only really picture her as a weak creature framed by the nineteenth-century artistic tradition: she is the half-light, the twilight, and the dawn. She is certainly not an exciting electric light. Sarah Hayden is right when she briefly includes "Pazzarella" in her discussion of a series of works where "Loy, as a female artist, reflects upon male Futurist modelings of artisthood."[48] For Hayden, who makes an en passant connection between "Pazzarella" and Marinetti's writings on women, Loy's short story conflates "the feminine" with "the (reviled) natural world" in her female protagonist.[49] But this prose work is about Futurism just as much as it is about the aesthetic sensibilities women are allowed to aspire to. Loy, writing this parody of Futurist men, deliberately portrays Pazzarella as a daughter of Parisian decadence and of French-inflected *crepuscolarismo* in Italy (see Chapter Two). Her story becomes a work about gender as well as aesthetics.

The Futurists attacked the Symbolist conception of woman as the moon and hoped to detach women as much as possible from this self-identification. In the famously controversial text by the Futurist leader, "Le mépris de la femme" ("Contempt for Woman," 1911), which has been often taken at face value as a manifesto against women, Marinetti initiates war against the idea of woman-as-moonlight, certainly a widespread idea of woman in early twentieth-century Italy, but not against the symbol of woman per se.[50] In this text, the lunar symbolism is associated with a certain romanticized conception of women: "Oui, nous méprisons la femme-réservoir d'amour, engin de volupté, la femme-poison, la femme-bibelot tragique, la femme fragile, obsédante et fatale, dont la voix lourde de destinée et la rêveuse chevelure se prolongent et se continuent dans les frondaisons des forêts baignées de clair de lune" (We feel contempt for woman conceived as the reservoir of love, engine of lust, woman-poison, woman as a tragic bibelot, fragile woman, obsessing and fatal, whose voice, heavy with destiny, and whose dreamy tresses reach out and mingle with the foliage of forests bathed in moonlight).[51] Marinetti's text deals with the role played by romantic love and gender politics in the construction of women's inequality up to that point. Marinetti's attack works in two ways: on the one hand, as we saw in Chapter Two, it is aimed at Symbolist and Decadent conceptions of women; on the other, it is an exhortation to the women of the new century to free themselves from their current state of "intellectual and erotic slavery."[52] Futurism's "allies are the suffragettes, because the more rights and powers they win for woman, the more will she be drained of love and cease to be a magnet for sentimental passion or an engine of lust."[53] Marinetti expands on this refrain in his 1916 book-length essay *Come si seducono le donne* (How to Seduce Women), where he says loud and clear that men should prefer women who are strong and intellectually (as well as emotionally) independent.[54] Loy reprises Marinetti's idea in her "Feminist Manifesto," where she exhorts fellow women to rise from the "conditions" of "Parasitism, Prostitution, or Negation" and demolish the boundaries of the two social classes in which women are subdivided, "**the mistress, & the mother**" (*LLB* 154; Loy's own emphasis). It is against this backdrop of gendered aesthetics that we need to read "Pazzarella." Geronimo, who explicitly sees Pazzarella as an artwork and himself as a new Pygmalion, "a creator" (*SEML* 96), has however failed to make her a woman according to his standards: "As a painter, struck for the first time with a higher conception of his art, regards his 'earlier' work with disparagement, I contemplated my *Pazzarella de le* [*sic*] *Scala di Pietra* critically" (*SEML* 94).[55] Symbolist tropes still haunt Geronimo's work: Pazzarella spends her days in the house, waiting for him; only thrives in the half-lights; feels like "the heroine of a melodrama" (*SEML* 94); weeps and seems to lack the strong confidence Marinetti was advocating for the new Futurist woman.

Would Mina Loy have attracted the attention of Futurist men (especially Marinetti) for her independence of thought, and vitality, rather than just her pretty and vaguely foreign looks? Possibly. Her poems from 1914–15 seem to tell a different story, of various Pazzarellas who, while courting Futurism, fail to be altogether Futurist. Simultaneously, in these poems Loy appears concerned with the condition of women who could not or would not embrace these Futurist ideals of sexual liberation and intellectual renovation. This attitude shines through two poems in particular, "Virgins Plus Curtains Minus Dots" and "At the Door of the House," both of which display Loy's feminist position toward women's condition in the 1910s and her careful observation of the Italian women around her. The first poem tackles the issue of virgins without a dowry ("dots" in French), destitute women financially unable to have themselves married off to a man.[56] Loy depicts these lower-class Italian women, whom she could have observed from her Costa San Giorgio house in Florence, as quite literally locked indoors and spying street life through curtains:

> Somebody who was never
>   a virgin
> Has bolted the door
> Put curtains at our windows
> See the men pass
> [. . .]
> Some   behind curtains
> Throbs to the night
> Bait   to the stars
> Spread it with gold
> And you carry it home
> Against your shirt front
> To   a shaded light
> With the door locked
> Against virgins who
> Might   scratch   (*LLB* 22-23, lines 44-48, 54-63)

The houses come to represent what Scuriatti aptly terms the "tyranny of domesticity," which encloses and imprisons these women ("Houses hold virgins / The door's on the chain," *LLB* 21, lines 1-2).[57] In the poem, Loy transforms this tyranny into her own unusual set of Chinese boxes: the houses make the outer box; at the center are the secluded women, hidden by curtains and well protected by locked doors; the innermost layer is made up by the indoor lights, necessarily "shaded" so as to be appropriate for the domestic space that contains them and replicating the social propriety of the houses and women alike. While lampshades protect the eyesight from the otherwise naked lights, Loy's women can only dream of "'transparent nightdresses made all of lace'" to make them feel like unshaded lights burning away in the night. With the "plus" and "minus" of the poem's scientific-sounding title signaling the dynamic relationship between women and ambient accessories, "Virgins Plus Curtains Minus Dots" represents the moment Loy begins to elaborate on domestic lighting as an appropriate way to visualize the condition of women at the time of her "conversion to Futurism."

In "At the Door of the House," Loy reprises the Futurist idea of woman-as-moonlight to further her critique of women's position in a patriarchal society. The "thousand women" (*LLB* 33, line 1) in the poem have been waiting for "the Man of the Heart" (*LLB* 33, line 21) to appear in the cards spread by the fortune teller as well as for him to physically show up at the doors of their houses. After shuffling her "Tauro cards" (*LLB* 34, line 46), the poem's fortune teller leads the Florentine women back to their passive condition governed by the moon:[58]

> The wheels with wings
> The rows on rows of goblets
>   Passionate magenta blossoms
> Hermits   —bring luck—
> Moons Prison-fortresses
> Cudgels
> A man cut in half
>   Means a deception
> And the nude woman
>   Stands for the world   (*LLB* 34, lines 47-56)

The tarot cards spread across the "wash-stand" (*LLB* 33, line 3) like jigsaw pieces that, when combined, ought to provide a complete picture to the women anxiously waiting all around the fortune teller. As the cards are dealt across the page, Loy places "moons" on the same line as "prison-fortresses." Traditionally, the moon card in the tarot deck would not signify the patriarchal prison Loy refers to here but rather feminine nature.[59] The combination of these two signifiers is, however, the target of Loy's critique: the role of women in a traditional society as 1910s Florence would have been encasing woman in her own prison; women are raised and made to believe that marriage ("Virgin Plus Curtains Minus Dots") and romance ("the Man of the Heart" in "At the Door of the House") represent the essence of their lives. The final card turned over by the fortune teller, where "the nude woman/ Stands for the world," may be pointing toward the usual mystificatory gender order, while also encouraging woman to emancipate by stripping off all her romantic and domestic constrictions. In these early poems, Loy harnesses natural light and artificial lighting to further nuance her feminist position.

Loy's early reflections on the condition of women, domesticity, and technology are even more vivid in her hilariously "savage satire" of her relationship with Papini.[60] The longer poem "The Effectual Marriage or The Insipid Narrative of Gina and Miovanni," which, according to Loy, was "inspired" by the "home of a mad woman" (*LLB* 39, lines 124-125), satirizes the couple's gendered division of labor in their domestic life:

> In the evening they looked out of their two windows
> Miovanni out of his library window
> Gina from the kitchen window
> From among his pots and pans
> Where he so kindly kept her
> Where she so wisely busied herself   (*LLB* 36, lines 11-16)

The domestic space, with its traditionally gendered duality, marks a physical and psychosocial divide between the two lovers: separate windows matching their different perspective on life; the man in the library, the woman in the kitchen; the man owning the crockery the woman needs for cooking and for "bus[ying] herself" with. Loy presents us, as Scuriatti notes, with a parody of gender roles in the domestic sphere which at the same time represents the stereotypes of men's and women's own "intellectual abilities and skills."[61] In the tenth (irregular) stanza of this poem, Loy further illustrates the gender divide within the couple while taking a mocking stance on the Futurists' love of electricity:

> While Miovanni thought alone in the dark
> Gina supposed that peeping   she might see
> A round light   shining   where his mind was
> She never opened the door
> Fearing that this might blind her
> Or even
> That she should see   Nothing at all
> So while he thought
> She hung out of the window
> Watching for falling stars
> And when a star fell
> She wished   that still
> Miovanni would love her to-morrow   (*LLB* 38, lines 67-79)

It is no coincidence that T. S. Eliot, the writer of *The Waste Land* and the careful observer of lights (see Chapter One), should think this poem "extremely good" and include these very lines in his review of *Others: An Anthology of the New Verse* (1917) for the *Egoist*.[62] Loy's fierce satire of gender roles has Gina imagine Miovanni's body separated from his mind, which is, perhaps obviously, "a round light"—a globe of light, a light bulb, a lamp—the source of his intellectual activity and of his being. Miovanni, who sits in his library and lives "outside time and space" (*LLB* 37, line 45), is the archetypical male avant-garde intellectual. Miovanni is not just any light; his "masculine intellectualism," as Julie Gonnering Lein calls it, is an electric light, "a bare light bulb" shining in the dark.[63] Gina may be overawed by Giovanni's light, but, in Loy's witty representation, Gina doubts Miovanni's intellectual potential: it might be he is a light so strong to blind everyone with his knowledge, or it may be just a visual ruse, like one of the illusions in the Café du Neant, threatening to offer Gina's opinion of the intellectual side of the pair. Perhaps, as Rowan Harris observes, "Miovanni's genius is [. . .] a mere posture, an empty pose."[64] In this stanza, Loy resorts again to the trope of the virgins who "bait   to the stars" from "Virgins Plus Curtains Minus Dots" to depict Gina in the same attitude and position, romantically looking out her window and wishing upon falling stars that her love for Miovanni should live on. Gina cannot be a blinding light, nor understand Miovanni's lofty speeches, and can only connect to the natural feminine of the stars in the sky.

In the last days of 1914, perhaps a time suitable for self-reflections, Loy wrote to Van Vechten: "For three weeks I have been suffering from an unhappy love & getting quite passatist—But I am too modern to despair of the future—."[65] The breakup with Marinetti and Papini had taken its toll on Loy, both emotionally and artistically. If she had found herself in the "throes of conversion to Futurism" a few months before, the unhappy ending of her love affairs now placed her in a mood that was quite the opposite of the Futurist ideals advocated by her two ex-boyfriends. Her "passatism" (from Italian *passatismo* and French *passéisme*) or passéism is present in all her portrayals of women I have explored thus far: in the poems of 1914-15, Loy oscillates between an attraction to Futurism and a tendency toward passéism. Yet it is relevant Loy should find strength in being "too modern to despair of the future." After all, in her response to Marinetti's movement, "Aphorisms on Futurism" (1914), published in the January 1914 edition of *Camera Work*, Loy professed: "DIE in the Past/Live in the Future./[. . .]/BUT the Future is only dark from outside./*Leap* into it—and it EXPLODES with *Light*" (*LLB* 149, lines 1-2, 14-15).[66] Although Loy's printed copy at the Beinecke Rare Books and Manuscript Library shows the words "Futurist" and "Futurism" replaced with "Modernist" and "Modernism"—an unequivocal mark of Loy's subsequent formal reconsideration of "her Futurist allegiance"—at the point of writing "Aphorisms," Loy imagined the future as the Futurists imagined it: up to date with the latest technological developments, fast, and of course blindingly bright with electricity.[67]

In her very early work, Loy was clearly intrigued by the ideological gendering of light and illumination as brought forward by the Futurists. In her play *Collision*, for example, she takes a further opportunity to associate the white glare of arc lighting with Futurism. The play, written in 1914 in Florence and published in 1915 in *Rogue* jointly with *Cittàbapini* as *Two Plays*, was never performed.[68] The play begins with "a central arc-light" illuminating a Marinetti-like character, appropriately identified as "MAN."[69] While the arc light is, at first, essentially a backdrop, it soon becomes apparent that it is more than just that, as it can be controlled by MAN, who consequently "stares blankly into arc-light—presses electric button—shattering insistant [*sic*] noise surrounds room—intermittently arc-light extinguishes" (Loy's spelling).[70] MAN, qua Marinetti, qua the primordial Futurist man, has technology at his fingertips: no more flickers or intermittences, the technology is first extinguished, then sublimated and perfected. After MAN's final cry for "CREATION—[. . .]/The vibrations accelerate to super-velocity— reach the static—the light is uniform."[71] As we saw in Chapter Two, in his text "Tuons le clair de lune!!" arc lighting functions for Marinetti as the futuristic, hyper-technological answer to moonlight. For Loy, aesthetically sensitive to different types of lights (as we see throughout this chapter), arc lighting is likewise *the* Futurist technology: bold, aggressive, masculine, public, and unstable without supervision. But then, what is the light appropriate for women, according to Loy?

Woman, Electric

In the review of *The Last Lunar Baedeker* mentioned earlier in which Kenner criticizes Loy for wanting to be "the Brancusi of poetry," he attempts another lunge to understand her. Comparing her to Marianne Moore, Kenner writes: "Both are female, yes, polysyllabic, yes, ironic, yes, both 'precise': but Moore's bias is always ethical, to a degree that flawed her late work, and Mina Loy is no more ethical than an arc light."[72] Kenner's likening here of Loy's supposed lack of ethics to a technology by then quite obsolete is tantalizing but also misleading. The metaphor equates the arc light's crude power of illumination with Loy's forensic precision and lack of ethical warmth, implying that her concerns were purely aesthetic; in support of his claim, Kenner adduces a few sensual, slightly blasphemous, clearly ironic lines from *Songs to Joannes.* This is a crude misunderstanding of poems that frequently and cogently construct and communicate their ethics via imagery of light and illumination, including the arc light associated in her play with "MAN," and Marinetti.

Hitherto I have traced Loy's Futurist allegiances via her poetic engagement with natural light and artificial illumination during her crucial *Bildungs-jahre* of 1914-15. Turning now to the poetic phase which parallels Loy's breakup with the Futurists and detachment from Futurist poetics, 1915-19, I propose that Loy, after her disillusionment with Futurism, gives a more explicit significance to natural and artificial illumination in her poetry and that this is a way of bridging the inequalities, both aesthetic and social, brought about by the gender divisions of the time, as well as of rebutting the masculinism of the Futurists. In doing this, Loy appropriates electric light for women and domesticates it in her poetry as well in the lamp art on which she embarks at this time. Virginia Kouidis's 1980 claim that Loy was "unconcerned with technology" has been largely superseded by the work of Julie Gonnering Lein.[73] In her study of Loy's poetics, Gonnering Lein concedes that Loy may not have been interested in all technologies, or even in conceptualizing technology per se, but shows that her poetry displays a command of basic physics and knowledge of electricity, in particular in their application to lamps.[74] This was for Loy a distinct aspect of modern life, representative of, and necessary for, the development of a Modern Woman.[75]

What did women in general think of the new electric light? Would the association of women and electricity have been generally welcome at the turn of the twentieth century? The picture is too complex to be analyzed in detail here, but I will offer a brief sketch of the historical context to situate Loy's own imagining of the new light. Tending the lights in the house had been, historically, a woman's business: women would hitherto have looked after candles, oil lamps, and gas lighting and would consequently find themselves in charge of managing the electric light in the domestic space.[76] Yet, with the arrival of electrical technologies, women were often portrayed as technologically illiterate, especially in electrical journals.[77] At the same time, technical literature went on to report a certain dislike of the electric light among women. Robert Hammond of the Hammond Electric Light and Power Supply Company (UK), reported in *The Electric Light in Our Homes* (1884) that women in particular took a dislike to the electric light (and, understandably, arc light more than other types of light) because of its harsh glare. Hammond recalls a ball lit by arc light, at which some ladies decided "to sit in the shade, rather than in the full effulgence of the arc light."[78] A similar scene is replicated in the satirical magazine *Punch* in 1889, where we see a number of high-society ladies sitting in an electrically lit room and using Japanese parasols to shield themselves from the unwelcome rays of electricity.[79] Edith Wharton, who in *The Decoration of Houses* (1897) declared electric light "of great service" only to "passageways and offices," hints in her novel *The House of Mirth* (1905) at similar popular opinions on the aesthetic effect of electric light on women.[80] Her protagonist, Lily Bart, looking at herself in the mirror, is "frightened by two little lines near her mouth": "'Oh, I must stop worrying!' she exclaimed. 'Unless it's the electric light—' she reflected, springing up from her seat and lighting the candles on the dressing-table."[81] The narrator, however, does not fail to inform us that, even with the electric wall lights off, "the two lines about the mouth remained."[82] Historian Graeme Gooday explains how in the 1880s and 1890s the general public perceived the aesthetic difference of electric light in gendered terms, which can be summarized according to the adage "men typically relished brightness and directness whilst women generally favoured muted elegance."[83] For Gooday, a case in point is Alice Gordon, who, in her introduction to *Decorative Electricity* (1891), confirms that "the master wishes to get all the light possible, and the mistress to have the light as becoming and pleasant as possible"; "it is rather difficult to reconcile these two wishes."[84] These two wishes give way to a "gendered battle [. . .] over whether the electric light in the domestic realm should be shaded [. . .] (as women preferred), or left unshielded and as brilliant as possible," with women covering themselves up to protect themselves against its light (as men preferred).[85]

Around the same time, however, others saw an opportunity to aestheticize the electric light for women beyond the domestic realm. In 1884, Gustave Trouvé, a French electrical engineer, had started producing in Paris electrical jewelry—or, in Maureen Dillon's words, "miniature lamps for personal adornment."[86] From his 1885 brochures, we know Trouvé was producing an array of electrical jewels, ranging from luminous diamonds to butterflies in hairpins, tiaras, electrical flowers, and many more, all powered by pocket batteries.[87] These jewels found an immediate use as special effects in the more sensationalist theater of the operettas and the music hall but also, for a time, among the wealthier women who could afford them. Two of them were Alice Gordon, who, in the previously mentioned *Decorative Electricity*, recounts her mishaps with electrical jewels, and Alice Vanderbilt (also known as Mrs. Cornelius Vanderbilt), famously pictured in 1883 in her "Electric

Light" ball gown of blue velvet, satin, and electrical lamps, a creation of the English fashion designer Charles Frederick Worth (see fig. 3.5).[88] In her electrically flamboyant dress, which we can only partly enjoy in this black-and-white photograph, Alice Vanderbilt embodies the new light in all her brimming femininity, showing how it can be made becoming, pretty, womanly. Electricity could thus be perceived more positively as able to produce "enlivened, attractive-looking, transformed women."[89] In the pre-electrical era, women had often "appeared as goddesses of light and truth" in the visual arts, but by the 1890s, according to Julie Wosk, these goddesses metamorphose into "emblems of the modern electrical age," exported worldwide thanks to the various world fairs and electrical exhibitions.[90] In tandem with electrical development more generally, we witness a proliferation of posters and advertisements portraying electrical goddesses or electricity fairies. The most popular exemplar of the electricity fairy in the modern literary imagination must be Tinker Bell, the twinkling light fairy from J. M. Barrie's play *Peter Pan; or, the Boy Who Wouldn't Grow Up* (1904), which is simultaneously effect and cause of this gendered process of electrification. Murray Pomerance explains how, "in the 1904 production, Tink is a winking light that moves about the stage, but a light that is intended to be understood as emanating from a tiny fairy figure, [. . .] a tiny, barely visible Galvanic source shaped like a woman."[91] Electricity fairies were particularly common at the end of the nineteenth and in the early twentieth century, but the trend of advertising electric light with images of electrical women continued into the mid-1920s (see plate 10, the poster of the Milan-based electrical company Edison, dated 1924).

By the point Loy started writing in the 1910s, on top of the Futurists' call to destroy the woman-as-moonlight, Loy would have encountered several instances of women carrying, tending, and embodying electric light, from the tale of Peter Pan she might have read to her children Giles and Joella to the various advertisements of the electrical age she would have seen in the many European cities she was waltzing through. As I have shown in the previous section, in her very early poems, Loy still saw women in general as imprisoned within their traditionalist, old-fashioned, lunar condition. She seems to consider herself complicit in this too, especially in her passéist reactions following her awakening to the avant-garde and her consciously feminist self-positioning. Her attitude changes somewhat in her first long poem, or rather song cycle of thirty-four songs, *Songs to Joannes* (1915–17).[92] The cycle is effectively a "collaged" narration of Loy's own experience of

Fig. 3.5. Mrs. Cornelius Vanderbilt (a.k.a. Alice Claypoole Gwynne) as "Electric Light" at the Vanderbilt Ball, March 26, 1883. Electrical gown designed by Charles Frederick Worth. Photograph by José María Mora. PR 223, Costume Ball Photograph Collection, New-York Historical Society, 39500. Photograph © New-York Historical Society.

Plate 1. Mich Mich, "Westinghouse Lampe: La plus élégante—La moins fragile" (Westinghouse Lamp: The most elegant—The least fragile). Poster, c. 1912 [?], 145 × 119 cm (57 × 47 in.). Digital image © Alamy.

Plate 2. Amédée Guillemin, "Le ciel de l'horizon de Paris (Côté Sud) vu à Minuit le 20 juin," in *Le ciel: notions elementaires d'astronomie physique* (Paris: Hachette, 1877). Photograph courtesy of Philippe Garcelon.

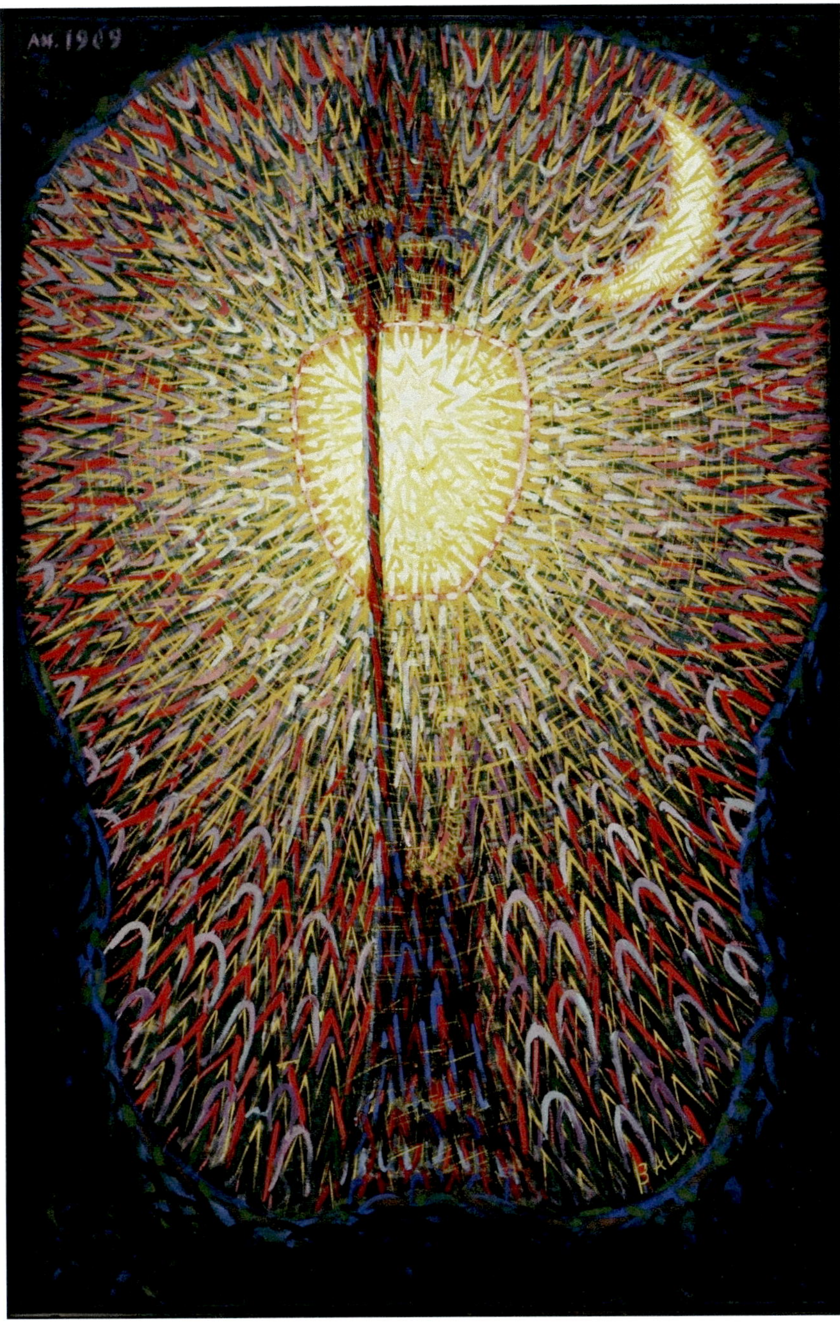

Plate 3. Giacomo Balla, *Lampada ad arco* (*Street Light*), c. 1910–11 (date on painting 1909). Oil on canvas, 174.7 × 114.7 cm (68.8 × 45.2 in.). Hillman Periodicals Fund. Museum of Modern Art, New York. Digital Image © The Museum of Modern Art/Art Resource, New York. Credit © 2023 Artists Rights Society (ARS), New York/SIAE, Rome.

Plate 4. Giacomo Balla, *Le torri del museo Borghese* (*The Towers of the Borghese Museum*), c. 1905. Pastels on paper, 37 × 26.5 cm (14.5 × 10.4 in.). Private collection. Digital image courtesy of Archivio Gigli, Rome. Credit © 2023 Artists Rights Society (ARS), New York/SIAE, Rome.

Plate 5. Natalia Goncharova, *Ткачиха. Ткацкий станок и женщина* (*The Weaver: Loom and Woman*), 1913. Oil on canvas, 154.4 × 99.8 cm (60.7 × 39.2 in.). Amgueddfa Cymru/National Museum of Wales, Cardiff. Digital image © National Museum of Wales. Credit © 2023 Artists Rights Society (ARS), New York/UPRAVIS, Moscow.

Plate 6. Natalia Goncharova, *Электрическая лампа* (*The Electric Lamp*), 1913. Oil on canvas, 105 × 81.5 cm (41.3 × 32 in.). Collection Centre Pompidou, Musée National d'Art Moderne, Paris. Photo © Centre Pompidou, MNAM-CCI, Dist. RMN-Grand Palais/Philippe Migeat. Credit © 2023 Artists Rights Society (ARS), New York/UPRAVIS, Moscow.

Plate 7. Rosa Rosà (Edyth von Haynau), Plate 3, from Mario Carli, *Notti filtrate: 10 liriche di Mario Carli con 10 disegni di Rosa Rosà* (Florence: Edizioni de *L'Italia futurista*, 1918), 11. Digital image courtesy of Beinecke Rare Book & Manuscript Library, Yale University. Credit © Famiglia Fornari (Heirs of Rosa Rosà).

Plate 8. Rosa Rosà (Edyth von Haynau), Plate 10, from Mario Carli, *Notti filtrate: 10 liriche di Mario Carli con 10 disegni di Rosa Rosà* (Florence: Edizioni de *L'Italia futurista*, 1918), 39. Digital image courtesy of Beinecke Rare Book & Manuscript Library, Yale University. Credit © Famiglia Fornari (Heirs of Rosa Rosà).

Plate 9. Růžena Zátková, *Marinetti—sluneční světlo* (*Marinetti—Sunlight*), c. 1922. Oil on canvas, 101 × 89 cm (39.7 × 35 in.). Private collection. Digital image © Francesca Barbi Marinetti.

Plate 10. Poster advertising Edison Light Bulbs: an allegorical figure illuminates the city lof Milan. Signed by San Marco and printed by Grafiche di Pavani Vanone, Milan, Italy, 1924. © Fototeca Gilardi, Milan.

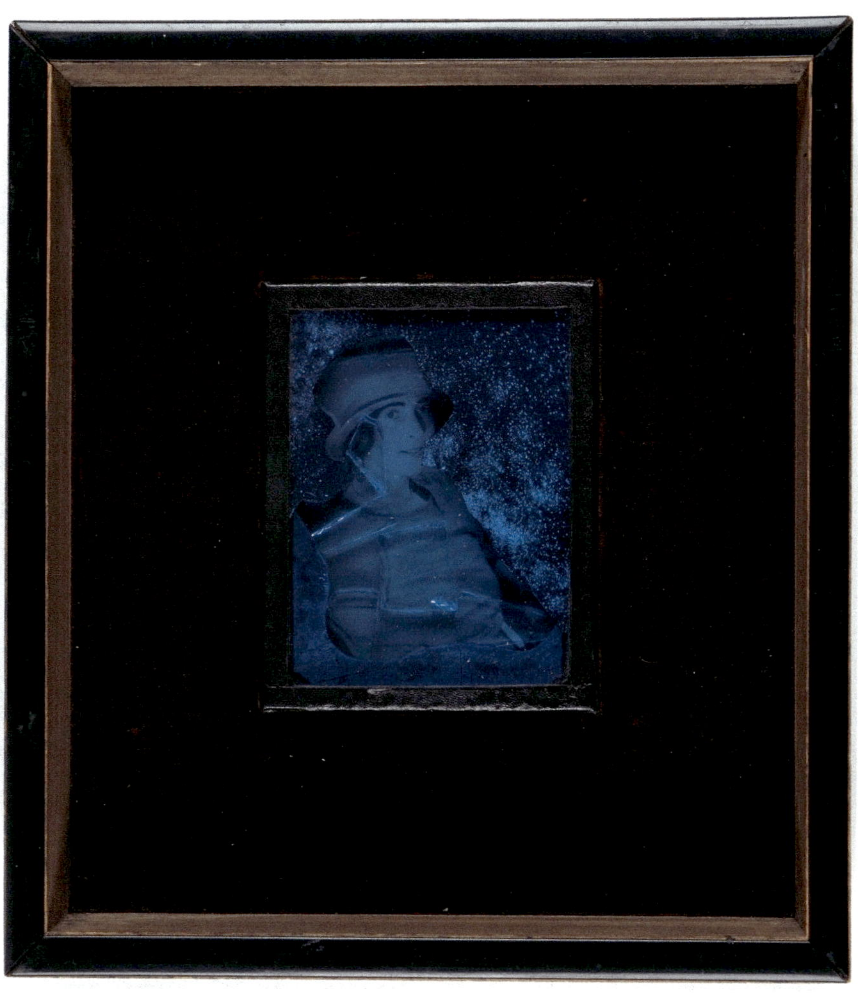

Plate 11. Joseph Cornell, *"Imperious Jewelry of the Universe" (Lunar Baedeker): Portrait of Mina Loy (Daguerreotype Object)*, 1936. Assemblage of silvered glass, glass shards, cut-out printed illustration, and gelatin silver print, in artist's frame, and including Man Ray photograph of Mina Loy, 13.2 × 10.6 × 2.5 cm (5 3/16 × 4 3/16 × 1 in.). Philadelphia Museum of Art: 125th Anniversary Acquisition. The Lynne and Harold Honickman Gift of the Julien Levy Collection, 2001, 2001-62-3. Image courtesy of the Philadelphia Museum of Art. © The Joseph and Robert Cornell Memorial Foundation/VAGA at ARS, New York, and DACS, London 2023.

Plate 12. Charles Demuth, *I Saw the Figure 5 in Gold*, 1928. Oil, graphite, ink, and gold leaf on paperboard, 90.2 × 76.2 cm (35 1/2 × 30 in.). Alfred Stieglitz Collection, the Metropolitan Museum of Art, New York. Digital image courtesy of the Metropolitan Museum of Art and Wikimedia Commons.

Plate 13. Georgia O'Keeffe, *New York with Moon*, 1925. Oil paint on canvas, 122 × 77 cm (48 × 30 in.). Carmen Thyssen-Bornemisza Collection, Museo Thyssen-Bornemisza, Madrid. Photo courtesy of Museo Thyssen-Bornemisza. © Georgia O'Keeffe Museum/ DACS 2023.

Plate 14. Georgia O'Keeffe, *City Night*, 1926. Oil on canvas, 121.92 × 76.2 cm (48 × 30 in.). Gift of funds from the Regis Corporation, Mr. and Mrs. W. John Driscoll, the Beim Foundation, the Larsen Fund, and by public subscription. Minneapolis Institute of Art, Minneapolis. Digital image courtesy of Minneapolis Institute of Art. © Georgia O'Keeffe Museum/DACS 2023.

Plate 15. Georgia O'Keeffe, *Radiator Building—Night, New York*, 1927. Oil on canvas, 121.92 × 76.2 cm (48 × 30 in.). Alfred Stieglitz Collection, co-owned by Fisk University, Nashville, Tennessee, and Crystal Bridges Museum of American Art, Bentonville, Arkansas. Photography by Edward C. Robison III. Digital image © Crystal Bridges. © Georgia O'Keeffe Museum/DACS 2023.

Plate 16. James Van Der Zee, *Portrait of a Young Woman*, 1930. Gelatin silver print with applied color, 17.3 × 11.8 cm (6 13/16 × 4 5/8 in.). Pepita Milmore Memorial Fund, National Gallery of Art, Washington. Digital image courtesy of National Gallery of Art. © James Van Der Zee Archive, the Metropolitan Museum of Art.

"failed relationships with several male lovers," lightened by the poet's mordant use of irony and peppered with her personal takes on Futurist syntax.[93] Loy, I argue, uses this cycle to finally put her passéism aside, in a literary work that mocks and ultimately surpasses the work of her Futurist boyfriends and of her artist ex-husband. Her use of a new palette of natural and technological light exemplifies this change in attitude.

When the poem's voice claims to be "the jealous store-house of the candle-ends / That lit your adolescent learning" (*LLB* 56, VIII, lines 1–2) or labels one of the boys as "a haloed ascetic" (*LLB* 55, V, line 10), we feel we are back in the setup of "The Effectual Marriage," with Gina looking at the stars and hoping Miovanni will love her again, as Miovanni's head turns into a light bulb in the dark of his library. Yet we are not. If storing candle ends signals both, on the one hand, the bittersweetness of a woman's clinging to memories of candlelit encounters and, on the other, her feminine chore of tending domestic lights, it is at this junction that Loy's poetics of light start diverging. The moon, clearly gendered female in her previous poems, now shines for the men of these songs. In the ninth song, we read:

When we lifted
Our eye-lids on Love
A cosmos
Of coloured voices
And laughing honey

And spermatozoa
At the core of Nothing
In the milk of the Moon   (*LLB* 56, IX, lines 1–8)

Loy throws romantic love back at the male body, making us ask: is romance a product of women's fantasies, or is it to be understood as men's fabrication? Lucia Re is correct in considering this poem a typical example of Loy's engagement with Futurist poetics and in deeming her attitude toward love, moonlight, and sentimentalism "consistent with the futurist polemic."[94] While the image of the spermatozoa swimming "in the milk of the Moon" could be merely a "dated euphemism for 'semen,'" as Eric Murphy Selinger points out, Loy's voice here is not criticizing the woman for believing semen to be "the milk of the Moon" but the couple, together, for imagining their relationship in terms tinted by a stereotyped "pink-love" (*LLB* 56, X, line 2).[95] Loy's masculine "milk of the Moon" in effect satirizes the Decadent perception of lunar, dreamy, lustful women by reversing the usual gendered association.

Toward the end of the cycle, Loy's disillusion with romantic love is complete. In Song XXIX, she writes:

> Unnatural selection
> Breed such sons and daughters
> As shall jibber at each other
> Uninterpretable cryptonyms
> Under the moon   (*LLB* 65, lines 5-9)

As earlier, in song XXIII, where "Irredeemable pledges/Of pubescent consummations/Rot/To the recurrent moon" (*LLB* 62, lines 4-6), the lovers carry on the traditional narrative of moonlit romantic love, and the poet casts a disillusioned look at her own relationships with men—or rather adolescent boys, as she herself calls them.[96] The moon maintains its facilitating role of sensual, Decadent rendezvous. If Loy's persona was initially enchanted with honeyed words and sex under the moonlight, by now men have revealed themselves as what they are, and their chatter in coded language has become unattractive to the speaker. By the third-to-last song in the cycle, the moon has turned cold ("The moon is cold/Joannes/Where the Mediterranean — — — — —," *LLB* 67, XXXII, lines 1-3): it no longer exudes its sensual, warm, carnal light abhorred by the Futurists but looks indifferently at the unhappy ending of Loy's love affair. If women are moonlight, she should, surely, receive some comfort from looking at the moon, stars, and fading lights, as Gina did in "The Effectual Marriage" and Pazzarella in her eponymous story?

Surely, yes, and yet this does not occur to the Loy of *Songs to Joannes*. Instead, her persona starts off by associating herself with a lamp of sorts:

> I must live in my lantern
> Trimming subliminal flicker
> Virginal   to the bellows
> Of Experience
>
>   Coloured   glass   (*LLB* 53, Song I, lines 14-18)

The figure of the woman with the lantern in the opening of *Songs to Joannes* has been variously identified as an allusion to the mythical tale of Eros and Psyche, or to the "wise virgin pose [with] an investigatory lantern."[97] The gendering of lamps and electric light I referred to above works as a clear influence on Loy's woman living in a lantern, who bears clear similarities to the Tinker Bells of the early twentieth century. There are, however, caveats to these readings. Loy's persona neither *carries* a lantern (like the wise virgin or an electrical goddess) nor accidentally *pours* it over the skin of her "Pig Cupid" lover (as Psyche would do), and nor *is* she the lantern itself (like Tinker Bell). She fends off her lover instead, acknowledging she "must live in [her own] lantern" (line 14), her "flicker" staying only "subliminal." The lantern, with its shade of colored glass, brings us back to "Virgins Plus Curtains Minus Dots," where the unmarried women are doubly protected and imprisoned by the curtains in their houses. These women are shaded lights themselves: beautiful lights burning with emotions, desires, and "subliminal flicker," longing to be naked lights, or perhaps lights with only some see-through "shade" ("'Transparent nightdresses made all of lace'", *LLB* 21, line 23) between them and the passing men's eyes.

At the time of writing *Songs to Joannes*, Loy has been speaking more openly about the aesthetic value of lamps and lampshades. In the first stanza of Song IV, for instance, Loy reinvents her early days caring for her children and her husband, Stephen:

> Once in a mezzanino
> The starry ceiling
> Vaulted an unimaginable family
> Bird-like abortions
> With human throats
> And Wisdom's eyes
> Who wore lamp-shade red dresses
> And woolen hair   (*LLB* 54, Song IV, lines 1–8)

The trapezoidal dresses Loy might have made for her own children turn into red lampshades for this "unimaginable family." Loy started making her own lampshades in 1917, by which time she had *Songs to Joannes* published in *Others: A Magazine of the New Verse* in its final version.[98] In a brief cameo of Mina Loy in Paris, Sylvia Beach would recount, many years later, how her millinery skills had a twofold purpose, satisfying Loy's desire for an artistic life while also sustaining her in the more practical needs of dressing herself and her children: "When you went to Mina's apartment you threaded your way past lamp shades that were everywhere: she made them to support her children. She made all her own clothes, also, and perhaps theirs. Her hats were very like her lamp shades; or perhaps it was the lamp shades that were like her hats. She wrote poetry whenever she had time."[99] I think it is possible to speculate that some of Loy's own self-made clothes (and not just her hats) might have looked a little like lamp shades. Carolyn Burke tells us that Neith Boyce, upon first meeting Loy in Florence in 1914, subsequently wrote in her diary that "Mrs. Haweis [was] looking like a Futurist poster—pretty and very talkative," in what, Burke assumes, was one of Loy's own "versions of the fashionable new skirts that bared the wearer's ankle."[100] Loy was always rather adventurous in her fashion style, and in 1917, shortly after relocating to New York from Florence, she attended a masquerade held by the Dada magazine the *Blind Man*, called the Blindman's Ball, in a costume of her own design, which was—to use Burke's words—"a cross between a Pierrot and a lampshade" (see fig. 3.6).[101] The silhouette of the lampshade appeals to Loy as an A-line that is at once feminine and modern: if the light inside the lamp comes to signify women's selves, the lampshade becomes for Loy the ideogram of women's clothing—it reminds us that lighting needs to be shielded, covered, made pretty. As in my history of the gendering of electric light, the question was whether to protect the women from the light or to cover up the light; in her dress, Loy decides to play with the covering up of both the light and the female body.

Julie Gonnering Lein, who employs Loy's arc-light metaphors and similes as a key to *Songs to Joannes*, is less concerned with the lamp as technological artifact than with the connection between the workings and physics of arc lighting and Loy's sexual desire, whose resemblance to one another would mold Loy's "electro-sexual metaphor[s]" in the cycle.[102] It is true that, throughout *Songs to Joannes*, Loy's lights, whether covered or not, emphasize the physicality of men's and women's desire: the "subliminal flicker" (*LLB* 53, Song I, line 15) of the beginning marks the excitement of early sexual attractions, while the moon grown cold marks the end of the relationship as well as the end of the poem. In July 1917 Francis Picabia, the French avant-garde artist introduced to Loy in New York that year by Marcel Duchamp (part of the *Blind Man* circle), published his own illustration of an Edison Mazda light bulb, entitled *Américaine* (American woman), as the cover of his own art magazine, *391* (fig. 3.7).[103] According to Mariea Caudill Dennison, the French artist "equate[s] American women with radiant high energy, modern advances and unconstrained openness to change" and "asserts that American women are sexually charged technological beauties."[104] Picabia's light bulb also bears two words on its glass, "flirt" and "divorce," alongside the name

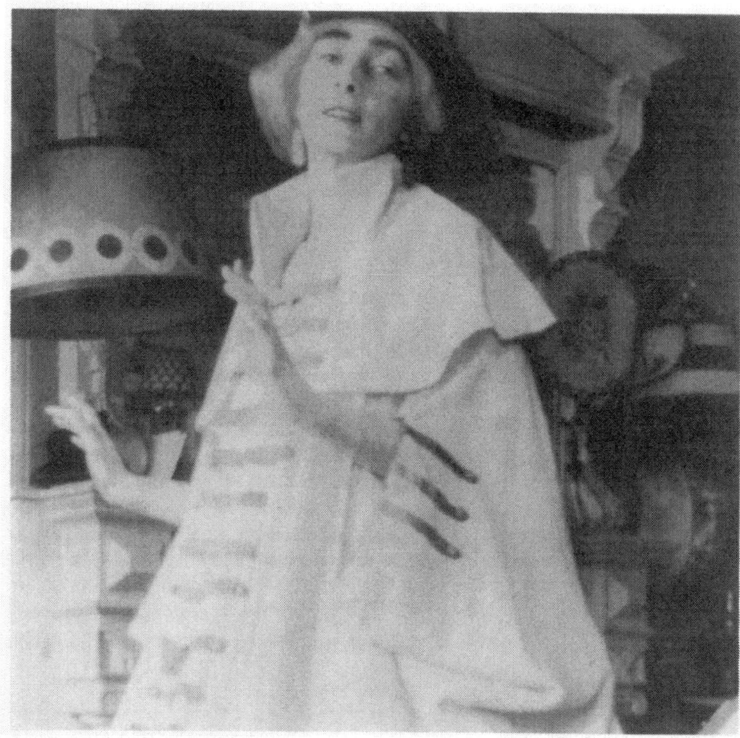

Fig. 3.6. Unknown photographer, *Mina Loy dressed for the Blindman's Ball*, 1917. Image as in Jennifer R. Gross, ed., *Mina Loy: Strangeness Is Inevitable* (Princeton: Princeton University Press, 2023), 37. Gelatin silver print on paper, 14 × 21.5cm (5 1/2 × 8 7/16 in.). Private collection. © Roger Conover.

of the Edison Mazda brand upside down at the bottom of the bulb.[105] These two words may well suggest the American woman's changeable, fickle attitude on the relationship front, as Dennison argues, although these features are equally typical of the moon, and corroborate "the ambivalence about the modern American woman," as Alex Goody thinks.[106] But "flirt" and "divorce" also represent the on-and-off switches of modern American women, suggesting erotic tensions commencing with a flirt and terminating with a divorce, as happens in Loy's *Songs to Joannes*. The typically feminine phases of the moon have been superseded by the velocity and immediacy of a modern light bulb's switch, and the lengths of relationships and erotic tensions have shortened. In Song XIV, the lights heighten the couple's sexual tension by way of an electrical metaphor, only to be reduced to vague romantic street lighting by Song XVI:

> No love or the other thing
> Only the impact of lighted bodies
> Knocking sparks off each other
> In chaos   (*LLB* 59, Song XIV, lines 6-9)

> We might have lived together
> In the lights of the Arno
> Or gone apple stealing under the sea
> Or played
> Hide and seek in love and cob-webs
> And a lullaby on a tin-pan   (*LLB* 59, Song XVI, lines 1-6)

The bodies of the couple are "lighted" and give off sparks much like carbon rods, turning sex into impact without love: for Gonnering Lein, the phrase "lighted bodies" detaches the two lovers (one wonders if we should even call them such) from the previously employed personal pronouns of "you" and "I."[107] Yet the bodies' "lighted" quality also helps us picture them as naked lights without shades, simply bodies electrically attracted to each other. If, however, Loy's persona and her Joannes "might have" had a romantic happy ending by the streetlamps constellating the Arno riverside in Florence, we should remember that the "natural incandescence" of the fireflies, to which the couple is suggestively compared (*LLB* 61, Song XIX, lines 15-22), never lasts very long.[108] By Song XXVIII the Loy figure is "burnt quite white / In the climacteric / Withdrawal of your sun" (*LLB* 64, lines 10-12). Since no one and nothing can get burnt in the absence of a light or heat source, it is her excess of unsatisfied passion that consumes her like a fire turned into ashes or a light bulb blown out on the spot. The trajectory of the two lovers is now complete: from being a "Pig Cupid," her lover Joannes has turned into a sun of near-classical beauty, distant and unreachable, while the woman, who initially prudently trimmed the lantern of her own desire, has now burnt herself out completely in the attempt at becoming a Modern Woman.

Lampisterie

In 1923, Loy decided to open a *lampisterie* (an old-fashioned term for a lamp shop) in Paris, at 52 rue de Colisée.[109] This event marks a new phase

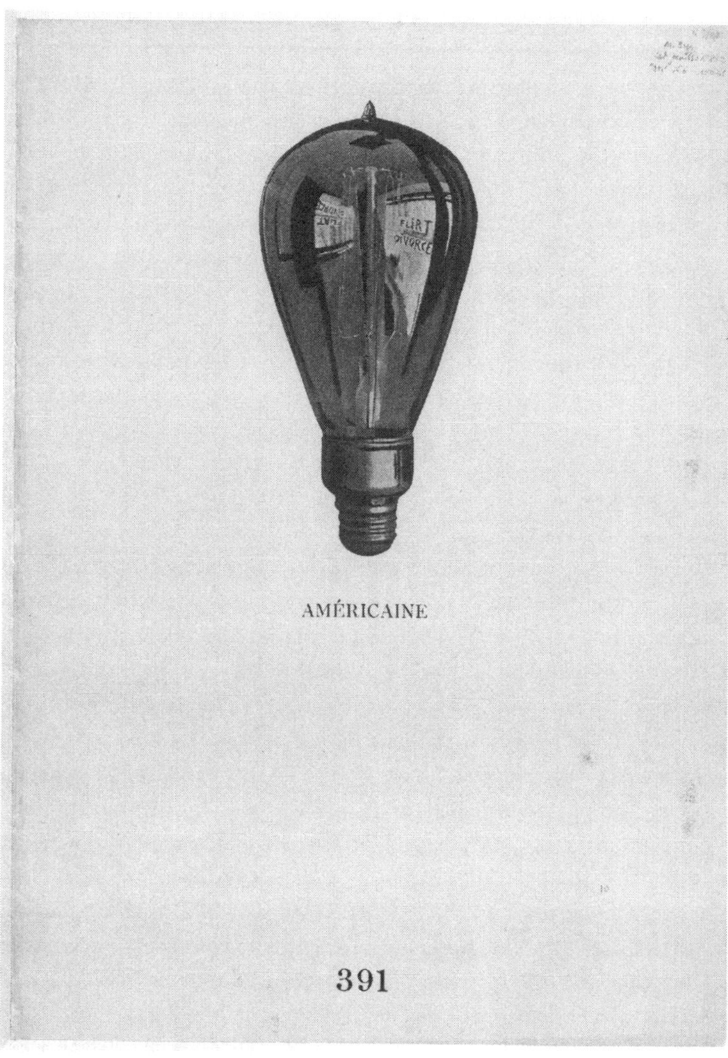

Fig. 3.7. Francis Picabia, *Américaine*, in *391*, vol. 6 (July 1917). Digital image courtesy of Bibliothèque nationale de France (BNF), Paris.

in Loy's engagement with electric light. During this period, the French-American Dadaist circles she had begun to frequent in New York and Paris influenced her engagement with lights and lighting more directly: Francis Picabia and Man Ray, for example, deployed lamps as the most "magical and mysterious products of technological modernity," while Tristan Tzara called his satirical notes or stories precisely *lampisteries*, playing on the double meaning of the French word *lampiste* as both someone making lamps and "a downtrodden underling."[110] It is with all of this in mind that Conover labels this period in Loy's life, from 1923 to 1930, as "Lampisterie."[111] As we have seen, Loy was not a stranger to the art of making lamps, having worked in a lampshade studio in 1917, the same year she presented her painting *Making Lampshades*, now sadly lost, at the Society of Independent Artists Exhibition in New York (April 10 to May 6, 1917).[112] As Susan Dunn points out, Loy was fascinated by fashion's double-faced potential as art and trade: the setting up of her own lamp shop was predominantly tied to her material and financial constraints, though her business had aesthetic purposes as well.[113] By making and selling her own lamps, Loy actively participated in some of the new cultural developments of her time: she contributed to the domestication of electric light, as well as the gendering of its discourse, both through her poetry and artwork.

By the time Loy came up with the idea of starting her own lamp business, the increasing number of electrified houses in Europe and the United States was accompanied by a growing interest in the ways in which electric light could be domesticated into something valuable and appropriate for the home. Several books were published on the subject. One of these was Henry Collins Brown's *Book of Home Building and Decoration* (1912), edited by his wife Clara Brown Lyman. One chapter was dedicated to the topic of how "to get full advantage from electric light in the home," while another tackled only lighting fixtures, clearly targeting women as the principal interior lighting designers (see fig. 3.8).[114] A year later, *The House in Good Taste* (1913), by Elsie de Wolfe, an American actress and interior decorator, advised women on how to decorate their own homes according to agreeable standards of taste that took the challenges of modern technologies into account. In her chapter dedicated to lighting fixtures, de Wolfe admits that "there is nothing more difficult than the problem of artificial light."[115] But, she goes on to affirm, "if properly considered, there is no reason why one's lighting fixtures should not be beautiful as well as utilitarian," although "it is seldom indeed that one finds lights that serve the purposes of utility and beauty."[116] By 1917, however, this "problem of artificial light" had turned into an aesthetic game for women. Clara Brown Lyman wrote in *The Art World* about the equivalent aesthetic value held of paintings and lamps:

The quest of the right kind of lamp for a home was never, perhaps, more interesting or more vigorously pursued than now, when the problem of the night lighting of various rooms for varying purposes has taken its rightful place as an important factor in the scheme of interior decoration alongside the selection of rugs, hangings and wall coverings. To recognize the qualities that go to make a good lamp is as essential as it is to know what constitutes a good painting. It is not enough to dismiss the subject of lamp selection with "I don't know about lighting but I know what I like." A bad picture may offend one's taste or do violence to a sense of the fitness of things, but the wrong kind of lamp does actual physical violence to the eyesight as well as sinning against all the laws of harmony of line and color.[117]

Interior design discourse has by this point fully incorporated lamps, which now complement a house artistically and visually, and reveal the owner's taste, just as paintings or wallpapers would do. Brown Lyman's comparison with paintings is striking as it effectively implies that electrical lamps have not only entered the space of the home but also the world of art.

As the skilled and multifaceted artist that she was, it is remarkable that Loy should specifically turn to lamp design and lamp making, instead of opting for painting or illustrating, for which she had been trained in art college,

Fig. 3.8. "Lighting Fixtures," from Henry Collins Brown, *Book of Home Building and Decoration* (New York: Doubleday, 1912), 163.

first in Munich and then in Paris.[118] Jessica Burstein, who has produced the most accurate analysis of Loy's "marketing aesthetics" to date, indicates that Loy's decision to open a shop was not "original" in itself, as many women of the "so-called leisure class" were motivated to run their own clothing or accessory shops.[119] That said, Loy, as Burstein reminds us, "was not of the leisure class," and the business had as its principal aim to "supply [. . .] Loy with enough capital to pursue poetry."[120] Making lampshades at home appears to have been a fashionable activity, to save money as well as to distinguish one's taste from what was available on the mass market. Already in 1906, the *Ladies' Home Journal* had published a feature entitled "Lamp Shades You Can Make at Home," in which Helen Koues encouraged women to make their own.[121] *Vogue*, which from the mid-1910s to the 1920s kept ladies of fashion updated with articles on interior decoration, featured a piece in 1916 on how women "of limited income" could make their own soft furnishings, including, of course, lampshades. "Though the Shops Charge for Them Fabulous Sums, the Woman of Quick Wit and Deft Fingers May Bring the Smartest Fittings within the Range of a Limited Income," Edna Woolman Chase proclaimed, explaining in detail how to make a "lampshade which would cost over thirty dollars in a smart shop, but which she can herself construct for a fraction of that sum."[122] As someone who believed that "modernism has democratized the subject matter and *la belle matière* of art," Loy's enterprise as a businesswoman was to combine the delicacy (and price appreciation) of a luxury item with the handmade quality and aesthetic value of a work of art (opposed to the typically mass-produced lamps, also more widespread at the time).[123]

Loy's lamps have sadly not survived: they were often produced from fragile materials, making them "fleeting illuminations."[124] We have, however, drawings and pictures of some of her lampshades. These include her star-shaped ceiling lights and wall sconces called *Les Etoiles* (The Stars; fig. 3.9), presumably designed for her children's bedrooms, as similar lamps are still popular today for the same purpose; her ship-decorated lamp *La Galère* (The Galley), one of her most popular designs according to Burke, as well as "the illuminated globes she called *mappemondes* (world maps) and *globes célestes* (celestial globes)"; and her vases of flowers, primarily calla lilies and tulips.[125] These beautifully designed lights create a fascinating combination of natural (the star shape) and artificial (the electric light), conceptually working in a manner not unlike the electric light inside Marinetti's mosque lamp, or electric moons in lieu of the actual moon (Chapter Two). On the

Fig. 3.9. Mina Loy's design for ceiling light and wall sconces "Les Etoiles." Photograph by Jean-Loup Charmet. Carolyn Burke Collection on Mina Loy and Lee Miller, YCAL MSS 778, box 7. Digital image courtesy of Beinecke Rare Book & Manuscript Library, Yale University. © Roger Conover.

one hand, Loy's creation of her own lamps and lampshades contributes to the process of domesticating the electric light, embellishing the new technology and remaking it for the home. On the other, having learned the aesthetic and ideological lessons of the Futurists as well as of feminism, Loy clearly uses these lamp designs to pursue her project of becoming a Modern Woman. For the reasons outlined above, making lamps and lampshades was a natural choice for her, given her attraction to brilliant objects. But by running her own lamp business (albeit at first with Peggy Guggenheim's help) and managing "half a dozen 'factory' workers," she successfully combines art with utility and carves out a space for herself in the society of the time as a single mother *and* a Modern Woman.[126]

Although making lampshades may have seemed to many at the time a craft rather than an art, given its specific practical purpose, it had a clear aesthetic value for all women who, like Loy, were interested in adjusting the electric light to their domestic needs. With her design of the calla lily lamp (fig. 3.10), which was heavily copied in France despite Loy's efforts to have

Fig. 3.10. Joella Haweis Bayer, photograph of Mina Loy, *Calla Lily Lamp "Arum Lumineux,"* ca. 1927. Loy's lamp is adorned here with ribbons or folded fabric. Gelatin silver print on paper, 20 × 12.5 cm (7 7/8 × 4 15/16 in.). Carolyn Burke Collection on Mina Loy and Lee Miller, YCAL MSS 778, box 7. Digital image courtesy of Beinecke Rare Book & Manuscript Library, Yale University. © Roger Conover.

her design copyrighted, our poet-artist goes a step further.[127] Her new lamp design is barely recognizable as a lamp and engages directly with an artistic trend of the time, though not necessarily with trends in interior decoration. Burke is the only one to have recognized that Loy's shade designs and productions were reminiscent of prewar styles such as Art Nouveau, despite the fact that Loy "claimed to dislike" an artistic and architectural style she instinctively associated with her former husband.[128] Nonetheless, Loy's lamps in general have very little in common with the modernist aesthetic taste that was all the rage in the mid-to-late 1920s, Art Deco, a style "tied to the city" that privileged sharp lines and geometric forms; her lamps share much more with Art Nouveau, a style "linked to eternal Nature" that domesticated floral and other natural forms for home living.[129] The calla lily lamp's slim design and delicate shapes appropriate and adapt Art Nouveau decorative modes, such as, for instance, the Daum-Majorelle table lamps of the early 1900s, which, with their weak watt power and deep "coloured glass shades," were more illuminated "art objects" than proper illumination technologies.[130] With Art Nouveau having "run its course" by the 1920s, the calla lily lamp is not simply a product of Loy breathing new life into a decorative mode from earlier days but is the result of a close observation of new aesthetic trends in the visual arts, rather than in contemporaneous interior design.[131]

In effect, we ought to see Loy's calla lily lamp less as a mere lamp and more like an art object: the calla lily lamp at once domesticates the electric light for the home and elevates its subject matter to an artistic level. Loy, even while living in Europe, was always aware of the trends in American art, and the calla lily lamp deliberately engages with the contemporary visual popularity of the calla lily. Soon after its arrival from South Africa in the mid-nineteenth century, this elegant white flower became a recurrent obsession for American artists, painted and photographed from a variety of angles.[132] According to the art historian Barbara Buhler Lynes, the artistic popularity of the calla lily peaked in the 1920s and 1930s, appearing frequently in the paintings of Stanton Macdonald-Wright, Charles Sheeler, Preston Dickinson, Marsden Hartley, Charles Demuth, Piet Mondrian, and Georgia O'Keeffe, and in the photographs of Marjorie Content, Imogen Cunningham, Clara Sipprell, Edward Weston, Cecil Beaton, and Tina Modotti.[133] Burke reminds us that Loy knew some of these artists: Marsden Hartley, for example, who coincided with her in Paris and was part of Gertrude Stein's circle of American expats; and Charles Sheeler and Charles Demuth, whom Loy may have met via Walter Arensberg in New York in 1916-17.[134] Though we cannot be sure she ever met Georgia O'Keeffe, Loy would have been familiar with her work through O'Keeffe's husband, Alfred Stieglitz, who then sent O'Keeffe issues of his own *Camera Work*, in which Loy's poems were published, as well as a copy of *Songs to Joannes*.[135]

Studying callas in their details was a sexy topic at the time, and both Georgia O'Keeffe and Marsden Hartley may have been attracted to the flower precisely for its hermeneutic ambivalence of feminine purity and sexuality as well as for its clear aesthetic appeal.[136] Georgia O'Keeffe, who had been painting calla lilies since 1923, was nicknamed the Lady of the Lily after Miguel Covarrubias's eponymous caricature, which at once parodies O'Keeffe's looks and the elongated callas of her paintings, while Stieglitz, active promoter of her work as well as her partner, saw a financial opportunity in the popularity of the flower.[137] For the photographers mentioned above, the translucent semitransparency and soft shape of the calla lily's petals allows experimenting with light and exposure: Marjorie Content imbues her 1928 *Still Life (Calla Lily and Spotted Leaf)* with light, while Imogen Cunningham produces several studies of how light plays inside the flower's corolla, emphasizing all the lines on its petals and the pistils. In Tina Modotti's photograph of the same year as Loy's lamp, the black-and-white contrast accentuates the slender shape of the two flowers' stalks, with the two corollas of the calla lilies absorbing the chiaroscuro contrast—no longer bright white but adulterated by the surrounding blacks and grays (fig. 3.11). In surviving photographs of Loy's lily lamp, the corollas are of a stark whiteness closer to the actual flower's color, while the photograph flattens the flower to a mono-dimensional capsule of light. In actuality, her calla lilies had "filaments concealed in their pistils emerged from a base that looked like a vase until the light came on."[138] Loy's lamp perfectly blends in with the home, creating the illusion of a real vase of flowers.

Situating Loy's lamp against the backdrop of this white flower's popularity in the visual arts adds an important layer to her own lamp-making business. While her lamp designs may have looked reminiscent of Art Nouveau, Loy was very aware of contemporary artistic trends in painting and photography, from which she borrows to create a lamp that not only fits in the modern home but adorns it as an artwork, an objet d'art in its own right, permeating the surrounding space with its aesthetic appeal—not simply with its light when turned on. Although we should not forget that lamp making is for Loy a business that enables her to sustain her family, she harnesses it to

Fig. 3.11. Tina Modotti, *Calla Lilies*, c. 1927. Gelatin silver print, 23.5 × 17.8 cm (9 1/4 × 7 in.). Detroit Institute of Arts, Founders Society Purchase, Abraham Borman Family Fund, F77.18. Digital image courtesy of the Detroit Institute of Arts.

feminize, aestheticize, and domesticate the electric light. For Burke, Loy's lamps materialize the content of her own poems:

> The starry skies and cosmic reaches of her poems, their slow transit through states of being, their concern with the liberation of form could all be rendered

through design, just as the contemplative unfolding of her verse could be conveyed in the transformation scenes of these devices. Her increasingly abstract meditations on the theme of creativity (and creation) could be dramatized in the play of light and shadow—the moment of revelation when a *mappemonde* was lit from within. God of her universe, she was creating stages on which to replay the divine *fiat lux*.[139]

Burke is right to make this connection between Loy the poet and Loy the artist—whether as the inventor of new objets d'art or the maker of lampshades. Much of Loy's poetry from this time is constellated by lamps, lanterns, stars, and moons: a symbolism in open dialogue with the previous poetic and artistic traditions, while at the same time "domesticating" the new lightscape for her own purposes. Her poetic discussion of "creation" and "creativity" is closely tied to her engagement with sources of natural and artificial light.

The poem "Lunar Baedeker" (composed before 1921, published 1923) is a spectacular exemplar of poetic light reflections: the speaker wanders at night through an undefined modern city, brilliantly lit by luminous personages ("A silver Lucifer," the dark angel who etymologically "carries light," *LLB* 81, line 1), electrical advertisements, and other artificial lights alike ("Delirious Avenues/lit/with the chandelier souls/of infusoria," lines 12-15). In the midst of this "landscape of spectacle and consumption" that is the modern city, the moon fails to provide the guidance expected by her in her role as a Victorian-style Baedeker, but rather it is a relic only fit for its own museums: "And 'Immortality'/mildews . . ./in the museums of the moon" (*LLB* 82, lines 44-46).[140] The "museums of the moon" constitute another ironic parody of the Futurists, where the moon and the museum, two of the many forces against which Marinetti fulminated, are condensed in one single mildewing entity. As Rachel Blau DuPlessis notices, the moon, "Pocked with personification" (*LLB* 82, line 49), is undoubtedly a symbol of femininity, poetry, and sexuality, but, in the course of "Lunar Baedeker," it becomes a "modernist cabaret stage," paired up with "imagery [that] is decadent in a mannered, circusy way."[141] DuPlessis's suggestion of overlapping modernism and Decadence in this poem is accurate: if "Lunar Baedeker" is on the one hand reminiscent of the atmospheres of "Café du Néant," at the same time it propounds a new poetic association of "woman and modern technology" to replace the usual one of "woman and nature" (and, we might add, woman and moon), which was only at its initial stages in Loy's 1910s poetry.[142]

The urban lights all around the exploratory "Loy" figure in "Lunar Baedeker" manage to both orient and disorient her at the same time:

> the eye-white sky-light
> white-light district
> of lunar lusts
> — — — Stellectric signs
> "Wing shows on Starway"
> "Zodiac carrousel"   (*LLB* 81, lines 21-26)

While in Chapter One we saw a sputtering and muttering gas streetlamp advise and warn a young T. S. Eliot against vice ("Rhapsody on a Windy Night"), in "Lunar Baedeker" the electric signs guide Loy's persona through a street of pleasurable temptations.[143] The Decadent flâneur of the nineteenth century has been set down amid the technological developments of the twentieth century, as the new electrically lit advertisements ("Stellectric signs") guide the speaker and her company through a night of excess. For DuPlessis, the aim of Loy's portmanteau "Stellectric signs" is to "make 'beauty' something urban, commercial, and modern, verbally fusing the 'Stella' or woman of poetic tradition, 'stellae' or stars in nature, and the word 'electric.'"[144] In this way, then, Loy would gender the urban night as at once feminine and hospitable to the new women inhabiting it. The tenor and the vehicle of Loy's metaphorical expression are hard to disentangle from one another: have the stars in the night sky taken on a technological form in the modern city, or have the electrically lit advertisements become new urban stars? As Pryor suggests, "stars and electricity both give light: both the signs of the zodiac and the electric signs of a modern metropolis might light one's way—or lead one astray."[145] Loy deliberately opts for an ambivalent phrase so that she can sublimate the romantic and the sexual, the timeless and the recent, the Decadent and the modernist into a single powerful metaphor. The electrically illuminated city's "sky-light/white-light district" (*LLB* 81, lines 21-22), a reference to Broadway's nickname the Great White Way, combines with the "lunar lusts," the carnal, moon-inflected amusements of the modern city, to a similar effect. As she night walks in "Lunar Baedeker," Loy responds to modern urban electrification by forging a poetry of double brilliance in which the natural and the artificial converge.

Ideas of creation and creativity deeply fascinated Loy and tallied with experimentations of light, both artificial and natural, as is evident from her poem "Apology of Genius" (published 1922), a sort of contest between a speaking "we" of artists and a judging "you" of the general public. "Apology" effectively acts as a manifesto for Loy's art and poetics, and not as a mere response to the *Ulysses* obscenity trial of 1921, although this context certainly informed Loy's poem and spurred her to create a poetic manifesto for the modern artist.[146] The lights constellating the poem set the "ostracized [. . .] we" (*LLB* 77, line 1) apart "from the civilized masses":[147]

> Lepers of the moon
> all magically diseased
> we come among you
> innocent
> of our luminous sores
> [. . .]
> We are the sacerdotal clowns
> who feed upon the wind and stars
> and pulverous pastures of poverty   (*LLB* 77, lines 4-8, 15-17)

Loy avoids electric lights and other artificial lighting in this poem, opting for a more conventional moon and star imagery instead. The phrase "lepers of the moon" eerily brings back to mind Marinetti's identification of the Symbolists as the "last lovers of the moon," an idea compounded by the mention of a magical disease affecting these geniuses. Is this a way of dismissing the geniuses as mere Symbolists, or passéists? Not quite. The general public, the "you," inaccurately sees the "we" of contested literary and artistic geniuses—such as Loy herself and the likes of James Joyce, Wyndham Lewis, Gertrude Stein, Edgar Allan Poe, Constantin Brancusi, Nancy Cunard, and Jules Pascin (to all of whose artistry Loy dedicates individual poems), whom Loy obviously felt an artistic affinity with—as decaying and Decadent "lepers," enthralled with the moon and its lunar fantasies, and not with real-life issues. Certainly, "Apology of Genius" may fail to stay true to its title and read more as an "attack" than an "apology," but its raison d'être is for Loy to proclaim, loudly, the importance of luminosity and of light for her own poetry.[148] In the 1930s, Loy would reprise this image with her series of "fresco vero" luminous paintings, such as *Stars*, *Light*, and *Moons I* (all 1932), in which near-mystical bodiless "masklike faces" hold stars or the moon, or are simply enlightened by the light surrounding them.[149] The moon—first rejected as the representative of passéism and of a passive and stereotyped femininity, then harnessed to parody men and masculine sexuality—at last metamorphoses into the luminary that represents modernist art and literature for Loy: even though her phrase is peppered with a good dose of self-irony, the "lepers of the moon" have ultimately become the writers, poets, painters, photographers who go against the grain.

In an undated letter to Carl Van Vechten from Loy's Florentine period, our poet-artist comments richly and lovingly on her friendships with Mabel Dodge Luhan and Frances Stevens, and scathingly on Giovanni Papini and Stephen Haweis. Amid these reflections, as often in Loy's fragmentary epistolary style, she throws in the following remark: "You know I know nothing about myself—you once said I had a luminous quality."[150] We cannot know when Van Vechten said this or to whom. Perhaps he was adducing her brilliant personality to promote her work in America; perhaps he was referring to the shiny, fine glaze of her poetry; or perhaps he was simply teasing her about all the lights in her work. In any case, what is apparent is that Loy found Van Vechten's remark (dare we call it a compliment?) about her luminosity worth remembering—as flattering her and as saying something true and meaningful about herself. In 1938, the American artist Joseph Cornell, famous for his assemblages, made a formal tribute to Loy's luminosity, most likely without being aware of Van Vechten's words: a tiny wooden box made up of glass shards, gelatine silver print, and a mask of stars, with, at the bottom, a charming black-and-white Man Ray photograph of Mina Loy (plate 11).[151] An admirer of Loy since the early 1930s, when he saw her artwork at her son-in-law Julien Levy's gallery, Cornell shared with Loy an admiration for all things luminescent.[152] For him, Loy was not simply the author of "Lunar Baedeker": Loy *was* a moon. In a later letter he would never send to Loy, he wrote, "I could not help but think of you, looking up at the moon, when the first rays of the sun turn its gold into silver. A long time ago, you may remember, you told me that your destiny was ravelled up somehow with the lunar globe."[153] His artistic homage to Loy truly honors her for the multifaceted artist that she was. In the latter part of her career and life, however, Loy might have "shaded" herself too much so as to nearly disappear from the cultural scene and from later narratives of modernism, in which our poet-artist has been long conspicuously absent. The purpose of this chapter, the centerpiece of *Brilliant Modernism*, wholly dedicated to Loy's poetry and the lamp art of her earlier period, has also been to reconsider Loy's luminous poetics and work within its larger cultural context. We have come full circle from the photograph of Loy bathed in light in Brancusi's studio: Loy, by pulling the globe lamp toward herself, traces her trajectory as an electrically brilliant poet, artist, and woman.

 4   Bringing Down the Stars

American Modernists

Herman Spector, "YELLOW LAMPS" (1929)[1]

On a late June day in 1910, the transatlantic ocean liner *Lusitania* of the Cunard Line is slowly approaching American shores in the hours just before dawn. As it makes its way toward New York Bay, the coastline becomes gradually visible, and very nearly tangible. The night still wraps most passengers in sleep, but some are standing on the deck, awake, eagerly awaiting the first glimpse of America. The moon that has accompanied them all through the Atlantic slowly regresses behind the clouds. To some, New York City's skyline appearing at a distance resembles an imaginary woman covered in shimmering jewels: the switched-on lights from the buildings, shops, and streets tingle and sparkle, as though dancing on her dark skin, evidencing every contour and every line of her profile.[2] As the ship draws closer to the city, the extraordinary artificial suns of Coney Island first, and then of Brooklyn and Manhattan, blind the passengers, as another vision comes their way: Lady Liberty holding her famous light promises to dispel all darkness, for good. Among the passengers on the *Lusitania*, a returning American citizen finds the spectacle rich, strange, and intoxicating.[3] This passenger—one hand in his coat pocket to reach for his notebook, the other moving across his head to tame his unruly leonine mane—is the enfant terrible of modernism, Ezra Pound.

It was after spending over two years on the Old Continent that Pound returned to the United States in 1910.[4] A week after his arrival, Pound wrote to his friend and patron, fellow American Margaret Stevens, that "the country seems strange to my eyes that have grown more European than I knew—strange but not so unpleasant as I expected."[5] Many of Pound's reflections in his correspondence to Stevens from New York made their way into the published record of his homecoming impressions, "Patria Mia," a series of articles in the *New Age*.[6] In the fuller account of this passage, it becomes clear that for Pound to get used to this flamboyant display of electricity was the same thing as getting used to America, and American customs, all over again. He writes:

> They [Americans] are against all delicate things. They will never imagine beautiful plaisaunces [*sic*]. They will never "sit on a midden and dream stars," as the Irish peasant said to Joseph Campbell.
>
> This new metropolitan has his desire sated before it is aroused. Electricity has for him made the seeing of visions superfluous. There is the sham fairyland at Coney Island, and, however sordid it is when one is in it, it is marvellous against the night as one approaches or leaves it.[7]

The Romantic notion of man contemplating the night sky and feeling subdued to nature and yet at the same time deeply curious about it is evidently no longer relevant for Pound's understanding of modern American identity. "Poetry, like devilry, loves darkness," wrote Joseph Campbell, the contemporary Irish poet cited by Pound.[8] Campbell mainly sang of the Irish countryside as what remained of a premodern way of life, claiming that inspiration could only come to him on moonlit, starlit nights, while sitting in a field in the dark. Indeed, darkness stirs the faculty of imagination by demanding an active response. It is a site of active creation: as Noam Elcott reminds us in the introduction to *Artificial Darkness: An Obscure History of Modern Art and Media*, it is in darkness that many ancient cosmogonies begin precisely because it is in it and thanks to it that things can take shape.[9] Invisibility and inability to see cannot spoon-feed images or visions to the poet, but rather they enable the mind to create. A state of darkness requires active imagination. Light, vision, and visibility call for a more passive response: in full light, everything is available, and visible—we simply need to take things in. Herman Spector, a younger poet published by Pound, would write in "Yellow Lamps": "yellow lamps are manifest, are obvious./yellow lamps are definite./[. . .]/who gives a damn for dark/and deep, damp mysteries?" (lines 1-2, 5-6).[10] With the creative potential of darkness being eroded by modern lighting technologies, the city morphed into a readymade vision. For as much as poets might have wanted to observe, and write about, the stars softly illuminating the dark sky of the night, these are no longer where and what they used to be. The bright windows, signs, and lamps of the city at night make for a modern continuation of the night sky.

To be immersed in too much light, as when walking about the electrical displays of the Coney Island Luna Park or strolling along brightly lit-up Broadway, is to obliterate darkness. And to obliterate darkness altogether is to disrupt the independent faculty of imagination. In *Signatures of the Visible* (1990), Frederic Jameson claims that "the visual is *essentially* pornographic, which is to say that it has its end in rapt, mindless fascination" (emphasis in the original).[11] Jameson's statement sets the stage for his subsequent discussion of motion pictures, a technology dependent on sources of artificial illumination—and especially electric light. For the early twentieth-century urban poet, the intense technological and experiential overlap between the electrified city and the cinematic world stimulated an understanding of the illuminated street as a visual feast.[12] Electric lamps, electric signs, and electric advertisements function as film projectors. Rather than projecting celluloid frames on a white surface, however, they expose the real—sometimes alluring, sometimes sordid. This electrified reality enables modernists to mindlessly stare at the world, which suddenly appears in sharp focus. As modernists are relentlessly aware, it is artificial brilliance that facilitates this vision of the world, transforming reality itself into a cinematic dream, a projection of the poet's desire. Under the lights of the nocturnal city, every vision, every intimate desire, and every unusual fantasy appears as *prêt à servir*. In this sense, there *is* something vulgar—and indeed pornographic, to borrow Jameson's term—about the electrified city. At the very end of the nineteenth century, Edith Wharton had famously written against the use of the electric light in any home *de bon ton*, effectively because it made everything too visible and public-looking: electric light "makes the *salon* look like a railway-station, the dining-room like a restaurant" (emphasis in original).[13] Electricity not only dispels dark mysteries but is a light for the masses. It shows things too well, reverting the intimate into the publicly visible and available. By exposing the world in its terrifying detail, it makes us painfully aware of our vulgar desires.

While sharing a deep awareness of electric light's power to shape the world around them, modernist poets diverged about how exactly electric light might be conducive to their creative process. A certain distance from

the spectacle of electricity offered one possible solution to restore the be-
holder's independent imagination. For Pound, Coney Island can only reven-
dicate a certain beauty when approached from sea. Repositioning Coney
Island against darkness is a matter of perspective: not just what can be seen
and cannot be seen at a distance, but what can be imagined thence. Dis-
tance enables a new interaction between electric light and darkness, and
therefore between the visible (which is immediately discernible through the
eye) and the invisible (what may not be discernible but can be imaginable
through the intellect). The visible and material stir the viewer's desire for
the invisible and immaterial, calling for an articulation, explanation, and
interpretation of that desire. But how can language and poetry intervene
in this hypervisual world that has been seducing everyone into a passive,
mindless fascination rather than toward an active search for delicate, tran-
scendental mysteries? If poetry ought to be the night—that beautiful dark-
ness adjacent to a fragment of reality that expands ad infinitum—now it is
so vividly illuminated, how should the modernist poet begin to write it?

The question of distance from artificial lights, and of a new perspective
for the modernist writer, resurfaces later in the same section of "Patria Mia."
Pound would continue his reflections about writing the city in such way:

> And New York is the most beautiful city in the world?
>
> It is not far from it. No urban nights are like the nights there. I have looked
> down across the city from high windows. It is then that the great buildings lose
> reality and take on their magical powers. They are immaterial; that is to say, one
> sees but the lighted windows.
>
> Squares after squares of flame, set and cut into the ether. Here is our poetry,
> for we have pulled down the stars to our will.[14]

If Pound, however invariably attuned to different shades of light, only occa-
sionally embraced the illuminated city as neither content nor style for his
own poetry (think of the *Cantos*, for example), his words capture the essence
of the poetry and art that was about to be written in, and on, the modern
American city.[15] From the windows of a skyscraper, the modernist poet looks
down at the city at night, taking the opposite perspective of the poet typi-
cally looking up at the sky, into the darkness. Why bother looking at the sky
above when the illuminated city is our new night sky—the new canvas for
the modern artist? Technological modernity has reversed the direction in
which the poet should look—not at actual stars but rather at artificial star-
light. From afar, the city's light-on-darkness appears to Pound as a delicate,

beautiful thing that pleases the eye and has modeled the gross, dark buildings into something immaterial, unreal, and sublime, while still altogether discernible to the eye.

Vladimir Mayakovsky, the Russian Futurist, would have agreed with Pound. With eyes even more foreign to America than Pound's own Europeanized ones, adjusted as they were to the rather less vampish lights of Moscow, Mayakovsky visited New York City in 1925 and admired its light(s) from both within and without.[16] In *Мое открытие Америки* (*My Discovery of America*, 1926), Mayakovsky's description of New York to his Russian audience is "light, light and light."[17] It quickly becomes evident that there should be no doubt as to what variety of light he must have meant. Electric light's ubiquity in 1920s New York surprises and mystifies Mayakovsky: "You get dressed thanks to electricity, on the streets there is electricity, the buildings are bathed in electricity; the evenly chiselled windows are like a stencilled advertising poster."[18] The Great White Way, the stretch of Broadway famous for its flamboyant illumination, "really is white and there really is a feeling that it's brighter than day on it, since it's light all day [. . .] against the background of darkest night."[19] To be walking on Broadway is to be walking inside the electric lights which have turned temporal conventions on their head, making day and night coincide. Darkness no longer exists here, other than as a distant backdrop. But the real beauty of electricity for Mayakovsky, as it appeared to be for Pound, comes from looking at it from a distance. In "Бруклинский мост" ("Brooklyn Bridge," 1925), Mayakovsky's speaker observes New York's illuminated cityscape as it pops up against the darkening sky:

Нью-Йорк

   до вечера тяжек

      и душен,

забыл,

   что тяжко ему

     и высóко,

и только одни

   домовьи души

встают

   в прозрачном свечении óкон. (lines 43–52)

(New York,/ by day so funky and oppressive/Forgets/ to be hard/ and heavy/ by night—/Here and there/ an occasional house-elf/Silhouetted in a square of light. [lines 40–48])[20]

Brooklyn Bridge, the ultimate instance of "American technological sublime," offers the Russian poet a new vantage point.[21] From here, as from Pound's "high windows," the lights of New York City appear against the night, providing aesthetic comfort and relief from the oppressive daylight. It is a mysterious, magical scene of light framed by darkness. During the day, the city's modern architecture appears too sharp and overwhelming. At night, its heavy architectural structures give in to darkness, leaving room for a skyline that would not have existed quite in this form in gaslit, or lamplit, times. In near-cinematic luminous black-and-white, the electrical lightscape can inspire visions, with the observer's desires dancing around as sparkling lights over a dark canvas. The modern poet watching the illuminated city from a distance—a skyscraper or a bridge—discovers its sublime beauty as commensurate to the extinguished night sky. It is, again, a matter of perspective. The onlooker's distance from the illuminated city suggests a certain distortion of vision and juxtaposition of light and darkness that turns the city into a work of art stirring and arousing the imagination—something that cannot quite happen when one walks in the light, along the great white ways of America.

As the poet steps into the lit-up New York street, perspective changes, and the sublimating remoteness from the lights is erased. To be *inside* electric light is to be literally within light, surrounded, embraced, infused by the excessive brightness of electricity. The visions and desires stirred by watching light from afar suddenly appear within easy reach on the illuminated street. In the early twentieth century, this experience of the modern electrified city was new and mystifying—repelling to some and exhilarating to others. As hinted in both Pound's prose and Mayakovsky's poem, inhabiting an electrified world creates new aesthetic challenges, but also opportunities. A number of poets and artists take up this provocation, making electricity a key element of modernist poetics. This reliance on electrification enables a discussion of American modernists belonging to different contexts and backgrounds. In order to offer as comprehensive a picture of these electrified American poetics as possible, this chapter looks at poems and artworks produced in the 1920s, in a geographical place (New York City) in which electric light was newly but fully domesticated, and hence a pervasive presence in both public places and the homes of individuals. This chapter thus takes a necessarily wide-angle view of American modernism, bringing together a number of poets and artists who—while they have all been considered modernist by scholars—did not always belong to the same literary and artistic circles, often because of their gender or racial identity. These American modernists, I argue, coincided in placing electrical brilliance at the very center of their new art. They may not have cosigned an intellectual program, as did the Futurists of Chapter Two, but they embraced electric light as the hinge of their visionary poetics. In what follows, I map the electrical imagination across a range of American modernists of different gender, race, background, and artistic affiliation. In the first section, I turn to modernists who explicitly theorize the electrical imagination and poetics in their works, William Carlos Williams and E. E. Cummings, alongside work by Francis Picabia. In the remaining three sections, I look at poems and artworks that exemplify the position of the poet and artist in and out of the city lights. In section two, I discuss the distant electrified landscapes of sensuality and masculine desire in the works of Alfred Stieglitz, Williams again, and Jean Toomer, while in section three I show how Georgia O'Keeffe and Lola Ridge actively embrace the same electrified skylines and streetscapes as a way to overturn gender conventions and artistic tradition. In the fourth and final section, I consider how, within the context of African American modernism, James Van Der Zee, Langston Hughes, and Gwendolyn B. Bennett harness artificially brilliant nightness as an instrument to update and reverse notions of blackness.

The Imagination Electric

In 1923, William Carlos Williams published *Spring and All*, an experimental manifesto mixing short poems with prose commentaries on his poetic practice and art, in a chopped-up style à la Gertrude Stein's *Tender Buttons* (1914).[22] *Spring and All* is the practical consummation of the statement "poetry feeds the imagination and prose the emotions, poetry liberates the words from their emotional implications, prose confirms them in it."[23] In section XI, Williams first frames his writing and the poetic imagination in terms of electrical force:

> The imagination is an actual force comparable to electricity or steam, it is not a plaything but a power that has been used from the first to raise the understanding of—it is, not necessary to resort to mysticism—In fact it is this which has kept back the knowledge I seek—
>
> The value of the imagination to the writer consists in its ability to make words. Its unique power is to give created forms reality, actual existence. (*CPI* 207)

According to Williams, imagination is comparable to electricity and to other forces readily available in nature but cultivated by man, such as steam, in at least two ways. First, the idea of electricity allows him to understand poetic imagination *not* as what he calls "a conscious recording of the day's experiences" (*CPI* 207; not, then, as a Wordsworthian "emotions recollected in tranquillity") but rather as pure enjoyment of the world—as quick, full, and instantaneous as a spark of electricity through the body. Secondly, and more importantly, imagination is for Williams a life-giving force comparable to electricity in that it is not just "derivative literary mimesis," as Slater aptly calls it, but generative: imagination and electricity both share a power to transform—in an almost Platonic sense—the world of shadows around us into reality.[24] Williams's equation of imagination with electricity further implies that imagination in and of itself does not belong strictly to the intellectual, the spiritual, or the abstract. Rather, imagination exists and operates in the same physical way as electricity. Imagination is at once a force freely existing in nature and in life, and one that people can control and harness for the purpose of creating new energy in the shape of new words and new ideas.

At the end of *Spring and All* (XXVI), Williams rhetorically reprises his initial position, stating that "imagination is not to avoid reality, nor is it description nor an evocation of objects or situations" (*CPI* 234). Imagination is "a force, an electricity or a medium, a place" (*CPI* 235). In this sense, poetic creation itself can be seen as a process of electrification. On the one hand, imagination electrifies poets, enabling them to be creative. On the other, imagination as electricity illuminates the material world around them by bringing it into existence, articulating its essence and meaning. The electrical imagination enables new visions of the world around us; it both precedes and incandesces, conditions and explains reality. Sheaves of electric light or an electromagnetic field at once emanating from poets and enveloping them bring the world into being. In short, modern reality ontologically depends on electrical imagination.

Williams brilliantly demonstrates this foundational quality of electric light in his free-flow prose "Notes in Diary Form" (1927): "STOP in black letters surrounded by a red glow, letters with each bulb a seed in the shaft of the L of the A lights on the river streaking the restless water lights upon pools of rainwater by the roadside a great pool of light full of overhanging sparks into whose lower edge a house looms its center marked by one yellow window-bright their faces!"[25] Another nocturnal landscape, but one quite unlike those we have encountered so far. The self is disembodied and fluid, flowing with the light through the luminous vascular system of the city, ricocheting from one object to the next, and in the process shaping space and creating reality. The real city can only appear in relation to the speed and glow of erratic electricity. As a consequence, the realist urban nightscape is deconstructed into a series of cubist abstractions: glowing geometrical forms such as the rigid letter shapes, rectangular edges of houses and windows, streaks of light, and circles of glowing pools. Williams's formalist insistence on electric light as the force structuring urban reality works as a direct manifestation of the famous phrase coined by media theorist Marshall McLuhan in the 1960s: "the medium is the message."[26] Intriguingly, McLuhan sees electric light as "pure information."[27] For him, electric light is "a medium without a message, [. . .] unless it is used to spell out some verbal ad or name," in which cases we can easily recognize its content and message.[28] Except that, McLuhan goes on to add, electric light does carry a message, which is "totally radical, pervasive, and decentralized."[29] Williams might have agreed with McLuhan. As he opens his piece with fragments of illuminated language ("STOP in black letters"), electricity as a medium still communicates legible content, but that meaning soon disintegrates into mere characters, letter shapes, and pure light forms of the city street. Williams's equation of imagination to electricity, and of electricity to a medium, in *Spring and All* is perfectly demonstrated in these diary notes, where both the electric light and the poet's imagination are self-referentially reproducing itself. The message, intrinsic to the medium (both poetic imagination and electric light), is the way that the medium structures and brings reality into being. As a force of imagination, electricity helps Williams aesthetically to articulate the everyday experience of a modern city, as well as to understand and appreciate things as they really are. We are not just watching city lights: we are deep inside the lights of the city. The writing that was following the light has become the light.

Poetic imagination, then, has become electrical, and the act of writing poetry in turn has become strictly connected to artificial illumination. Writing is light. Indeed, in "A Note on the Art of Poetry" (1929), Williams remarked that "there is very little light in literature today," implicitly complaining about the lack of depth, meaning, and relevance in contemporary poetry.[30] Who then should the poet be if not one whose creativity at once emanates and is nourished by light? Poem XIV of *Spring and All* (also known as "Death the Barber") enacts a conversation between the poet-physician speaker and his barber, in a sequence of chopped-up lines that recreate the dialogue as interrupted and regulated by the cutting of hair. Here, a particular kind of lamp—a "quartz lamp"—reaffirms the speaker's masculinity as well as the spark of his poetic creativity:

> Of death
> the barber
> the barber
> talked to me
>
> cutting my
> life with
> sleep to trim
> my hair—
>
> It's just
> a moment
> he said, we die
> every night—
>
> And of
> the newest
> ways to grow
> hair on
>
> bald death—
> I told him
> of the quartz
> lamp   (*CPI* 212-213, lines 1-20)

At the time of writing *Spring and All*, the nearly forty-year-old doctor had begun balding at the forehead and temples, as his passport photograph of 1921 attests. In his autobiography *I Wanted to Write a Poem* (1958), Williams, reminiscing on his first meetings with Pound and Moore, recalls with vivid clarity (and a hint of jealousy) the lushness of both friends' hair.[31] Williams, as a balding man in his forties and as a physician, would have been familiar with Henry Lewis Jones's *Medical Electricity: A Practical Handbook for Students and Practitioners*, at its eighth edition in 1920, which contained detailed findings on electric light as an aid to hair growth, or with Richard W. Müller's *Baldness: Its Causes, Its Treatments and Its Prevention* (1917). The barber might have suggested better sleeping habits and no exciting night life ("the barber / talked to me / cutting my / life with / sleep"), but physicians of the time believed electric light, filtered by a quartz screen (i.e., quartz lamps), to be an ally in fighting baldness and making life come back into the area of the scalp previously thought dead.[32] When Williams's speaker updates the barber on "newest / ways to grow / hair on / bald death" (lines 14-17), nearly an anagram for "head," he would have conjured up one of the illustrations from Müller's book, showing the bald patients' heads right inside this so-called Alpine Sun (fig. 4.1). From the outside, such images would have re-called ancient ones of blind death (rather than bald); but for the man whose scalp was being treated, the experience of having his head inside the Alpine Sun was as close to entering light as one could possibly get at the time. If keeping your head inside an electric lamp was thought to enable your hair to grow, what other things could it nourish? Williams sees artificial lighting feeds his writing: his head is the light in which ideas, thoughts, and poems can grow.

Half in jest, Williams might have reimagined himself as an illuminated head—not unlike Zátková's "Electrical Marinetti" (see Chapter Two) or Loy's parody of Papini in "The Effectual Marriage" (see Chapter Three). Light bulbs, imagination, and poetry were at the time deeply entangled ideas. The French avant-garde artist Francis Picabia frequently bestowed human traits on lamps and artificial lights, as in *Lampe* (Lamp, 1923) and *Américaine* (see Chapter Three). He likewise connected artificial light with the irruption and power of artistic creativity, as in *Magnéto Anglaise* (English Magneto, 1921-22). He portrayed his artist friends either as or with lamps, as in the "mechano-morphs" (or "object-portraits") he prepared for the July-August 1915 issue of Alfred Stieglitz's magazine *291*, such as *De Zayas! De Zayas! Je suis venu sur les rivages du Pont-Euxin* (De Zayas! De Zayas! I Came to the Shores of the Black Sea, 1915) and *Ici, c'est ici Stieglitz foi et amour* (Here, This Is Stieg-litz Here Faith and Love, 1915).[33] But it is the photographer Paul Haviland he reimagines as a wired table lamp and as poetry in *Voilà Haviland—La poésie est comme lui* (Here is Haviland—Poetry Is Like Him, 1915; fig. 4.2). Haviland's genius, Picabia implies, can be barely contained within the lamp's wire, which is left open, hinting both at the possibility of a question mark and the silhouette of an actual head. As in the case of Williams as quartz lamp, Haviland as table lamp suggests that imagination is powered by elec-tric light and that electric light in turn is poetry. No electric light, then no modern imagination, or poetry.

In this context of imagination as electricity and of the poet's head as a lamp, Williams's poem "Struggle of Wings" (1926; *The Dial*, July 1926, and subsequently in *Poems 1922-1928*) gains new significance. This poem, re-

Fig. 4.1. "Patient being rayed by suspended quartz lamp for deficient hair on crown," illustration from Richard W. Müller's treatise *Baldness: Its Causes, Its Treatment and Its Prevention* (New York: E. P. Dutton & Company, 1917), plate 98, 117.

markably underdiscussed given its complexity or, some would say, obscurity, is often deemed "too long," "heavy," "slack," and even an example of Williams below his best.[34] Beset by writer's block and at a stressful time in his medical practice, Williams was—his biographer tells us—finally "at work

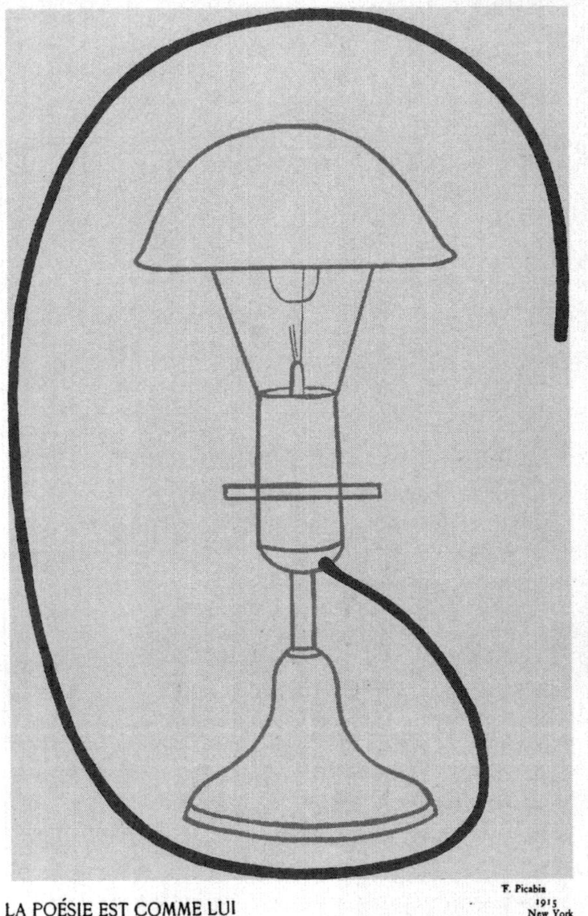

Fig. 4.2. Francis Picabia, *Voilà Haviland—La poésie est comme lui* (Here is Haviland—Poetry Is Like Him), 1915, print, from *291*, no. 5-6 (July-August 1915), 5.

on a long poem—the first [. . .] in months: a poem about the illogical and the vitality of the creative process."[35] At the center of this poem full of ellipses and excisions—partly suggested, partly imposed by Marianne Moore—and ekphrastic moments, Williams hinges the following stanza:

> And it is Inness on the meadows and fruit is
> yellow ripening in windows every minute
> growing brighter in the bulblight by the
> cabbages and spuds—
>
> And all there is is won   (*CPI* 261, lines 48-52)

In these lines, Williams pays a brief homage to that other celebrity of Rutherford, New Jersey, the nineteenth-century landscape painter George Inness.[36] In the poem, Inness's realistic bucolic scene is incongruously compared to a brightly lit window frame, glowing in yellow "bulblight": an epithet whose playfulness was warranted by the familiarity by 1926 of the noun "light bulb." With a single word, Williams erases the imagined distinction between nature and artifice, transforming the manmade source of light into the growth organ of an onion or tulip, or even of hair. We have seen how in "Notes in Diary Form," he imagined the light bulbs that make up the letters of electric signs as seeds emanating light. In "Struggle of Wings," a poem written before that diary entry, however, Williams is much more ambiguous about the tenor and vehicle of his metaphor. Although causing plants to grow, botanical bulbs do not emanate light; the same can be said of hair bulbs and follicles. A bald head can look much like a translucid globe or light bulb. Yet a sphere that does shine and cause fruit to ripen and grow is of course the sun. And the sun was, to be sure, a defining feature of Inness's paintings, as most of his work portrayed the New Jersey countryside basked in a warm embrace of yellow-coloring light. Williams's word "bulblight" therefore comes to describe both the glow of an electric light bulb illuminating a still life and the light of the setting sun over a garden observed through the window. The creative process begins with the "bulblight" of the poet's imagination—an electrical sun head enabling the vision in the window frame, growing things, ideas, and verse. At the same time, "bulblight" is not a principle generating difference but oneness: "all there is is won" and inevitably one. Electric light enables Williams to create a landscape that may well jar with Inness's vestigially Romantic pastoral, but at the same time it is a landscape that does not exclude it. We can still see Inness and feel longing in Williams's window frame, but there is no ekphrasis, only light and life.

Edward Estlin Cummings, Williams's modernist comrade-in-arms, like-wise saw electricity as a creative force. In the foreword to his collection *is 5* (1926), which is reminiscent of parts of *Spring and All*, Cummings echoes Williams:

> If a poet is anybody,he is somebody to whom things made matter very little—somebody who is obsessed by Making.   Like all obsessions,the Making obsession has disadvantages;for instance,my only interest in making money would be to make it. Fortunately,however,I should prefer to make almost anything else,including locomotives and roses.   It is with roses and locomotives(not to mention acrobats Spring electricity Coney Island the 4th of July the eyes of mice and Niagara Falls)that my "poems" are competing.[37]

Poems are not abstract entities but are created, made, molded into a shape. Given his studies of ancient Greek, Cummings naturally understands the poet as someone "obsessed by Making."[38] The poet is a craftsman, a demiurge, an inventor—an Edison or a Tesla. Ontologically, Cummings's poems have the same value as all the things (to use the broadest term available) in his list: roses, locomotives, but also the nocturnal extravagance of Coney Island, the fireworks of the 4th of July, the force of nature controlled by men at Niagara Falls . . . Most of these things would not quite qualify as artifacts (how can you make a rose? Or spring?) but are still products of creation. Like Williams earlier, Cummings is concerned with non-imitative creation, rather than mimesis: poetry is not an imitative art; like electricity, it is a creative force. In a much later poem, "brIght" (*No Thanks*, 1935), about the gradual appearance of a solitary star in the night sky, Cummings would get as close as possible to actually *making* electricity on the page.[39] Graphically avant-garde, Cummings broadcasts a generous number of question marks, the punctuation most similar to a lamp's filament, so that its bright star could be switched on and begin to glow: "near deep whO big alone soft near/deep calm deep/???? Ht????? T)/Who(holy alone)holy(alone holy)alone" (*CP* 485, lines 12-15).[40] Cummings's poem does not simply *reproduce* the effect of a glowing star's halo slowly appearing on the page, but rather it enacts the effect of an actual light bulb turning on in a room, or a real star becoming visible in the night sky. In its near-Futurist organization of words and punctuation, Cummings's poem is the thing itself, a star, a light bulb—the poem is electric light on a page. The non-mimetic creative potential of making poetry is the experience of electricity; it can only be properly comprehended and harnessed in an electrified world.

That Cummings sees artificial light as a force analogous to poetic creativity is evident in "i was sitting in mcsorley's" (1922). This "sketch," or "poempainting" as it is often called, was inspired by the men-only Manhattan bar that opened in 1854 and is still famous today for its nineteenth-century homey feel.[41] In Cummings's poem, an intoxicated man looks around the space of the bar which is both illuminated and created by a lamp:

> and i was sitting in the din thinking drinking the ale,which never
> lets you grow old blinking at the low ceiling my being pleasantly was
> punctuated by the always retchings of a worthless lamp.
>
> when With a minute terrif   iceffort one dirty squeal of soiling light
> yanKing from bushy obscurity a bald greenish foetal head established
> [. . .]
> (spattered)by this instance of semiluminous nausea A vast wordless
> nondescript genie of trunk trickled firmly in to one exactly-mutilated
> ghost of a chair,
> [. . .]
> gone Darkness   it was so near to me,i ask of shadow won't you have a
> drink?   (*CP* 120-121, lines 18-22, 25-27, 32-33)

The "worthless lamp" of Cummings's imagination retches light. Its bouts of "semiluminous nausea" create the environment around the speaker, making it visible but also "establish[ing]" it in a particular way. The "bald greenish foetal head" is at once the lucid, egg-like head of the bartender preparing drinks or of one of the bar's aging patrons, and the perfectly round shape of the globe hanging from the ceiling and illuminating McSorley's bar. With their lucid whiteness, the lamps, already visible in John Sloan's 1920s series of paintings of McSorley's, pop out of the darkened environment in the photographs of Berenice Abbott, who managed to penetrate this exclusively masculine space in 1937 (see fig. 4.3). The ambience of McSorley's bar, despite being connected to electricity, was of gaslight "flicker[ing] fitfully" well into the 1940s.[42] Unlike T. S. Eliot's lamppost in "Rhapsody on a Windy Night" (Chapter One), incidentally a poem Cummings much admired, the lamp inside McSorley's bar does not formulate words that can be intelligibly understood by the drunken speaker of Cummings's poem.[43] In conjuring up Eliot's ghost—and that of his lamppost—Cummings reminds us that McSorley's belongs to the nineteenth century. But Cummings's lamp is not there to warn him against vice or sin, as Eliot's would have done. In-

Fig. 4.3. Berenice Abbott, *McSorley's Ale House, 15 East 7th Street, Manhattan*, 1937. Gelatin silver print, 20.3 × 25.4 cm (8 × 10 in.). The Miriam and Ira D. Wallach Division of Art, Prints and Photographs: Photography Collection, the New York Public Library. Photograph courtesy of the New York Public Library Digital Collections. Sponsor: Federal Art Project, New York.

stead, it shapes the space around itself and the speaker by focusing the poet's perspective through illumination. The lamp may be retching, but it effectively channels the disharmony of the poem's first part into a more coherent and sharpened vision of McSorley's interior. Light, by generating reality, is not simply offering the poet material with which to work. The perspective of the lamp and the speaker are interdependent, merged into one; creative light is linked to poetic invention. As the poem draws to a close, the poet's vision of the bar is eaten up by the dark: the light of the gas lamp goes off, and the poet is left with Darkness as an unresponsive drinking companion.

For Cummings, as for Williams and those writers considered in this chapter, the lived experience of a brightly artificially lit society supports the theorization of the electrical imagination and of modern electrical poetics.

Electricity and the poetic imagination work as correlated forces, allowing an articulation of poetry as a productive—rather than purely mimetic—process. Like an electric light switch, electric imagination instantaneously illuminates the world and actualizes reality.

Lightscapes of Desire

At the turn of the twentieth century, one American photographer was able to immortalize electrified cityscapes in a way that perfectly captured the experience and meaning of scrutinizing the city at night: Alfred Stieglitz. His iconic visions of a lucidly black, wonderfully glossy New York, in such works as *Picturesque Bits of New York and Other Studies* (1897), *The Glow of Night—New York* (1896, printed 1897), and *Night—New York* (1897, printed 1929/1932), established him as "photography's leading light" of the period, and *the* photographer of the night.[44] Stieglitz had learned from the Impressionists the importance of being able to modulate light and understood that, in order to capture the essence of the night, he had to put lighting technologies at the center of his compositions.[45] Stieglitz's lights celebrate darkness: the electric lights from the lampposts or from the skyscrapers make the dark visible. Had it not been for New York's electrification, Stieglitz would have found it impossible to photograph the night with such sharpness. In *Night—New York*, as in *Reflections—Night, New York* (1897; fig. 4.4), Stieglitz tricks the eyes of the viewer by playing with the illuminated Savoy Hotel in the background: what is the intended subject of these photographs, the brilliant lamps at the front of the hotel or the dark silhouette of the bare tree in the foreground? Nature and artifice are once again in opposition in this photograph: nature, represented by the tree, the blackest thing in the photograph, embraces the lights of the Savoy Hotel in a web of darkness. By contrast, Stieglitz's streetlights frame the dark (rather than vice versa), practically making it visible to the camera lens: artificial lighting enables a new artificial darkness, one that is necessarily created and intensified by electricity.[46]

Stieglitz's treatment of artificial darkness eroticizes nighttime New York. The radiant pointed bulbs, piercing through the darkness and reverberating against the greasy pavement glistening after rain, anticipate the aesthetic of the American film noir. Throughout Stieglitz's early output, the electric night works as the extended space of male desire and imagination. Perhaps precisely because Stieglitz found 1910s Paris a more strongly feminine city than New York, he constantly frames New York vertically.[47] The choice of angle from below (generally from the ground, though sometimes from the windows

Fig. 4.4. Alfred Stieglitz, *Reflections: Night—New York*, 1897. First published in Alfred Stieglitz, *Picturesque Bits of New York and Other Studies* (New York: R. H. Russell, 1897). Photogravure, 20.5 × 27.4 cm (8 1/16 × 10 13/16 in.). Princeton University Art Museum. Gift of David H. McAlpin, Class of 1920. Digital image courtesy of Princeton University Art Museum.

of his flat at the Shelton Hotel) in *The Flatiron* (1903), *Two Towers—New York* (1911), *From the Back-Window—291* (1915; fig. 4.5), *From the Shelton, New York, 30th Floor—Looking North* (1927), and *From My Window at an American Place, North* (1930) throws into relief the phallic masculinity of the sleek skyscrapers. By contrast, Stieglitz's disciple Paul Haviland avoids such vertical angles. His *New York at Night* (1914), for example, enhances the beauty of the illuminated skyscrapers from an elevated perspective, harnessing the width of a landscape format and highlighting the horizontal dimension of a sprawling metropolis. In most of the nocturnal photographs mentioned above, whether by Stieglitz or Haviland, the monumental height of the buildings displaces the photographer from the urban subject. Humanity necessarily becomes miniscule, and ultimately vanishes. All other people gone, the modern photographer is now the voyeur of the city. From the lower levels of the street or from some faraway terrace, the distance between the

Fig. 4.5. Alfred Stieglitz, *From the Back-Window—291*, 1915. Platinum print, 25.1 × 20.2 cm (9 7/8 × 7 15/16 in.). Alfred Stieglitz Collection, the Metropolitan Museum of Art, New York. Digital image courtesy of the Metropolitan Museum and Wikimedia Commons.

photographer and the city—its lights, its skyscrapers, its electrical signs— heightens the desire to know the city and to make it the playground of his desires (because the photographer is, more often than not, a "him").

The trope of the illuminated city attracting people like moths to a flame had been gaining currency for decades, but the sudden presence of electric signs and advertisements intensified its allure, and its atmosphere of consumption—"the huge signs play/to make our city smile, be gay,/and BUY [. . .] TODAY," to borrow Spector's lines from "Cash or Credit" (1931).[48] *From the Back-Window* is a case in point. With its brightly lit rectangles, the photograph anticipates Mayakovsky's vision of New York as an advertising poster. Zooming in on the illuminated windows and advertisements in Stieglitz's composition allows us better to distinguish which is a window and which an advertisement: the face of a seemingly female Pierrot pops out of the illuminated advertisement for the New York branch of the French perfumery Riviera.[49] That the advertisement should have the face and pointed hat of a Pierrotian figure, which would have been visible to Stieglitz, makes for a (possibly inadvertent) tongue-in-cheek reference to the lunar mood of the previous century still lingering well into the 1910s and 1920s, as we have seen elsewhere in this book. Taking this series of photographs from the back window of his office, Stieglitz would have seen the lit-up signs and windows clearly, but in the blurred white-and-blackness of his image, the lights are just blurred flashes of whiteness. Stieglitz would sit at the window of his 291 studio and pry on his neighbors while "waiting for the right moment to photograph the evening."[50] *From the Back-Window* vividly transmits the sense of intimacy and erotic pleasure the big modern city affords both its observers and its inhabitants. The verticality of the enormous, brilliantly illuminated skyscrapers in the background thrusts us into the more intimate, dark, Baudelairean backyard in the foreground, with the Riviera poster and a line of laundry creating a feeble contrast in the blackness of the photograph. The brightly lit rectangles of light invite us to look inside and observe the private lives of New Yorkers.

Stieglitz's photographs celebrate an urban voyeurism that observes the night from a position of safety. While the photographer is safely hidden in the dark of his studio, the lights around him invite him to look at the city as if peering through a hole and discovering an inviting, sensual body. As we shall see, Stieglitz's voyeuristic art paves the way for a reimagining of the urban night as an electrified, and electrifying, temptation for the male modernist poets gravitating around him.

Electricity, unlike the gaslight of Eliot's "Rhapsody on a Windy Night" (Chapter One), gives wing to men's desires and imagination. It exposes the objects of desire without warning of pitfalls. It enables them to inspect darkness—both that of the city and that of their own thoughts and yearnings. The poet Williams, an attentive member of Stieglitz's circle, adopted his friend's disposition toward the electrified cityscape.[51] His work was often seen as the poetic equivalent of a Stieglitz photograph.[52] In earlier works— *The Tempers* (1913), *Poems 1909-1917* (1917), and *Al Que Quiere!* (1917)—he had been, as had Eliot and F. T. Marinetti (see Chapters One and Two), legibly under the influence of Symbolist, Laforguean lunar dandyism.[53] *Sour Grapes* also marks a shift to a more avant-garde, effectively more modernist Williams.[54] Whatever Laforguean attitude might have been part of Williams's poetry writing, by 1921 he had come to the conclusion that "Laforgue is a new Laforgue in America."[55] This was, after all, the reason why Williams disliked Eliot's poetry, and to some extent Pound's too: theirs was too European, a "rehash[ing]" of French poetry.[56] But, if the moon over the city prettified and Frenchified his early poetry, it is the electrified city of the 1920s that fuels his modernism. In "To a Friend Concerning Several Ladies" (from *Sour Grapes*, 1921), for example, we read:

> Here is what they say: Come!
> and come! and come! And if
> I do not go I remain stale to
> myself and if I go—
>   I have watched
> the city from a distance at night
> and wondered why I wrote no poem.
> Come! yes,
> the city is ablaze for you
> and you stand and look at it.   (*CPI* 165, lines 17-26)

To go or not to go to the city tonight? The decision is stalled by the act of watching the city. For this poet-doctor living a sheltered life in the small town of Rutherford, New Jersey, electrically illuminated New York works as a *distant* temptation.[57] Looking at the city "ablaze" stirs and enables his poetry imagination, providing a compromise between going into the city and not going into the city. Indeed, in this new poetic phase, as Mike Weaver tells us, Williams had been "aestheticiz[ing] his sexual approach to life"; he had been "writing sexually."[58] The sexual impulse and the act of writing poetry were two processes strictly associated in Williams's mind. "I knew nothing at all about the sexual approach but I had to do something about it. I did it in the only terms I knew, through poetry."[59] Does New York City, then, incarnate all the opportunities the male speaker does not dare to seize?[60] Sure, but not in such a disappointing and disheartening way as we might be led to think. The imagination-as-electricity enables those opportunities on the poetic level: watching the city equals watching his desires play out on the revealing backdrop of the night.

If Williams typically observes the city at a distance, in "The Great Figure" (1921), perhaps his best-known city poem, we find the speaker thrown into the midst of an aggressively illuminated and loud urban environment. Famously recalled in Williams's autobiography as the result of a sudden moment of inspiration as he was walking down Ninth Avenue, on his way to Marsden Hartley's studio on Fifteenth Street, the poem revels in proximity to the light and dark of the city:[61]

> Among the rain
> and lights
> I saw the figure 5
> in gold
> on a red
> firetruck
> moving
> tense
> unheeded
> to gong clangs
> siren howls
> and wheels rumbling
> through the dark city.   (*CPI* 174, lines 1–13)

The electric illumination shining through the rain and reflected by the fire truck are responsible for abstracting and fragmenting the poet's vision of the city, which turns into multiple shards of golden light. This extreme brightness illuminates all corners of the city: the number may be golden, but the city remains dark even with all its flamboyant illumination—the city that was "ablaze" for the poet in the earlier poem, once one is in it, appears dark. In Charles Demuth's adaptation of this poem, the poster portrait *I Saw the Figure 5 in Gold* (1928; plate 12), the American artist gives us overlapping layers of perfectly round globes of New York lampposts, brightly illuminated electrical signs, and toweringly tall, disquietingly darkened skyscrapers.[62] Demuth's electrical signs point to William Carlos Williams's name, with the neon-lit "BILL" and the exposed-lamp "CARLO[S]" placed in the top bit of the painting.[63] This time, in "The Great Figure" as in *I Saw the Figure 5 in Gold*, the darkness of the city frames the brilliance of the urban illumination. Inside the city lights, Williams is not just *the* poet of the city: he *is* the city, with all its brilliant illuminations and its pockets of darkness. Demuth bestows onto Williams an electrical apotheosis.

For Jean Toomer, also part of the Stieglitz circle, an electrifying, electrified, city-woman embodies the night's exciting possibilities.[64] If Williams had been cautiously and surreptitiously watching the night from afar, only imagining women in it, for Toomer the experience of the modern night equals that of seeing and approaching an attractive woman. Initially written as a response to Richard Aldington's essay on the poetic phrase and metaphor as a "shock of illumination," the poem "Her Lips Are Copper Wire" (written 1920; published 1923) celebrates a sensual union between a presumably male speaker and an electrifying city-woman:[65]

> whisper of yellow globes
> gleaming on lamp-posts that sway
> like bootleg licker drinkers in the fog
>
> and let your breath be moist against me
> like bright beads on yellow globes
>
> telephone the power-house
> that the main wires are insulate
>
> (her words play softly up and down
> dewy corridors of billboards)
>
> then with your tongue remove the tape
> and press your lips to mine
> till they are incandescent   (*CPJT* 6, lines 1–13)

Recent readings of this poem have revolved around its possible racial meanings, particularly Toomer's use of the word "incandescent" as deriving from Latin "candescere" (literally, to turn white).[66] But while Toomer may have had racial aesthetics in mind elsewhere, as I discuss later in this chapter, in "Her Lips Are Copper Wire," I would argue, "incandescent" is used as a synonym for electrical blaze, fittingly for a poem on the modern city at night. Norman Fitts, then editor of the little magazine *S4N*, calls Toomer's poem "one of the first attempts to write machinery poetry" in the US and one "that showed indications of [Filippo Tommaso Marinetti's] own disease."[67] Fitts's excitement about landing this first machine poem made in America spurred him to translate it into Italian and send his translation off to Marinetti.[68] To reiterate this, Fitts combined publication of "Her Lips Are Copper Wire" with a text by Marinetti and translated by Fitts himself. Restoring the poem's publication context offers a fresh perspective to understanding its textual content and imagery.

Readers of the quadruple *S4N* issue of Summer 1923 would have found remarkable coincidences between Toomer's poem and Marinetti's text. On top of the usual Marinettian claims against "old-fashioned beauty (romantic, symbolist and decadent)," "*la Femme Fatale et le Clair de lune*," and in favor of "geometric splendor," the Italian Futurist discusses the aesthetic importance of the electrified city at night, in the context of "electricity's lyric initiative":[69] "We prefer the luminous advertisements, futurist gems and face-paint, under which each night cities hide their wrinkles of age. [. . .] Nothing is more beautiful than a great humming powerhouse, which contains within itself the hydraulic pressure of a mountain-chain and the electric force of an entire horizon, synthesized on distribution boards bristling with switches and glittering commutators. These formidable switchboards are our only models in poetry."[70] The modern city at night looks like a woman covered in "futurist gems"—the electrical signs switching and twinkling on and off are the jewels embellishing her. Toomer, who was keen to get published, would have knowingly drawn on this notion of the modern, hyper-technological, electrical city as a Futurist invention. But Toomer was no Futurist himself, and when Fitts suggested changing the "yellow globes" of the poem to "bulbs"— ostensibly to avoid a repetition but perhaps also to give the poem a more techno-Futurist twang—Toomer rejected his editor's proposal.[71] "Bulbs" would have conjured up naked lights, but "globes" was immediately suggestive of the round, moony shapes of lampposts, the new urban stars, the Futurist gems adorning the night-woman. Moreover, Toomer wanted his vision of the city-woman to be only gradually transformative. First, his electric woman lights up the round globes of the lampposts and then the billboards glowing with messages in the night. In this way, she fulfills her promise of anticipated desire by removing the insulating tape and finally transferring electrical current from her body to that of the poet-speaker, whose lips also turn incandescent. The bright kiss in "Her Lips Are Copper Wire" marks the successful transfer of current between the electrical city-woman and the poet. Electricity works two ways on the poet's imagination, at once eroticizing the city and urbanizing the woman. But which is the tenor and which is the vehicle in this metaphor? Both are luminously electrified and brilliantly exciting. Under electric light, the woman and the city have become the poet's single object of desire.

The electrified cityscape glows with the temptations and seductions of modern life. Its play of light on darkness and the different perspectives on the city inspire the poet to witness and write the new experience of the illuminated nightscape. Darkness frames the light, and to get closer to the lights means to become one with them, and to become one with the light means to satisfy that desire. Drawing on visual representations of the New York night such as Stieglitz's, modernist poets such as Toomer and Williams eroticize a city gendered female and embodying their desires. But what of the women artists and poets inspired by the sight of the modern electrified nightscape? Modernist women, too, were walking about New York at night, nose up at the lights.

Streetlighting the Night

As soon as Georgia O'Keeffe moved into a flat on the thirtieth floor of the newly finished Shelton Hotel in 1925, she felt the urge to begin painting New York. This was a new challenge for an artist who had, up to that moment, mainly dedicated herself to flower enlargements. For O'Keeffe, the challenge brought its own gender trouble: "I had never lived up so high before and was so excited that I began talking about trying to paint New York. Of course, I was told that it was an impossible idea—even the men hadn't done too well with it. From my teens on I had been told that I had crazy notions so I was accustomed to disagreement and went on with my idea of painting New York."[72] The men with the "impossible idea" of portraying New York included 1920s painters Charles Sheeler, John Marin, Niles Spencer, and Stefan Hirsch.[73] Painting or photographing New York was perceived to be the realm of male artists, mainly because of the controlling and commanding perspective enforced by the phallic shape of skyscrapers.[74] O'Keeffe's first New York painting was, in her own words, "a night scene of 47th Street, *New York Street with Moon*" (plate 13), showing "a street light in the upper foreground at about the Chatham Hotel."[75] Perhaps unsurprisingly, Stieglitz, who had achieved celebrity with his photographs of lighted avenues and tall skyscrapers, rejected O'Keeffe's *New York Street with Moon* for the exhibition *Seven Americans* he was preparing for the Anderson Galleries in 1925.[76] Stieglitz et al. thought city streets were not a suitable, nor profitable, subject for women artists.[77] He reportedly claimed that "the Woman receives the World through her Womb [. . .] Mind comes second": women for him could only paint expressions of their intrinsic femininity (such as flowers as women's sex).[78] For this tastemaker of the American art scene, in other words, O'Keeffe's art was to be interpreted as a direct representation of her—womanly—sexuality.[79] Even though O'Keeffe may have, for marketing and popularity reasons, partly subscribed to this narrative, her paintings of New York, and especially those of the electrically lit city at night, tell a different story.

O'Keeffe's numerous city paintings are a testament to her creative stubbornness as well as artistic flair and independence. Apart from being attracted, like other artists, to New York's ambitious evolution, O'Keeffe was drawn to the luminous possibilities of the sprawling city—in ways unlike the men that preceded her.[80] In her series of New York paintings, skyscrapers are often sketched, windowless figures cutting through the sky—"sky shapers," as William Chapman Sharpe nicknames them—marking the outline of the New York sky.[81] In her first cityscapes, such as *New York Street with Moon*, O'Keeffe depicts a lamppost shining brightly white on 47th Street, near the now-defunct Chatham Hotel, against a crepuscular sky with a full moon retreating amid the clouds. But the skyline simply does not glow with the magical, glittery lights of the numerous electrical signs and illuminated windows that would have been present at the time (no matter the time of evening). O'Keeffe mutes her windows or even erases them from her paintings, effectively creating a skyline of darkness against which the solitary figures of an electric globe and the moon appear as the real protagonists of the city, and the only focus of her art. If, in Stieglitz, or even Edward Hopper (simply think of his *Night Windows*, from 1928), the city is a sensual, eroticized body, object of modernism's voyeurism, this aspect of urban modernity loses relevance in O'Keeffe. Her gaze does not spy or peer through shutters; rather, she observes the city from below. Notwithstanding her account of the painting's genesis, O'Keeffe's perspective is decidedly not from high up but rather with nose and chin up to the sky. Her observation point is from below and necessarily from within the lights—either walking along the streets of New York or watching them from the Chatham Hotel windows. Despite being inside light, O'Keeffe's eye aims for the sky, blocking out all life, and all light, from New York streets and buildings. Instead, the gaze focuses on one lamppost and one traffic light, which she morphs into modern stars—stars brought down to earth. What Pound proposed in poetry, O'Keeffe effectively achieves in her paintings of New York.

With *New York Street with Moon*, O'Keeffe deliberately sets herself to overturn Stieglitz and contemporary portraits of New York—something that would not have been lost on him.[82] In its vertical format and visual reference to clouds, O'Keeffe's painting is openly in dialogue with Stieglitz's series *Equivalents* (1922-35), *The Flatiron Building* (1902-03), and his other New York skyscrapers.[83] But Stieglitz's photographs of the sky are always—out of technical necessity—moonless, his skyscrapers always brilliantly illuminated, and his lampposts always present in multitudes. In O'Keeffe's painting, by contrast, the only detail of photographic realism present is the elegant, near-rococo hook of her lamppost, which is indeed typical of Manhattan lights, as still visible today in some streets.[84] With this painting, O'Keeffe conveyed a visual experience without the need for theorizations or complex layers of mediation, something she associated with the work of male artists.[85] It is effectively a manifesto for a new type of art about the city. Much like Balla's *Lampada ad arco* (Chapter Two), O'Keeffe wants her painting to make a statement about painting the modern city and its relationship to the new lights, and for this reason the darkened skyline of New York creates a visual ricochet effect between the traffic light, the lamppost, and the moon, which forces the observer to consider the special relationship between these lights in the context and perspective of the city. Unlike Stieglitz's night photography, which harnesses electric light purely to make darkness visible, O'Keeffe's art is effectively interested in the lights themselves: their new shapes, their brilliance, and their meaning for the modern city. For O'Keeffe, to paint New York in the 1920s meant to paint light in all its forms. And to paint the new lights together with the old ones meant to understand the larger implications of this superimposition of lights for modern art and its relationship to tradition, and gender roles.

While in *New York Street with Moon*, the traffic light, the lamp, and the moon are in a luminous conversation with one another—three softly round, glowing shapes that take the viewer's eyes from below right up to the sky— in *City Night* (1926; plate 14), painted a year later, O'Keeffe goes a step further in (con)fusing the moon with street lighting. In *City Night*, the observer is again looking at the city nose up, while the vertical angle created by the blackened skyline lures us into the irresistible vanishing point of the brilliant moon and its halo. Except that the moon reminds us rather of a lantern attached to the dark arm coming out of the building to the left. The "artificial light," as Sharpe says, "carves out the buildings, particularly the white one in the background."[86] The moon is O'Keeffe's own version of Williams's "bulb-light," which combines natural and artificial light in its oneness. O'Keeffe blocks out all the lights of the city to refocus our attention on the central source of light: a distant round light, half moon, half lamp, tucked into the folds of the skyscrapers at the bottom of the painting. Because the round light resists immediate identification as either a natural or artificial body, O'Keeffe represents a vision of the city that defies heteronormative gender paradigms. With its hard, sculpted silhouette, frighteningly perpendicular perspective, and ambiguous, half-natural, half-artificial light at the centre, *City Night* queers the erotic notion of American city à la Stieglitz. It offers O'Keeffe an opportunity to push back against the essentializing readings of her art and of herself as a woman dabbling in representing the American metropolis, a pursuit that was up to that point perceived as overtly masculine. O'Keeffe's bulb-moon thus signals a further move toward a position of resistance against the essentializing of her art as feminine. Not only does O'Keeffe want to be able to paint New York just like and better than the other men, but she also pushes for a different interpretation of herself as an artist of the modern city.[87] In her city of darkness, the muting of all other lights leads the eyes to the painter's absolute desire—the moon as vanishing point.

In her later work about nighttime New York, O'Keeffe changes her perspective on the city and begins to adhere more closely to that of the men who had been painting and writing New York. In *Radiator Building—Night, New York* (1927; plate 15) and *Ritz Tower* (1928), O'Keeffe proposes a new observation point at street level, as well as a fully electrified lightscape, following Stieglitzian perceptions of the city (such as the phallic skyscrapers in both paintings), only to defy the sensual eroticization forced upon it by the hands of fellow male artists. In *Ritz Tower*, the pear-shaped streetlight creates a visual rhyme that is much reminiscent of *New York Street with Moon*: the tiny half moon tucked away at the top left of the painting nearly dissolves in the copious illumination of the skyscraper below, and the lamppost at the center of the picture becomes singled out by its conspicuous halation. But here the city lights nearly annul the moon's presence along with its role as marker of femininity. The moon here is just another light in a skyline that is no longer simply dark but punctuated by numerous illuminations marking the contours of the street and the tall buildings. The stars, too, lose their relevance to the urban landscape, but rather have effectively been brought down to earth, and constellate the dark city. In this illuminated city of desire, the abnormally sized lamppost takes center stage once again, projecting a halo of darkness that obliterates all other lights behind it. The phallic skyscraper of Stieglitzian memory in the background is partly obliterated by the darkness made visible by the streetlamp's halo. In this silent dialogue between the lamppost and the city, the former strives to become the moon, in an attempt to recreate the appropriate background against which it can shine. In painting the lights of New York, O'Keeffe paints the struggle to disrupt conventional gender-driven views of the city at night.

With *Radiator Building—Night, New York* in particular O'Keeffe tackles head-on the gendering of the illuminated city. She does this by reorganizing its lights around the pitch darkness of the night sky, thus doing away with the feminine moon. If, in *New York Street with Moon*, *City Night*, and even *Ritz Tower*, artificial and natural lights eventually merge into one "stellectric" source of light (to borrow Loy's portmanteau), where the lamppost appeared lunar and the moon looked more like a lightbulb, in this painting the moon is nowhere in sight. As in Stieglitz's night photography, the moon is effectively written out of the composition of the city sky by the compresence of lights, advertisements, and lampposts. The artificially glowing Radiator Building, with its striking Gothic and Art Deco features exposed by the electric light and contoured by the surrounding darkness, offers the vivid impression of a woman's silhouette and, with it, the vivid representation of a modern subjectivity.[88] The name of O'Keeffe's then husband, Alfred Stieglitz, glows in red to the left.[89] If for Stieglitz, Williams, and Toomer the advertisements of the electrified city were feminine and therefore sexually attractive, in O'Keeffe's painting her husband's presence as an electrical sign sheds an ominous light over the scene, like a bleeding hemorrhage, or even a phallic attempt to penetrate her beautifully effeminate skyscraper. O'Keeffe disrupts the typically phallic symbolism of the skyscraper by investing it with a feminine silhouette adorned with spotlights.[90] It is New York in drag. The erect stature of O'Keeffe's building, combined with its feminized attire, points toward the artist's subversion of the identity of the city: New York is neither hyperfeminine nor hypermasculine, but a radical, queer fusion of the two. Much like the ambiguous moon as artificial light, O'Keeffe merges feminine and masculine traits of the electrified city to challenge its gendered identity and liberate her work from the essentializing discourses that had controlled and dominated perceptions of it up to that point.

In poetry, it is Irish-born Lola Ridge who, walking along New York City lights, harnesses urban illumination to disrupt essentialist ideas about women, feminine creativity, and tradition. Going a step further than O'Keeffe, Ridge understands vividly electrified New York also as a figure of resilience and social empowerment. In Kaniere (South Island, New Zealand), where Ridge grew up in the 1880s, the main source of illumination in her house, as she recalls in her diary, was kerosene lamps.[91] Even though Ridge witnessed the coming of electric light in the larger cities of New Zealand and Australia, and experienced electrified San Francisco in 1907, it was illuminated New York that she found particularly inspiring. Ridge, the "immigrant flâneuse," walked about New York astonished yet excited to witness modernity sprawling and sparkling in front of her—a view she found, according to Nancy Berke, profoundly fascinating in its extreme contradictions.[92] Ridge was intrigued by America's artistic, social, and political possibilities, feeling much like a modern American, empowered by a new appreciation of national belonging.[93] As the legend goes, upon arrival in the United States, Ridge changed her name and, in a clear symbolical gesture, destroyed the poems she had brought with her from Australia.[94] From that moment, her poetry would focus on light.[95] Light appears everywhere in her verse, as it would have been literally everywhere on the streets of New York. In her city poetry, electric light becomes a polemical tool, empowering the feminist artist and activist, and providing her with an iconography capable of articulating her unique social vision.

In Ridge's poems, artificial light delineates figures and buildings as rising against the American urban spectacle of power and brilliance. Often, her speakers exist thanks to light—they are figures forged out of the city illuminations. In "To the Others," Ridge imagines some mysteriously bright people "Like big white arc lights . . ./[. . .] | Each his ray—/Your tracery of light,/Making a shining way about America" (lines 3, 7-9).[96] The speaker governs this constellation of other lights as "a torch blown along the wind,/Flickering to a spark/But never out" (lines 17-19). Ridge's speaker becomes a darker and more fragile version of Lady Liberty, her torch infusing courage and action to these other lights with its brightness, and illuminating the way to the common good. If not as strong as a marble statue against the winds that may blow, she still is a symbol of resilience in the face of adversity, as her flame is never extinguished. In the poem "The Ghetto," on the improved social freedom afforded to Jewish women in America, Ridge makes a direct wordplay with electricity and the Statue of Liberty, as the Jewish immigrants of Hester Street are "ever pursuing/The great white Liberty" (*CEW* 59, 7, lines 49-50). In this poem, freedom speaks the ideological—and racially charged—language of bright electricity to these new

Fig. 4.6. Charles Graham, "BARTHOLDI'S STATUE OF LIBERTY—THE ILLUMINA-
TION OF NEW YORK HARBOR," *Harper's Weekly*, vol. 30 (1886), 716-717. Digital
image courtesy of Library of Congress Prints and Photographs Division, Washing-
ton, DC.

Americans. To immigrants arriving in New York by ocean liner after dark,
since November 1886 when it was inaugurated with a display of electrical
illumination and fireworks (fig. 4.6), the Statue of Liberty had been appear-
ing to visitors and prospective American citizens as a gigantic vision of em-
powerment, as well as womanhood and of course electric light.[97] With the
phrase "the great white Liberty," however, Ridge also creates a conscious
pun on Broadway, which by 1910 had more than twenty blocks fully illumi-
nated by electricity and had for some time been known as the Great White
Way.[98] The electrified Liberty is the high point of technological sublime. This
embodied and electrified America is at once the symbol of social, religious,
and political emancipation and of personal independence, embodying the
possibility for entertainment and prosperity that also lies at the cusp of
these immigrants' pursuits. While these immigrant aspirations might not
always be rapidly attainable, they remain available to them as a distant yet
persistent, brightly lit vision. Electrified, nighttime New York is a skyline of
desire for social justice and empowerment.

Ridge's previous experience as a factory worker, her radical left affiliations, and sympathy for the marginalized—women, homosexuals, workers, Jews, and African Americans—shaped her into a poetic spokeswoman for these communities.[99] Ridge's contemporaries saw her in this role, as a "Lady Liberty" of sorts. In 1922 William Saphier caricatures the radical poet as towering over an illuminated industrial space, back straight and chin up, this time holding not a torch but a vase of carnations, a symbol of the labor movement (fig. 4.7). The electrical skyline as eroticized by Stieglitz and Williams, and revendicated by O'Keeffe, is transformed here into the illuminated darkness of urban factories and workers, often working long hours into the night. Saphier's image effectively parodies this radical woman's revolutionary eschatology, with the stars embodying, this time, the collective lights of the workers in the factory. The lit-up windows of the factory are miles away from Pound's magical squares of light: they symbolize the workers' long shifts, their fatigue, and physical labor at night. Against the little lights at her back, Ridge stands as a monumental and empowering force, carrying the whole of proletariat in the seams of her skirt. This illustration, however parodic, captures the poet at the height of her popularity: Ridge is imagined much in the way she would have seen herself in her role as defender of the marginalized—a leftist, darkened Lady Liberty who rises over illuminated factories gathers and leads all the dispersed individual lights of the proletariat toward a brighter future.

Ridge understood the electrified night not only as a socially empowering force for the masses but also as an opportunity to reverse poetic tradition and to reorganize gender dynamics. In "Nocturne" (*Sun-Up and Other Poems*, 1920), Ridge overturns the traditional gender roles of love poetry, showing her speaker as an empowered flâneuse not only who is assertively walking about the city but who also affirms her own desire through her handling of lights.[100] The poem begins with a description of the urban night that anticipates O'Keeffe's paintings of New York's illuminated street-canyons:

> Indigo bulb of darkness
> Punctured by needle lights
> Through a fissure of brick canyon shutting out stars,
> And a sliver of moon
> Spigoting two high windows over the West river. . . .   (*CEW* 202, lines 1–5)

From a perspective similar to that adopted by O'Keeffe in *New York Street with Moon*, the speaker looks up to the sky from the street, her eyes zigzagging through the many lights and the buildings to aim for the moon, which

Fig. 4.7. A caricature of Lola Ridge by William Saphier, from Margaret Widdemer, *A Tree with a Bird in It: A Symposium of Contemporary American Poets on Being Shown a Pear-Tree on Which Sat a Grackle, With Illustrations by William Saphier* (New York: Harcourt, Brace, and Company, 1922), 43.

only appears as a distant "sliver." As in O'Keeffe, Ridge's is a vision of a dark skyline that frames the starless yet moonlit night sky, with the "bulb of darkness" making for a nearly oxymoronic pairing and punning on its usual compound with "light." The stars have been once more brought down to earth:

removed from the sky by the buildings that are "shutting [them] out," they make a novel appearance as the "needle lights" of the electric signs below. But the speaker and her lover also turn into lights breaking through the darkness:

> Boy, I met to-night,
> Your eyes are two red-glowing arcs shifting with my vision. . . .
> [. . .]
> What are you to me, boy,
> That I, who have passed so many lights,
> Should carry your eyes
> Like swinging lanterns?   (*CEW* 202, lines 6-7, 14-17)

The boy's eyes have transformed into red (arc?) lights of desire, while the speaker's experience is synthesized by the "many lights," which, if we were to read this autobiographically, may well be hinting at the age difference between Ridge and her partner, David Lawson, or at the fact that Ridge had, at the age of nearly fifty, already spent quite a few of her feline lives.[101] Ridge plays with the idea of women's task of tending lights, shifting this gendered practice out of the domestic sphere and into the city nightscape. Her handling of artificial lights puts her speaker at the center of the night, of the city, and of her life. Ridge's night-woman figure experiences the nocturnal city in novel ways. She is a strong, self-confident figure, who refuses to carry her lover's eyes as lanterns because she wants to see the world with her own eyes and be able to follow her own light. Ridge's woman holds her own fate in her hands and is free to express her own desire, rather than being simply prey to the city, and other men.

Within the context of her poetics of social empowerment, Ridge, as an active promoter of feminism, sees electric light as an excellent tool to endow her female personae—and, therefore, other women—with enhanced creative power and agency. In 1919 she toured the Midwest for a series of lectures, stopping in Chicago to give a speech entitled "Woman & the Creative Will."[102] In this lecture, Ridge discusses at length the patriarchal structures and Western Weltanschauung that prevented women from developing their full creative and artistic potential. Men have an advantage, argues Ridge, in that they have been holding "the organizing of the world," making "mental order [. . .] instinctive" for men, an action that has shaped them into "more spiritually articulate" beings than women (*CEW* 147). This fact, according to Ridge, has been a cause of women's spiritual, artistic, and intellectual inferiority over the centuries: "Only ready-made ideas come to the mind in ready words. Creative thought floats in vaguely luminous masses that must be pressed and rounded into shape. [. . .] This means that the creator must hold—without slipping once—infinite mental parts, building each in its appointed place. This requires a highly organized mind—one that can be a perfect executive to the creative will" (*CEW* 147). According to Ridge, creative will requires a mental agility only men can fully practice because of their historical privilege. They know exactly how to turn creative thoughts into properly shaped energy, high-powered light bulbs if you will, rather than simple "luminous masses." For this radical poet, the burning, illuminating force of light also works as an impetus for her writing and is a core part of her poetics. This metaphor of writing as a bright, burning force would make a comeback in a 1935 interview, where she would declare that, when writing, you should "let anything that burns you come out."[103] Burning symbolizes the light coming out of the poet—an autogenerated desire that is realized by "letting it out" through writing, thus becoming intelligible, organized light. As we have seen, for Williams and Cummings creative imagination was an electrical force, one they felt they could master and employ in their poetry; in Chapter Two, we saw that *futurista* Maria Ginanni imagined her feminine creative energy as electrical glowworms that could irradiate and go everywhere. For Ridge, women must reappropriate their creative energy and transform it from free, uncontrolled light into sharp, directed, organized spotlights. Creativity is pointless as an impetuous, boundless passion; in order for creativity to be meaningful, it must resemble electricity and be organized light with a message.

In "Electricity," Ridge plies the idea of a passive femininity by thinking about the actual workings of electricity. In this short poem, organized light is generated by the opposite poles of electricity:

Out of fiery contacts . . .
Rushing auras of steel
Touching and whirled apart . . .
Out of the charged phalluses
Of iron leaping
Female and male,
Complete, indivisible, one,
Fused into light.   (*CEW* 208, lines 1–8)[104]

The semantic connection between electricity and sex had been established since the early days of studies on electricity in the eighteenth century.[105] In the previous chapter, we saw Loy criticize the electrical union between lovers in *Songs to Joannes*, but for Ridge, the passionate embrace of the "fiery contacts" sublimates into a final union in which the two lovers effectively radiate electric light (much as in Goncharova's painting discussed in Chapter Two). Ridge manipulates the bipolar nature of electricity to express a sexual union that is mutually fulfilling for both men and women. Electricity is for Ridge the product of two complementary halves—the female and the male—and emblematizes a feminist union of equal with equal.[106] Ridge's speakers actively generate light, eventually becoming one in light: the electricity of sexual intercourse between the two opposites equals the creative process, a fusing of different lights into a single, organized light.

For both O'Keeffe and Ridge, electrified New York is a source of wonder and fascination that leads them to closely scrutinize the relationship between the electric lights and the city, and between the electrified city, artistic tradition, and gender roles. To bring down the stars is for them an act of substitution: electricity is the light of the night, bringing starlight and moonlight closer to us, and therefore effectively substituting them. For O'Keeffe, starting a new dialogue between natural and artificial lights within the modern city in her painting enables her to challenge and disrupt an essentialist critical understanding of her work. In her poetry, Ridge harnesses electricity's potential as an organized and controlled light, as a way to incentivize women's artistic creation in particular but also to mark the resilience and empowering efforts of minorities and the marginalized. O'Keeffe rewrites the streetlights by observing them at a distance, as she walks along the city at night or watches it from her window. Ridge sees herself as an embodied, burning light of the modern city. New York streetlights offer a way to recast poetic and artistic tradition, and place it at the service of their nonconformist agendas.

A Luminous Blackness

Filippo Tommaso Marinetti's invitation to murder the moonlight and replace it with electricity, echoed in Ezra Pound's imperative to bring the stars to earth, resonated on the other side of the Atlantic. In 1922, with some delay in transatlantic literary communications, the Jamaican-American poet Claude McKay published a poem, "Moon Song," whose content appears to be knowledgeable of the Futurist lesson. As the speaker walks about the city at night, he cannot but burst into an indignant cry against the moon:

> There is no magic from your presence here,
>> O moon, mad moon, tuck up your trailing robe,
> Its silver seems so ancient and severe
>> Against the glow of one electric globe.[107]

The poem, as it turns out, is the opposite of a lyrical moon song, as the speaker joins the large chorus of lunicidal poets we have encountered in this book. One single electric globe is enough to estrange the light of the moon from the cityscape. What's a poet got to do to write decent poems if the moon has become an austere presence? The speaker's eyes are directed not so much toward the bright lights around him, but upward, toward the mad moon. It is certainly poetic tradition that incites McKay to write "Moon Song," as Sharpe suggests.[108] But not quite in the way that Marinetti would have wished for. To this poet and observer of the modern city, while the moon lacks in power to beautify its urban surroundings, electricity equally fails to provide him with a suitable, and different, pathway to writing the city. McKay's street-level perspective exposes an inability to connect to what is above him (the night sky) as well as what surrounds him (the illuminated city). Where many of our New York artists have reveled in the feeling of being *inside* the lights of the city, McKay's speakers appear to be unable to. "Moon Song" adopts a point of view comparable to that of O'Keeffe's *New York Street with Moon*, in which the moon and a single lamppost are in an open visual dialogue with one another, observed from a lower angle. But for McKay, even as he acknowledges the moon as obsolescent, he does not find electricity to be equally inspiring. For McKay the electric light appears purely as a disturbance to the moonlit urban scene he had hoped to frame in his poetry. The moon, even with its "ancient and severe" light, is still at the center of his writing.

Langston Hughes, who wrote so often and so eloquently about the moon that we might call him, with T. S. Eliot (Chapter One), another votary of lunar dandyism, dedicated a series of poems about moonstruck Pierrot.[109] But in "A Black Pierrot" (1923), he reimagines Pierrot not only as Black but as moonless too: "I am a black Pierrot:/She did not love me,/So I crept away into the night/And the night was black, too."[110] Yet, as we know, no moon, no Pierrot—it is as simple as that. This Pierrot melts into a moonless, starless, lamp-less night because if Pierrot the French pantomime character loves the moon, this Black Pierrot cannot, and should not, love the moon in its whiteness. The traditional Pierrot thrives in contrasts: the night and the moon, white and black, laughter and tears. Hughes's Pierrot feels comfortable in an environment in which he can melt away, and disappear, becoming invisible black on black.

These two examples of a certain resistance against poetic lunar tradition point toward a friction between the aesthetics of the moon and those of the electrified night. In Toomer's story "Bona and Paul" (from *Cane*, 1923), the author uses a specific palette choice that reinforces racial difference by way of light sources, presenting us with the characters of the lunar black and the electrical white. Art, the protagonist's (Paul's) blond Norwegian friend, is "like the electric light which he snaps on."[111] White, quick, smart Art seems to have all the characteristics of electricity within him; he fits well within the environment of the hyper-technological city. He is brilliantly white like any electric lamp. Paul, a mixed-race character seemingly molded on Toomer's own mixed-heritage profile, on the other hand, is repeatedly compared to natural lights—he is "moony" (*C* 98), "a candle" (*C* 95), and "cool like the dusk, and like the dusk, detached" (*C* 99). In the eyes of the white onlookers, Paul is a natural light, embodying the archetype of the primitive, decadent African American.[112] Under the electric lights of a Chicago nightclub, his racial difference is reinstated: "Suddenly [Paul] knew that he was apart from the people around him. [. . .] Suddenly he knew that people saw, not attractiveness in his dark skin, but difference. [. . .] He saw himself, cloudy, but real. He saw the faces of the people at the tables round him. White lights, or as now, the pink lights of the Crimson Gardens gave a glow and immediacy to white faces. The pleasure of it, equal to that of love or dream, of seeing this. Art and Bona and Helen? He'd look. They were wonderfully flushed and beautiful" (*C* 102). Within the space of the electrically illuminated nightclub, Paul feels distanced from his electrical-white friends: the colors of modern electricity suit the complexion of white people's faces, giving them the same glow as in early cinematic portrayals of white people on screen.[113] They appear to him as a vision he can mindlessly stare at, almost in awe, but they also reinforce the feeling that his skin tones do not belong to the aesthetics of electricity. In spite of being inside the lights of the nightclub, Paul feels as distant to these lights as though he were watching a distant skyline. In "Bona and Paul," the binary contrast between artificial and natural lights allows him to aesthetically comment on the American racial dynamics of his time. What Toomer further implies with this aesthetic choice is that the night of pre-electrical times favored darker skin tones in ways that the electrified night could not, becoming instead a white, translucent space in which everything is illuminated, visible, and controlled.

Richard Dyer, who has written eloquently on the racial dimension of light and its whiteness, comments on the significance of illumination technologies and cultures for crafting and reimagining the human self, while also stressing how these technologies and cultures of light seem to appear unique to white people.[114] In her rich analysis of Black skin through the figure of eclectic dancer, model, and actress Josephine Baker, Anne Anlin Cheng argues that we need to turn to a different "cult of light" for Black bodies in the 1920s and 1930s.[115] By closely observing the various presentations of Baker's body in photographs and visuals of the time, Cheng makes the suggestive proposition that *"the 'glittery' and the 'blackened' may be uncannily equivalent"* (emphasis in original).[116] Due to the pairing of her glittery clothing and accessories with the luminous effects chosen in photographic and cinematic representations of this extraordinary dancer, Baker's skin effectively turns golden—a problematic reinscription, for Cheng, of colonial discourses onto her luminous Black body.[117] But the pairing of Black and luminous could be extended to women other than divas of Baker's status and charisma, and went beyond the language of colonial gold and exoticism. The artificial brilliance of electric light reinvented blackness.

The idea that the glittery and the blackened may be opposite yet unifying aesthetic categories finds its poetic realization in Langston Hughes's poem "To the Black Beloved" (first published in *Crisis* in 1925; *CPLH* 627). Here the contrast between darkness and light, black and white, night and electricity is reconciled in the aestheticized Black body. The dark and the luminous are one and the same:

> Ah,
> My black one,
> Thou art not luminous
> Yet an altar of jewels,
> An altar of shimmering jewels,
> Would pale in the light
> Of thy darkness,
> Pale in the light
> Of thy nightness.   (*CPLH* 58, lines 13-21)

Though still associated with the night, here the Black body is brilliant with unequivocal light. Hughes at first denies the possibility of the "luminous" Black body, but then reframes blackness as an illumination of its own. In this marvelously electrified America, the night can no longer be considered a purely dark affair, so why should Black skin be read in terms of dimness or opaqueness? Hughes makes it clear that artificial brilliance can be, and is, an essential attribute of the Black body. Seeing the body of his beloved as in a photographic negative, Hughes turns the traditional notion of chiaroscuro on its head, reimagining darkness—and therefore "nightness"—as shining dark light. The oxymoronic juxtaposition is necessary and stems from the experience of the newly lit environment around the poet, in which the night's blackness becomes at once visible and illuminated. The electrified nightscape challenges previous conceptions of blackness, making this visible and luminous darkness a more suitable iconography for the Black body in the poetry and art of the time.

So far in this book, I have given many examples of direct identification between the poet and a lamp or other source of light. These men and women, however, were largely white. Electricity enables a new construction of whiteness—luminous, brilliant, radiant, electrified—while also allowing white people to feel they have conquered the space of the night under the principle of what Dyer terms "controlled visibility."[118] But, as I have shown in this final chapter, questions of distance and proximity to the electric light influence the way in which intense electricity was often able to generate a new vision of darkness and therefore of nightness. In Ralph Ellison's *Invisible Man* (1952), for example, a much later novel about Harlem's African American community in the early twentieth century, its Black protagonist basks in the luminosity created by the abducted electric power he (unlawfully) directed to his flat.[119] While in actuality any extreme electric illumination gives shape and visibility to the Black body, the protagonist is socially as well as effectively invisible, absorbed as he becomes so by the excessive illumination in which he finds himself. Many African Americans would have experienced the early twentieth-century electrical, hypermodern environments of American cities in terms of displacement and of disassociation.[120] Yet, as I show in the following pages, African American modernist poets and artists were able to repurpose the electrically illuminated nightscape in the service of reinventing blackness as a source of light of its own.

James Van Der Zee, the "official" photographer of 1920s and 1930s Harlem, directly harnessed artificial brilliance to illuminate his portrait photographs of women. In many of his photographs, what appears to be a brilliant jewel, shining through the photograph due to studio lighting, turns out to be an artifice in the artifice: Van Der Zee would retouch the negatives by drawing imaginary bracelets, rings, and necklaces onto the skin of the women he photographed—most of whom were African American, but not all of them, as is the case of *Blumstein's Sales Girls* (1930), for instance, a photograph he also retouched. As photograph conservator Laura Panadero points out, the hand-drawn jewels attract the observer's attention as brilliant presences on these women's skin, creating a particularly strong visual contrast in the photographs of African American women, such as in *Portrait of a Young Woman* (1930; see plate 16), in which Van Der Zee added a bracelet and a ring.[121] Our eyes are drawn to the center of the picture, with the sparkling jewels illuminating the woman's Black skin, in a game of contrasts that Van Der Zee pioneered in order to render the various tones of women's complexions.

Unlike many other photographers of the time, Van Der Zee employed a ground-floor studio, in which he had to become proficient in the use of different types of electric light bulbs to render precise gradations of color and shade.[122] He also liked to use artificial brilliance to promote a surreptitiously avant-garde portrayal of the Harlem community. At first glance, *Nude by Fireplace* (1923; see fig. 4.8) represents an African American woman warming up to a brightly warm, roaring fire: the beauty of firelight illuminating her naked body immediately conjures up passion and natural instinct. When we look more closely, however, it becomes clear that the fire is not real but part of a painted backdrop Van Der Zee used many times. The warm light of the "fire" is due to the photographer's virtuosity with electric lights.[123] Van Der Zee would often disrupt the viewer's assumptions and combine primitivist African elements with "a cognizance of the American cultural present" in a way that combined the past and present of the Harlem community.[124] In this photograph, I argue, the artificially illuminated fire fashions and modernizes a new idea of feminine sensuality, which is at once natural and artificial. Van Der Zee's woman, whose naked body and proximity to fire suggests natural associations, is rather warmed and sexualized by the electric light hiding away from the frame of the composition. Proximity to the artificial light renders Van Der Zee's photographed subject luminous, glittery, translucent: the naked woman becomes light as her skin is caressed by the beams of the hidden electric lamp. As a photographer, Van Der Zee saw the opportunity offered by electricity to alter conventional associations of luminosity with white femininity, making Black skin glow with artificial brightness.

Fig. 4.8. James Van Der Zee, *Nude by Fireplace*, 1923. Gelatin silver print, 23.5 × 18.42 cm (9 1/4 × 7 1/4 in.). Gift of Regenia A. Perry, 2021.979, Virginia Museum of Fine Arts, Richmond. Digital image courtesy of Virginia Museum of Fine Arts. © James Van Der Zee Archive, the Metropolitan Museum of Art, New York City.

Back in the context of the electrified city, poets Hughes and Gwendolyn Bennetta Bennett reimagine and reinvent the contrast created by the intense new brightness of the urban lightscape against the darkness of the night sky. In "The Fascination of Cities" (1926), an article—part memoir, part self-reflection—written for the magazine *Crisis: A Record of Darker Races*, Langston Hughes conjures up all the important cities of his life: Kansas City, Chicago, Mexico City, New York, and Paris. All these cities when lit up at night cast a special charm on the poet, whether observed from afar or from right within the lights of the streets. Hughes remembers watching the lights and the people in the "cool night air" of Kansas City when he first realized he had been seized by "fascination of cities [. . .] burning like a fever in the blood."[125] In all these cities of his heart, dark skin and bright lights combine into an exciting mix that fascinates and inspires Hughes's writing. Both New York and Paris appear to Hughes as beautiful visions of their distant skylines. He first sees New York from the sea, until Manhattan holds the writer in a tight embrace, made up of the two contrasting nocturnal districts: "Broadway and its million lights. Harlem and its love-nights, its cabarets and casinos, its dark, warm bodies."[126] Paris, on the other hand, is first enjoyed from the windows of a typically French attic room at dusk: "In the darkening day she becomes like an enchantress-city adorning herself with lights. She becomes like a sorceress-city making herself beautiful with lights."[127] Hughes's privileged viewpoint allows him to make a modern night-woman out of the sight of electrified Paris. In this case, the texture of the night sky becomes a woman's skin—an African American woman's skin, we might add, as the purpling light of dusk was often perceived to be suited to describe a Black woman's skin.[128] Her skin becomes darker and at the same time more brilliant thanks to the lights adorning her as though they were jewels—imaginary jewels recreating the idealized contrast of brightness against nightness. In this wide-eyed, dreamy description of Hughes's Paris, Black skin made artificially luminous—whether by shiny jewels or glowing lamps—becomes the vivid embodiment of the modern electrified nightscape.

Only a few months after the publication of Hughes's article "The Fascination of Cities" in *Crisis*, Bennett's poem "Street Lamps in Early Spring" (1926) was published in the Art issue of *Opportunity: Journal of Negro Life*.[129] Even sandwiched as it is between an illustrated article on the somber African masks of "Primitive Negro Sculpture" and a translation from Blaise Cendrars's *Anthologie Nègre* (Negro Anthology, 1921), Bennett's poem glows on and off the page:

> Night wears a garment
> All velvet soft, all violet blue . . .
> And over her face she draws a veil

> As shimmering fine as floating dew . . .
> And here and there
> In the black of her hair
> The subtle hands of Night
> Move slowly with their gem-starred light.[130]

The image Bennett conjures up very much resembles Hughes's jeweled Parisian night. It is very likely Bennett would have known Hughes's poem, as she contributed both artwork and poetry not just to *Opportunity* but also to *Crisis* all through the 1920s.[131] The image is remarkably similar to Hughes's: the Black Night, wearing electric streetlamps as shiny jewels. The terms in which Bennett is thinking about blackness, femininity, and the city are congruent with Hughes's: she is, too, thinking about an electrified city (most probably Paris, again as for Hughes) in the present moment. But if for Hughes the illuminated city at night appears as the embodiment of urban seductions and temptations, for Bennett the night sky appears rather as a friendly and tender presence: a woman is caressing the city below her, making beautiful jewels out of the brilliant starlike streetlamps below. Bennett's night-woman does not live in "a world outside electric light," as Alex Goody claims but rather, I contend, inhabits one in which darkness frames light and in which electric light makes Black skin glow.[132] This night-woman actively brings down the stars, lowering them to street level. She does not adorn herself of stars but rather of artificial lamps, which make her luminous—she is in and around the lights. Night's shining jewel-lamps emphasize the empowering force of the cityscape for the modern flâneuse. During Bennett's stay in France in 1925, she recalls how on one occasion at the beginning of her stay in Paris, "it was dark and I became afraid and thought I was lost."[133] Walking the streets of an unknown foreign city at night must have felt hazardous, whereby reimagining the urban night as a feminine beauty with thick black hair and luminous jewels becomes an important gesture to reestablish the confidence of night-walking women. More importantly, Bennett makes this African American Night at once visible and invisible precisely by virtue of electricity: her skin and hair comfortably melting away in the darkness of the night sky, her jewelry molds her into an illuminated, and highly visible, spectacle. To be Black does not mean to live outside electricity; blackness thrives in the pairing with its opposite—light.

The changes brought about by US electrification reverberated in the poetic practices of these poets who wanted, in turn, to create change for themselves—in poetry, the arts, and within society. Galvanized by the evolving cityscape around them, these Brilliant Modernists saw in electric light an opportunity to recast and reshape their writing, their poetics, and their identities as poets. The perspective of the poet and artist zigzagging through the streets of the illuminated city allows them to observe and sometimes satiate their desires, to reshape gender roles and notions of aesthetics. Electrified darkness becomes a malleable oxymoron to modernize and reconceptualize poetry and art about the city and its people. This chapter has purposefully included as wide a range of poets and artists as possible to show the different ways in which electric light brought about change in modernism, from more established names to lesser-known ones, and across the divides of artistic and literary labels. The artificial brilliance of electricity further created a deep line of demarcation with the previous literary and artistic traditions: if in the twentieth century Laforgue had to necessarily become American, and Pierrot Black, poetry *had* to turn electric.

Conclusion

Shining to the Full

A Light-Conscious Modernity

Our century is light-conscious, as was no other.

Elizabeth Bowen, "NEW WAVES OF THE FUTURE" (1969)[1]

At the very beginning of my research for this book, during my time as a postdoctoral fellow, I came across a few essays by novelist Elizabeth Bowen on the subject of light and illumination, published in various periodicals between the late 1920s and the end of her life. In the dimly lit lower level of the National Library of Scotland reading room, I slightly jumped off my chair. Reading Bowen, it becomes apparent that, for her, each period is necessarily experienced through a specific kind of light.[2] She sensed that each mode of illumination did not simply point to a historically specific atmosphere; each lighting meant something different. In her literary examples, light is the result of specific cultural practices from the time: light in literature is culture, as well as history. What would *Madame Bovary* be without a French *crépuscule*, or *Wuthering Heights* without its frenzied firelight, or, indeed, Marcel Proust's *À la recherche du temps perdu* (*In Search of Lost Time*) without its numerous light reflections, shades of twilight, and different sorts of lamps?[3] "What a trouvaille," I thought, "I shall save it for the conclusion of my book."

In the very last of these nonfiction pieces Bowen wrote on light and culture, "New Waves of the Future" (1969), the modernist novelist looks back on past decades and their relationship with light, while reflecting on the present moment. Thinking back on the relationship between light(ing) and the twentieth century from her privileged position as direct eyewitness, Bowen identifies the developments, and anticipates the conclusions, of this book. In a very few sentences, she gets to the heart of the matter:

> Our century is light-conscious, as was no other. We react more knowingly than
> our forefathers to light's dramas, variations, and possibilities. True, far back goes
> the association with Nature, with poetry, with romance—where would genera-
> tions of lovers have been without the moon or the sunset, or children without
> the miracle of the rainbow? But we moderns love light with an extra ardour,
> seeking it out. We like best to go, to be, where it shines to the full. We construct
> our homes, so far as may be, of glass. And when, day ended, darkness blackens
> our windows, we make play with *lighting*: twentieth-century art which trans-
> forms rooms.[4]

Bowen, who was highly susceptible to light in all its forms, identifies an in-
stinctive connection between sensitivity to light and the modern project.
The key word in the passage, and the key idea of this book, is the adverb
"knowingly": the moderns, and the moderns of the early twentieth century
especially, display a new attitude to light because they are more aware of
it, in all its possibilities. A child of the turn of the twentieth century, Bowen
experienced firsthand the changes in the cultures of light described in this
book. For her, living in the twentieth century means having an acute aware-
ness and in-her-bones understanding of the time period's multiple forms of
light, their interactions and juxtapositions, as well as their different qualities
and meanings. Light, of course, has always been a human necessity. But the
twentieth century explodes with electric light, and with it comes a need to
reconfigure existing attitudes toward light, natural or artificial, as well as to
darkness. To bask in the period's multiple sources of light—diurnal and noc-
turnal, natural and artificial—means to realize that, beyond this biological
necessity, twentieth-century people crave *all* of "light's dramas, variations,
and possibilities." The waning, flickering streetlamp, the bright lamp on the
bedside table, electrically lit advertisements, the glowing vista of skyscrap-
ers at night, the moon reduced to a miniature luminous dot in the brighter-
than-ever nocturnal sky: all are significant aspects of a modern sensibility.

Bowen's idea of "shin[ing] to the full" becomes another term for bril-
liance, or brightness, as a yearning strictly pertinent to the twentieth cen-
tury. Not only is it a conscious act of wanting to be where light is at its
brightest, it is also a striving for added brilliance in order to attempt to lessen,
if not completely obliterate, the darkness against which light shines. Many
modernist poets and artists, as we have seen, turn to the new illuminations
of the period as an expression of their desire for artificially constructed and
manipulated brightness and darkness. Across *Brilliant Modernism*, I have

shown how this attraction to light across its spectrum is crucial to modernist artistic and poetic practices. Different approaches to natural and artificial lights mark a sharp temporal and cultural division between Bowen's "forefathers" (whom we might identify as the Victorians) and her generation. There is a temporal specificity to the aesthetics of lighting technologies. While Victorian aesthetics celebrated the corners of darkness created by oil lamps, gaslight, and so on, the distinctive aesthetic trait of the new century is brightness above all else. The old poetic and artistic disposition toward moonlit darkness and natural light yields to a compulsive fascination for what Bowen aptly calls the "artful naturalism" of illuminating and being illuminated.[5] So why and how does this twentieth-century obsession with light matter? What can it tell us about contemporary ideas, attitudes, and poetic practice? During the first age of electrification, electric light disrupted established relationships between people and light. But exactly in what ways and with what effects?

Electric light, Bowen explains, "does not dictate our moods" as gaslight or earlier versions of electricity might have done but rather "expresses them, eloquently."[6] Electric light does not simply affect or influence us. Modern subjectivity is not just reactive toward electric light as an external phenomenon. Instead, the electric light is conceived and manipulated as an extension of the self. Rather than the self being molded by the light bulb, which might force the beholder to adopt a particular affectation or a sense of oneself, the bulb is already a synecdoche of the self: it is an external part of the self representing the whole. For this reason, it is particularly apt to look closely at poetry and artificial light together, as both are expressions of the self and of subjectivity. In many ways, Bowen's aperçu on the light consciousness of the twentieth century shows how this book has magnified this topic, therefore making it more legible to readers today. Yet this book also marks the limits of Bowen's statements. If there is a specific twentieth-century art of artificial light, as Bowen calls it, what about the poetry of this light-obsessed, electrified period? As I have shown throughout this book, early twentieth-century poetry moved on from traditional associations with nature, and turned to the new artificial lights as an expression and an extension of modern subjectivity. Light and artificial illumination in prose often set up an ambience or an atmosphere; in poetry, they frequently tell us something unique and specific about the poetic self. For William Carlos Williams, for example, electric light functions both as the source of poetic matter *and* the agency of the poetic self. This function of the electrified nightscape is evident in the poem "To a Friend Concerning Several Ladies" (from *Sour Grapes*, 1921), in which the speaker, bereft of the muse, is invited not only to watch but to live and experience the illuminated city: "Come! yes,/the city is ablaze for you/and you stand and look at it."[7] This new urban night of electric lights, which eroticizes illuminated darkness, was not only the setting and topic of much of this poetry of the 1920s, but also a verbalization of masculine desire and sexuality.

The poets and artists discussed in this book exemplify a particular social and cultural phenomenon: at the turn of the twentieth century, with the coming of electrification, artificial brilliance and the illuminated nightscape were not just interesting external phenomena to be admired or abhorred; rather they initiated actual cultural change and heralded an unprecedented identification between sensitive beholders and the new technology. Electrification, as has often been remarked, substantially changed life rhythms by transforming the night into active time (think of major nighttime cultural shifts, such as extended working hours and the multiplying of nocturnal entertainments) but also into aesthetic time. The electrified night made for a new time for art, which included artistic development and poetic inspiration. Zdeněk Pešánek, an avant-garde artist, sculptor, architect, as well as light theorist and illumination enthusiast from what is now the Czech Republic, recorded in *Kinetismus* (*Kineticism*, written 1924-27; published 1941) that "by using light, which encompasses light advertising, we have extended the artistic life of urban spaces by as much as 1000 hours a year during the evening hours, which are much easier to devote to meditation than the working hours, with their hustle and bustle."[8] Observing the electrified nightscape from a window in New York or during a stroll along the Arno in Florence in the early decades of the twentieth century, or pausing to admire the shape and brilliance of electric lamps in the home: all such activities contributed to the development of a new poetic and artistic disposition.

For the majority of poets and artists of this period, the new nightscape equates to the self. As such, the ways in which they articulate the experience of the early twentieth-century night can tell today's reader much about individual poets' and artists' disposition toward art and literature. For some, electricity prompts a firmer return to the old aesthetics of gas—as is the case of young T. S. Eliot, who, highly sensitive to the variation of different light sources, decided to turn his eyes away from the electrified America of his time to bask in the poetic past of a gaslit world instead. At the start of his poetic career, the appeal of nineteenth-century lunar and gaslit aesthetics was too strong in him: before he could appreciate, and write about, the current moment, he needed to master—ultimately to overturn—the aesthetics of the poets preceding him. The friction between the fuzzy gaslit aesthetics of the nineteenth century and the twentieth century's bold electrified glare complicated modernism's liaison with artificial brilliance. As Ezra Pound and Vladimir Mayakovsky stopped to watch—entranced—the electrical lightscape of New York, they became aware that, just as nighttime had changed, broader cultural shifts were taking place and that their writing, too, could no longer abide by the aesthetics of the previous century: "Here is our poetry," Pound would write, "for we have pulled down the stars to our will."[9] Poetry happened where electric light illuminated the city.

As the night turns into an actual bright second day, expectations of gender mutate and are often inverted. Electric light transformed not only the night but also representations and conceptions of women: the passive, palefaced, sexually dormant lunar woman as she was dreamed of, imagined, and worshipped by the Symbolists could no longer exist under electric light. Intellectually astute, sexually active, and emotionally independent, the Modern Woman came onto the stage as, to borrow Mina Loy's portmanteau term, a "stellectric" figure:[10] part star, part electric light; part conventional beauty, part awakened feminist and unstoppable force of nature. In her life and art, Loy revolutionized the traditional, and by that point old-fashioned, concept of lunar femininity by embracing electric light as a way of life. Not only did she make her own lamps, which were to her both an artform and means to financial independence, but she reimagined her sexuality as at her own command, almost a matter of flipping on or off a switch. The Futurist women at Marinetti's court and beyond embraced the revolution offered by the electric light much in the same way: like Loy in "Pazzarella" and *Songs to Joannes*, they responded to the Futurist view of women as naturally and passively lunar by identifying with the active vitality of electric light. For Futurist women artists and poets, the bare nakedness of the light bulb makes for an attractive symbol of the new poetic and artistic practice, as well as an unabashed metaphor for sensual union. The poetic trope of woman as graceful moon, to be admired and revered at a distance, was consigned to the past; she now walks the street-lit night, electrified and electrifying in body and soul.

The modern city, so sharp, gray, and geometrical by day, becomes at night a new site for self-creation. As Alfred Stieglitz, Jean Toomer, and William Carlos Williams watched American city streets both up close and from a distance, their desires were projected onto the urban nightscape. Nighttime electricity is not only an invitation for bolder manifestations of desire; it is a direct expression of the observer's sexuality. In Jean Toomer's poem "Her Lips Are Copper Wire," the speaker's desire transforms into the embodiment of the electrified cityscape after dark. A final kiss marks the sublimation of the encounter between the poet and the electrified city-woman of his desires: "then with your tongue remove the tape/and press your lips to mine/till they are incandescent."[11] But if the new urban space fosters masculine imagination and desire, for women artists and writers it invites contradiction, subversion, and reappropriation. For O'Keeffe and Ridge, the electric lights of New York shaped and expressed a new, more independent and conscious, and even queerer, form of femininity. The new urban mise-en-scène of hard lines and sharp contrasts generates a poetic repertoire, and a sexual politics, of resistance. "Out of the night you burn, Manhattan,/In a vesture of gold——" writes Ridge, reimagining nighttime Manhattan as an artificially brilliant beauty.[12] In the hands of O'Keeffe and Ridge, as in those of Loy and the Futurist women, city lights became a symbol of rebellion against normative and traditional perceptions of gender.

At the same time, the illuminated dark develops as a distinct, alternative aesthetic category. Electric light enables African American modernist poets and artists to reconceptualize darkness in a way that challenges and ultimately overturns the traditional, archetypal association of the Black body with natural darkness and lunar dimness. Although the electrified night might have appeared to those experiencing it for the first time as an intrinsically whiter space due to its increased luminosity and seeming erasure of darkness, some poets and artists of the Harlem Renaissance harnessed the new lightscape to a modern African American sensibility. Langston Hughes, Gwendolyn B. Bennett, and James Van Der Zee engaged the aesthetics of artificial light to challenge lazy associations between darkness and the Black body. The Black body dancing under electric light shines like the body of the night, wearing electric streetlights as jewels. This powerful image of artificially illuminated darkness, which crops up in both Bennett and Hughes, signals another act of resistance, this time in the hands of African American modernists, against traditional associations of natural darkness, moonlight, and the Black body.

Looking at modernist poetry slant, by way of its lights, I have told the story of a group of artists and poets at a tangent from the canonical version of modernism: one for which artificial brilliance is a driving force. Though this is necessarily a very particular and in some ways eccentric grouping of poets and artists, together they make for a composite and transnational picture of modernism, brought together by a shared consciousness of light in all its forms. My book offers a reconstellation of modernism: one pretty exclusively attracted to urban life, celebrating human ingenuity, and perceiving technology as a fundamental reflection and extension of the self.[13] My focus, too, has for the most part been confined to poetry and the visual arts, to see how they interacted with each other and how they reflected on, and shaped, light cultures of the early twentieth century. Scholars have said surprisingly little about these issues so far. Early cinema, and its role in early twentieth-century cultures of light, has, by contrast, attracted considerable commentary. Chapter One touched on the work of Georges Méliès, but we might equally have drawn on Thomas Edison's commercial pictures or the remarkable innovations in dance and film of Loïe Fuller.[14]

As this work draws to a close, I ponder the afterlife of poetry and art's role in shaping early twentieth-century cultures of light, as well as the cultural legacies of its principal characters, my Brilliant Modernists. How did various forms of light figure in poetry once electric light got settled in the 1930s home? Did electric light matter in poetry after the Second World War, and how? Who are the late twentieth- and twenty-first-century equivalents of the Brilliant Modernists? Did the *Apollo* landings generate a new mode of lunar poetry? How do city lights contribute to the texture of twenty-first-century poetry? How did ecopoetics and environmentalism impact the place and purpose of light in poetry? Is light perceived as gendered today? What cultures of light do poets embrace today?

It would be easy to conclude in a somber vein: to worry, as we must, about everything from screen time to urban light pollution and the environmental crisis. I want to end, however, on a brighter note, with one luminous example of the intellectual legacy of Brilliant Modernists. American poet, artist, and editor Lawrence Ferlinghetti can be seen as another poet of light, one directly engaging with the inheritance of modernist brilliance. In 1953, together with college tutor Peter D. Martin, Ferlinghetti founded America's best-known independent bookshop: the City Lights Bookstore and Publishers in San Francisco.[15] The launch of the store was followed by that of the City Lights Pocket Poets Series, in which Ferlinghetti published his own work and that of numerous poets who had attained, or thanks to City Lights would go on to attain, international recognition.[16] City Lights still exists today and still is considered an important tastemaker in contemporary poetry; it also remains a beacon of activism. As the story goes, the inspiration for the bookstore's name came from Charlie Chaplin's eponymous film of 1931.[17] But the image the name conjures up is surely an illuminated skyline at night—something that remarkably never appears in Chaplin's film. For Ferlinghetti and Martin, the name signaled to their readers and customers intellectual empowerment and artistic resistance in the face of cultural obscurantism. In adopting this image, Ferlinghetti followed the modernist poets and artists of *Brilliant Modernism*, who harnessed their instinctive light consciousness to investigate specific preoccupations of the age: social change and inequality, gender, and aesthetics. Though Ferlinghetti's motives, in the postwar era, were different from those of my book's generation of modernists, he nevertheless embraced the urban artificial lightscape as a distinctive trait of twentieth-century aesthetics.

Having lived to the venerable age of 101, Ferlinghetti was effectively eyewitness to most of the twentieth century and to a significant part of the twenty-first. His text "What Is Poetry?" (2007), part of *Poetry as Insurgent Art*, is a testament to his continuous work in the field of poetry and poetics throughout the century. Ferlinghetti began this text as part of a broadcast in the 1950s and then went on revising it until the early 2000s. In it, he compiled a list of aphorisms in response to the titular question. The plurality of his answers notwithstanding, Ferlinghetti is adamant that, while poetry can certainly be many things, it cannot exist without light. For Ferlinghetti, poetry *is* all forms of light. All poems are "lumina, emitting light," whether "a bare light bulb" or "a lighthouse" or "the moon weeping because it must fade away in the day."[18] Writing after the modernists, Ferlinghetti is less interested in fighting the moon as a standing vestige of an earlier style in poetry. He is, however, keen on using artificial illumination as a medium for self-discovery in the urban nightscape, as is the case in "The Long Street" (from *A Coney Island of the Mind*, 1958):

> Thru the light of the world
> Thru the night of the world
> With lanterns at crossings
> Lost lights flashing
> Crowds at carnivals
> Nightwood circuses
> Whorehouses and parliaments
> Forgotten fountains

> Cellar doors and unfound doors
> Figures in lamplight[19]   (lines 80–89)

In the illuminated darkness of the street, fleeting stills of the nocturnal reality around the speaker come alive. With the lightscape of the twentieth-century night, the lost, the forgotten, the unfound become visible, legible, and ultimately rediscoverable. For Ferlinghetti, as for the Brilliant Modernists, poetry as light is born out of its combination with darkness. Poetry is "the shadow cast by our streetlight imaginations," as well as "the light at the end of the tunnel and the darkness within."[20] Poetry cannot and should not obliterate darkness; rather, it should make the dark more visible. This claim resonates thoroughly with the poetry and art of *Brilliant Modernism*: the early twentieth-century electrified nightscape expressed the poetic self and human condition in ways that had simply not been possible before.

Acknowledgments

Growing up in the extravagant lights of Milan and dreaming of electrified nightscapes elsewhere, I simply do not remember a time in my life when I was not utterly fascinated with illuminated darkness. It is this personal fascination with life after dark that set me off across the world. Writing this book would not have been possible without the constant inspiration of the towns and cities I lived in and visited during its gestation period. In some (Milan, Florence, Rome, Toronto, Edinburgh, and York), I produced many of the pages you see in this book; and to the lit-up streets of these cities, my imagination is forever grateful.

But of course, I do not have just cities to thank. This book would never have been possible without the constant encouragement, support, and practical help of institutions, colleagues, friends, and family members. Firstly, I should like to express my gratitude to the Institute for Advanced Studies in the Humanities (IASH) at the University of Edinburgh for believing in the early life of this project and for providing me with the space and time to conceptualize this project as a book. After IASH, this project found a comfortable and congenial home in the Department of English and Related Literature at the University of York, which nurtured it and made it grow. It is no exaggeration to say that, without the help of three colleagues in particular—Trev Broughton, Hugh Haughton, and Helen Smith—you would not be able to read this book in its current form. Trev has been the most scrupulous reader, mentor, and friend I could have ever wished for. If I have been able to succeed in finishing this book, it is largely thanks to her and her ability to always be constructive and encouraging while critical. Throughout the COVID-19 pandemic, my numerous international travels, and the negotiation of motherhood with academia, Trev has always had more than just words of advice: she has always been able to tell me the thing I needed to hear at the time I needed to hear it. That is a rare gift, and without her resourcefulness and encouragement this book may have never been finished. She has also read and proofread large portions of this book, so if there are still any errors or infelicities of expression, they are solely my fault. From my first days at York, Hugh has been spurring me to write the book I wanted to write. I will never forget his unwavering reassurance and inspiration, nor the chats about poetry during our walks along various rivers of North Yorkshire. Finally, Helen has been a most supportive and generous head of department, always encouraging me to believe in the strengths of this project. I am thankful to her for letting me take the time I needed to finish the first full draft and for all her comments, support, and guidance along the way. In my department I also wish to thank Emilie Morin, for her mentorship and friendship; Matt Campbell, for his wisdom and collegiality; Alexandra Kingston-Reese, for her cheerleading; and Freya Sierhuis, for her nudges to "just go for it" at the right times. Thanks are also in order for Fran Brooks, Lola Boorman, Brian Cummings, Catherine Evans, Shazia Jagot, Erica Sheen, and JT Welsch for their assistance at key moments in the progress of this project. In the Department of Art History, I am extremely thankful to Michael White for reading parts of my early manuscript, and for his advice on how to best incorporate images into the later and final versions. In the English Office, I must thank Naomi Myers, Anne Chantry, and Nicola Long, who, during my two stints as chair of the Board of Examiners, were always understanding of my work as a researcher and helped me make time in a very busy administrative schedule. Many thanks also to Cathy Moore for purchasing the numerous books I needed for this project, but especially to Helen Barrett for not only obtaining the books but also for processing the numerous permission and copyright invoices for payment. The Library Team at York was absolutely wonderful, coping patiently with my many book requests during the COVID-19 pandemic. Special thanks go to Carmen in the Interlending Team, who was nothing short of extraordinary in dealing with my varied urgent requests as I prepared my final manuscript for publication. My thanks to the York community would not be complete if I did not express my gratitude for the many students who took my module, Modernism and Technology, over the years 2017-18, 2018-19, and 2019-20. Thank you for our inspiring conversations in seminars and office hours, and for rooting for this book to be written!

Further afield, I would like to thank colleagues at other institutions who have read drafts of book proposals and chapters, or helped me by asking the right sort of questions: in particular, I should like to thank William Chapman Sharpe, Victoria Bazin, Katrin Wehling-Giorgi, Rebecca Woods, and Ann-Marie Einhaus. I am also grateful to all the audiences to whom I have been able to present snippets of my research for this book: the Institute for Advanced Studies in the Humanities at the University of Edinburgh (2016); the History and Politics Doctoral Workshop Series at Università Cattolica del Sacro Cuore, Milan (2017); the British Association of Modernist Studies conference at the University of Birmingham (2017); the Technology and Imagination workshop at the Institute for the History and Philosophy of Science and Technology at the University of Toronto (2017); the Historicizing Modernism/Modernist Archives conference at the Norwegian Study Centre of the University of York (2018); the Modern School Research Seminar at the University of York (2018); and the Women and Transnational Modernism workshop at the Netherlands Research School for Literary Studies (2021). Among these audiences, I should like to add the group of students at Masaryk University in Brno, Czech Republic, who took my intensive module New Technologies and Modernist Literature in 2016. *Děkuji* to Filip Krajník, who kindly invited me to Brno on that occasion and supported me with the Czech material for this project, sometimes generously posting me books that I could not easily access in the United Kingdom. I am grateful, too, to the History of Technology Reading Group at the University of Leeds, and especially to Graeme Gooday and Daniel Pérez Zapico for making me feel welcome, even as a non-historian!

This project found a welcoming home and nurturing environment at Johns Hopkins University. I would like to thank Douglas Mao for his patience, guidance, and dedication to this project. I could not have wished for a more sensitive and attentive reader in the lead-up to the submission of my full manuscript for peer review, or as I was preparing the final version of my manuscript. I am deeply grateful to Doug for helping me shape this work into its current form, as well as for allocating research funds from Johns Hopkins University to partially subsidize the numerous illustrations you will find in this book. I am also extremely thankful to the anonymous readers for their generous and insightful comments in the final editing stages of the manuscript. At Johns Hopkins University Press, I would like to give a warm thank-you to my editor, Matthew McAdam, and his acquisitions assistant, Adriahna Conway, whom it has been a real pleasure to work with, and who have helped behind the scenes.

This book would be very different without its many illustrations, so I would like to record my thanks to the various librarians, archivists, and international institutions that have either kindly supplied me with high-resolution images or have helped me clear permission to republish those images. These include: the Cecil Beaton Archive at Condé Nast; the National Gallery of Art; the Metropolitan Museum of Art; the State Library of Victoria; Musée Carnavalet; the Centre Pompidou; the New-York Historical Society; Bibliothèque nationale de France; the Beinecke Rare Book and Manuscript Library, Yale University; the Detroit Institute of Arts; the New York Public Library; the Princeton University Art Museum; the Library of Congress Prints and Photographs Division; the Virginia Museum of Fine Arts; the James Van Der Zee Archive at the Metropolitan Musem of Art; the Museum of Modern Art; Biblioteca Nazionale Centrale; Amgueddfa Cymru / National Museum of Wales; Fototeca Gilardi; the Philadelphia Museum of Art; Museo Thyssen-Bornemisza; the Minneapolis Institute of Art; Fisk University Galleries and Crystal Bridges Museum of American Art; Marina Giorgini; Alena Pomajzlová; Francesca Barbi Marinetti; Roger Conover; Philippe Garcelon; Elena Gigli and Archivio Gigli di Giacomo Balla; and Luca and Cristina Fornari.

I gratefully acknowledge permission to reprint the following works, in whole or in part:

"Street Lamps in Early Spring" (1926) by Gwendolyn B. Bennett, copyright © NYPL, reprinted by permission of the Manuscripts, Archives, and Rare Books Division at the Schomburg Center for Research in Black Culture, the New York Public Library.

"Nocturne" and "Rhapsody on a Windy Night" from *The Poems of T. S. Eliot Volume I: Collected and Uncollected Poems*, by T. S. Eliot, edited by Christopher Ricks and Jim McCue, copyright © 2015 by Faber and Faber Ltd.

"Spring and All: XIV" ("Death the Barber") and "The Great Figure" from *The Collected Poems of William Carlos Williams: Volume I 1909-1939* by William Carlos Williams, edited by Walton Litz and Christopher MacGowan, copyright © 1938 by New Directions Publishing Corp., reprinted by permission of New Directions Publishing Corp. for North America and Carcanet Press for the United Kingdom and Commonwealth.

I am grateful to the Department of English and Related Literature at the University of York and to Johns Hopkins University for covering permissions costs.

Finally, none of this would have been possible without the never-failing support of my friends and family, who were there for me as I was writing this book. I am particularly grateful to Andrea Bellini, Francesca Bratton, Poppy Cullen, Kit Fan, Juliana Mensah, Pauline Trouillard, and Lydia Zeldenrust. Heartfelt thanks go to my extended family in Slovenia, who pushed me to reach the finish line: Cvetka and Zdravko Jakovac, Anja and Miha Jakovac, and little Živa, *hvala lepa*. *Grazie di cuore* to my parents, Gabriella Manconi and Fabrizio Asciuto, for always being my warmest fans. I owe the biggest debt of gratitude to my husband, Gašper Jakovac, without whose backing, patience, and eagle-eyed reading skills this book simply would not have seen the light of day. Thank you for being there for me, reading my numerous drafts, and always being ready to chat about my Brilliant Modernists. But thanks especially for enabling me to finish this book at a time in which we were both navigating parenthood, ill health, and living overseas. I dedicate this book to you and to our son, Leone, whose instinctive love of lights and streetlamps was an inspiring force through my final months of writing.

Notes

Introduction

1. Pound, *Selected Prose: 1909-1965*, 107. The section of "Patria Mia" from which this sentence is extracted was originally published in *The New Age* (September 19, 1912), 491-492.

2. On the kind of light bulb used by Cecil Beaton for this photograph, see Lewis, *Isms: Understanding Photography*, 47.

3. Somerville, "Camera Artist: The Portraiture of Cecil Beaton," 69; Muir, *Cecil Beaton's Bright Young Things*, 31.

4. Muir, *Cecil Beaton's Bright Young Things*, 31-32.

5. Photographing the Bright Young Things gave Beaton a chance to "experiment with lighting, props, poses, and background"; Somerville, "Camera Artist: The Portraiture of Cecil Beaton," 69.

6. Beaton, *The Book of Beauty*, 34.

7. Muir, *Cecil Beaton's Bright Young Things*, 11.

8. Edison's subsequent experiments with a light bulb lasted for more than forty hours. Schivelbusch, *Disenchanted Night*, 58; French, *When They Hid the Fire*, 94. Nye, *American Illuminations*, 59; Bazerman, *Languages of Edison's Light*, 179; Barnaby, *Light Touches*, 136. In the most recent biography of Edison, Edmund Morris also marks the beginning of 1880 as the start of Edison's lighting business enterprise, following the successful experiments of autumn and winter 1879; see Morris, *Edison*, 361. In this first successful experiment, taking place in Edison's laboratories at Menlo Park, New Jersey, the electric light shone bright and uninterrupted for over thirteen hours, an important benchmark in the rush to perfect incandescent electricity for lighting purposes. Freeberg, *The Age of Edison*, 2-3.

9. Freeberg, *The Age of Edison*, 62.

10. Luckiesh, *Artificial Light*, 116-125; Gibson, *The Romance of Modern Electricity*, 184; Munro, *The Romance of Electricity*, 278. For more on arc lighting and its use, see: Hannah, *Electricity before Nationalisation*; Munro, *Electricity and Its Uses*.

11. Nye, *Technology Matters*, 5.

12. I am indebted here to the concept of thick description (and the example of the stratified meanings of a wink) as it was first theorized by anthropologist Clifford Geertz; see *The Interpretation of Cultures*, 6-7.

13. Nye, *Technology Matters*, 2-3.

14. Unfortunately, not much is known of Alfred Lee, the second author cited on the music score. For Frank W. Green, whose pantomimes were regularly attended by Lewis Carroll, see Foulkes, "Lewis Carroll, E. L. Blanchard and Frank W. Green," in Davis, *Victorian Pantomime*, 62.

15. Green and Lee, *The New Electric Light*.

16. Schlör, *Nights in the Big City*, 68-69.

17. Caledoniensis, *Gas and the Electric Light*, 4.

18. Otter, *The Victorian Eye*, 261.

19. Walkowitz, *City of Dreadful Delight*, 1, 230; Nead, *Victorian Babylon*, 83-84; Benjamin, "On Some Motifs in Baudelaire," 167, 170.

20. Sharpe, *New York Nocturne*, 9.

21. Woolf, "Character in Fiction," 421.

22. Jones, *Imagist Poetry*, 48 (line 4).

23. For reasons of space and focus, this book does not consider moonlight as the expression of a parallel musical phenomenon, beginning with the Romantics and Ludwig van Beethoven and continuing right up to Claude Debussy and Gabriel Fauré. For an interesting recent take on the impact of Beethoven's moonlight sonata on literary modernism, see Waddell, *Moonlighting*.

24. Dale, *Poems of Jules Laforgue*, 206-207. Ronald Schuchard, too, uses this term from Laforgue very briefly in his discussion of Eliot's early Symbolist-inflected poems; see *Eliot's Dark Angel*, 77-79.

25. Laforgue, "Clair de lune" ("Moonlight"), in *L'Imitation de Notre-Dame la Lune*, 22 (lines 3-4). My translation.

26. Loy, *The Lost Lunar Baedeker*, 81 (line 47); Cunard, *Selected Poems*, 9 (line 11).

27. Mirrlees, *Collected Poems*, 16 (lines 414-415).

28. Cunard, *Selected Poems*, "Ballad of 5 Rue de l'Etoile," 45 (line 42).

29. Yeats, "A General Introduction for My Work," 526.

30. Scappettone, *Killing the Moonlight*, 10.

31. Seifert, *On the Waves of TSF. Na vlnách TSF*, 42.

32. Salinas, *Poesías complétas*, 147. My translation.

33. Wosk, *Women and the Machine*, 88; Gooday, *Domesticating Electricity*, 1-6.

34. See Steen, "Die 'fée electricité' trifft Prometheus."

35. Marvin, *When Old Technologies Were New*, 30.

36. Hardy, *Diaries*, 26.

37. Stevenson, "A Plea for Gas Lamps," 259.

38. Stevenson, "A Plea for Gas Lamps," 258.

39. Stevenson, "A Plea for Gas Lamps," 262.

40. For more on the reception of electric light and electricity in the latter half of the nineteenth century, see Simon, *Dark Light*, 70-95; Gooday, *Domesticating Electricity*, 61-89.

41. For more on some of the qualitative differences between gas and electric light, see Otter, *The Victorian Eye*, 173-213, and Schivelbusch, *Disenchanted Night*, 15-78.

42. Stevenson, "A Plea for Gas Lamps," 261.

43. Marinetti, *Teoria e invenzione futurista*, 31. English translation: Rainey, Poggi, and Wittman, *Futurism*, 47.

44. Marinetti, *Teoria e invenzione futurista*, 30; Rainey, Poggi, and Wittman, *Futurism*, 47.

45. Scappettone, *Killing the Moonlight*, 10-11.

46. Moody, *Ezra Pound: Poet*, xiv.

47. Indeed, Pound told his friend Margaret Cravens that after this long spell abroad America "seems strange to my eyes that have grown more European than I knew—strange but not so unpleasant as I expected," Moody, *Ezra Pound: Poet*, 127.

48. Pound, *Selected Prose*, 107.

49. Bensaude-Vincent and Newman, "The Artificial and the Natural: State of the Problem," in *The Artificial and the Natural*, 18; Mumford, *Technics and Civilization*, 367.

50. de Maupassant, "La nuit (cauchemar)," 307. This story was first published in the periodical *Gil Blas* (IX, no. 2765, June 14, 1887) but subsequently placed as the last piece of de Maupassant's fittingly titled collection *Clair de lune* (second edition, 1888). The English translation of this passage is taken from Benjamin, *The Arcades Project*, 570.

51. The French term *clair de lune* is clearly suggestive of the nineteenth-century poetic and musical tradition, from Verlaine to Debussy. Marinetti, *Le Futurisme*, 170; English translation: Rainey, Poggi, and Wittman, *Futurism*, 59.

52. Luckiesh, *Lighting the Home*, caption to plate I, frontispiece.

53. Luckiesh, *Lighting the Home*, 280.

54. Mumford, *Technics and Civilization*, 371. Throughout this book, ellipses in square brackets are used to indicate an omission in quoted material. Ellipses that are not bracketed appear in the original source text.

55. Adorno, *Aesthetic Theory*, 62.

56. Adorno, *Aesthetic Theory*, 62.

57. Adorno, *Aesthetic Theory*, 62.

58. Toomer, *The Wayward and the Seeking*, 43.

59. Emerson, *Essays, Poems, Addresses*, 235.

60. Woolf, *A Room of One's Own and Three Guineas*, 13-14.

61. Bachelard, *The Flame of a Candle*, 1-2.

62. Bachelard, *The Flame of a Candle*, 63-64.

63. Kenner, *The Mechanic Muse*, 14. Later scholars of American modernism and of Italian Futurism in particular, including Cecelia Tichi, Lisa M. Steinman, and Günter Berghaus, noted the typically technological imagination of early twentieth-century writers.

64. See Armstrong, *Modernism, Technology, and the Body*; Trotter, *Literature in the First Media Age*, and *The Literature of Connection*; Goody, *Technology, Literature, and Culture*, and *Modernist Poetry, Gender and Leisure Technologies*.

65. Goody, *Technology, Literature, and Culture*, 2-7.

66. See McCabe, *Cinematic Modernism*; Perlow, *The Poem Electric*; Allen, *Modernist Invention*.

67. Elcott, *Artificial Darkness*, 1-16; Bach and Degenring, "Introduction: Dark Nights, Bright Lights," 6.

68. Brevda, *Signs of the Signs*; Leahy, *Literary Illumination*, 190.

69. See Nead, *Victorian Babylon*, and *The Haunted Gallery*.

70. See Flint, *The Victorians and the Visual Imagination*, and *Flash! Photography, Writing, and Surprising Illumination*.

71. Sharpe, *New York Nocturne*, 4.

72. Geertz, *The Interpretation of Cultures*, 3-32.

73. Stephen Greenblatt and Catherine Gallagher have famously identified a connection between historicist research and the "broadening of the field" to recover previously neglected authors—especially women—in their introduction to *Practicing New Historicism*, 10-11.

74. Mao and Walkowitz, "The New Modernist Studies," 737-738.

75. See, among others, Mao and Walkowitz, "The New Modernist Studies," 738-739; Sonita Sarker, "Absence and Containment"; see also Stanford Friedman, "Planetarity," 471-499.

76. Saint-Amour, "Weak Theory, Weak Modernism," 453.

77. Mao, "Introduction: The New Modernist Studies," 2. See also Mao and Walkowitz, "Introduction: Modernisms Bad and New," 1-2.

78. Feldman, "Introduction to Historicizing Modernists: Approaches to 'Archivalism,'" 4. This digital turn in the archives of modernism enabled and permitted this book's historicizing efforts, even more so during the difficult time of the COVID-19 pandemic.

79. Kenner, *The Mechanic Muse*, 19.

Chapter 1. Observing Light

1. Eliot, "What France Means to You," trans. Iman Javadi, in *The Complete Prose of T. S. Eliot: The Critical Edition: The War Years, 1940-1946: Volume 6*, 12, 514.

2. On the debate about Eliot's itinerary on his first trip to Europe see *The Com-*

plete Prose of T. S. Eliot: The Critical Edition: The War Years, 1940-1946: Volume 6, 515; Hargrove, *T. S. Eliot's Parisian Year*, 9; Crawford, *Young Eliot*, 145.

3. Only a few months earlier, his mother, Charlotte Champe Stearns Eliot, had expressed typical maternal reservations on her youngest son's journey to France. Eliot's original letter is lost, as is all his correspondence from Milton Academy, Harvard, and Paris, but Mrs. Eliot's reply makes it clear not only that he had he expressed a desire to go to Paris but that this was linked to the fulfillment of his literary ambitions: "I have rather hoped you would not specialize later on French literature. [. . .] I cannot bear to think of your being alone in Paris, the very words give me a chill. English speaking countries seem so different from foreign. I do not admire the French nation, and have less confidence in individuals of that race than in English," letter from Charlotte Eliot to T. S. Eliot, April 3, 1910, in *The Letters of T. S. Eliot: Volume 1, 1898-1922*, 11-12.

4. The list could very easily continue and fill several pages, with more poems by Paul Verlaine ("Croquis Parisien" ["Sketch of Paris"], "La lune blanche" ["White Moon"], "Impression fausse" ("False Impression"), part IV of "Soleil et chair" ("Sun and Skin") by Arthur Rimbaud, and Stéphane Mallarmé's "Apparition" ("Apparition"). Moonlight, or *clair de lune*, was certainly a recurring trope in much French poetry of the nineteenth century (think only of Théophile Gautier's poems "Clair de lune sentimental" ["Sentimental Moonlight"] and "La lune" ["The Moon"], and Victor Hugo's "Clair de lune" ["Moonlight"]). For more on French Symbolism, see Lehmann, *The Symbolist Aesthetic in France, 1885-1895*, Peyre, *Qu'est-ce que le symbolisme?*, and Cándida Smith, *Mallarmé's Children*.

5. Sharpe, *New York Nocturne*, 81.

6. Sharpe, *New York Nocturne*, 86. That Decadent poets relied on moonlight as a source of inspiration is clear from again the poetry of Jules Laforgue but also Oscar Wilde's *Salomé* (1891), discussed later in this chapter, and Ernest Dowson's *The Pierrot of the Minute* (1897).

7. Eliot, *Fireside* 1, no. 2 (January 29, 1898), 5, 11, in MS Am 1635.5 "T. S. Eliot's Juvenilia," Houghton Library, Harvard University.

8. Crawford, *Young Eliot*, 56.

9. Hargrove, *T. S. Eliot's Parisian Year*, 6. "I remember getting hold of Laforgue years ago at Harvard, purely through reading Symons, and then sending to Paris for the texts," in a letter to Robert Nichols, August 8, 1917, in *The Letters of T. S. Eliot: Volume 1*, 212. Eliot further glosses his relationship to Arthur Symons's book in his 1930 review of Peter Quennell's book *Baudelaire and the Symbolists*, saying: "I myself owe Mr. Symons a great debt: but for having read his book, I should not, in the year 1908, have heard of Laforgue or Rimbaud; I should probably not have begun to read Verlaine; and but for reading Verlaine, I should not have heard of Corbière," in *The Complete Prose: Volume 4*, 11-14. For a fuller account of the influence of French poetry on Eliot, see Romer, "French Poetry," in *T. S. Eliot in Context*, 211-220;

for a detailed account of the influence of Jules Laforgue on young Eliot, see Soldo, "T. S. Eliot and Jules LaForgue," 137-150, and *The Tempering of T. S. Eliot*.

10. T. S. Eliot and Donald Hall, "T. S. Eliot, The Art of Poetry No. 1," *Paris Review*, issue 21 (Spring-Summer 1959), accessed October 6, 2020, https://www.theparisreview.org/interviews/4738/the-art-of-poetry-no-1-t-s-eliot. The bookshop Eliot refers to may well have been Schoenhof's Foreign Books, which used to be in Cambridge rather than Boston, selling foreign books at 76 Mt. Auburn St. from 1856 to 2017. Alison W. Steinbach and Katherine E. Wang, "Schoenhof's Foreign Books to Close Brick-and-Mortar Store," *Harvard Crimson*, February 22, 2017, https://www.thecrimson.com/article/2017/2/22/schoenhofs-books-closing/. In *Eliot's Dark Angel*, Ronald Schuchard is certain Eliot purchased his copy of Laforgue at Schoenhof's (70).

11. Eliot, "What France Means to You," in *The Complete Prose of T. S. Eliot: The Critical Edition: The War Years, 1940-1946: Volume 6*, 512-514.

12. Eliot and Hall, "T. S. Eliot, The Art of Poetry No. 1."

13. Eliot and Hall, "T. S. Eliot, The Art of Poetry No. 1."

14. Marx, "Paris," 27.

15. Hargrove, *T. S. Eliot's Parisian Year*, 33.

16. Marx, "Paris," 27.

17. McAlmon and Boyle, *Being Geniuses Together, 1920-1930*, 7.

18. Hargrove, *T. S. Eliot's Parisian Year*, 14, 30.

19. Eliot, "A Commentary" (April 1934), in *The Complete Prose of T. S. Eliot: The Critical Edition: Tradition and Orthodoxy, 1934-39: Volume 5*, 81.

20. Eliot, "What France Means to You," trans. Iman Javadi, in *The Complete Prose of T. S. Eliot: The Critical Edition: The War Years, 1940-1946: Volume 6*, 512, 514.

21. Blühm and Lippincott, *Light!: The Industrial Age 1750-1900*, 182; Nye, "The Artificial Lighting Available to European and American Museums, 1800-1915," 39; Holcombe, "The Electric Lighting System of Paris," 122; Downie, *Paris, Paris*, 215. For more on gaslight in Paris during the nineteenth century, see Bressani, "Paris—Light into Darkness: Gaslight in Nineteenth-Century Paris," 28-36. For more on electrification in France, see Beltran and Carré, *La fée et la servante*.

22. Clayson, "Bright Lights, Brilliant Wits," 32.

23. Apollinaire, *Alcools suivi de Le Bestiaire illustré par Raoul Dufy et de Vitam impendere amori*, 31. My translation.

24. Hargrove, *T. S. Eliot's Parisian Year*, 72.

25. Thacker, *Modernism, Space and the City*, 30-31.

26. Downie, *Paris, Paris*, 263, 314. Historian Chris Otter has convincingly argued that the "nineteenth century is the history [. . .] of the proliferation, concatenation, and spatial juxtaposition of multiple light forms," in *The Victorian Eye*, 261.

27. I have been able to trace two instances in his early work: in part II of the unfinished prose poem "The Engine," the rather vanguardistically titled "Machinery: Dancers" (1915), the speaker "switched on the light" (*P* 274, line 5), the use of the verb "to switch on" entering the English language in the 1880s, signaling that the light is electric and operated by a "switch" (*Oxford English Dictionary*, https://www.oed.com); a letter from London, dated October 31, 1920, where Eliot very mundanely complains to his mother about taking a flat over from an "old spinster," who "maliciously had the electricity, gas, and telephone cut off," in *The Letters of T. S. Eliot: Volume 1, 1898–1922*, 515. For more on light in T. S. Eliot's poetry, see Asciuto, "The Sun Also Sets," and "Light and Mystical Writing."

28. Kenner, *The Mechanic Muse*, 19.

29. Keegan, "Emily of Fire & Violence."

30. Kennedy, *T. S. Eliot and the Dynamic Imagination*, 149. Letter to John Hayward, dated September 7, 1942, HB/V/12, The Hayward Bequest, King's College Archives, University of Cambridge. The passage referred to here has also been published in Gardner, *The Composition of* Four Quartets, 177.

31. Compare usage of the more modern "streetlights" in contemporary English with "streetlamp," often referring to older types of lamps (i.e., gas), and "lantern" now used more evocatively, as it represents an obsolete lighting technology, see *Oxford English Dictionary*, accessed January 29, 2021, https://www.oed.com.

32. Letter to John Hayward, dated September 9, 1942, HB/V/12, The Hayward Bequest, King's College Archives, University of Cambridge; also published in Gardner, *The Composition of* Four Quartets, 178.

33. Gardner, *The Composition of* Four Quartets, 178.

34. The poem, while written in Paris in 1910–11, was first published in *Blast* in 1915; *The Poems of T. S. Eliot: Volume I: Collected and Uncollected Poems*, 18. Further references to Eliot's poems are from this edition and will be indicated in parentheses in the text.

35. Eliot and Hall, "The Art of Poetry No. 1."

36. Wilde, *Poems*, 85 (lines 13–16).

37. Baudelaire, *The Painter of Modern Life*, 15.

38. *Larousse Dictionnaire de Français*, accessed February 6, 2019, https://www.larousse.fr/dictionnaires/francais; *Oxford English Dictionary*, accessed October 15, 2020, https://www.oed.com.

39. Thacker, *Modernism, Space, and the City*, 29; Brooker, "Seduction and Disenchantment," 29.

40. Childs, "Rhapsody of Matter and Memory"; Yang, "Rhapsody on a City of Dreadful Night," 9.

41. It is worth remembering that different lighting technologies did not only impact the eye but also the ear, as they could produce different types of noises. According to Chris Otter, gas and argand burners made "singing noises," closer to

human voices, while early arc light produced a buzzing sound, and incandescent electric light was silent; see Otter, *The Victorian Eye*, 206. Jewel Spears Brooker in passing identifies Eliot's streetlamp as a gas lamp, in "Seduction and Disenchantment," 31.

42. Paccoud, "Planning, law, power, and practice," 341.

43. Harvey, *Paris, Capital of Modernity*, 96.

44. Carmona, *Haussmann*, 404.

45. Carmona, *Haussmann*, 404.

46. Carmona, *Haussmann*, 404; Harvey, *Paris, Capital of Modernity*, 275.

47. Baudelaire, *Le spleen de Paris or Les cinquante petits poèmes en prose de Charles Baudelaire*, 84–85; English translation: Baudelaire, *Paris Spleen*, 52.

48. Berman, *All That Is Solid Melts into Air*, 152.

49. Kennel, "Charles Marville, Hidden in Plain Sight," 10; Rice, *Parisian Views*, 85.

50. de Thézy, *Marville*, 21. In 1862, the French architect Victor Baltard would write to his colleague Constant Dufeux, who had introduced him to Marville's work, that the French photographer was a master in "cette ingénieuse pratique qui nous fait saisir les défauts et comprendre les mérites de certaines œuvres devant lesquelles nous étions passés indifférents et de nos œuvres mêmes en nous les présentant sous un nouvel aspect" (this ingenious practice which makes us notice the flaws and understand the merits of certain works we had been passing by indifferently, as well as of our own works which are presented to us in a new light [my translation]), letter dated October 23, 1862, qtd. in de Thézy, *Marville*, 18.

51. de Wolf, "Paris on Display," 219.

52. Kennel, "Charles Marville," 37; the lamps were designed by the French architect Jean-Antoine-Gabriel Davioud, see Carmona, *Haussmann*, 405.

53. Downie remarks how "Haussmann-style streetlamps" are still being produced today so that Paris can retain its "warm, and welcoming [atmosphere] infused with nostalgia," in *Paris, Paris*, 216.

54. Rice, *Parisian Views*, 88; de Thézy, *Marville*, 207.

55. Kennel, "Charles Marville," 37.

56. Clayson, *Illuminated Paris*, 18.

57. Rice, *Parisian Views*, 96.

58. Dyer, "On Atget," 31.

59. Dyer, "On Atget," 33.

60. Clayson, *Illuminated Paris*, 7.

61. Blake, *George Augustus Sala*, 1, 51, 81, 260. Sala's book on Paris, *Paris Herself Again in 1878-9* (1880) was extremely popular at the time, "still remembered a generation after it was published," and mentioned in *The Old Wives' Tale* (1908) by Arnold Bennett, who overlapped with Eliot in Paris, see Edwards, *Dickens's "Young Men,"* 108; "The articles which George Augustus Sala wrote under the title 'Paris Herself Again' ought to have been paid for in gold by the hotel and pension-keepers

of Paris. They awakened the English curiosity and the desire to witness the scene of terrible events. Their effect was immediately noticeable," in Bennett, *The Old Wives' Tale*, 416.

62. *Punch*, July 8, 1882, qtd. in Blake, *George Augustus Sala*, 3.

63. Nead, *Victorian Babylon*, 108.

64. Blake, *George Augustus Sala*, 82; Nead, *Victorian Bablyon*, 108.

65. Sala, "The Secrets of the Gas," from *Gaslight and Daylight*, 156.

66. Sala, "The Secrets of the Gas," 159.

67. Schlör, *Nights in the Big City*, 68-69.

68. Delattre, *Les douze heures noires*, 91.

69. Schlör, *Nights in the Big City*, 76.

70. Nead, *Victorian Babylon*, 83.

71. Letter from T. S. Eliot to Conrad Aiken, December 31, 1914, in *The Letters of T. S. Eliot: Volume 1, 1898-1922*, 82.

72. Brooker, "Mimetic Desire and the Return to Origins in *The Waste Land*," 137.

73. Eliot, "Talk on Dante [What Dante Means to Me]," in *The Complete Prose of T. S. Eliot: The Critical Edition: A European Society, 1947-1953: Volume 7*, 483.

74. Baudelaire, *The Flowers of Evil*, 192-193. Laforgue, too, remembers this precise line of "Le Crépuscule de soir" when reflecting on the "damned" Baudelaire and his depiction of life in the city of Paris; see Laforgue, "Notes sur Baudelaire," from *Œuvres Complètes: Mélanges Posthumes*, 111.

75. Bachelard, *The Flame of a Candle*, 66.

76. Schlör, *Nights in the Big City*, 206.

77. Blaschko, *Die Prositution im 19. Jahrhundert*, 38, as quoted in Schlör, *Nights in the Big City*, 226.

78. Eliot, *The Poems of T. S. Eliot: Volume II: Practical Cats & Further Verses*, 316.

79. Childs, *Modernism and Eugenics,* 123.

80. Schlör, *Nights in the Big City*, 204; Walkowitz, *City of Dreadful Delight*, 1. Walkowitz returns to this trope of gaslight and Victorian streets when discussing the "Yorkshire Ripper" (230).

81. Bachelard, *The Flame of a Candle*, 10.

82. Schlör, *Nights in the Big City*, 239, 247.

83. Benjamin, *Charles Baudelaire,* 50.

84. "I am not I, but rather the street, the lampposts," from Döblin, "An Romanautoren und ihre Kritiker: Berliner Programm," 18. My translation.

85. Brooker, "Seduction and Disenchantment," 29; Beasley, *Theorists of Modernist Poetry*, 42.

86. Bachelard, *The Flame of a Candle*, 69.

87. Bachelard, *The Flame of a Candle*, 29-30.

88. Untermeyer, "New Poetry," qtd. in Lockerd, *Decadent Catholicism*, 76.

89. For more on Eliot and Oscar Wilde, see Bush, "In Pursuit of Wilde Possum,"

469-485, and Riquelme, "T. S. Eliot's Ambiviolences," 353-379. For an account of
Eliot's decadence see Schuchard, *Eliot's Dark Angel*, and Sherry, *Modernism and the
Reinvention of Decadence*. For a detailed comparison of Aubrey Beardsley's and Eliot's
"Decadent Catholicism," see Lockerd, "'A Satirist of Vice and Follies': Beardsley,
Eliot, and Images of Decadent Catholicism," 143-165, and *Decadent Catholicism and
the Making of Modernism*. For a succinct consideration of Decadent influences on
Eliot, see Boyiopoulos, *The Decadent Image*, 182-190. For a more recent account of
Modernism's (but not Eliot's) broader engagement with Decadence, see *Decadence
in the Age of Modernism*, eds. Kate Hext and Alex Murray.

90. Romer, "French Poetry," 215.

91. Dale, *Poems of Jules Laforgue*, 206-207.

92. Villiers de l'Isle-Adam, qtd. in Symons, *The Symbolist Movement in Literature*,
114. According to Schuchard, the moon for Laforgue also represents "the Uncon-
scious," in *Eliot's Dark Angel*, 77.

93. Grojnowski, "Sur quelques comptes rendus oubliés des 'Complaintes' et de
'L'imitation de Notre-Dame la Lune' de Jules Laforgue,", 112. My translation.

94. Schuchard, *Eliot's Dark Angel*, 77.

95. Corbière, *Selected Poems and Prose*, 44-45.

96. Schuchard, *Eliot's Dark Angel*, 77.

97. Yeats shows a deep interest in the astrological and esoteric meanings of
the moon as apparent in "The Phases of the Moon" (published in *The Wild Swans
at Coole*, 1919), among others, and makes use of more ancient, traditional lunar
imagery (e.g., "The purity of the unclouded moon / Has flung its arrowy shaft upon
the floor," in "Blood and the Moon" [1928], published in *The Winding Stair* [1929]);
Yeats, *Collected Poems*, 158-162 and 244-246.

98. Yeats, *Collected Poems*, 76.

99. Moody, *Thomas Stearns Eliot: Poet*, 18-19; the retelling is entitled "Hamlet,
ou les suites de la piété filiale" and is part of *Moralités Légendaires* (*Moral Tales*).
Schuchard, *Eliot's Dark Angel*, 78; Soldo, "T. S. Eliot and Jules LaForgue," 142-143.

100. Moody, *Thomas Stearns Eliot*, 18; Laforgue, *Moralité Légendaires*, 71. The
English translation is from Laforgue, *Moral Tales*, 41.

101. I am grateful to Dr. Trev Broughton for this second reading of the poem.

102. Laforgue, *Poems*, 256-257.

103. Nead, *The Haunted Gallery*, 209. For a brief account of moon voyages in
science fiction and photographs, see also Taunton, "Moon Voyaging, Selenography,
and the Scientific Romance."

104. Whitfield, *Mapping the Heavens*, 167; Nead, *The Haunted Gallery*, 211.

105. Nead, *The Haunted Gallery*, 211.

106. Whitfield, *Mapping the Heavens*, 177. Flammarion's titles ranged from pop-
ularizing texts for a general audience (*Études et lectures sur l'astronomie*, 1866-1880;
Astronomie Populaire, 1880), books to educate women in astronomy (*Astronomie des*

dames, 1903), books on spiritualism (*La Mort et son mystère*, 1920-22), and even science fiction (*La fin du monde*, 1893). Some of his most popular titles were also translated into several languages, including Italian, Spanish, Hebrew, and Czech, and English titles such as *Popular Astronomy* (1894) and *Astronomy for Amateurs* (1903) were extremely popular in the Anglophone world. (NB: *Astronomy for Amateurs* had been published in French as *Astronomie des dames*, "Astronomy for Women").

107. Nead, *The Haunted Gallery*, 221, 223. The exact tricks and light plays are explained in detail, along with some evocative accompanying illustrations, in Hopkins, "A Trip to the Moon," *Magic*, 348-353.

108. "Systematic Photographic Map of the Moon, Increasing and Decreasing Phases," Metropolitan Museum of Art, accessed November 2, 2020, https://www .metmuseum.org/art/collection/search/705881.

109. "Systematic Photographic Map of the Moon, Increasing and Decreasing Phases," Metropolitan Museum of Art, accessed November 2, 2020, https://www .metmuseum.org/art/collection/search/705881.

110. These maps are believed to be the inspiration for Dunkin's *The Midnight Sky over London* (1879). Whitfield, *Mapping the Heavens*, 176.

111. Ebury, "Eliot's Cosmology," 143.

112. Eliot, *Fireside* 1, nos. 13-14. For more on *Fireside*, but not on this particular short narrative by young Eliot, see Soldo, "Jovial Juvenilia," 25-37.

113. I have checked the sky from both Paris and Boston for all dates of August 1910 by using the interactive planetarium Your Sky, available here: https://www .fourmilab.ch/yoursky/.

114. "O Moon the blest / Of sleepless rest, / White medallion / Of Endymion," *Poems of Jules Laforgue*, 192-193.

115. Ebury, "Eliot's Cosmology," 143, 145.

116. Peter Dale, "Introduction," *Poems of Jules Laforgue*, 19.

117. Flammarion, *Astronomie des dames*, 268. Flammarion, *Astronomy for Amateurs*, 235.

118. Janes, *Oscar Wilde Prefigured*, 212, 214; Snodgrass, *Aubrey Beardsley*, 276. Interestingly, Aymer Vallance, who compiled an early list of all drawings by Beardsley, indicated the title of the *Salomé* illustration *The Woman in the Moon* as *The Woman (or Man) in the Moon*, hinting at the illustration's ambiguous representation of the moon as well as the conventional trope of the "Man in the Moon"; see Ross, *Aubrey Beardsley, with Sixteen Full-Page Illustrations and a Revised Iconography by Aymer Vallance*, 88.

119. In *Aubrey Beardsley*, Snodgrass suggests it is an "inverted rose-gem" or perhaps, in tune with the Wildean association, "a green carnation" (282).

120. Wilde, *Salomé: Drame en un acte*, 9. English translation from Wilde, *Salomé: A Tragedy in One Act: Translated from the French of Oscar Wilde*, 11.

121. Georges Méliès's films got immediately pirated, and on the back of this

the French film director had even to open an office in New York to monitor and legalize the US distribution of his films; see Solomon, "Negotiating the Bounds of Transnational Cinema with Georges Méliès, 1896-1908," 159-160. David Trotter, in "T. S. Eliot and Cinema" (*Modernism/modernity* 13, no. 2, 2006), does not consider Georges Méliès as a possible influence on T. S. Eliot and neither does Susan McCabe in *Cinematic Modernism*. Nancy Hargrove also does not mention the French film director in her two-page section on Parisian cinema in *T. S. Eliot's Parisian Year*. Scholars of modernism have, however, often compared Méliès's early cinematic experiments with James Joyce's narrative, such as Hanaway-Oakley's chapter "Machine-Humans and Body-Subjects" in *James Joyce and the Phenomenology of Film*; Baron, "Flaubert, Joyce"; Marco Camerani, *Joyce e il cinema delle origini*. John Frazer was the first one to explore how the films of Georges Méliès could be considered as "progenitors of modernism," in "Cubism and the Cinema of Georges Méliès," 95.

122. For John Paul Riquelme, "*Salomé* had a particularly intense effect on Eliot," in "T. S. Eliot's Ambiviolences," 354; for Lockerd, Beardsley mostly influenced Eliot "through the medium of Wilde" with the *Salomé* illustrations, in *Decadent Catholicism and the Making of Modernism*, 80, 88.

123. Schuchard, *Eliot's Dark Angel*, 77.

124. Jones, *Imagist Poetry*, 48.

125. Christopher Ricks, in his notes to the new edition of T. S. Eliot's *Poems*, suggests an echo with T. E. Hulme's poem "Above the Dock," but this is published for the first time in 1912, while "Conversation Galante," if published in *Poetry* in 1916, was written in 1909 (*P* 447-448). Certainly, the moon-as-balloon image is strikingly similar but may be a confirmation that Imagist Hulme, too, reflects on this aesthetic shift and that perhaps he had not been so impermeable to the Futurist texts that had been circulating since 1909.

126. Lee Scrivner is one of the very few critics to dare to give us a brief discussion of Eliot and Marinetti together, as two insomnia-driven modernist poets, but for him the two are in sharp contrast with one another; see *Becoming Insomniac*, 10.

127. I am thinking here in particular of the much-quoted review essay by Eliot, "Reflections on Contemporary Poetry," published in the *Egoist* in 1919, in which he discusses "a feeling of profound kinship, or rather of a peculiar personal intimacy, with another, probably a dead author"; *The Complete Prose of T. S. Eliot: The Critical Edition: The Perfect Critic, 1919-1926: Volume 2*, 67.

Chapter 2. Killing the Moonlight

1. Marinetti, *Teoria e invenzione futurista*, 30; English translation from Rainey, Poggi, and Wittman, *Futurism*, 47. Further references to the translations in this anthology will be indicated as *F* and followed by page numbers.

2. Agnese, *Marinetti: Una vita esplosiva*, 74. My translation.

3. Salaris, *Storia del futurismo*, 13.

4. Marinetti, "Le Futurisme," *Le Figaro*, February 20, 1909, https://gallica.bnf .fr/ark:/12148/bpt6k2883730.item#. English translation from "The Founding and Manifesto of Futurism," *F* 51. On this occasion, I have edited Lawrence Rainey's translation so as to be closer to the original text (for close-reading purposes).

5. Niebisch, *Media Parasites in the Early Avant-Garde*, 22-23.

6. Perloff, "The Audacity of Hope," 15; Poggi, *Inventing Futurism*, 6; Salaris, *Storia del futurismo*, 14; Palazzeschi, "Marinetti e il Futurismo," in Marinetti, *Teoria e invenzione futurista*, vii.

7. d'Orlando, "Réflexions autour d'un astricide: Marinetti, poète mal luné," 143.

8. For more on the concept of avant-garde art and literature, see Poggioli, *The Theory of the Avant-Garde*, although a little dated; Bürger, *Theory of the Avant-Garde*. For more specifically on Futurism and its wider ramifications as an avant-garde movement, see Lista, *Le futurisme: Création et avantgarde*; White, *Literary Futurism*; Perloff, *The Futurist Moment*.

9. *Decadentismo* is the Italian variant of the Decadent movement, deriving from its French counterpart (*Décadence*); the most notable Italian Decadent poet was Gabriele D'Annunzio. For more on Decadentismo, see Binni, *La poetica del decadentismo* and Marzot, *Il decadentismo italiano*. *Simbolismo* is the Italian trans- lation of French *Symbolisme*, and Italian writers who show Symbolist influence in their works are Giovanni Pascoli and Gabriele D'Annunzio. *Crepuscolarismo* (from Italian *crepuscolo*, "twilight"; "Twilightism") was a literary sentiment more than an actual movement, specific to early twentieth-century Italy, concerned with the idea that Italian poetry was at its (albeit glorious) twilight. *Crepuscolari* detached themselves from the grand epics and sensual novels of Gabriele D'Annunzio and preferred a melancholic poetry of dusks and everyday life, although still formalistic. Peter Davidson rather more flourishingly describes them as "elegists for things lost and superseded in the modernizations of the new century, a group who would have wished only to prolong the lingering evening of the past" (in *The Last of the Light*, 38). A number of Crepuscular poets flowed into the Futurist movement, and a significant part of Marinetti's first Futurist anthology is still crepuscular in tones. For more on *Crepuscolarismo* and in particular its ties with Futurism, see Livi, *Tra crepuscolarismo e futurismo*. Salaris, *Storia del futurismo*, 14.

10. Apelian, "Modern Mosque Lamps," 187.

11. Apelian, "Modern Mosque Lamps," 188.

12. Poggi, *Inventing Futurism*, 7.

13. Perloff, "The Audacity of Hope," 15.

14. Berghaus, "Futurism and the Technological Imagination," 16; Colombo, *Milano si accende*, 27; Pasca, "Le forme della luce," 45, 46; Pavese, "Dalla luce ad arco alle lampade al sodio," 15, 20. It is worth noting here that the illumination

history of the city of Milan is similar to that of most other European cities when it comes to the superimposition of gas, arc, and electric (incandescent) lighting. Pasca explains how new gas lamps were installed in the streets of Milan up to 1922, while incandescent lamps began replacing both gas and arc lamps from 1911, in "Le forme della luce," 47.

15. Niebisch, *Media Parasites*, 23.

16. Poggi, *Inventing Futurism*, 7.

17. Berghaus, "Futurism and the Technological Imagination," 2; Pizzi, *Italian Futurism and the Machine*, 35.

18. Marinetti, *La grande Milano tradizionale e futurista*, 11. My translation.

19. Sartini Blum, "Transformations in the Futurist Technological Mythopoeia," 77.

20. Marinetti, "Le Futurisme," *Le Figaro*, February 20, 1909, https://gallica.bnf.fr/ark:/12148/bpt6k2883730.item#. Marinetti never acknowledges Morasso's debt on his theoretical writings, despite clear echoes and even though he published his essay "L'artigliere meccanico" in *Poesia* in 1906; see Berghaus, "Futurism and the Technological Imagination," 16; Pizzi, *Italian Futurism and the Machine*, 57.

21. Marinetti, "Le Futurisme," *Le Figaro*, February 20, 1909, https://gallica.bnf.fr/ark:/12148/bpt6k2883730.item#.

22. Pietropaolo, "Science and the Aesthetics of Geometric Splendour in Italian Futurism," 49.

23. Berghaus, "Futurism and the Technological Imagination," 22.

24. Berghaus, "Futurism and the Technological Imagination," 27.

25. Sartini Blum, "Transformations in the Futurist Technological Mythopoeia," 77-97.

26. The full title of the first edition of Marinetti's manifesto was "La rassegna internazionale Poesia pubblica questo proclama di guerra, come risposta agli insulti di cui la vecchia Europa ha gratificato il Futurismo trionfante" (in French: "La revue internationale Poesia publie cette proclamation de guerre en réponse aux insultes dont la vieille Europe a gratifié le Futurisme triomphant"; in English: "The international journal *Poesia* publishes this proclamation of war in response to the insults with which aged Europe has gratified triumphant Futurism"). The title "Let's Murder the Moonlight!!" would only be used to indicate this second manifesto/proclamation from its publication in French in instalments in *Poesia* no. 7, 8, and 9 (August, September, and October 1909), "Tuons le clair de lune!!," and in Italian afterward, published by *Poesia* as a separate pamphlet in 1911 with the title *Uccidiamo il chiaro di luna!!* For more on the publishing history of the Futurist manifestos, see Tonini, *I manifesti del Futurismo italiano*.

27. Marinetti, *Le Futurisme*, 169. Further references to this French edition will be indicated as *LF* and followed by page numbers. Rainey, Poggi, and Wittman, "Introduction to Part Three," *Futurism*, 412. The list of Marinetti's friends as it appears in the 1909 edition comprises Paolo Buzzi (1874-1956), Federico de Maria

(1885-1954), Enrico Cavacchioli (1885-1954), Corrado Govoni (1884-1965), and Libero Altomare (real name Remo Mannoni, 1883-1942). The list, however, changes according to the year and Marinetti's artistic allegiance. In the 1911 version, Marinetti adds the names of painters Umberto Boccioni (1882-1916), Carlo Carrà (1881-1966), Luigi Russolo (1885-1947), Giacomo Balla (1871-1958), and Gino Severini (1883-1966), who, according to art historian Maurizio Calvesi, would all paint their own take on Marinetti's manifesto. The only one to portray electric light's conquest of the night is, however, Balla's *Lampada ad arco* (Arc Lamp), discussed later in this chapter; see Calvesi, "Attraverso Marinetti," 18. In the 1914 version, for example, the list no longer includes Federico de Maria, who had meanwhile left the group, and has as new "friends" Aldo Palazzeschi (1885-1974), Luciano Folgore (real name Omero Vecchi, 1888-1966), Francesco Balilla Pratella (1880-1955), Auro D'Alba (1888-1965), and Armando Mazza (1884-1964); see Rainey, Poggi, and Wittman, *Futurism*, 6, 524.

28. The French term *clair de lune* is of course clearly suggestive of the nineteenth-century poetic and musical tradition, from Verlaine to Debussy.

29. See my discussion of noises made by gas and arc lighting, compared to the silence of incandescent electricity in the previous chapter; d'Orlando, "Réflexions autour d'un astricide," 147.

30. Shakespeare, *Romeo and Juliet*, Act 2, Scene 1, line 50, 379.

31. d'Orlando, "Réflexions autour d'un astricide," 147.

32. Poggi, *Inventing Futurism*, 12. Conti, "Marinetti in France between Symbolism and Futurism," 54. Marinetti's French poetry has been collected in the Italian edition *Scritti francesi*, ed. Pasquale A. Jannini. For more on the relationship between French Symbolism and select Futurist writers, please see Vinall, "Marinetti, Soffici, and French Literature," 15-38.

33. Panteo, *Il poeta Marinetti*, 15; Somigli, "The Poet and the Vampire," 572, 584. Luca Somigli's translation.

34. See, among others, Poggi, *Inventing Futurism*, 184-186, and Sartini Blum, *The Other Modernism*, 7.

35. Marinetti, *La ville charnelle*, 191. My translation.

36. "Soudain la lune blanche et juteuse de lumière, / éclatant en plein ciel / ainsi qu'une fabuleuse noix de coco, / oscille et roule sur le dos mouvant du dromadaire" (Suddenly the moon, white and juicy with light, / Cracking in the open sky / Like a fabulous coconut, / Swings and rolls on the moving back of a dromedary) from the poem "Mon âme est puérile" (My Soul is Puerile), and "O Lune verte, ô mystique araignée / dont les pattes laborieuses enlacent mes cordages, / souffre donc que je rende mon âme frénétique / sur la bouche en triangle!" (Oh green moon, oh mystical spider / whose laborious legs wrap cordage around me, / suffer so that I make my soul wild / on the triangle-shaped mouth), in Marinetti, *Destruction*, 28. My translation.

37. Marinetti, *Destruction*, 146-147. My translation.

38. Marinetti, *La ville charnelle*, 151. My translation.

39. Marinetti, *La ville charnelle*, 155-156. My translation.

40. The text is rather meaningfully entitled "Nous renions nos maîtres les Symbolistes, derniers amants de la lune" (We Abjure Our Symbolist Masters, the Last Lovers of the Moon), Marinetti, *Le Futurisme*, 82; Rainey, Poggi, and Wittman, *Futurism*, 93. *Le Futurisme* was published in 1911 and consequently translated into Italian as *Guerra, sola igiene del mondo* and published in 1915. The text was republished in Italian in *L'Italia futurista* in 1917 (II, no. 25; August 5, 1917,1): clearly, Futurists felt that the threat of neo-Symbolist literature had not been eradicated yet. Further references of this 1911 edition of *Le Futurisme* will be indicated in text as *LF* and followed by page numbers.

41. Berghaus, "Futurism and the Technological Imagination," 15; Pizzi argues that Émile Zola held "the most enduring influence" on Marinetti's "mechanical mach(in)ismo," *Italian Futurism and the Machine*, 53-54; Vera Castiglione explores Marinetti's Futurist appropriation of Emile Verhaeren's "celebration of the technological world," in "A Futurist before Futurism: Émile Verhaeren and the Technological Epic," 104; and also Vinall, "Marinetti, Soffici, and French Literature," 25. For more on Marinetti and Mallarmé specifically, see Suter, "Mallarmé and His Futurist 'Heir' Marinetti."

42. Livi, *Poesia (1905-1909)*, 64-65; Agnese, *Marinetti: Una vita esplosiva*, 51. For more about Marinetti's ambivalent relationship with D'Annunzio the poet and D'Annunzio the man, see Bragato, " 'Figlio di una turbina e di d'Annunzio': Marinetti edipico?," 61-78.

43. Livi, *Poesia (1905-1909)*, 64-65.

44. Conti, "Marinetti in France between Symbolism and Futurism," 62.

45. Conti, "Marinetti in France between Symbolism and Futurism," 62. The English translation from both Italian and French is by Claudia M. Clemente, as in Conti, "Marinetti in France between Symbolism and Futurism," 75. Marinetti's French translation was published as "Les villes terribles" in *Vers et prose: recueil trimestriel de littérature* V (March-April-May 1906), 80-83.

46. Bragato, "Marinetti edipico," 75.

47. Ricoeur, *The Rule of Metaphor*, 213.

48. Ricoeur, *The Rule of Metaphor*, 213.

49. Ricoeur, *The Rule of Metaphor*, 186.

50. Ricoeur, *The Rule of Metaphor*, 174.

51. See Ada Negri's letters to Paolo Buzzi, where she frequently mentions *Poesia*, which she contributed to, and Marinetti, in Negri and Buzzi, *Diorami Lombardi*. Gipponi, *La poesia in Ada Negri*, 28. Ada Negri also contributed, albeit marginally, to the magazine *L'Italia futurista*. Ada Negri was often asked to feature

with short opinion pieces in *Poesia*. In 1917, however, Marinetti attacked Negri's sentimentalism, criticising her recent collection of short stories on the condition of Italian women, entitled *Le solitarie* (Solitary Women), in an open letter to Ada Negri, "Donne, non piagnucolate" ("Women, Do Not Whine"); *L'Italia futurista* 2, no. 32 (November 4, 1917), 1. According to Walter Adamson, Negri "remained [a] loyal friend of Marinetti to the end of [her] life"; in *Embattled Avant-Gardes*, 100. For more on Negri's reception in the 1910s, see Laura Scuriatti's first chapter in *Mina Loy's Critical Modernism*. For Negri's later profile (especially during Fascism in Italy in the 1920s and 1930s), see Pickering-Iazzi, *Politics of the Visible.*

52. Negri, *Dal Profondo*, 275. My translation.

53. Negri, *Esilio*, 207. My translation.

54. Negri, *Esilio*, 209. My translation. Negri moved to Zurich in 1913 to be with her daughter Bianca, after breaking up with her husband; see Sarzana, "La vita risolta in un grido," in Negri, *Poesie e Prose*, xvi–xvii.

55. In her early poetry, Negri uses the word "lampada" once in "Mistica" (Mystic; from *Fatalità*, Fate, 1892), once in "L'estasi" (The Ecstasis) and once as "lampadetta" (little lamp) in "Mara" (both from *Maternità*, Maternity, 1904), and once in "L'errante" (The Wanderer, *Dal profondo*). In her collection *Tempeste* (Storms, 1895) she makes no use of the word, and in *Esilio* she prefers the more ancient and more neutral "lume" (light, normally indicating an artificial light such as that of a candle). More interesting is when Negri uses the word "fanale," which she associates with the gaslit "sentinels" of the previous chapter: in "L'abbandonato" (from *Maternità*), for example, a ruddy streetlamp monitors an orphaned baby in the street; in "Il fanale nel vicolo" (from *Esilio*), another streetlamp sheds more red light over some prostitutes and other miserable women, while also warning them against their sinful behaviour.

56. *Divisionismo* (Divisionism) was a mostly Italian artistic movement, "a version of Neo-Impressionism," reminiscent of French *Pointillisme* (Pointillism), flourishing at the end of the nineteenth century and into the first decade of the twentieth century, in Lombardy and Piedmont first and then in Rome; Chilvers and Glaves-Smith, *A Dictionary of Modern and Contemporary Art*. Divisionism's aesthetic aim was to achieve maximum luminosity in their artwork. For more information on Italian Divisionist art, see Fraquelli, *Radical Light*. The title of this painting effectively means "arc lamp" in Italian, although in English this painting is generally known as *Street Light*.

57. Benzi, "Giacomo Balla," 14; Lista, "Divisionismo e visione fotografica," 13.

58. Pucci, "Street Light," in Fraquelli, *Radical Light*, 131–132.

59. Balla's painting was listed in the catalog for the first Futurist exhibition ("Les Peintres Futuristes Italiens"), at the Bernheim-Jeune Gallery in Paris (February 1912), but eventually not exhibited there, and would only be exhibited in 1913 at

the "Mostra futurista" in Rome's Teatro Costanzi; see Velani, "Balla alle soglie del secolo nuovo," 214; Poggi, *Inventing Futurism*, 117; Benzi, "Giacomo Balla," 14-15; Fraquelli, "Modified Divisionism: Futurist Painting in 1910," 81.

60. Boccioni, et al., "Pittura futurista: Manifesto tecnico," in Caruso, *Manifesti proclami, interventi e documenti teorici del futurismo, 1909-1944*, 12-15.

61. Temkin, "*Luce futurista*," 32; Lista, "Divisionismo e visione fotografica," 13.

62. Letter from Giacomo Balla to his fiancée Elisa, November 16, 1900. He thus continued describing his fascination for electrical signs and advertisements: "Quello che poi diventa addirittura fantastico è una specie di reclame a parole grandissime le quali sono scritte sui cornicioni in alto dei palazzi e le stesse parole sono composte di lampade elettriche [. . .] e il bello sta che ogni momento cambiano di colore e di posizione" (What then is really fantastic is a sort of advertisement with huge words which are written up on the cornices of buildings and the words themselves are made up of electric light bulbs [. . .] and the nice thing is that they keeping changing color and location), in Baldacci, *Ricostruzione di casa Balla*, 158. My translation.

63. Giovanni Lista puts forward the suggestion that Balla would have personally seen the "Mostra Internazionale d'Elettricità" (International Electricity Exhibition) in Turin in 1884; see Giovanni Lista, "Divisionismo e visione fotografica," 2, 7; Coen, "Light," 78. Marinetti and his wife would likewise name their third daughter Luce in 1932.

64. Fagiolo, *Balla: The Futurist*, 56.

65. Rampazzo, *Futurista al chiaro di luna*, 26.

66. Buzzi, *Poesie scelte*, 81. My translation.

67. Pasca, "Le forme della luce," 47. Arc lamps were consequently suppressed in Milan in 1917; Pavese, "Dalla luce ad arco alle lampade al sodio," 29.

68. Buzzi, *Poesie scelte*, 81.

69. Bohn, *Italian Futurist Poetry*, 38-39. Further references to this edition will be indicated as *IFP* and followed by page numbers.

70. Marinetti, "Manifesto tecnico della letteratura futurista," in *Teoria e invenzione futurista*, 41. This manifesto was published in the introduction to the anthology *I poeti futuristi*, 12-23.

71. D'Ambrosio, "Notes on 'Esoteric Futurism,'" 297.

72. Take, for example, Morpurgo's "Colloqui notturni" ("Nocturnal Conversations"), also from the 1925 anthology *I nuovi poeti futuristi*: "***l'uomo sorride sul mondo viola/Io no*** *guardo attentamente il violento sforzo di/un briciolo di pane che tenta mutarsi/in una lampadina elettrica*" (***the man smiles on the violet world/I do not*** *I watch a bread crumb's/violent efforts to become an/electric lightbulb*, IFP 126-127, lines 6-8, emphasis in the original).

73. For a brief history of scholarship on Futurist women in the last few decades, see Berghaus, "Futurism and Women: A Review Article," 401-410; and Carpi, "Le

scrittrice futuriste," 36. See, for example, Salaris, *Le futuriste: donne e letteratura d'avanguardia in Italia, 1909-1944*, which was the first book to establish the importance of studying Futurist women; Bentivoglio and Zoccoli, *Women Artists of Italian Futurism*, and then as *Le futuriste italiane nelle arti visive*; Bello Minciacchi, *Spirale di dolcezza + serpe di fascino*; Carpi, *Futuriste: Letteratura, Arte, Vita*; Berghaus, *International Yearbook of Futurism Studies: Volume 5: Women Futurists*; Re, "Maria Ginanni vs. F. T. Marinetti," and "Women at War: Eva Kühn Amendola (Magamal)," 275-308; Sica, *Futurist Women: Florence, Feminism, and New Science*; Gatti and Resch, *L'elica e la luce: le futuriste 1912-1944*.

74. Poggi, *Inventing Futurism*, 197.

75. Marinetti, "Le Futurisme," *Le Figaro*, February 20, 1909, https://gallica.bnf.fr/ark:/12148/bpt6k2883730.item#.

76. Salaris, *Storia del futurismo*, 52; Berghaus, "Futurism and Women: A Review Article," 401.

77. Wood, "'On or about December 1910,'" 143. I am following here Jamie Wood's redating of the London lecture as taking place in December 1910.

78. Marinetti, *Le futurisme*, 57.

79. Salaris, *Storia del futurismo*, 53.

80. Salaris, *Le futuriste*, 25.

81. Marinetti, *Le futurisme*, 58.

82. In their preface to *Come si seducono le donne*, Corra and Settimelli do not fail to stress that "Pochi uomini possono vantarsi di possedere in questo campo una esperienza vasta e varia quanto quella di Marinetti" (Few men can boast having such an ample and varied experience in this field as Marinetti's); Corra and Settimelli, "Marinetti intimo," in Marinetti, *Come si seducono le donne*, 21. My translation.

83. Corra and Settimelli, "Marinetti intimo," 22. My translation.

84. Corra and Settimelli, "Marinetti intimo," 23. My translation. In his notebooks, Marinetti jotted down some ideas to write *Il manuale della giovane sposa futurista* (The Young Futurist Bride's Handbook) in February 1919 and a book for women with the working title of *Come si devono dare agli uomini* (How to Give Yourself to a Man) in May 1920; Marinetti, *Taccuini, 1915-1921*, 407, 479.

85. Salaris, *Storia del futurismo*, 54-55; Resch, "Le futuriste: corpo moltiplicato e anima plurisensibile," in *L'elica e la luce*, 29-35. Poggi suggests de Saint-Point's manifesto might have been written by Marinetti himself, in *Inventing Futurism*, 223. For Bentivoglio, however, de Saint-Point's manifestos appear like a more natural trajectory from her work tackling women's issues, such as *Trilogie de l'amour et de la mort* (1906), *Un inceste* (1907), *Une femme et le désir* (1910), and the conference series *Donna e letteratura* (1910-11); in Bentivoglio and Zoccoli, *Le futuriste italiane nelle arti visive*, 12.

86. Pickering-Iazzi, *Politics of the Visible*, 208; de Saint-Point, "Manifesto della donna futurista," 82, 83.

87. de Saint-Point, "Manifesto futurista della lussuria," 89.

88. de Saint-Point, "Manifesto della donna futurista: Risposta a F. T. Marinetti," 81.

89. Salaris, *Storia del futurismo*, 56.

90. According to Claudia Salaris, the manifestos first appeared as a single publication in Russia brought out by the Union of Youth in 1912, see *Storia del futurismo*, 68-69; and also Budanova, "Penetrating Men's Territory," in Berghaus, *International Yearbook of Futurism Studies*, 169. According to Lapšin, however, the first excerpt of Marinetti's *Figaro* manifesto was translated for Večer as early as March 8, 1909, which then gave way to numerous translations of excerpts from the manifestos, culminating in the more comprehensive translations of Tastevin (*Futurizm*, published in Moscow in 1914), Šeršenevič (*Marinetti: Manifesty ital'janskogo futurizma*, also Moscow 1914), and M. A. Engel'gardt (*Marinetti F. T. Futurizm*, for Prometeo, Sankt Peterburg, also 1914); see Lapšin, *Marinetti e la Russia*, 253. In his memoirs, Roman Jakobson recalls how Marinetti's texts were translated by Genrik Tastevin, who had been his French instructor at the time, see *My Futurist Years*, 8, 20.

With regard to Russian names here and in Chapter Four, I follow English-language conventions for ease, especially with names of famous artists and writers.

91. This is reported by Goncharova's first biographer, Ilia Zdanevich, as quoted in Lapšin, *Marinetti e la Russia*, 170.

92. Jakobson, *My Futurist Years*, 20-21.

93. Jakobson, *My Futurist Years*, 20-21. See also Budanova, "Penetrating Men's Territory," 171-172, and Parton, *Goncharova: The Art and Design of Natalia Goncharova*, 98 (although Parton does not seem to know of a meeting between Goncharova, Larionov, and Marinetti). The couple met Marinetti later in the same year in Rome on their way to Paris and struck up a stronger friendship when working in Rome again in 1916-17, but it seems credible that the vodka-fueled meeting at the Alpine Rose in Moscow helped to ease the relationship between Larionov, Goncharova, and Marinetti. See Jakobson, *My Futurist Years*, 21; Sebregondi, "Goncharova and Italy: Controversy, Inspiration, Friendship," 124.

94. Vadim Gabrielevich Shershenevich, *Великолепный очевидец* (Great Eye-witness), 501, quoted in Lapšin, *Marinetti e la Russia*, 170.

95. "Marinetti [. . .] visti i quadri della Gončarova, esclamò: 'Bene! Molto fresco! Come noi!'. Guardò quelli di Larionov, fece una smorfia: 'Male!', si girò e se ne andò," quoted in Lapšin, *Marinetti e la Russia*, 170. English translation: "Viewing Goncharova's pictures, Marinetti had exclaimed: 'Great! A breath of fresh air! Just like us!' and on viewing Larionov's work 'Poor stuff!,' Sebregondi, "Goncharova and Italy," 201.

96. Parton, *Goncharova*, 192, 87. According to Parton, Goncharova develops a broader interest in painting different technologies, like the Futurists: see, for example, *Автомобиль* (*The Automobile*, 1911), and her 1913 paintings *Электрический*

орнамент (*Electric Ornament*), Электричество (*Electricity*), Велосипедист (*The Bicyclist*), Ткачиха. Ткацкий станок и женщина (*The Weaver: Loom and Woman*), and Динамо (*The Dynamo*).

97. Chamot, *Goncharova: Stage Designs and Paintings*, 51.

98. Although the painting Ткачиха. Ткацкий станок и женщина (*The Weaver: Loom and Woman*) is dated 1910 by the author at the back of the painting, scholars generally agree on the actual composition date as 1913; see also "Art Collections Online," Amgueddfa Cymru/National Museum of Wales, accessed February 2, 2021, https://museum.wales/art/online/?action=show_item&item=653.

99. The women featured in this magazine are Maria Ginanni, Irma Valeria, Fulvia Giuliani, Enif Robert, Fanny Dini, Mina Della Pergola, Emma Marpillero, Enrica Piubellini, Marj Carbonaro, Shara Marini, Rosa Rosà, and Magamal. See Sica, *Futurist Women*, 1-2; Salaris, *Le futuriste*, 55-62.

100. Pickering-Iazzi, *Politics of the Visible*, 207; Adamson, *Embattled Avant-Gardes*, 102-104.

101. Re, "Maria Ginanni vs. F. T. Marinetti," 104.

102. Dini, "Al futurismo trionfante," 2. My translation. For biographical information on Dini, see Bello Minciacchi, *Spirale di dolcezza + serpe di fascino*, 261-262.

103. The position of Futurist men on the role of women were varied and too complex to be discussed here in detail, as the discussion in the column "Donna + Amore + Bellezza" (Woman + Love + Beauty), which unfolded in the pages of *L'Italia futurista* over the year 1917, demonstrates. For more on this topic, see in the first instance Sica, *Futurist Women*, 25-29.

104. Re, "Maria Ginanni vs. F. T. Marinetti," 106. For further bibliographical information on Ginanni, see Bello Minciacchi, *Spirale di dolcezza + serpe di fascino*, 87-90.

105. Re, "Maria Ginanni vs. F. T. Marinetti," 106.

106. Re, "Maria Ginanni vs. F. T. Marinetti," 117; Sica, "Maria Ginanni," 346.

107. Ginanni, "Frammento di novella colorata," 2. My translation.

108. Marinetti, "Manifesto tecnico della letteratura futurista," *Teoria e invenzione futurista*, 40-48 (for the English translation see Rainey, Poggi, and Wittman, *Futurism*, 119-125); Sica, "Maria Ginanni," 346.

109. "Lùcciola," Vocabolario della lingua italiana Treccani, accessed February 11, 2021, https://www.treccani.it/vocabolario/lucciola/.

110. Sica, *Futurist Women*, 129, 128, 133.

111. Ginanni, "Frammenti di novelle colorate," 2. My translation.

112. Ginanni, "Frammenti di novelle colorate," 2. My translation.

113. Sica, "Maria Ginanni," 348.

114. Sica, *Futurist Women*, 10; also see Sica, "Nocturnal Itineraries," 145-158.

115. Ginanni, "Le lucciole," 2. My translation.

116. Settimelli, "Maria Ginanni prima grande scrittrice italiana," 1-2. Fellow

Futurist Emilio Settimelli, editor of *L'Italia futurista*, hails Ginanni as "la prima grande scrittrice italiana," the first great Italian woman writer, reviewing and sponsoring her first published collection of poetry, *Montagne trasparenti* (Transparent Mountains). Settimelli, promoting Ginanni, clarifies first off what her poetry is not: "In lei niente dei simbolisti, dei decadenti, niente dei russi, niente insomma di tutto quello che tanto ha influenzato la poesia italiana in questi ultimi tempi. La sua lirica è completamente nostra" (Settimelli, "Maria Ginanni," 1). While Ginanni's poetry has got nothing to do with Symbolism, or Decadence, or Russian literature, the influences he identifies as still dominant in Italian poetry, and is "completely ours," he seems reluctant to attach the word "Futurist" to her work, a fact he had already discussed in his preface to her collection of poetry, saying she seems to be wanting to establish her own movement, with a style of her own; see Sica, "Maria Ginanni," 339. Two years later, after the publication of Ginanni's prose poem in the pages of *L'Italia futurista*, the magazine proposes the only piece by another woman writer who is clearly influenced by, and is clearly responding to, Ginanni's style: Marj Carbonaro's "Luci nel buio." Carbonaro reprises the theme of glowworms in the night but this time with an Occultist twist; see Carbonaro, "Luci nel buio," 2, and Sica, *Futurist Women*, 141.

117. For more on Rosa Rosà's life, see also Zoccoli, "Futurist Women Painters in Italy," 378-379, and Re, "Rosa Rosà's Futurist-Feminist Short Novel *A Woman with Three Souls*," in Re, ed., and Dominic Siracusa, trans., "Rosa Rosà's *A Woman With Three Souls* in English Translation," 2-8, as well as Simonetta Proietti, "Edyth Von Haynau (Rosa Rosà)" (PhD diss., Università di Roma Tre, 2017).

118. Zoccoli, "Futurist Women Painters in Italy," 379.

119. Giuliani, *Il poeta futurista Mario Carli*, 97.

120. Sica, "Nocturnal itineraries," 145.

121. Carli, *Notti filtrate*, 10.

122. Carli, *Notti filtrate*, 14. My translation.

123. Giuliani, *Il poeta futurista Mario Carli,* 20.

124. Carli, *Notti filtrate*, 22. My translation.

125. Zoccoli, "Futurist Women Painters in Italy," 379.

126. Carli, *Notti filtrate*, 38.

127. Carli, *Notti filtrate*, 38.

128. For the French origins of Futurists' eroticizing of machines, see Pizzi, *Italian Futurism and the Machine*, 54; Sartini Blum, "Transformations in the Futurist Mythopoeia," 81.

129. Giovanni Gerbino's poem is entitled "Le donne sono tutte sul Corso" ("The Women Are All on the Avenue"), see *IFP* 174-175.

130. Enzo Mainardi may well have had Baudelaire's poem "Les chats" ("Cats") in mind: "Leurs reins féconds sont pleins d'étincelles magiques,/Et des parcelles d'or, ainsi qu'un sable fin,/Etoilent vaguement leurs prunelles mystiques" (Within their

potent loins are magic sparks, / And flakes of gold, fine sand, are vaguely seen / Behind their mystic eyes, gleaming like stars, lines 12-14), in Baudelaire, *The Flowers of Evil, With Parallel French Text*, 134-135. I am grateful to Hugh Haughton for the suggestion.

131. Pomajzlová, *Růžena*, 285, 292, 331, 363. Zátková's mixed-media assemblages have much in common with Mina Loy's own assemblages.

132. Pomajzlová, *Růžena*, 294, 336. Zátková's assemblages are comparable to the ones Loy also made, around the same time. The ephemerality of the materials chosen by both artists made it such that only very few copies have survived the test of time.

133. Pomajzlová, *Růžena*, 357.

134. Giorgini, *Růžena Zátková: Un'artista dimenticata*, 221.

135. Zoccoli, "Futurist Women Painters in Italy," 386.

136. Pomajzlová, *Růžena*, 398; letter from Benedetta Cappa Marinetti to Zátková, February 3, 1922. The original is held at the Beinecke Rare Book and Manuscript Library of Yale University, in the Filippo Tommaso Marinetti Collection. According to Franca Zoccoli, Marinetti encouraged Zátková to make a coloured version of her black-and-white portrait of himself; see Bentivoglio and Zoccoli, *Le futuriste italiane nelle arti visive*, 129.

137. Pomajzlová, *Růžena*, 225, 226, 436.

Chapter 3. Living with Lanterns

1. Loy, *The Last Lunar Baedeker*, 314.

2. Barthel, "The Paris Studio of Constantin Brancusi," 35; McAuley, "The Artists and their Alley."

3. Potter and Hobson, "Introduction," *The Salt Companion to Mina Loy*, 1.

4. Barthel, "The Paris Studio of Constantin Brancusi," 35.

5. Barthel, "The Paris Studio of Constantin Brancusi," 35.

6. I am grateful to Michael White for further discussing the technicalities of this shot with me.

7. Conover, "Notes on the Text," *The Lost Lunar Baedeker*, 198. Further references to this edition will be indicated in the text as *LLB* and followed by page numbers. Elkins, "From the Gutter to the Gallery," 1094.

8. Rosenbaum, "Paris 1923." Churchill, Kinnahan, and Rosenbaum, "Digital Baedeker," 63-80. Churchill further reprises this in "Ghost in an Avant-Garde Alley."

9. Burke, *Becoming Modern*, 224.

10. After Roger Conover, Sara Crangle argues this draft was probably "written in the late 1930s or early 1940s," in "Notes," *Stories and Essays of Mina Loy*, 222, 370. Further references from this edition will be indicated in the text as *SEML* and

followed by page numbers. For more on when Loy and Brancusi may have met for the first time, please see Prescott, *Poetic Salvage*, 85-86.

11. Roger Conover was the first to point out the relevance of Loy's later recollection to the earlier poem (*LLB* 199). Margherita Andreotti previously claimed Loy "could have easily seen the sculpture in a show held that spring (March-April [1922]) in the Sculptor's Gallery in New York, if not in [John] Quinn's own collection," in "Brancusi's *Golden Bird*," 136; Burke, *Becoming Modern*, 316; "Mariette Mills," *Mapping the Practice and Profession of Sculpture in Britain and Ireland 1851-1951*; Loy, "Phenomenon in American Art," YCAL MSS 6, box 6, folder 172, and reprinted in *The Last Lunar Baedeker*, 300-302. It is my speculation, however, that Mina Loy met Brancusi through Mariette Mills, who was a sculptor and medalist active in Paris and Florence.

12. Burke, *Becoming Modern*, 308.

13. Lazevnick, "Impossible Descriptions," 192.

14. Lazevnick, "Impossible Descriptions," 193.

15. Prescott, *Poetic Salvage*, 91.

16. Pound, "Brancusi," 6.

17. The original photograph in the Brancusi Collection at the Centre Pompidou carries the following clarification on its reverse: "L'oiseau d'or photo pris [*sic*] en plein so[leil]" (The golden bird photograph taken in full sun, my translation). For more on Brancusi's specific use of lighting effects for his own pictures of his sculptures, see Brown, *Brancusi Photographs Brancusi*, 4-17, and Tabart and Monod-Fontaine, *Brancusi photographe*, 10-12. For more on Brancusi's photographs of his sculptures in general, also see Paret, "Sculpture and Its Negative."

18. Prescott, *Poetic Salvage*, 90.

19. Marcoci, *The Original Copy*, 98; Lazevnick, "Impossible Descriptions," 198.

20. Scuriatti, *Mina Loy's Critical Modernism*, 85.

21. Hugh Kenner, "To Be the Brancusi of Poetry," 30.

22. Potter and Hobson, "Introduction," 1.

23. Shreiber and Tuma, "Introduction," 13-14.

24. Potter and Hobson, "Introduction," 1.

25. Mina Loy to Mabel Dodge Luhan, February 1914, YCAL MSS 196, box 24, folder 664 (pp. 2-3).

26. Mina Loy to Stephen Haweis, March 22 [?] 1914, YCAL MSS 196, box 42, folder 1276.

27. Mina Loy to Mabel Dodge Luhan, 1914, YCAL MSS 196, box 24, folder 665 (p. 3).

28. Mina Loy to Carl Van Vechten, undated, YCAL MSS 1050, box 76, folder 1082-1083. Loy's own emphasis, and bracketed text is circled and marked as "private" in her original.

29. Harris, "Futurism, Fashion, and the Feminine," 24. For more on *Lacerba*, see Adamson, *Avant-Garde Florence*, 166–180.

30. Burke, *Becoming Modern*, 151–154.

31. Conover, "Notes on the Text," 178.

32. Prescott, *Poetic Salvage*, 5; "Mina Loy Chronology," *The Salt Companion to Mina Loy*, 12; Conover, "Notes on the Text," 178.

33. At a distance of nearly twenty years from each other, Andrew Michael Roberts and Tara Prescott have gone a long way toward clarifying that Loy's Café du Néant is far from being the "imaginary" place hypothesized by Carolyn Burke (*Becoming Modern*, 103). Roberts, " 'How to Be Happy in Paris': Mina Loy and the Transvaluation of the Body," 140; Prescott, *Poetic Salvage*, 6. Although Prescott references Roberts's essay, she does not discuss the importance of Roberts's findings, and argument, for her own reading of Loy's poem. I offer here a new reading that goes beyond what both scholars have said.

34. Nadis, *Wonder Shows*, 15; "In the Cabaret du Neant: A Ghastly Parisian Diversion," *New York Sun*, as republished in *Current Literature*, 250. When, in the autumn of 1937, the café eventually closed down its business, now unappetizing to a generation who had gone through a world war, the *Observer* saluted its closure as putting an end to "the fashions of yesterday," and showing some surprise at the fact that it had "lasted so long," in "PARIS WEEK BY WEEK: FAMOUS CABARET CLOSES DOWN," *Observer*, October 31, 1937, 14.

35. Roberts, " 'How to Be Happy in Paris': Mina Loy and the Transvaluation of the Body," 137; Burke, *Becoming Modern*, 177.

36. Hoeckley, "Quaint Inns and Cabarets," 9.

37. Hoeckley, "Quaint Inns and Cabarets," 9.

38. Hoeckley, "Quaint Inns and Cabarets," 9; Nadis, *Wonder Shows*, 15–16; "THE CABARET DU NEANT," 152.

39. "THE CABARET DU NEANT," 152; Hopkins, *Magic*, 55–60.

40. See Tara Prescott's own photographic collection as published in *Poetic Salvage*, 7–10.

41. Hopkins, *Magic*, 55. A summary of Hopkins's section on the Cabaret du Néant appeared in *Scientific American* (see note 33).

42. Prescott, *Poetic Salvage*, 11–12. Contrarily to Prescott, however, I do not think there is any ancient Egyptian undercurrent to the scene in the poem.

43. Chancellor, *How to Be Happy in Paris*, 125, 127. Chancellor recalls how, in the Salle d'Intoxication, "the coffin-worms [i.e., the spectators] are asked to give their attention to some large paintings, which represent dancers at the old Moulin Rouge, an absinthe drinker, a battlefield, and so on. Lights are switched on behind these pictures, and the figures in them change to skeletons," 125.

44. Chancellor, *How to Be Happy in Paris*, 127.

45. Roberts, "'How to Be Happy in Paris': Mina Loy and the Transvaluation of the Body," 141.

46. "Pazzarella/Pazzerella" means "mad woman" in Italian, and both spellings are acceptable in current Italian. The manuscript of "Pazzarella" (now at the Beinecke Rare Book and Manuscript Library) is undated, but Potter hypothesizes it was "likely [. . .] written during the latter part of Loy's stay in Florence," in *Modernism and Democracy*, 157.

47. For more on Loy's irony and self-irony in her works, including a brief mention of "Pazzarella," see Pryor, *Poetry, Modernism, and an Imperfect World*, 97–100.

48. Hayden, *Curious Disciplines*, 25.

49. Hayden, *Curious Disciplines*, 40.

50. For a more ample discussion of woman's issue in the Futurist movement, please refer to the preceding chapter, "Killing the Moonlight: F. T. Marinetti and the Futurist Avant-Garde."

51. Marinetti, *Le futurisme*, 57; Rainey, Poggi, and Wittman, *Futurism*, 86.

52. Marinetti, *Le futurisme*, 57; Rainey, Poggi, and Wittman, *Futurism*, 86–87.

53. Rainey, Poggi, and Wittman, *Futurism*, 86. For more on Marinetti's engagement with the suffragette movement, especially in the UK, please see Wood, "F. T. Marinetti's Onslaught on London and Recursive Structures in Modernism."

54. This is apparent throughout the book, where Marinetti exhorts women against modesty and elasticity of morals, and in favor of intellectual strength, in Marinetti, *Come si seducono le donne*.

55. There are many similarities between T. S. Eliot's 1916 poem "La Figlia Che Piange" and this passage in Loy's "Pazzarella," as Sean Pryor interestingly suggests in *Poetry, Modernism, and an Imperfect World*, 100.

56. Loy glosses the meaning of "dots" herself by calling it "Marriage Portions" (*LLB* 21). Conover, "Notes on the Text," 181; Alex Goody, *Modernist Articulations*, 108; Burke, *Becoming Modern*, 191–192. Alex Goody correctly points out that the meaning of Loy's "dots" triangulates missing dowries (in French), Marinetti's call to abolish punctuation, and the "censored reality of sex," in *Modernist Articulations*, 108.

57. Scuriatti, *Mina Loy's Critical Modernism*, 41.

58. Scholars have too often neglected this poem, which must have given birth to the Madame Sosostris passage in T. S. Eliot's *The Waste Land*. As far as I am aware, the only scholars who noted (albeit rather nonchalantly) that this poem by Loy predates *The Waste Land*, as it was published in *Others: A Magazine of the New Verse* in 1917, are Powell in "Basil Bunting and Mina Loy," 10, and Ricks and McCue, in their notes to *The Poems of T. S. Eliot: Collected & Uncollected Poems: Volume I*, 609–610.

59. For more on readings of the tarot card of the moon, see Kelly, *Tarot Card Combinations*, 32, and Fairfield, *Everyday Tarot*, 99–100.

60. Re, "Mina Loy and the Quest for a Futurist Feminist Woman," 810.

61. Scuriatti, "Negotiating Boundaries," 74.

62. Eliot, "Observations," in *The Complete Prose of T. S. Eliot: The Critical Edition: Apprentice Years, 1905–1918: Volume 1*, 712. In the article, Eliot cites Loy's poem from "While Miovanni thought alone in the dark" to "That she should see   Nothing at all." Perhaps Loy's poems made more of an impression on Eliot than he would have liked to admit.

63. Gonnering Lein, "Shades of Meaning," 625.

64. Harris, "Futurism, Fashion, and the Feminine," 36.

65. Mina Loy to Carl Van Vechten, December 27, 1914, YCAL MSS 1050, box 76, folder 1082, 2.

66. Conover, "Notes on the Text," 215.

67. Loy, "Aphorisms on Futurism."

68. Schmid, "Mina Loy's Futurist Theatre," 3; Churchill, "Courting an Audience." Certainly, the presence of a searching arc light on the stage (on any stage, really) would have been hard to accomplish, unless Loy imagined her play ought to have been performed in some public space (such as a square), but we have no indication this might have been her intention.

69. Loy, "Two Plays," 8. Churchill, "Courting an Audience."

70. Loy, "Two Plays," 8.

71. Loy, "Two Plays," 8.

72. Kenner, "To Be the Brancusi of Poetry," 30.

73. Kouidis, "The Poetry of Mina Loy," 176.

74. Gonnering Lein, "Shades of Meaning," 617.

75. Loy appeared in the *New York Evening Sun* (February 17, 1917) as a "prototype of 'Modern Woman,'" as reported in Conover, "Time-Table," lxix. On Mina Loy and the concept of Modern Woman, see Parmar, *The Autobiographies of Mina Loy*.

76. Gooday, *Domesticating Electricity*, 75.

77. Marvin, *When Old Technologies Were New*, 23.

78. Hammond, *The Electric Light in Our Homes*, 76.

79. See illustration by George Du Maurier, *HAPPY THOUGHT. The Electric Light, so favourable to Furniture, Wall Papers, Pictures, Screens, &c., is not always becoming to the Female Complexion. Light Japanese Sunshades will be found invaluable.*, published in *Punch*, July 20, 1889.

80. Wharton and Codman Jr., *The Decoration of Houses*, 126.

81. Wharton, *The House of Mirth*, 30.

82. Wharton, *The House of Mirth*, 30.

83. Gooday, *Domesticating Electricity*, 154.

84. Gordon, *Decorative Electricity*, 4.

85. Gooday, *Domesticating Electricity*, 159.

86. Dillon, "'Like a Glow-Worm,'" 77.

87. Desmond, *Gustave Trouvé*, 95–96.

88. Wosk, *Women and the Machine*, 71–72; Gordon, *Decorative Electricity*, 121–122; Dillon, " 'Like a Glow-Worm,' " 77. In *New York Nocturne*, Sharpe comments on this photograph of Mrs. Vanderbilt as a personification of the Statue of Liberty, 139.

89. Wosk, *Women and the Machine*, 74.

90. Wosk, *Women and the Machine*, 69–71.

91. Pomerance, "Tinker Bell, the Fairy of Electricity," 15.

92. Conover, "Notes on the Text," 188.

93. The male lovers recognizable in the poem are however yet again her ex-husband Stephen Haweis, Marinetti, and Giovanni Papini. Conover, "Notes on the Text," 193.

94. Re, "Mina Loy and the Quest for a Futurist Feminist Woman," 807.

95. Selinger, "Love in the Time of Melancholia," 28.

96. Loy identified one of her lovers as a "boy" in Song V, line 5, and then as an "adolescent" in Song VIII, line 2.

97. Gonnering Lein, "Shades of Meaning," 617; DuPlessis, *Genders, Races, and Religious Cultures*, 62; Shreiber, " 'Love is a lyric,' " 96–97.

98. *Songs to Joannes* was published in *Others* in April 1917, vol. 3, no. 6.

99. Beach, *Shakespeare and Company*, 113.

100. Burke, *Becoming Modern*, 171.

101. Burke, *Becoming Modern*, 245.

102. Gonnering Lein, "Shades of Meaning," 621.

103. Burke, *Becoming Modern*, 213; Goody, *Modernist Articulations*, 101.

104. Dennison, "Francis Picabia's *Américaine*," 622.

105. Dennison, "Francis Picabia's *Américaine*," 621.

106. Dennison, "Francis Picabia's *Américaine*," 621; Goody, *Modernist Articulations*, 108.

107. Gonnering Lein, "Shades of Meaning," 621.

108. Gonnering Lein, "Shades of Meaning," 621.

109. Dunn, "Mina Loy, Fashion, and the Avant-Garde," 447; Conover, "Time-Table," lxxiii–lxxiv. Initially, Loy was financially aided by Peggy Guggenheim and Laurence Vail; consequently, her son-in-law Julien Levy financed Loy's enterprise from 1927 until the closing down of her business between 1929 and 1930.

110. Wood, "Brancusi's White Studio," 272–273. For further exploration of Francis Picabia's lamps, see also Chapter Four of this book.

111. Conover quoted in Burstein, *Cold Modernism*, 187.

112. The painting was presented for the first time at the Society of Independent Artists Exhibition in New York (April 10 to May 6, 1917), Dunn, "Mina Loy, Fashion, and the Avant-Garde," 445; *Catalogue of the First Annual Exhibition of the Society of Independent Artists*, 166.

113. Beach alluded to it in the previous quotation, and Burke also discusses it. Dunn, "Mina Loy, Fashion, and the Avant-Garde," 444.

114. Brown and Brown Lyman, *Book of Home Building and Decoration.*

115. de Wolfe, *The House in Good Taste*, 109.

116. de Wolfe, *The House in Good Taste*, 109.

117. Brown Lyman, "Lamps and Lighting," 185.

118. Dunn, "Mina Loy, Fashion, and the Avant-Garde," 447-448. For more on Mina Loy's artistic training and her time spent in Munich and Paris, see Burke, *Becoming Modern*, 53-87. For Loy and illustrations, see Goody, "Ladies of Fashion/Modern(ist) Women," and "'Consider Your Grandmothers.'"

119. Burstein, *Cold Modernism*, 187.

120. Burstein, *Cold Modernism*, 188.

121. Koues, "Lamp Shades You Can Make at Home," 37.

122. Woolman Chase, "Decorating," 58.

123. Loy, "Gertrude Stein," *The Last Lunar Baedeker*, 298; Burstein, *Cold Modernism*, 188.

124. Burke, *Becoming Modern*, 343.

125. Burke, *Becoming Modern*, 342-343; Gross, *Mina Loy*, 60-63.

126. Burke, *Becoming Modern*, 365.

127. Burstein, *Cold Modernism*, 189.

128. Burke, *Becoming Modern*, 342.

129. Fischer, *Designing Women*, 14, 16.

130. Escritt, *Art Nouveau*, 345. For more on Art Nouveau objects and architecture, see also Duncan, *Art Nouveau.*

131. Duncan, *Art Deco Complete*, 6.

132. Buhler Lynes, "Introduction. Georgia O'Keeffe and the Calla Lily in American Art, 1860-1940," in *Georgia O'Keeffe and the Calla Lily*, 1.

133. Buhler Lynes, "Introduction," 1-2; Eldredge, "Calla Moderna," 22, 24-25, 28-29.

134. Burke, *Becoming Modern*, 329, 213.

135. Grasso, *Equal under the Sky*, 56.

136. Both artists make the calla "an important focus of their art during the 1920s," Buhler Lynes, "Georgia O'Keeffe and the Calla Lily," 2; Eldredge, "Calla Moderna," 13, 19.

137. Eldredge, "Calla Moderna," 26; Moore, "The Pale Beauty of Priceless Flowers," 46-47.

138. Burke, *Becoming Modern*, 365.

139. Burke, *Becoming Modern*, 343.

140. Kinnahan, *Mina Loy, Twentieth-Century Photography, and Contemporary Women Poets*, 59.

141. Kouidis, "Rediscovering Our Sources," 183. For Loy's allusions to the

poetry of Charles Baudelaire and Jules Laforgue in *Lunar Baedeker,* see Kouidis, *Mina Loy: American Modernist Poet*. DuPlessis, *Genders, Races, and Religious Cultures*, 41.

142. DuPlessis, *Genders, Races, and Religious Cultures*, 41.

143. Eliot's "Rhapsody on a Windy Night" and "Preludes" were published together with Loy's poems "At the Door of the House," "The Effectual Marriage or the Insipid Narrative of Gina and Miovanni," and "Human Cylinders" in Kreymborg, *Others*.

144. DuPlessis, *Genders, Races, and Religious Cultures*, 41.

145. Pryor further argues that Loy's "Stellectric signs" represent "the stars in the night sky." Pryor, *Poetry, Modernism, and an Imperfect World*, 93.

146. For Harriet Monroe, this poem addressed "the world in general," in "Guide to the Moon: Review of *Lunar Baedecker* by Mina Loy," 101; for Burke, in *Becoming Modern*, it is "a defense of modern art's creations," 309; for Prescott, in *Poetic Salvage*, it works as a manifesto where Loy "reaffirms kinship with a remote band of intellectual outlaws," 109; Scuriatti ultimately defends a *Ulysses* reading of the poem, *Mina Loy's Critical Modernism*, 89.

147. Churchill, *The Little Magazine* Others, 197.

148. Goody, *Modernist Articulations*, 140.

149. Gross, "Truant of Heaven," in *Mina Loy*, 70. Gross defines "fresco vero" as "a new type of painting technique using a mixture of sand, gesso, and plaster" invented by Loy that enabled her to create "the luminosity essential to her conception of the series."

150. Mina Loy to Carl Van Vechten, undated, YCAL MSS 1050, box 76, folder 1082-1083.

151. The box is now on display at the Philadelphia Museum of Art. Prescott, *Poetic Salvage*, 107.

152. Burke, *Becoming Modern*, 404. According to art historian Kirsten Hoving, Cornell "produced hundreds of works with references to astronomy," and "developed a deep knowledge and love of the stars" during his life, in Hoving, *Joseph Cornell and Astronomy*, 1.

153. Joseph Cornell to Mina Loy, draft letter, July 3, 1951, in *Joseph Cornell's Theater of the Mind: Selected Diaries, Letters, and Files*, ed. Mary Ann Caws (New York: Thames and Hudson, 1993), 175, as quoted in Hoving, *Joseph Cornell and Astronomy*, 46. For more on Cornell's friendship with Loy, see Gross, "Truant of Heaven," in *Mina Loy*, 92-95.

Chapter 4. Bringing Down the Stars

1. Spector, *Bastard in the Ragged Suit*, 51. The poem "Yellow Lamps" was first published in Charles Henri Ford's *Blues: A Magazine of New Rhythms* in 1929.

2. This image takes its cue from Langston Hughes's words about Paris, in "The

Fascination of Cities" (1926), from *The Collected Works of Langston Hughes: Volume 9*, 31, as well as Gwendolyn B. Bennett's poem "Street Lamps in Early Spring," both of which I discuss later in the chapter.

3. Moody, *Ezra Pound*, 126.

4. From early 1908, Pound had been spending time in Europe, mostly in England, France, and Italy. After arriving in the United States in June 1910, he spent about eight months there, of which six weeks were in Pennsylvania with his family and the rest in New York. He returned to Europe in February 1911. See Moody, *Ezra Pound*, xiv.

5. Letter from Ezra Pound to Margaret Cravens, dated June 30, 1910, in Pound and Spoo, *Ezra Pound and Margaret Cravens*, 41.

6. Pound and Spoo, *Ezra Pound and Margaret Cravens*, 7.

7. Pound, *Patria Mia and the Treatise on Harmony*, 14.

8. Campbell, *Mearing Stones*, 3.

9. Elcott, *Artificial Darkness*, 1.

10. Johns and Clancy, "Introduction," in Spector, *Bastard in the Ragged Suit*, 6; Spector, *Bastard in the Ragged Suit*, 51.

11. Jameson, *Signatures of the Visible*, 1.

12. For more on the intersections between cinema and modernism, see, among others, Trotter, *Cinema and Modernism*, Marcus, *The Tenth Muse*, and *Dreams of Modernity*, and McCabe, *Cinematic Modernism*.

13. Wharton and Codman Jr., *The Decoration of Houses*, 126.

14. Pound, *Patria Mia and the Treatise on Harmony*, 19.

15. For my recent short article on Ezra Pound's half-watt light in *Hugh Selwyn Mauberley* (1920), see Asciuto, "A Half-Watt Light for Photography in Ezra Pound's 'Medallion' (1920)," 347-351.

16. When visiting Paris in 1922, Mayakovsky was already shocked to find that "lamps in the bars of Montmartre alone would suffice to light all the schools in Russia"; see Woroszylski, *The Life of Mayakovsky*, 333.

17. Mayakovsky, *My Discovery of America*, 53.

18. Mayakovsky, *My Discovery of America*, 47.

19. Mayakovsky, *My Discovery of America*, 52.

20. Mayakovsky, *Собрание сочинений в двенадцати томах* (Collected Works in Twelve Volumes), 232. English translation: Mayakovsky, *"Vladimir Mayakovsky" & Other Poems*, 161-162.

21. Nye, *American Technological Sublime*, 83-86.

22. Slater, "Technology and the Rise of the Vernacular Object in William Carlos Williams's *Spring and All*," 189. Compare Williams's prose commentaries to the poetry in *Spring and All* and the "Objects" section in Stein, *Tender Buttons*, 11-31. For comparative work on Stein and Williams (although not *Spring and All*), see Perlow, "Description as Chance Operation," 573-598.

23. Williams, *The Collected Poems of William Carlos Williams: Volume I 1909-1939*, 231 (XIII, lines 7-12). Further references to this edition will be indicated in brackets in the text, as *CPI*, and followed by page numbers.

24. Slater, "Technology and the Rise of the Vernacular Object," 195.

25. Entry for October 27, "Notes in Diary Form (1927)," in Williams, *Selected Essays*, 64.

26. McLuhan, *Understanding Media*, 7.

27. McLuhan, *Understanding Media*, 8.

28. McLuhan, *Understanding Media*, 8.

29. McLuhan, *Understanding Media*, 8.

30. Williams, "A Note on the Art of Poetry," 78.

31. "I remember exactly how [Ezra Pound] looked. No beard, of course, then. He had a beautifully heavy head of blond hair of which he was tremendously proud. Leonine. It was really very beautiful hair, wavy," and "I met Marianne Moore for the first time in the *Others* days. She had a head of the most glorious auburn hair and eyes—I don't even know to this day whether they were blue or green—but these features were about her only claim to physical beauty," in Williams, *I Wanted to Write a Poem*, 6, 20.

32. At first, the quartz lamp was thought to replace common arc lamps, with a shell of fused quartz instead of glass; see Pierce, "The Quartz Lamp," 133. Subsequently, however, after Kromayer's and Nagelschmidt's modification, quartz lamps were deployed to cure baldness; see Müller, "The Nagelschmidt Modification of the Kromayer Quartz Lamp," 774. For more on this usage of the quartz lamp and "light showers," see Ingold, *Lichtduschen*, 87-92. For Williams's barber, "sleep is a nightly slice of death"; Cirasa, *The Lost Works of William Carlos Williams*, 216.

33. Wong, "Powering Portraiture," 118; Perloff, "Williams and the Visualization of Poetry," 174.

34. Doyle, *William Carlos Williams*, 52, 171. An exception is Victoria Bazin's chapter "Poetic 'Struggle' as Modernist Production" in *Modernism Edited: Marianne Moore and the* Dial *Magazine*, where she discusses for the first time the publication history of "Struggle of Wings" as well as Marianne Moore's editorial intervention on Williams's poem, 197-231.

35. Doyle, *William Carlos Williams*, 51; Mariani, *William Carlos Williams*, 250-251. When Williams approached Marianne Moore, then editor of the *Dial*, to offer "Struggle of Wings" and other shorter poems for publication, he confessed he had "not done any verse for three years," admitting it was taking him "a little time to work back into any sort of fluidity of thought in that medium"; letter from William Carlos Williams to Marianne Moore, dated January 14, 1926, YCAL MSS 34, series I, box 8, folder 283.

36. Weaver, *William Carlos Williams*, 8; in the later lines, Williams would also

mention "a fractured Picasso" and may have been referring to an unidentified Renaissance painting of the Ascension; see Bazin, *Modernism Edited*, 209.

37. Cummings, *Complete Poems 1904-1962*, poem XVI, 235. Further references to this edition will be indicated in brackets in the text as *CP* and followed by page numbers. I follow Cummings's punctuation and formatting as in this edition, unless otherwise stated.

38. Cummings studied ancient Greek at Harvard University, where he also attempted at translations of Euripides; see Sawyer-Lauçanno, *E. E. Cummings*, 43-45; Kennedy, *Dreams in the Mirror*, 53-54.

39. Norman, *E. E. Cummings*, 147; Sawyer-Lauçanno, *E. E. Cummings*, 393.

40. Norman, *E. E. Cummings*, 147.

41. Sawyer-Lauçanno, *E. E. Cummings*, 280; "History of McSorley's," McSorley's Old Ale House, accessed April 16, 2021, https://mcsorleysoldalehouse.nyc/history/. For some later creative responses on the theme of women's access to McSorley's, see Quagliano, "Tony Quagliano Presents Reuel Denney and 'McSorley's Bar,'" and Schorb, "A Tall One."

42. Mitchell, "The Old House at Home."

43. Cummings liked Eliot's poem "Rhapsody on a Windy Night." According to his biographer Christopher Sawyer-Lauçanno, Cummings had read *Prufrock and Other Observations* in the copy sent to him by Scofield Thayer. Subsequently, in some of his notes from the army, Cummings appears to have singled out Eliot's "Rhapsody on a Windy Night" and "Preludes" among the works of the new art that showed "certain vital musical gestures"; see Sawyer-Lauçanno, *E. E. Cummings*, 150-151. In the June 1920 issue of the *Dial*, Cummings ends his awkward review of Eliot's *Poems* (1920) with "our final like, which it must be admitted is also our largest," which goes to Eliot's section from "Rhapsody," beginning with "The lamp hummed: / 'Regard the moon'"; see Cummings, *A Miscellany Revised*, 28-29, and Kennedy, *Dreams in the Mirror*, 209.

44. Burke, *Foursome*, 20; Davis, *Night Light*, no page numbers. Many of Stieglitz's photographs can be accessed at the website of the National Gallery of Art here: https://www.nga.gov/research/online-editions/alfred-stieglitz-key-set .html.

45. Dijkstra, *The Hieroglyphics of a New Speech*, 91-92; Sharpe, *New York Nocturne*, 120; Valance, *Nocturne*, 61.

46. Elcott, *Artificial Darkness*, 12.

47. Norman, *Alfred Stieglitz*, 69-70, and Halter, *The Revolution in the Visual Arts*, 147.

48. Spector, *Bastard in the Ragged Suit*, 83.

49. The New York shop was on Fifth Avenue and started launching its own fragrances from approximately 1920; "Perfume Houses, Volume Q, R," Perfume

Intelligence—The Encyclopaedia of Perfume, accessed June 28, 2021, https://www.perfumeintelligence.co.uk/library/perfume/q/q7/q7p5.htm. According to the advertisements appearing in *Vogue* from 1913 to 1920, this perfumery often relied on images of masked figures for its advertisement. It also had branches in Chicago and Boston, and prided itself on bringing French products to an American audience.

50. Berman, "City Lights," 40.

51. Dijkstra, *The Hieroglyphics of a New Speech*, 104.

52. Dijkstra, *The Hieroglyphics of a New Speech*, 166.

53. This is evident in "A la lune" (1914), "Night" (1916), "Summer Song," and "To a Solitary Disciple" (1917). In his earlier poetry, Williams frequently harnesses the moon to raise the poetic profile of the American urban space, as for instance in "Night," in which houses appear with "the dark silhouetted / on flashes of moonlight!" (*CPI* 58, lines 2-3).

54. Williams would recall, in slightly psychoanalytical terms, how his early poetic phase before *Sour Grapes* (1921) was "a quiet period, a pre-sex period, although I was married"; he was still "finding out about life"; in Williams, *I Wanted to Write a Poem*, 23. Even though "Williams' attitude towards Freud" was "complex, perhaps even contradictory," Terence Diggory has aptly shown in his article how Williams was in fact familiar with Freudian theories, "William Carlos Williams' Early 'References to Freud,'" 3.

55. Williams to Kenneth Burke, January 26, 1921, *The Selected Letters of William Carlos Williams*, 48.

56. Mariani, *William Carlos Williams*, 153. Williams knew French well, and his mother spoke both Spanish and French in the household; see Robinson, "'I like the Spanish title': William Carlos Williams's *Al Que Quiere!*," 95, 97.

57. Mariani, *William Carlos Williams*, xiii; Cirasa, *The Lost Works of William Carlos Williams*, 209; Ahearn, *William Carlos Williams and Alterity*, 50.

58. Weaver, *William Carlos Williams*, 37, 44.

59. Williams, *I Wanted to Write a Poem*, 14.

60. Sharpe, *New York Nocturne*, 258.

61. Williams, *The Autobiography*, 172.

62. On this painting, see Dijkstra, "Introduction," in Williams, *A Recognizable Image*, 3; Schwarz, "Painting Williams, Reading Demuth," 17, 27; Agee, *Modern Art in America, 1908-68*, 123. On the friendship between Williams and Demuth, see Marling, *William Carlos Williams and the Painters*, 15-18. Demuth also dedicated his painting *Machinery* to Williams; see Marling, *William Carlos Williams and the Painters*, 34.

63. For more on the technicalities and history of exposed-lamp electric signs, see Jakle, *City Lights*, 212-215. In his autobiography, Williams remembers how

Charles Demuth would always call him Carlos and "once painted a 'literary' picture around my name"; see Williams, *The Autobiography*, 152.

64. Burke, *Foursome*, 139; Scruggs, "The Photographic Print, the Literary Negative," 61, 64.

65. North, *The Dialect of Modernism*, 171; Baker Jr., *Afro-American Poetics*, 36; Toomer, *Collected Poems*, 105. Further references to the poetry of Jean Toomer are from this edition and will be indicated as *CPJT* in the text in brackets and followed by page numbers.

66. Trotter, *Literature in the First Media Age*, 25; Jackson Ford, *Split-Gut Song*, 80-83; Beeston, *In and Out of Sight*, 105.

67. Whalan, "Jean Toomer, Technology, and Race," 467-468; Foley, *Jean Toomer*, 301. Letter from Norman Fitts to Jean Toomer, dated Good Friday 1923, MSS 1, box 3, folder 79. For more on *S4N*, Fitts's editorship, and Marinetti's involvement with this American magazine, see Brooker, "Growth through Disagreement," 655-675.

68. Letter from Fitts to Toomer, dated Good Friday 1923, MSS 1, box 3, folder 79.

69. Marinetti, "Futurism," translated by Norman Fitts, *S4N*, May-August 1923, 11-12, 14. For more on Marinetti in this book, see Chapter Three.

70. Marinetti, "Futurism," 14.

71. Letter from Fitts to Toomer, dated Good Friday 1923, MSS 1, box 3, folder 79.

72. O'Keeffe, *Georgia O'Keeffe*, 17.

73. Dijkstra, *O'Keeffe and the Eros of Place*, 231.

74. Chave, "'Who Will Paint New York?,'" 74.

75. O'Keeffe, *Georgia O'Keeffe*, 17.

76. Barson, "O'Keeffe's Century," 13. As the story goes, he was soon proved mistaken in his judgment, because, when O'Keeffe was finally given the chance to exhibit this painting a year later, *New York Street with Moon* sold immediately; see O'Keeffe, *Georgia O'Keeffe*, 18; Barson, "O'Keeffe's Century," 13.

77. Greenough, "Touching the Centre," 57-58; Barson, "O'Keeffe's Century," 13.

78. Dijkstra, "America and Georgia O'Keeffe," 123. For more on the politics of gender in O'Keeffe's flowers, see also 125-126. Stieglitz made this claim in his essay "Woman in Art" (1919); see also Buhler Lynes, "The Language of Criticism," 47.

79. Buhler Lynes, *O'Keeffe, Stieglitz and the Critics, 1916-1929*, 23-24. For more on Stieglitz's opinions of women, see also Dijkstra, "America and Georgia O'Keeffe," 115-116. Pollock, "Seeing O'Keeffe Seeing," 105.

80. Dijkstra, *O'Keeffe and the Eros of Place*, 231.

81. Sharpe, *New York Nocturne*, 251.

82. Greenough, "Touching the Centre," 58. For more on Stieglitz's painting selection criteria, see Dijkstra, "America and Georgia O'Keeffe," 105–130.

83. Barson, "O'Keeffe's Century," 13; Whitaker Peters, *Becoming O'Keeffe*, 279.

84. Troyen, "Common Ground," 40. The same light fixture appears in O'Keeffe's painting *A Street* (1926).

85. Dijkstra, "America and Georgia O'Keeffe," 117; Sharpe, *New York Nocturne*, 251.

86. Sharpe, *New York Nocturne*, 253. For a discussion of the moon and moonlight in nineteenth-century American art, see Sharpe, *New York Nocturne*, 80–131, and Leeds, *Dreams and Dramas*.

87. I am thinking here especially of a certain "gendered critical discourse" articulated by contemporary reviewers of O'Keeffe's work, establishing her work as necessarily feminine; see Bazin, *Modernism Edited*, 175, 178–179, but also Buhler Lynes, "The Language of Criticism," 43–54, and, in the same volume, Chave, "O'Keeffe and the Masculine Gaze," 29–42.

88. Whitaker Peters, *Becoming O'Keeffe*, 292; Sharpe, *New York Nocturne*, 254; Cheng, *Second Skin*, 84.

89. In the 1920s, O'Keeffe incorporates Stieglitz in many of her paintings "as the line of her vision," something that becomes explicit in *Radiator Building*; see Bazin, *Modernism Edited*, 179.

90. Green Fryd, "Georgia O'Keeffe's *Radiator Building*," 270.

91. Ridge, diary entry May 2, 1940, "Diaries 1940–1941," 67.

92. Berke, "'Electric Currents of Life,'" 27–28.

93. Berke, "'Electric Currents of Life,'" 31.

94. Tobin, "An Unfinished Tower," 73; Tante, *Living Authors*, 340; Tobin, "Introduction," in Ridge, *To the Many*, 17.

95. As Caroline Maun notices, light *is* one of the main unifying patterns in Ridge's American poetry; see Maun, *Mosaic of Fire*, 26.

96. Ridge, *Collected Early Works*, 108. Further references to this edition will be indicated in parentheses in the text, as *CEW*, and followed by page numbers. The title "To the Others" might be a reference to the poets of Alfred Kreymborg's leading magazine, *Others: A Magazine of the New Verse* (1915–1919), see Churchill, "An Introduction to *Others: A Magazine of the New Verse*"; for more on Ridge's involvement with the magazine, see Svoboda, *Anything That Burns You*, 121–127.

97. Nye, *Electrifying America*, 32. The statue was officially unveiled on October 28, 1886, but because of the stormy weather in the bay the firework-and-electric-light spectacle was postponed until November 1; see "The Statue of Liberty," *Harper's Weekly*, 714. Not only was the torch itself illuminated with "eight lamps [. . .] with an aggregate power of 48,000 candles," but "six other lamps of 6,000 candle power each" and "parabolic reflectors" were placed all around the base of the statue: a truly amazing spectacle to anyone witnessing it. See "Liberty's Torch

Lighted," 1. The reporter calls it "the most striking and impressive [pageant] ever seen in the country, and fitting the occasion it honored."

98. Nye, *Electrifying America*, 50, 52. According to John A. Jakle, the term Great White Way was coined by O. J. Gude, "whose company pioneered the street's electric sign"; *City Lights*, 201. Marston, "ELECTRIC SIGNS Have Given 'The Great White Way' Its Name," 8.

99. Svoboda, *Anything That Burns You*, 5; Berke, *Women Poets on the Left* 71. For more on Ridge's political activism, see Svoboda, *Anything That Burns You*, 73-86, 218-226.

100. In 1920s New York, Lola Ridge would have already embodied the second generation of the late nineteenth-century middle-class working women whom Deborah L. Parsons describes as starting to walk more assertively around the city at night, as a result of changes in women's lifestyle; see *Streetwalking the Metropolis*, 83, and elsewhere. When using the French term in the feminine, here and elsewhere in the book, I am indebted to Lauren Elkin's conceptualizing in *Flâneuse*.

101. Ridge met Lawson at the Ferrer Center in 1910. He was born in 1886, while Ridge was born in 1873. On their first meeting, see Svoboda, *Anything That Burns You*, 73-86.

Unsurprisingly, Daniel Tobin chose the phrase "light in hand" as title for the first collection of Ridge's early poetry to be republished after her death, as it truly testifies Ridge's feminist vision that women should be the masters of their own lives.

102. Svoboda, *Anything That Burns You*, 5.

103. Tante, *Living Authors*, 341.

104. In the original 1920 edition of *Sun-Up and Other Poems*, "phalluses" is spelled "phallases." Daniel Tobin then corrected it in his new edition of Ridge's early works, in an effort to "negotiate between making reasonable corrections and keeping the texts of her work as authentic as possible" (*CEW* 392). I am following here Tobin's spelling.

105. Fairclough, *Literature, Electricity and Politics 1740-1840*, 79-105.

106. Electricity might hint at Ridge's common-law union with David Lawson, who worked as a civil engineer but who would sometimes pass for "an electrician from Wales" (Kreymborg, *Troubadour*, 326; Svoboda, *Anything That Burns You*, 122), making electricity a possible inside joke for the couple. Ridge married Lawson in 1919. According to Ridge's biographer, Lawson worked in New Jersey and New York as "a low-paid engineer." But "in 1918 he was a toolmaker, a machine designer in 1924, and in 1929, a consulting engineer in the employ of the New Jersey State Highway Commission"; Svoboda, *Anything That Burns You*, 74. According to my private correspondence with Elaine Sproat, he was a civil engineer.

107. McKay, *Complete Poems*, 150-151 (lines 7-16). Further references to this edition will be indicated as *CP* in the text and followed by page numbers.

108. Sharpe, *New York Nocturne*, 90.

109. On Hughes's lunar imagery, see Koprince, "Moon Imagery in *The Ways of White Folks*"; Moreno, "Gypsy Moon over Harlem." On the French Symbolists' influence on Hughes, see Patterson, *Race, American Literature and Transnational Modernisms*, 100.

110. Hughes, *The Collected Poems of Langston Hughes*, 31 (lines 1-4). Further references to this edition will be indicated as *CPLH* in the text and followed by page numbers.

111. Toomer, *Cane*, 97. Further references to this edition will be indicated as *C* in the text and followed by page numbers.

112. Baker Jr., *Afro-American Poetics*, 37; Douglas, *Terrible Honesty*, 83.

113. Dyer, *White*, 84.

114. Dyer, *White*, 103.

115. Cheng, *Second Skin*, 115.

116. Cheng, *Second Skin*, 64.

117. Cheng also points out that the golden effects of Baker's skin contribute to exoticizing her appearance and reinscribing colonial discourses back onto her; Cheng, *Second Skin*, 152-153. For more on Josephine Baker's body as an indicator of colonial discourse typical of the modern primitivist imagination, see Lemke, *Primitivist Modernism*, 97-99.

118. Dyer, *White*, 86.

119. Ellison, *Invisible Man*, 6.

120. Harlem, New York's Black neighborhood and center of American nightlife, remained a dimly lit space, as it had been relying heavily on gas lighting both outside and indoors well into the twentieth century; Wintz, *Black Culture and the Harlem Renaissance*, 17; Sharpe, *New York Nocturne*, 177; Burrows and Wallace, *Gotham*, 1069.

121. Panadero, "James Van Der Zee's Retouched Portraits."

122. Haskins, *James Van DerZee*, 99.

123. Willis-Braithwaite, "They Knew Their Names," 18-21. James Van Der Zee's studio was, unlike many photographers' studios at the time, on the ground floor and so necessitated electric lights, and he was extremely well attuned to the different shades of light cast by different lights available to him; see Haskins, *James Van DerZee*, 99.

124. Willis-Braithwaite, "They Knew Their Names," 18; Siddons, "African Past or American Present?," 441.

125. Hughes, "The Fascination of Cities," in *The Collected Works of Langston Hughes*, 27. The essay was originally published in *Crisis: A Record of Darker Races* 31, no. 3 (January 1926), 138-140.

126. Hughes, "The Fascination of Cities," in *The Collected Works of Langston Hughes*, 30.

127. Hughes, "The Fascination of Cities," in *The Collected Works of Langston Hughes*, 31.

128. I am thinking here of Toomer's poem "Karintha" but also elsewhere in *Cane*, where we read: "Her skin is like dusk on the eastern horizon," 97. Moreover, the night-woman association was for most African American poets, and even those of the Harlem Renaissance, generally natural (rather than artificial), with no other lights to prettify women barring that of the moon (as, for example, in the poetry of Helene Johnson, Angelina Weld Grimké, and before them, Paul Laurence Dunbar). See Miller, *Making Love Modern*, 214, 217; Johnson, *This Waiting for Love*; Weld Grimké, *Selected Works*; Dunbar, *Collected Poetry*.

129. Bennett, "Street Lamps in Early Spring," 152.

130. Bennett, *Heroine of the Harlem Renaissance and Beyond*, 27 (quoted in full).

131. Wheeler and Parascandola, "Art," in Bennett, *Heroine of the Harlem Renaissance and Beyond*, 35.

132. Goody, "Poetry and Technology," 364.

133. Diary entry, June 26, 1925, in Bennett, *Heroine of the Harlem Renaissance and Beyond*, 179.

Conclusion

1. Bowen, "New Waves of the Future," in *People, Places, Things*, 42. The essay was first published in *American Home*, no. 72 (October 1969), and is one of the last essays to be written by Bowen; see Hepburn, "Notes," in Bowen, *People, Places, Things*, 420.

2. Bowen, "Modern Lighting," in *People, Places, Things*, 26–28.

3. These are all examples used by Bowen: see Bowen, "Modern Lighting," in *People, Places, Things*, 26–27.

4. Bowen, "New Waves of the Future," in *People, Places, Things*, 42.

5. Bowen, "New Waves of the Future," in *People, Places, Things*, 45.

6. Bowen, "New Waves of the Future," in *People, Places, Things*, 45.

7. Williams, *The Collected Poems: Volume I*, 165 (lines 17–26).

8. Pešánek, *Kineticism*, 69.

9. Pound, *Patria Mia and the Treatise on Harmony*, 19.

10. Loy, "Lunar Baedeker," *The Lost Lunar Baedeker*, 81 (line 24).

11. Toomer, *Collected Poems*, 6 (lines 11–13).

12. Ridge, *To the Many*, 66 (lines 1–2).

13. The slanted reading of *Brilliant Modernism* does not include, for example, instances of rural modernisms, such as those discussed in *Rural Modernity in Britain*, Kristin Bluemel and Michael McCluskey, eds., or Andree, "Cripping the Pastoral," 12–34.

14. See, for example, Gunning, "Light, Motion, Cinema!," 106-129; Gunning, "Loïe Fuller and the Art of Motion," 75-90; Ronetti, "'Chromo-culture,'" 72-83; Willis, "'What the Moon is Like,'" 175-203.

15. "A Short History of City Lights," City Lights Bookstore and Publishers.

16. Morgan, "Bookstore Tour."

17. Morgan, "Bookstore Tour."

18. Ferlinghetti, *Poetry as Insurgent Art*, 37, 48, 66. "What Is Poetry?" was initially a transcript of a 1950s broadcast. It was first published in 1975, and then republished with additions in 2007 by New Directions.

19. Ferlinghetti, *A Coney Island of the Mind*, 72-73.

20. Ferlinghetti, *Poetry as Insurgent Art*, 50, 39.

Bibliography

Introduction

Adorno, Theodor. *Aesthetic Theory*. Edited by Gretel Adorno and Rolf Tiedemann. Translated by Robert Hullot-Kentor. Minneapolis: University of Minnesota Press, 1997.

Allen, Edward. *Modernist Invention: Media Technology and American Poetry*. Cambridge: Cambridge University Press, 2020.

Armstrong, Tim. *Modernism, Technology, and the Body: A Cultural Study*. Cambridge: Cambridge University Press, 1998.

Bach, Susanne, and Folkert Degenring. *Dark Nights, Bright Lights: Night, Darkness, and Illumination in Literature*. Berlin: De Gruyter, 2015.

Bachelard, Gaston. *The Flame of a Candle*. Translated by Joni Caldwell. Dallas, TX: Dallas Institute of Humanities and Culture, 2012.

Barnaby, Alice. *Light Touches: Cultural Practices of Illumination, 1800–1900*. London: Routledge, 2017.

Bazerman, Charles. *Languages of Edison's Light*. Cambridge, MA: MIT Press, 2002.

Beaton, Cecil. *The Book of Beauty*. London: Duckworth, 1930.

Beltran, Alain, and Patrice A. Carré. *La fée et la servante: La société française face à l'électricité XIXᵉ-XXᵉ siècle*. Paris: Belin, 1991.

Benjamin, Walter. *The Arcades Project*. Translated by Howard Eiland and Kevin McLaughlin. Cambridge, MA: Belknap Press of Harvard University Press, 1999.

Benjamin, Walter. "On Some Motifs in Baudelaire." In *Illuminations*, edited by Hannah Arendt and translated by Harry Zorn, 152–196. London: Vintage, 2015.

Bensaude-Vincent, Bernadette, and William R. Newman. *The Artificial and the Natural: An Evolving Polarity*. Cambridge, MA: MIT Press, 2007.

Brevda, William. *Signs of the Signs: The Literary Lights of Incandescence and Neon*. Lewisburg, PA: Bucknell University Press, 2011.

Caledoniensis. *Gas and the Electric Light*. Edinburgh, UK: Maclachlan and Stewart, 1879.

Cunard, Nancy. *Selected Poems.* Edited by Sandeep Parmar. Manchester, UK: Carcanet/Fyfield Books, 2016.

de Maupassant, Guy. "La nuit (cauchemar)." In *Clair de lune,* 303-316. Paris: Paul Ollendorff, 1894.

Dowson, Ernest. *The Pierrot of the Minute: A Dramatic Phantasy in One Act.* London: Leonard Smithers, 1896.

Elcott, Noam Milgrom. *Artificial Darkness: An Obscure History of Modern Art and Media.* Chicago: University of Chicago Press, 2016.

Emerson, Ralph Waldo. *Essays, Poems, Addresses.* Edited by Gordon S. Haight. New York: Van Nostrand Company, 1941.

Feldman, Matthew. "Introduction to *Historicizing Modernists: Approaches to 'Archivalism.'*" In *Historicizing Modernists: Approaches to "Archivalism."* Edited by Matthew Feldman, Anna Svendsen, and Erik Tonning, 1-19. London: Bloomsbury, 2021.

Flint, Kate. *Flash! Photography, Writing, and Surprising Illumination.* Oxford: Oxford University Press, 2017.

Flint, Kate. *The Victorians and the Visual Imagination.* Cambridge: Cambridge University Press, 2000.

Foulkes, Richard. "Lewis Carroll, E. L. Blanchard and Frank W. Green." In *Victorian Pantomime: A Collection of Critical Essays.* Edited by Jim Davis, 54-69. Basingstoke, UK: Palgrave Macmillan, 2010.

Freeberg, Ernest. *The Age of Edison: Electric Light and the Invention of Modern America.* New York: Penguin Press, 2013.

French, Daniel. *When They Hid the Fire: A History of Electricity and Invisible Energy in America.* Pittsburgh: University of Pittsburgh Press, 2017.

Gallagher, Catherine, and Stephen Greenblatt. *Practicing New Historicism.* Chicago: University of Chicago Press, 2000.

Geertz, Clifford. *The Interpretation of Cultures: Selected Essays.* New York: Perseus Books, 1973.

Gibson, Charles R. *The Romance of Modern Electricity: Describing in Non-Technical Language What is Known About Electricity and Many of Its Interesting Applications.* London: Seeley and Co. Limited, 1906.

Gooday, Graeme. *Domesticating Electricity: Technology, Uncertainty, and Gender, 1880-1914.* Pittsburgh: University of Pittsburgh Press, 2016.

Goody, Alex. *Modernist Poetry, Gender and Leisure Technologies: Machine Amusements.* New York: Palgrave Macmillan, 2019.

Goody, Alex. *Technology, Literature, and Culture.* Cambridge: Polity, 2013.

Green, Frank W., and Alfred Lee. *The New Electric Light: The Popular Comic Song Sung by Nellie Power, &c. &c.* London: C. Sheard, 1879.

Hannah, Leslie. *Electricity before Nationalisation: A Study of the Development of the Electricity Supply Industry in Britain to 1948.* London: Macmillan, 1979.

Hardy, Emma. *Diaries*. Edited by Richard H. Taylor. Manchester, UK: Mid Northumberland Arts Group and Carcanet New Press, 1985.

Jones, Peter, ed. *Imagist Poetry*. London: Penguin, 2001.

Kenner, Hugh. *The Mechanic Muse*. Oxford: Oxford University Press, 1987.

Laforgue, Jules. *L'Imitation de Notre-Dame la Lune: Des Fleurs de bonne volonté*. Edited by Pascal Pia. Paris: Gallimard, 1970.

Laforgue, Jules. *Poems*. Translated by Peter Dale. London: Anvil Press Poetry, 2001.

Leahy, Richard. *Literary Illumination: The Evolution of Artificial Light in Nineteenth-Century Literature*. Cardiff, UK: University of Wales Press, 2018.

Lewis, Emma. *Isms: Understanding Photography*. London: Bloomsbury, 2017.

Loy, Mina. *The Lost Lunar Baedeker*. Edited by Roger L. Conover. Manchester, UK: Carcanet, 1997.

Luckiesh, Matthew. *Artificial Light: Its Influence Upon Civilization*. London: University of London Press, 1920.

Luckiesh, Matthew. *Lighting the Home*. New York: The Century Co., 1920.

Mao, Douglas, ed. *The New Modernist Studies*. Cambridge: Cambridge University Press, 2021.

Mao, Douglas, and Rebecca L. Walkowitz. *Bad Modernisms*. Durham, NC: Duke University Press, 2006.

Mao, Douglas, and Rebecca L. Walkowitz. "The New Modernist Studies." *PMLA: Publications of the Modern Language Association of America* 123, no. 3 (2008): 737-748.

Marinetti, Filippo Tommaso. *Le Futurisme*. Paris: E Sansot, 1911.

Marinetti, Filippo Tommaso. *Teoria e invenzione futurista*. Edited by Luciano de Maria. Milan: Mondadori, 1968.

Marvin, Carolyn. *When Old Technologies Were New: Thinking About Electric Communication in the Late Nineteenth Century*. Oxford: Oxford University Press, 1988.

McCabe, Susan. *Cinematic Modernism: Modernist Poetry and Film*. Cambridge: Cambridge University Press, 2008.

Mirrlees, Hope. *Collected Poems*. Edited by Sandeep Parmar. Manchester, UK: Carcanet, 2011.

Moody, A. David. *Ezra Pound: Poet: A Portrait of the Man and His Work: Volume I: The Young Genius 1885-1920*. Oxford: Oxford University Press, 2007.

Morris, Edmund. *Edison*. New York: Random House, 2019.

Muir, Robin. *Cecil Beaton's Bright Young Things*. London: National Portrait Gallery Publications, 2021.

Mumford, Lewis. *Technics and Civilization*. New York: Harcourt, Brace and Company, 1934.

Munro, John. *Electricity and Its Uses*. London: The Religious Tract Society, 1887.

Munro, John. *The Romance of Electricity*. London: The Religious Tract Society, 1893.

Nead, Lynda. *The Haunted Gallery: Painting, Photography, and Film, c. 1900*. New Haven, CT: Yale University Press, 2007.

Nead, Lynda. *Victorian Babylon: People, Streets and Images in Nineteenth-Century London*. New Haven, CT: Yale University Press, 2011.

Nye, David Edwin. *American Illuminations: Urban Lighting, 1800-1920*. Cambridge, MA: MIT Press, 2018.

Nye, David Edwin. *Electrifying America: Social Meanings of a New Technology, 1880-1940*. Cambridge, MA: MIT Press, 1990.

Nye, David Edwin. *Technology Matters: Questions to Live With*. Cambridge, MA: MIT Press, 2006.

Otter, Chris. *The Victorian Eye: A Political History of Light and Vision in Britain, 1800-1900*. Chicago: University of Chicago Press, 2008.

Palmer, Bryan D. *Cultures of Darkness: Night Travels in the Histories of Transgression, from Medieval to Modern*. New York: Monthly Review Press, 2000.

Perlow, Seth. *The Poem Electric: Technology and the American Lyric*. Minneapolis: University of Minnesota Press, 2018.

Pound, Ezra. *Selected Prose: 1909-1965*. Edited by William Cookson. New York: New Directions, 1973.

Rainey, Lawrence, Christine Poggi, and Laura Wittman, eds. *Futurism: An Anthology*. New Haven, CT: Yale University Press, 2009.

Saint-Amour, Paul K. "Weak Theory, Weak Modernism." *Modernism/modernity* 25, no. 3 (2018): 437-459.

Salinas, Pedro. *Poesías complétas*. Edited by Solita Salinas de Marichal. Madrid: Debolsillo, 2011.

Sarker, Sonita. "Absence and Containment: English-Language Transnational Literary Modernist Studies Today." *Modernism/modernity PrintPlus* 4, cycle 3 (2019). https://doi.org/10.26597/mod.0134.

Scappettone, Jennifer. *Killing the Moonlight: Modernism in Venice*. New York: Columbia University Press, 2014.

Schivelbusch, Wolfgang. *Disenchanted Night: The Industrialization of Light in the Nineteenth Century*. Translated by Angela Davies. Berkeley and Los Angeles: University of California Press, 1995.

Schlör, Joachim. *Nights in the Big City: Paris, Berlin, London, 1840-1930*. Translated by Pierre Gottfried Imhof and Dafydd Rees Roberts. London: Reaktion Books, 2016.

Schuchard, Ronald. *Eliot's Dark Angel: Intersections of Life and Art*. New York: Oxford University Press, 1999.

Seifert, Jaroslav. *On the Waves of TSF: Na vlnách TSF*. Edited by Karel Teige. Remake by Zdeněk Trinkewitz. Translated by Dana Loewy. Prague: Akropolis, 2011.

Sharpe, William Chapman. *New York Nocturne: The City After Dark in Literature,*

Painting, and Photography, 1850-1950. Princeton, NJ: Princeton University Press, 2008.

Simon, Linda. *Dark Light: Electricity and Anxiety from the Telegraph to the X-Ray.* San Diego: Harcourt, 2004.

Somerville, Kristine. "Camera Artist: The Portraiture of Cecil Beaton." *The Missouri Review* 35, no. 4 (2012): 61-80.

Stanford Friedman, Susan. "Planetarity: Musing Modernist Studies." *Modernism/modernity* 71, no. 3 (2010): 471-499.

Steen, Jürgen. "Die 'fée electricité' trifft Prometheus—Die internationale Elektrotechnische Ausstellung 1891 und die 'Neue Zeit.'" In *Unbedingt modern sein: Elektrizität und Zeitgeist um 1900*, edited by Rolf Spilker, 38-49. Bramsche: Rasch Verlag, 2003.

Stevenson, Robert Louis. *Virginibus Puerisque and Other Papers.* New York: Scribner's, 1912.

Tichi, Cecelia. *Shifting Gears: Technology, Literature, Culture in Modernist America.* Chapel Hill, NC: University of North Carolina Press, 1987.

Toomer, Jean. *The Wayward and the Seeking: A Collection of Writings.* Edited by Darwin T. Turner. Washington, DC: Howard University Press, 1980.

Trotter, David. *Literature in the First Media Age: Britain between the Wars.* Cambridge, MA: Harvard University Press, 2013.

Trotter, David. *The Literature of Connection: Signal, Medium, Interface, 1850-1950.* Oxford: Oxford University Press, 2020.

Waddell, Nathan. *Moonlighting: Beethoven and Literary Modernism.* Oxford: Oxford University Press, 2019.

Walkowitz, Judith R. *City of Dreadful Delight: Narratives of Sexual Danger in Late-Victorian London.* Chicago: University of Chicago Press, 1992.

Woolf, Virginia. "Character in Fiction." In *The Essays of Virginia Woolf: Volume III: 1919-1924*, edited by Andrew McNeillie, 420-438. London: Hogarth, 1988.

Woolf, Virginia. *A Room of One's Own and Three Guineas.* Edited by Morag Shiach. Oxford: Oxford University Press, 2000.

Wosk, Julie. *Women and the Machine: Representations from the Spinning Wheel to the Electronic Age.* Baltimore, MD: Johns Hopkins University Press, 2001.

Yeats, William Butler. "A General Introduction for My Work." In *Essays and Introductions*, 509-526. New York: Macmillan Company, 1961.

Chapter 1. Observing Light

Apollinaire, Guillaume. *Alcools suivi de Le Bestiaire illustré par Raoul Dufy et de Vitam impendere amori.* Paris: Gallimard, 2005.

Asciuto, Nicoletta. "Light and Mystical Writing: T. S. Eliot's Poetic Practice in *Four Quartets*." *Religion & Literature* 52, no. 3 (2021): 47-69.

Asciuto, Nicoletta. "The Sun Also Sets: The Violet Hour in T. S. Eliot's *The Waste Land*." *Literary Imagination* 18, no. 2 (2016): 150–165.

Bachelard, Gaston. *The Flame of a Candle*. Translated by Joni Caldwell. Dallas: Dallas Institute of Humanities and Culture, 1988.

Baron, Scarlett. "Flaubert, Joyce: Vision, Photography, Cinema." *Modern Fiction Studies* 54, no. 4 (2008): 689–714.

Baudelaire, Charles. *The Flowers of Evil: Bilingual Edition*. Translated by James McGowan. Oxford: Oxford University Press, 2008.

Baudelaire, Charles. *Le spleen de Paris or Les cinquante petits poèmes en prose de Charles Baudelaire*. Paris: Emile-Paul, 1917.

Baudelaire, Charles. *The Painter of Modern Life*. Translated by P. E. Charvet. London: Penguin Books, 2010.

Baudelaire, Charles. *Paris Spleen*. Translated by Louise Varèse. New York: New Directions Publishing, 1970.

Beasley, Rebecca. *Theorists of Modernist Poetry: T. S. Eliot, T. E. Hulme and Ezra Pound*. London: Routledge, 2007.

Beltran, Alain, and Patrice A. Carré. *La fée et la servante: La société française face à l'électricité XIXe-XXe siècle*. Paris: Belin, 1991.

Benjamin, Walter. *Charles Baudelaire*. Translated by Harry Zohn. London and New York: Verso, 1997.

Bennett, Arnold. *The Old Wives' Tale*. London, Edinburgh, and New York: Thomas Nelson and Sons Ltd., 1917.

Berman, Marshall. *All That Is Solid Melts into Air: The Experience of Modernity*. London: Verso, 2010.

Blake, Peter. *George Augustus Sala and the Nineteenth-Century Periodical Press: The Personal Style of a Public Writer*. London: Routledge, 2016.

Blühm, Andreas, and Louise Lippincott. *Light!: The Industrial Age 1750–1900: Art & Science, Technology & Society*. New York: Thames and Hudson, 2001.

Boyiopoulos, Kostas. *The Decadent Image: The Poetry of Wilde, Symons, and Dowson*. Edinburgh, UK: Edinburgh University Press, 2015.

Bressani, Martin. "Paris—Light into Darkness: Gaslight in Nineteenth-Century Paris." In *Cities of Light: Two Centuries of Urban Illumination*, edited by Sandy Isenstadt, Margaret Petty, and Dietrich Neumann, 28–36. New York: Routledge, 2015.

Brooker, Jewel Spears. "Mimetic Desire and the Return to Origins in *The Waste Land*." In *Gender, Desire, and Sexuality in T. S. Eliot*, edited by Cassandra Laity and Nancy K. Gish, 130–149. Cambridge: Cambridge University Press, 2004.

Brooker, Jewel Spears. "Seduction and Disenchantment: Eliot in the Bergsonian World." In *T. S. Eliot, France, and the Mind of Europe*, edited by Jayme Stayer, 24–38. Newcastle-upon-Tyne, UK: Cambridge Scholars, 2015.

Bush, Ronald. "In Pursuit of Wilde Possum: Reflections on Eliot, Modernism, and the Nineties." *Modernism/modernity* 11, no. 3 (2004): 469–485.

Camerani, Marco. *Joyce e il cinema delle origini: Circe.* Fiesole: Cadmo, 2008.

Cándida Smith, Richard. *Mallarmé's Children: Symbolism and the Renewal of Experience.* Berkeley: University of California Press, 1999.

Carmona, Michel. *Haussmann: His Life and Times, and the Making of Modern Paris.* Translated by Patrick Camiller. Chicago: Ivan. R. Dee, 2002.

Childs, Donald J. *Modernism and Eugenics: Woolf, Eliot, Yeats, and the Culture of Degeneration.* Cambridge: Cambridge University Press, 2004.

Childs, Donald J. "Rhapsody of Matter and Memory." *American Literature* 63, no. 3 (1991): 474-488.

Clayson, Hollis. "Bright Lights, Brilliant Wits: Caricature and Electric Light in Later Nineteenth-Century Paris." In *Electric Worlds/Mondes électriques: Creations, Circulations, Tensions, Transitions*, edited by Alain Beltran, Léonard Laborie, Pierre Lanthier, and Stéphanie Le Gallic, 17-38. Bern: Peter Lang, 2016.

Clayson, Hollis. *Illuminated Paris: Essays on Art and Lighting in the Belle Époque.* Chicago: University of Chicago Press, 2019.

Corbière, Tristan. *Selected Poems and Prose: The Centenary Corbière: Bilingual Edition.* Translated by Val Warner. Manchester, UK: Carcanet, 2003.

Crawford, Robert. *Young Eliot: From St Louis to* The Waste Land. London: Vintage, 2015.

Dale, Peter. "Introduction." In *Poems of Jules Laforgue.* Translated by Peter Dale, 7-23. London: Anvil Press Poetry, 2009.

Delattre, Simone. *Les douze heures noires: La nuit à Paris au XIXe siècle.* Paris: Albin Michel, 2000.

de Thézy, Marie. *Marville: Paris.* Paris: Hazan, 1994.

de Wolf, Joke. "Paris on Display: Marville's Photographs at the Universal Exhibitions." In *Charles Marville: Photographer of Paris*, edited by Sarah Kennel, 209-219. Chicago: University of Chicago Press, 2014.

Döblin, Alfred. "An Romanautoren und ihre Kritiker: Berliner Programm." *Der Sturm* 4, no. 158/159 (May 1913): 17-18.

Downie, David. *Paris, Paris: Journey into the City of Light.* New York: Broadway Books, 2011.

Dyer, Geoff. "On Atget." In *Eugène Atget: Old Paris,* 31-36. Madrid: TF Editores, 2011.

Ebury, Katherine. "'In this valley of dying stars': Eliot's Cosmology." *Journal of Modern Literature* 35, no. 3 (2012): 139-157.

Edwards, Peter David. *Dickens's "Young Men": George Augustus Sala, Edmund Yates, and the World of Victorian Journalism.* Aldershot, UK: Ashgate, 1997.

Eliot, Thomas Stearns. *The Complete Prose of T. S. Eliot: The Critical Edition: The Perfect Critic, 1919-1926: Volume 2.* Edited by Ronald Schuchard and Antony Cuda. Baltimore, MD: Johns Hopkins University Press, 2014.

Eliot, Thomas Stearns. *The Complete Prose of T. S. Eliot: The Critical Edition: English*

Lion, 1930-1933: Volume 4. Edited by Jason Harding and Ronald Schuchard. Baltimore, MD: Johns Hopkins University Press, 2015.

Eliot, Thomas Stearns. *The Complete Prose of T. S. Eliot: The Critical Edition: Tradition and Orthodoxy, 1934-39: Volume 5*. Edited by Iman Javadi, Ronald Schuchard, and Jayme Stayer. Baltimore, MD: Johns Hopkins University Press, 2017.

Eliot, Thomas Stearns. *The Complete Prose of T. S. Eliot: The Critical Edition: The War Years, 1940-1946: Volume 6*. Edited by David E. Chinitz and Ronald Schuchard. Baltimore, MD: Johns Hopkins University Press, 2017.

Eliot, Thomas Stearns. *The Complete Prose of T. S. Eliot: The Critical Edition: A European Society, 1947-1953: Volume 7*. Edited by Ronald Schuchard and Iman Javadi. Baltimore, MD: Johns Hopkins University Press, 2019.

Eliot, Thomas Stearns. *Fireside: A Weekly Magazine* 1, no. 2 (January 29, 1898). In MS Am 1635.5 "T. S. Eliot's Juvenilia," Houghton Library, Harvard University.

Eliot, Thomas Stearns. *Inventions of the March Hare*. Edited by Christopher Ricks. London: Faber and Faber, 1996.

Eliot, Thomas Stearns. *The Letters of T. S. Eliot: Volume 1, 1898-1922*. Edited by Valerie Eliot and Hugh Haughton. London: Faber and Faber, 2009.

Eliot, Thomas Stearns. Letters to John Hayward (HB/V/12). The Hayward Bequest, King's College Archives, University of Cambridge.

Eliot, Thomas Stearns. *The Poems of T. S. Eliot: Volume I: Collected and Uncollected Poems*. Edited by Christopher Ricks and Jim McCue. London: Faber and Faber, 2015.

Eliot, Thomas Stearns. *The Poems of T. S. Eliot: Volume II: Practical Cats & Further Verses*. Edited by Christopher Ricks and Jim McCue. London: Faber and Faber, 2015.

Eliot, Thomas Stearns, and Donald Hall. "T. S. Eliot, The Art of Poetry No. 1." *Paris Review* 21 (Spring-Summer 1959). https://www.theparisreview.org/interviews/4738/the-art-of-poetry-no-1-t-s-eliot.

Flammarion, Camille. *Astronomie des dames: précis d'astronomie descriptive*. Paris: Flammarion, 1921.

Flammarion, Camille. *Astronomy for Amateurs*. Translated by Frances A. Welby. New York and London: D. Appleton and Company, 1908.

Flammarion, Camille. *Popular Astronomy: A General Description of the Heavens*. Translated by J. Ellard Gore. London: Chatto and Windus, 1907.

Frazer, John. "Cubism and the Cinema of Georges Méliès." *Millennium Film Journal* 19 (1987-88): 94-102.

Gardner, Helen. *The Composition of* Four Quartets. London: Faber and Faber, 1978.

Grojnowski, Daniel. "Sur quelques comptes rendus oubliés des *Complaintes* et de *L'imitation de Notre-Dame la Lune* de Jules Laforgue." *Revue d'Histoire littéraire de la France* 1 (1970): 108-113.

Hanaway-Oakley, Cleo. *James Joyce and the Phenomenology of Film*. Oxford: Oxford University Press, 2017.

Hargrove, Nancy Duvall. *T. S. Eliot's Parisian Year*. Gainesville, FL: University Press of Florida, 2009.

Harvey, David. *Paris, Capital of Modernity*. London: Routledge, 2006.

Hext, Kate, and Alex Murray. *Decadence in the Age of Modernism*. Baltimore, MD: Johns Hopkins University Press, 2019.

Holcombe, Arthur Norman. "The Electric Lighting System of Paris." *Political Science Quarterly* 26, no. 1 (1911): 122-132.

Hopkins, Albert A. *Magic: Stage Illusions and Scientific Diversions, including Trick Photography*. London: Sampson Low, Marston and Company, 1897.

Janes, Dominic. *Oscar Wilde Prefigured: Queer Fashioning and British Caricature, 1750-1900*. Chicago: University of Chicago Press, 2016.

Jones, Peter, ed. *Imagist Poetry*. London: Penguin Books, 2001.

Keegan, Paul. "Emily of Fire & Violence." *London Review of Books* 42, no. 20 (October 22, 2020). https://www.lrb.co.uk/the-paper/v42/n20/paul-keegan/emily -of-fire-violence.

Kennedy, Sarah. *T. S. Eliot and the Dynamic Imagination*. Cambridge: Cambridge University Press, 2018.

Kennel, Sarah. "Charles Marville, Hidden in Plain Sight." In *Charles Marville: Photographer of Paris*, edited by Sarah Kennel, 2-41. Chicago: University of Chicago Press, 2014.

Kenner, Hugh. *The Mechanic Muse*. Oxford: Oxford University Press, 1987.

Laforgue, Jules. *Essential Poems & Prose of Jules Laforgue*. Translated by Patricia Terry. Boston: Black Widow Press, 2010.

Laforgue, Jules. *Moral Tales*. Translated by William Jay Smith. London: Picador Classics, 1984.

Laforgue, Jules. *Œuvres Complètes de Jules Laforgue: Moralités Légendaires*. Paris: Société du Mercure de France, 1902.

Laforgue, Jules. *Œuvres Complètes: Mélanges Posthumes*. Paris: Société du Mercure de France, 1902.

Laforgue, Jules. *Poems of Jules Laforgue*. Translated by Peter Dale. London: Anvil Press, 2011.

Larousse Dictionnaire de Français. https://www.larousse.fr/dictionnaires/francais.

Lehmann, Andrew George. *The Symbolist Aesthetic in France, 1885-1895*. Oxford: Blackwell, 1968.

Le Morvan, Charles. *Carte photographique et systématique de la lune*. Paris: L'Académie des Sciences, 1914.

Lockerd, Martin. *Decadent Catholicism and the Making of Modernism*. London and New York: Bloomsbury, 2020.

Lockerd, Martin. "'A Satirist of Vice and Follies': Beardsley, Eliot, and Images of Decadent Catholicism." *Journal of Modern Literature* 37, no. 4 (2014): 143-165.

Lynn, W. T. "The Moon as Seen from Mount Hamilton." *Leisure Hour*, September 1893.

Marx, William. "Paris." In *T. S. Eliot in Context*, edited by Jason Harding, 25-32. Cambridge: Cambridge University Press, 2011.

McAlmon, Robert, and Kay Boyle. *Being Geniuses Together, 1920-1930.* London: Michael Joseph, 1968.

McArthur, Murray. "Symptom and Sign: Janet, Freud, Eliot, and the Literary Mandate of Laughter." *Twentieth-Century Literature* 56, no. 1 (2010): 1-24.

McCabe, Susan. *Cinematic Modernism: Modernist Poetry and Film.* Cambridge: Cambridge University Press, 2008.

McIntire, Gabrielle. *Modernism, Memory, and Desire: T. S. Eliot and Virginia Woolf.* Cambridge: Cambridge University Press, 2008.

Méliès, George. *Le voyage dans la lune (A Trip to the Moon).* 1902.

Metropolitan Museum of Art. "Systematic Photographic Map of the Moon, Increasing and Decreasing Phases." https://www.metmuseum.org/art/collection /search/705881.

Moody, Anthony David. *Thomas Stearns Eliot: Poet.* Cambridge: Cambridge University Press, 1979.

Nead, Lynda. *The Haunted Gallery: Painting, Photography, Film c. 1900.* New Haven, CT, and London: Yale University Press, 2007.

Nead, Lynda. *Victorian Babylon: People, Streets, and Images in Nineteenth-Century London.* New Haven, CT: Yale University Press, 2000.

Nye, David Edwin. "The Artificial Lighting Available to European and American Museums, 1800-1915." In *From Darkness to Light: Writers in Museums, 1798-1898,* edited by Rosella Mamoli Zorzi and Katherine Manthorne, 25-40. Cambridge: Open Book Publishers, 2019.

Otter, Chris. *The Victorian Eye: A Political History of Light and Vision in Britain, 1800-1910.* Chicago: University of Chicago Press, 2008.

Oxford English Dictionary. https://oed.com.

Paccoud, Antoine. "Planning, Law, Power, and Practice: Haussmann in Paris (1853-1870)." *Planning Perspectives* 31, no. 3 (2016): 341-361.

Peyre, Henri. *Qu'est-ce que le symbolisme?* Paris: Presses universitaires de France, 1974.

Rice, Shelley. *Parisian Views.* Cambridge, MA: MIT Press, 1997.

Riquelme, John Paul. "T. S. Eliot's Ambiviolences: Oscar Wilde as Masked Precursor." *Hopkins Review* 5, no. 3 (2012): 353-379.

Romer, Stephen. "French Poetry." In *T. S. Eliot in Context*, edited by Jason Harding, 211-220. Cambridge: Cambridge University Press, 2011.

Ross, Robert Baldwin. *Aubrey Beardsley, with Sixteen Full-Page Illustrations and a Revised Iconography by Aymer Vallance*. London and New York: John Lane, 1909.

Sala, George Augustus. *Gaslight and Daylight, with Some London Scenes They Shine Upon*. London: Chapman and Hill, 1859.

Sala, George Augustus. *Twice Round the Clock; Or the Hours of the Day and Night in London*. London: Richard Marsh, 1862.

Scarfe, Francis. "Eliot and Nineteenth-Century French Poetry." In *Eliot in Perspective: A Symposium*, edited by Graham Martin, 45–61. London: Macmillan, 1970.

Schlör, Joachim. *Nights in the Big City: Paris, Berlin, London 1840–1930*. Translated by Pierre Gottfried Imhof and Dafydd Rees Roberts. London: Reaktion Books, 2016.

Schuchard, Ronald. *Eliot's Dark Angel: Intersections of Life and Art*. Oxford: Oxford University Press, 1999.

Scrivner, Lee. *Becoming Insomniac: How Sleeplessness Alarmed Modernity*. Basingstoke, UK: Palgrave Macmillan, 2014.

Sharpe, William Chapman. *New York Nocturne: The City After Dark in Literature, Painting, and Photography, 1850–1950*. Princeton, NJ: Princeton University Press, 2008.

Sherry, Vincent. *Modernism and the Reinvention of Decadence*. Cambridge: Cambridge University Press, 2015.

Snodgrass, Chris. *Aubrey Beardsley: Dandy of the Grotesque*. Oxford: Oxford University Press, 1995.

Soldo, John J. "Jovial Juvenilia: T. S. Eliot's First Magazine." *Biography* 5, no. 1 (1982): 25–37.

Soldo, John J. *The Tempering of T. S. Eliot*. Ann Arbor, MI: UMI Research Press, 1983.

Soldo, John J. "T. S. Eliot and Jules LaForgue." *American Literature* 55, no. 2 (1983): 137–150.

Solomon, Matthew. "Negotiating the Bounds of Transnational Cinema with Georges Méliès, 1896–1908." *Early Popular Visual Culture* 14, no. 2 (2016): 155–167.

Steinbach, Alison W., and Katherine E. Wang. "Schoenhof's Foreign Books to Close Brick-and-Mortar Store." *Harvard Crimson*, February 22, 2017. https://www.thecrimson.com/article/2017/2/22/schoenhofs-books-closing/.

Symons, Arthur. *The Symbolist Movement in Literature*. London: William Heinemann, 1899.

Taunton, Matthew. "Moon Voyaging, Selenography, and the Scientific Romance." In *Late Victorian into Modern,* edited by Laura Marcus, Michèle Mendelssohn, and Kirsten E. Shepherd-Barr, 218–231. Oxford: Oxford University Press, 2016.

Thacker, Andrew. *Modernism, Space and the City: Outsiders and Affect in Paris, Vienna, Berlin, and London*. Edinburgh, UK: Edinburgh University Press, 2019.

Trotter, David. "T. S. Eliot and Cinema." *Modernism/modernity* 13, no. 2 (2006): 237-265.

Walker, Nathaniel Robert. "Lost in the City of Light: Dystopia and Utopia in the Wake of Haussmann's Paris." *Utopian Studies* 25, no. 1 (2014): 24-51.

Walkowitz, Judith R. *City of Dreadful Delight: Narratives of Sexual Danger in Late-Victorian London.* London: Virago, 1992.

Whitfield, Peter. *Mapping the Heavens.* London: The British Library, 2018.

Wilde, Oscar. *Poems.* London: David Dogue, 1881.

Wilde, Oscar. *Salomé: A Tragedy in One Act: Translated from the French of Oscar Wilde and Pictured by Aubrey Beardsley.* London: Melmoth and Co., 1904.

Yang, Carol L. "Rhapsody on a City of Dreadful Night: The Flâneur and Urban Spectacle." *Yeats Eliot Review* 26, no. 3/4 (2009): 3-14.

Yeats, William Butler. *Collected Poems.* London: Vintage, 1990.

Chapter 2. Killing the Moonlight

Adamson, Walter L. *Embattled Avant-Gardes: Modernism's Resistance to Commodity Culture in Europe.* Berkeley: University of California Press, 2007.

Agnese, Gino. *Marinetti: Una vita esplosiva.* Milan: Camunia, 1990.

Amgueddfa Cymru/National Museum of Wales. "Art Collections Online." https://museum.wales/art/online/?action=show_item&item=653.

Apelian, Colette. "Modern Mosque Lamps: Electricity in the Historic Monuments and Tourist Attractions of French Colonial Fez, Morocco (1925-1950)." *History and Technology* 28, no. 2 (2012): 177-207.

Baldacci, Paolo, ed. *Ricostruzione di casa Balla.* Milan: Mondadori, 1986.

Baudelaire, Charles. *The Flowers of Evil, With Parallel French Text.* Translated by James McGowan. Oxford: Oxford University Press, 1998.

Bello Minciacchi, Cecilia, ed. *Spirale di dolcezza + serpe di fascino: scrittrici futuriste: antologia.* Naples: Bibliopolis, 2008.

Bentivoglio, Mirella, and Franca Zoccoli. *Le futuriste italiane nelle arti visive.* Rome: De Luca, 2008.

Benzi, Fabio. "Giacomo Balla: Modernity and the Avant Garde." In *Giacomo Balla: Designing the Future,* translated by Christopher Adams, 9-35. Milan: Silvana Editoriale, 2017.

Berghaus, Günter. "Futurism and the Technological Imagination Poised between Machine Cult and Machine Angst." In *Futurism and the Technological Imagination,* edited by Günter Berghaus, 1-37. Amsterdam and New York: Rodopi, 2009.

Berghaus, Günter. "Futurism and Women: A Review Article." *Modern Language Review* 105, no. 2 (2010): 401-410.

Berghaus, Günter, ed. *International Yearbook of Futurism Studies: Volume 5: Women Futurists.* Berlin and Boston: DeGruyter, 2015.

Binni, Walter. *La poetica del decadentismo.* Florence: Sansoni, 1949.

Bohn, Willard, ed, trans. *Italian Futurist Poetry.* Toronto: University of Toronto Press, 2005.

Bragato, Stefano. "'Figlio di una turbina e di d'Annunzio': Marinetti edipico?" In *Archivio d'Annunzio* 5 (2018): 61–78.

Budanova, Natalia. "Penetrating Men's Territory: Russian Avant-Garde Women, Futurism and the First World War." In *International Yearbook of Futurism Studies: Volume 5: Women Futurists*, edited by Günter Berghaus, 168–198. Berlin and Boston: DeGruyter, 2015.

Bürger, Peter. *Theory of the Avant-Garde.* Translated by Michael Shaw. Manchester, UK: Manchester University Press, 1984.

Buzzi, Paolo. *Poesie scelte.* Edited by Emilio Mariano. Milan: Ceschina, 1961.

Calvesi, Maurizio. "Attraverso Marinetti." In *Marinetti*, edited by Claudia Salaris, 7–33. Florence: La Nuova Italia, 1988.

Cangiullo, Francesco. "Un aneddoto marinettiano: Il processo della luna." Undated. In "Libroni on Futurism: Slides." GEN MSS 475, box 20, slide 5. Filippo Tommaso Marinetti Papers, Beinecke Rare Book and Manuscript Library, Yale University.

Carbonaro, Marj. "Luci nel buio." *L'Italia futurista* 3, no. 38 (1918): 2.

Carli, Mario. *Notti filtrate: 10 liriche di Mario Carli con 10 disegni di Rosa Rosà.* Florence: Edizioni de *L'Italia futurista*, 1918.

Carpi, Giancarlo, ed. *Futuriste: Letteratura, Arte, Vita.* Rome: Castelvecchi, 2009.

Carpi, Giancarlo. "Le scrittrici futuriste: Reificazione, superamento del genere e feticismo." In *L'elica e la luce: le futuriste 1912–1944*, edited by Chiara Gatti and Raffaella Resch, 36–39. Milan: Officina libraria, 2018.

Caruso, Luciano, ed. *Manifesti proclami, interventi e documenti teorici del futurismo, 1909–1944.* Florence: Spes, 1990.

Castiglione, Vera. "A Futurist before Futurism: Émile Verhaeren and the Technological Epic." In *Futurism and the Technological Imagination*, edited by Günter Berghaus, 101–124. Amsterdam and New York: Rodopi, 2009.

Cesaretti, Enrico. "Back to the Future: Temporal Ambivalences in F. T. Marinetti's Writings." In *Italian Modernism: Italian Culture between Decadentism and Avant-Garde,* edited by Luca Somigli and Mario Moroni, 243–266. Toronto: University of Toronto Press, 2004.

Chamot, Mary. *Goncharova: Stage Designs and Paintings.* London: Oresko Books, 1979.

Chilvers, Ian, and John Glaves-Smith. *A Dictionary of Modern and Contemporary Art.* 3rd ed. Oxford: Oxford University Press, 2015.

Coen, Ester. "Light." In *FuTurBalla: Life, Light, Speed*, edited by Ester Coen, 75–101. Milan: Skira, 2016.

Colombo, Andrea. *Milano si accende: Quando la luce elettrica illuminò i sogni degli italiani.* Milan: Bompiani, 2014.

Conti, Eleonora. "Marinetti in France between Symbolism and Futurism: *Vers et Prose* and *Les Guêpes*." In *The History of Futurism: The Precursors, Protagonists, and Legacies*, edited by Geert Buelens, Harald Hendrix, and Monica Jansen, 35-51. Lanham, MD: Lexington Books, 2012.

D'Ambrosio, Matteo. "Notes on 'Esoteric Futurism': Marinetti and the Occultist Circle in Milan." In *International Yearbook of Futurism Studies: Volume 8*, edited by Günther Berghaus, Domenico Pietropaolo, and Beatrice Sica, 294-324. Berlin: DeGruyter, 2018.

D'Annunzio, Gabriele. "Les villes terribles." Translated by Filippo Tommaso Marinetti. *Vers et prose: recueil trimestriel de littérature* V (March-April-May 1906).

Davico Bonino, Guido. *Manifesti futuristi*. Milan: Rizzoli, 2009.

Davidson, Peter. *The Last of the Light: About Twilight*. London: Reaktion Books, 2017.

de Saint-Point, Valentine. "Manifesto della donna futurista." In *Futuriste: Letteratura, Arte, Vita*, edited by Giancarlo Carpi, 81-85. Rome: Castelvecchi, 2009.

de Saint-Point, Valentine. "Manifesto futurista della lussuria." In *Futuriste: Letteratura, Arte, Vita*, edited by Giancarlo Carpi, 87-90. Rome: Castelvecchi, 2009.

Dini, Fanny. "Al futurismo trionfante." *L'Italia futurista* 2, no. 31 (1917): 2.

d'Orlando, Vincent. "Réflexions autour d'un astricide: Marinetti, poète mal luné." *Chroniques italiennes*, nos. 47-48 (1996): 141-153.

Fagiolo, Maurizio. *Balla: The Futurist*. Translated by Margaret Kunzle. Milan: Nuove Edizioni Gabriele Mazzotta, 1987.

Fraquelli, Simonetta. "Modified Divisionism: Futurist Painting in 1910." In *Italian Futurism 1909-1944: Reconstructing the Universe*, edited by Vivien Greene, 78-82. New York: Guggenheim Museum Publications, 2014.

Fraquelli, Simonetta, Lara Pucci, and Linda Schädler. *Radical Light: Italy's Divisionist Painters, 1891-1910*. New Haven, CT: Yale University Press, 2008.

Gatti, Chiara, and Raffaella Resch, eds. *L'elica e la luce: le futuriste 1912-1944*. Milan: Officina libraria, 2018.

Ginanni, Maria. "Frammento di novella colorata." *L'Italia futurista* 1, no. 1 (1916): 2.

Ginanni, Maria. "Frammenti di novelle colorate." *L'Italia futurista* 1, no. 2 (1916): 2.

Ginanni, Maria. "Le lucciole." *L'Italia futurista* 1, no. 9 (1916): 2.

Giorgini, Marina. *Růžena Zátková: Un'artista dimenticata*. Brussels: Peter Lang, 2019.

Gipponi, Tino. *La poesia in Ada Negri*. Milan: Prometheus, 2017.

Giuliani, Francesco. *Il poeta futurista Mario Carli: Il mito della giovinezza*. Foggia: Edizioni Ro.Ma., 1991.

Jakobson, Roman. *My Futurist Years*. Edited by Bengt Jangfeldt. Translated by Stephen Rudy. New York: Marsilio Publishers, 1997.

Lakoff, George, and Mark Turner. *More than Cool Reason: A Field Guide to Poetic Metaphor*. Chicago: University of Chicago Press, 1989.

Lapšin, Vladimir Pavlović. *Marinetti e la Russia: Dalla storia delle relazioni letterarie e artistiche negli anni dieci del XX secolo*. Translated by Michela Trainini. Milan: Skira, 2008.

Lista, Giovanni. "Divisionismo e visione fotografica." In *Balla: La modernità futurista*, edited by Giovanni Lista, Paolo Baldacci, and Livia Velani, 1–13. Milan: Skira, 2008.

Lista, Giovanni. *Le futurisme: Création et avant-garde*. Paris: Terrail, 2001.

Livi, François, ed. *Poesia (1905–1909)*. Naples: Edizioni Scientifiche Italiane, 1992.

Livi, François. *Tra crepuscolarismo e futurismo: Govoni e Palazzeschi: Con le varianti de* Le Fiale *e le varianti complete della poesia di Palazzeschi*. Milan: Istituto propaganda libraria, 1980.

Marinetti, Filippo Tommaso. *Come si seducono le donne*. Milan: Excelsior, 2009.

Marinetti, Filippo Tommaso. *Destruction: Poèmes lyriques*. Paris: Leon Vanier, 1904.

Marinetti, Filippo Tommaso. "Donne, non piagnucolate (lettera aperta alla sig.ra Ada Negri)." *L'Italia futurista* 2, no. 32 (November 4, 1917): 1.

Marinetti, Filippo Tommaso, ed. *I poeti futuristi*. Milan: Edizioni futuriste di poesie, 1912.

Marinetti, Filippo Tommaso. *La grande Milano tradizionale e futurista. Una sensibilità italiana nata in Egitto*. Edited by Luciano De Maria. Milan: Mondadori, 1969.

Marinetti, Filippo Tommaso. *La ville charnelle*. Paris: Sansot and Co., 1908.

Marinetti, Filippo Tommaso. *Le futurisme*. Paris: E Sansot, 1911.

Marinetti, Filippo Tommaso. "Le Futurisme." *Le Figaro*, February 20, 1909. https://gallica.bnf.fr/ark:/12148/bpt6k2883730.item#.

Marinetti, Filippo Tommaso. *Scritti francesi*. Edited by Pasquale A. Jannini. Milan: Mondadori Editore, 1983.

Marinetti, Filippo Tommaso. *Taccuini, 1915–1921*. Edited by Alberto Bertoni. Bologna: Il Mulino, 1987.

Marinetti, Filippo Tommaso. *Teoria e invenzione futurista*. Edited by Luciano De Maria. Milan: Mondadori, 1968.

Marzot, Giulio. *Il decadentismo italiano*. Bologna: Cappelli, 1970.

Mengaldo, Pier Vincenzo, ed. *Poeti italiani del Novecento*. Milan: Mondadori, 1981.

Negri, Ada. *Dal Profondo*. Milan: Fratelli Treves, 1910.

Negri, Ada. *Esilio*. Milan: Fratelli Treves, 1914.

Negri, Ada. *Poesie e Prose*. Edited by Pietro Sarzana. Milan: Mondadori, 2020.

Negri, Ada, and Paolo Buzzi. *Diorami Lombardi: Carteggio 1896–1944*. Edited by Barbara Stagnitti. Padua: Il Poligrafo, 2008.

Niebisch, Arndt. *Media Parasites in the Early Avant-Garde: On the Abuse of Technology and Communication*. Basingstoke, UK: Palgrave Macmillan, 2002.

Oxford English Dictionary. www.oed.com.

Panteo, Tullio. *Il poeta Marinetti*. Milan: Società Editoriale Milanese, 1908.

Parton, Anthony. *Goncharova: The Art and Design of Natalia Goncharova*. Woodbridge, UK: Antique Collectors' Club, 2010.

Pasca, Vanni. "Le forme della luce." In *Milano illuminata: storia, immagini, urbanistica ed emozioni dell'illuminazione elettrica pubblica*, 44-63. Milan: AEM, 1993.

Pavese, Claudio. "Dalla luce ad arco alle lampade al sodio: Origini e sviluppo dell'illuminazione pubblica elettrica a Milano." In *Milano illuminata: storia, immagini, urbanistica ed emozioni dell'illuminazione elettrica pubblica*, 10-43. Milan: AEM, 1993.

Perloff, Marjorie. "The Audacity of Hope: The Foundational Futurist Manifestos." In *The History of Futurism: The Precursors, Protagonists, and Legacies*, edited by Geert Buelens, Harald Hendrix, and Monica Jansen, 11-22. Lanham, MD: Lexington Books, 2012.

Perloff, Marjorie. *The Futurist Moment: Avant-Garde, Avant Guerre, and the Language of Rupture*. Chicago: University of Chicago Press, 2003.

Pickering-Iazzi, Robin. *Politics of the Visible: Writing Women, Culture, and Fascism*. Minneapolis: University of Minnesota Press, 1997.

Pietropaolo, Domenico. "Science and the Aesthetics of Geometric Splendour in Italian Futurism." *Futurism and the Technological Imagination*, edited by Günter Berghaus, 41-62. Amsterdam: Rodopi, 2009.

Pizzi, Katia. *Italian Futurism and the Machine*. Manchester, UK: Manchester University Press, 2019.

Podavini, Davide. "The Anthology *Poeti futuristi*: Poetry of Transition." In *The History of Futurism: The Precursors, Protagonists, and Legacies*, edited by Geert Buelens, Harald Hendrix and Monica Jansen, 24-34. Lanham, MD: Lexington Books, 2012.

Poggi, Christine. *Inventing Futurism: The Art and Politics of Artificial Optimism*. Princeton, NJ: Princeton University Press, 2008.

Poggioli, Renato. *The Theory of the Avant-Garde*. Translated by Gerald Fitzgerald. Cambridge, MA: The Belknap Press of Harvard University Press, 1968.

Pomajzlová, Alena. *Růžena—Příběh malířky Růženy Zátkové: Story of the Painter Růžena Zátková*. Translated by Lawrence Wells, Magdalena Wells, Branislava Kuburović, David Brooker, and Alena Pomajzlová. Prague: Arbor Vitae and Porte, 2011.

Proietti, Simonetta. "Edyth Von Haynau (Rosa Rosà): Una donna tra futurismo e politica." Ph.D. diss., Università di Roma Tre, 2017.

Rainey, Lawrence, Christine Poggi, and Laura Wittman, eds. *Futurism: An Anthology*. New Haven, CT: Yale University Press, 2009.

Rampazzo, Elena. *Futurista al chiaro di luna: La poesia di Paolo Buzzi fra tradizione e avanguardia*. Trieste: Edizioni Università di Trieste, 2020.

Re, Lucia. "Maria Ginanni vs. F. T. Marinetti: Women, Speed, and War in Futurist Italy." *Annali d'italianistica* 27 (2009): 103-124.

Re, Lucia. "Women at War: Eva Kühn Amendola (Magamal)—Interventionist, Futurist, Fascist." *Annali d'italianistica* 33 (2015): 275-308.

Re, Lucia, ed., and Dominic Siracusa, trans. "Rosa Rosa's *A Woman with Three Souls* in English Translation." *California Italian Studies* 2, no. 1 (2011): 2-40.

Resch, Raffaella. "Le futuriste: corpo moltiplicato e anima plurisensibile." In *L'elica e la luce: le futuriste 1912-1944*, edited by Chiara Gatti and Raffaella Resch, 29-35. Milan: Officina libraria, 2018.

Richards, Ivor Armstrong. *The Philosophy of Rhetoric.* New York: Oxford University Press, 1965.

Ricoeur, Paul. *The Rule of Metaphor: Multi-disciplinary Studies of the Creation of Meaning in Language.* Translated by Robert Czerny, Kathleen McLaughlin, and John Costello. London: Routledge and Kegan Paul, 1978.

Roberti, Lello. "È morto il chiaro di luna?" *Roma*, March 9, 1920. In "Libroni on Futurism: Slides," box 24, slide 3. Filippo Tommaso Marinetti Papers, Beinecke Rare Book and Manuscript Library, Yale University.

Salaris, Claudia. *Le futuriste: donne e letteratura d'avanguardia in Italia, 1909-1944.* Milan: Edizioni delle donne, 1982.

Salaris, Claudia. *Storia del futurismo.* Rome: Editori Riuniti, 1985.

Sartini Blum, Cinzia. *The Other Modernism: F. T. Marinetti's Futurist Fiction of Power.* Berkeley: University of California Press, 1996.

Sartini Blum, Cinzia. "Transformations in the Futurist Technological Mythopoeia." *Philological Quarterly* 74, no. 10 (1995): 77-97.

Schnapp, Jeffrey Thompson. "Propeller Talk." *Modernism/modernity* 1, no 3 (1994): 153-178.

Scuriatti, Laura. *Mina Loy's Critical Modernism.* Gainesville, FL: University Press of Florida, 2019.

Sebregondi, Ludovica. "Goncharova and Italy: Controversy, Inspiration, Friendship." In *Natalia Goncharova*, edited by Matthew Gale and Natalia Sidlina, 123-129. London: Tate Publishing, 2019.

Settimelli, Emilio. "Maria Ginanni prima grande scrittrice italiana." *L'Italia futurista* 2, no. 3 (1917): 1-2.

Shakespeare, William. *The Oxford Shakespeare: The Complete Works.* Edited by John Jowett, William Montgomery, Gary Taylor, and Stanley Wells. Oxford: Clarendon Press, 2005.

Sica, Paola. *Futurist Women: Florence, Feminism, and New Science.* Basingstoke, UK: Palgrave Macmillan, 2016.

Sica, Paola. "Maria Ginanni: Futurist Woman and Visual Writer." *Italica* 79, no. 3 (2002): 339-352.

Sica, Paola. "Nocturnal Itineraries: Occultism and the Metamorphic Self in Florentine Futurism." In *Back to the Futurists: The Avant-Garde and Its Legacy,* edited by Elsa Adamowicz and Simona Storchi, 145-158. Manchester, UK: Manchester University Press, 2013.

Somigli, Luca. "The Poet and the Vampire: 'Roi Bombance' and the Crisis of Symbolist Values." *Italica* 91, no. 4 (2014): 571-589.

Sottong, Heather R. "Marinetti's Metaphorical Break with Tradition." *Carte italiane* 2, no. 6 (2010): 7-22.

Suter, Patrick. "Mallarmé and His Futurist 'Heir' Marinetti." In *International Yearbook of Futurism Studies: Volume 4,* edited by Günter Berghaus, 134-164. Berlin: DeGruyter, 2014.

Temkin, Ann. "*Luce futurista*: Art for an Electric Age." In *The Futurist Imagination: Word + Image in Italian Futurist Painting, Drawing, Collage and Free-Word Poetry*, edited by Anne Coffin Hanson, 30-39. New Haven, CT: Yale University Press, 1983.

Tonini, Paolo. *I manifesti del Futurismo italiano*. Gussago: Edizioni dell'Arengario, 2011.

Velani, Livia. "'Nous avions veillé tout la nuit . . .': Balla alle soglie del secolo nuovo: Dalla fotografia all'ilarità." In *Balla: La modernità futurista*, edited by Giovanni Lista, Paolo Baldacci, and Livia Velani, 311-323. Milan: Skira, 2008.

Vinall, Shirley W. "Marinetti, Soffici, and French Literature." In *International Futurism in Arts and Literature*, edited by Günther Berghaus, 15-38. Berlin: DeGruyter, 2000.

Vocabolario della lingua italiana Treccani. https://www.treccani.it/vocabolario.

White, John J. *Literary Futurism: Aspects of the First Avant Garde*. Oxford: Clarendon Press, 1990.

Wood, Jamie. "'On or about December 1910': F. T. Marinetti's Onslaught on London and Recursive Structures in Modernism." *Modernist Cultures* 10, no. 2 (2015): 135-158.

Zoccoli, Franca. "Futurist Women Painters in Italy." In *International Futurism in Arts and Literature*, edited by Günter Berghaus, 373-397. Berlin: DeGruyter, 2000.

Chapter 3. Living with Lanterns

Adamson, Walter L. *Avant-Garde Florence: From Modernism to Fascism*. Cambridge, MA: Harvard University Press, 1993.

Andreotti, Margherita. "Brancusi's *Golden Bird*: A New Species of Modern Sculpture." *Art Institute of Chicago Museum Studies* 19, no. 2 (1993): 134-152, 198-203.

Barthel, Albrecht. "The Paris Studio of Constantin Brancusi: A Critique of the Modern Period Room." *Future Anterior: Journal of Historic Preservation, History, Theory, and Criticism* 3, no. 2 (2006): 34-43.

Beach, Sylvia. *Shakespeare and Company*. London: Faber and Faber, 1960.

Brown, Elizabeth A. *Brancusi Photographs Brancusi.* London: Thames and Hudson, 1995.

Brown, Henry Collins, and Clara Brown Lyman. *Book of Home Building and Decoration Prepared in Cooperation with and under the Direction of the Leading Manufacturers of the Country.* New York: Doubleday, 1912.

Brown Lyman, Clara. "Lamps and Lighting." *The Art World* 2, no. 2 (May 1917): 185–188.

Buhler Lynes, Barbara. "Georgia O'Keeffe and the Calla Lily in American Art, 1860–1940." In *Georgia O'Keeffe and the Calla Lily in American Art, 1860–1940*, edited by Barbara Buhler Lynes, 1–3. New Haven, CT: Yale University Press, 2002.

Bürger, Peter. *Theory of the Avant-Garde.* Translated by Michael Shaw. Manchester, UK: Manchester University Press, 1984.

Burke, Carolyn. *Becoming Modern: The Life of Mina Loy.* Berkeley: University of California Press, 1997.

Burstein, Jessica. *Cold Modernism: Literature, Fashion, Art.* University Park, PA: Penn State University Press, 2012.

"THE CABARET DU NEANT." *Scientific American* 74, no. 10 (March 7, 1896): 152.

Catalogue of the First Annual Exhibition of the Society of Independent Artists. New York: William Edwin Rudge, 1917.

Chancellor, John. *How to Be Happy in Paris Without Being Ruined!* London: Arrowsmith, 1926.

Churchill, Suzanne Wintsch. "Courting an Audience: Loy's Plays." In *Mina Loy: Navigating the Avant-Garde*, edited by Suzanne W. Churchill, Linda A. Kinnahan, and Susan Rosenbaum. University of Georgia, 2020. https://mina-loy.com /chapters/courting-an-audience/.

Churchill, Suzanne Wintsch. "Ghost in an Avant-Garde Alley." In *Mina Loy: Navigating the Avant-Garde*, edited by Suzanne W. Churchill, Linda A. Kinnahan, and Susan Rosenbaum. University of Georgia, 2020. https://mina-loy.com/sightings /ghost-in-an-avant-garde-alley/.

Churchill, Suzanne Wintsch. *The Little Magazine* Others *and the Renovation of Modern American Poetry.* Farnham, UK: Ashgate, 2006.

Churchill, Suzanne Wintsch, Linda Kinnahan, and Susan Rosenbaum. "Digital Baedeker: A Feminist Experiment with Mina Loy's Archive." In *The Contemporary Poetry Archive: Essays and Interventions*, edited by Linda Anderson, Mark Byers, and Ahren Warner, 63–80. Edinburgh, UK: Edinburgh University Press, 2019.

Conover, Roger. "Time-Table." In *The Last Lunar Baedeker*, by Mina Loy, edited by Roger Conover, lxiii–lxxix. Asheville, NC: The Jargon Society, 1982.

Conover, Roger L. "Notes on the Text." In *The Lost Lunar Baedeker*, edited by Roger L. Conover, 175–219. Manchester, UK: Carcanet, 1997.

Crangle, Sara. "Notes." In *Stories and Essays of Mina Loy*, edited by Sara Crangle, 295-416. Champaign, IL: Dalkey Archive Press, 2011.

Dennison, Mariea Caudill. "Francis Picabia's *Américaine* from the Cover of *391*, July 1917." *Burlington Magazine* 146, no. 1218 (2004): 621-622.

Desmond, Kevin. *Gustave Trouvé: French Electrical Genius (1839-1902)*. Jefferson, NC: McFarland and Company, 2015.

de Wolfe, Elsie. *The House in Good Taste: Illustrated with Photographs in Color and Black and White*. New York: The Century Co., 1914.

Dillon, Maureen. " 'Like a Glow-Worm Who Had Lost Its Glow': The Invention of the Incandescent Electric Lamp and the Development of Artificial Silk and Electric Jewellery." *Costume: The Journal of the Costume Society* 35, no. 1 (2001): 76-81.

Duncan, Alastair. *Art Deco Complete*. London: Thames and Hudson, 2014.

Duncan, Alistair. *Art Nouveau*. London: Thames and Hudson, 2001.

Dunn, Susan E. "Mina Loy, Fashion, and the Avant-Garde." In *Mina Loy: Woman and Poet*, edited by Maeera Shreiber and Keith Tuma, 443-455. Orono, ME: National Poetry Foundation, 1998.

DuPlessis, Rachel Blau. *Genders, Races, and Religious Cultures in Modern American Poetry, 1908-1934*. Cambridge: Cambridge University Press, 2001.

Eldredge, Charles C. "Calla Moderna: 'Such a Strange Flower.' " In *Georgia O'Keeffe and the Calla Lily in American Art, 1860-1940*, edited by Barbara Buhler Lynes, 5-37. New Haven, CT: Yale University Press, 2002.

Eliot, Thomas Stearns. *The Complete Prose of T. S. Eliot: The Critical Edition: Apprentice Years, 1905-1918: Volume 1*. Edited by Ronald Schuchard and Jewel Spears Brooker. Baltimore, MD: Johns Hopkins University Press, 2014.

Eliot, Thomas Stearns. *The Poems of T. S. Eliot: Volume I: Collected & Uncollected Poems*. Edited by Christopher Ricks and Jim McCue. London: Faber and Faber, 2015.

Elkins, Amy E. "From the Gutter to the Gallery: Berenice Abbott Photographs Mina Loy's Assemblages." *PMLA* 134, no. 5 (2019): 1094-1103.

Escritt, Stephen. *Art Nouveau*. London: Phaidon, 2000.

Fairfield, Gail. *Everyday Tarot: Using the Cards to Make Better Life Decisions*. Boston: Weiser, 2002.

Fischer, Lucy. *Designing Women: Cinema, Art Deco, and the Female Form*. New York: Columbia University Press, 2003.

Gonnering Lein, Julie. "Shades of Meaning: Mina Loy's Poetics of Luminous Opacity." *Modernism/modernity* 18, no. 3 (2011): 617-629.

Gooday, Graeme. *Domesticating Electricity: Technology, Uncertainty, and Gender, 1880-1914*. Pittsburgh: University of Pittsburgh Press, 2016.

Goody, Alex. " 'Consider Your Grandmothers': Modernism, Gender and the New York Press." *Media History* 7, no. 1 (2001): 47-56.

Goody, Alex. "Ladies of Fashion/Modern(ist) Women: Mina Loy and Djuna Barnes." *Women: A Cultural Review* 10, no. 3 (1999): 266–282.

Goody, Alex. *Modernist Articulations: A Cultural Reading of Djuna Barnes, Mina Loy and Gertrude Stein.* Basingstoke, UK: Palgrave Macmillan, 2007.

Gordon, Alice. *Decorative Electricity.* London: Sampson Low, Marston, Searle and Rivington, 1891.

Grasso, Linda M. *Equal under the Sky: Georgia O'Keeffe & Twentieth-Century Feminism.* Albuquerque, NM: University of New Mexico Press, 2017.

Gross, Jennifer R., ed. *Mina Loy: Strangeness Is Inevitable.* Princeton, NJ: Princeton University Press, 2023.

Hammond, Robert. *The Electric Light in Our Homes.* London: Frederick Warne and Co., 1884.

Harris, Rowan. "Futurism, Fashion, and the Feminine: Forms of Repudiation and Affiliation in the Early Writing of Mina Loy." In *The Salt Companion to Mina Loy*, edited by Rachel Potter and Suzanne Hobson, 17–46. London: Salt Publishing, 2010.

Hayden, Sarah. *Curious Disciplines: Mina Loy and Avant-Garde Artisthood.* Albuquerque, NM: University of New Mexico Press, 2018.

Hoeckley, Albert Herman. "Quaint Inns and Cabarets of London and Paris." *New York Times*, July 28, 1901.

Hopkins, Albert A. *Magic: Stage Illusions and Scientific Diversions, including Trick Photography.* London: Sampson Low, Marston and Company Limited, 1897.

Hoving, Kirsten. *Joseph Cornell and Astronomy: A Case for the Stars.* Princeton, NJ: Princeton University Press, 2009.

"In the Cabaret du Neant: A Ghastly Parisian Diversion." *New York Sun*, as republished in *Current Literature, 1888–1912* 19, no. 3 (March 1896): 250.

Kelly, Dorothy. *Tarot Card Combinations.* Boston: Weiser, 2003.

Kenner, Hugh. "To Be the Brancusi of Poetry." *New York Times*, May 16, 1982.

Kinnahan, Linda A. *Mina Loy, Twentieth-Century Photography, and Contemporary Women Poets.* Abingdon, UK: Routledge, 2017.

Koues, Helen. "Lamp Shades You Can Make at Home." *Ladies' Home Journal*, April 1907.

Kouidis, Virginia M. *Mina Loy: American Modernist Poet.* Baton Rouge, LA: Louisiana State University Press, 1980.

Kouidis, Virginia M. "Rediscovering Our Sources: The Poetry of Mina Loy." *boundary 2* 8, no. 3 (1980): 167–188.

Kreymborg, Alfred, ed. *Others: An Anthology of the New Verse.* New York: Alfred A. Knopf, 1917.

Lazevnick, Ashley. "Impossible Descriptions in Mina Loy and Constantin Brancusi's *Golden Bird*." *Word & Image* 29, no. 2 (2013): 192–202.

Lista, Giovanni. *Le futurisme: Création et avant-garde.* Paris: Terrail, 2001.

Loy, Mina. "Aphorisms on Futurism." Mina Loy Papers YCAL MSS 6, Beinecke Rare Book and Manuscript Library, Yale University.

Loy, Mina. *The Last Lunar Baedeker*. Edited by Roger Conover. Asheville, NC: The Jargon Society, 1982.

Loy, Mina. Letter to Carl Van Vechten, undated. YCAL MSS 1050, box 76, folder 1082-1083. Carl Van Vechten Papers, Beinecke Rare Book and Manuscript Library, Yale University.

Loy, Mina. Letter to Carl Van Vechten, undated. YCAL MSS 1050, box 76, folder 1082-1083. Carl Van Vechten Papers, Beinecke Rare Book and Manuscript Library, Yale University.

Loy, Mina. Letter to Carl Van Vechten, December 27, 1914. YCAL MSS 1050, box 76, folder 1082-1083. Carl Van Vechten Papers, Beinecke Rare Book and Manuscript Library, Yale University.

Loy, Mina. Letter to Mabel Dodge Luhan, February 1914. YCAL MSS 196, box 24, folder 664. Mabel Dodge Luhan Papers, Beinecke Rare Book and Manuscript Library, Yale University.

Loy, Mina. Letter to Mabel Dodge Luhan, 1914. YCAL MSS 196, box 24, folder 665. Mabel Dodge Luhan Papers, Beinecke Rare Book and Manuscript Library, Yale University.

Loy, Mina. Letter to Stephen Haweis, March 22 [?], 1914. YCAL MSS 196, box 42, folder 1276. Mabel Dodge Luhan Papers, Beinecke Rare Book and Manuscript Library, Yale University.

Loy, Mina. *The Lost Lunar Baedeker*. Edited by Roger L. Conover. Manchester, UK: Carcanet, 1997.

Loy, Mina. "Phenomenon in American Art," 1950. YCAL MSS 6, box 6, folder 172. Mina Loy Papers, Beinecke Rare Book and Manuscript Library, Yale University.

Loy, Mina. *Stories and Essays of Mina Loy*. Edited by Sara Crangle. Champaign, IL: Dalkey Archive Press, 2011.

Loy, Mina. "Two Plays." *Performing Arts Journal* 18, no. 1 (1996): 8-17.

Luckiesh, Matthew. *Lighting the Home*. New York: The Century Co., 1920.

Marcoci, Roxana. *The Original Copy: Photography of Sculpture, 1839 to Today*. New York: The Museum of Modern Art, 2010.

Marinetti, Filippo Tommaso. *Come si seducono le donne*. Milan: Excelsior, 2007.

Marinetti, Filippo Tommaso. *Le futurisme*. Paris: E Sansot, 1911.

Marvin, Carolyn. *When Old Technologies Were New: Thinking About Electric Communication in the Late Nineteenth Century*. Oxford: Oxford University Press, 1988.

McAuley, James. "The Artists and their Alley." *New York Times*, September 25, 2016.

Monroe, Harriet. "Guide to the Moon: Review of *Lunar Baedecker* by Mina Loy." *Poetry* 23, no. 2 (1923): 100-103.

Moore, James. "The Pale Beauty of Priceless Flowers: Market and Meaning in O'Keeffe's Calla Lily Paintings." In *Georgia O'Keeffe and the Calla Lily in American Art, 1860-1940*, edited by Barbara Buhler Lynes, 39-57. New Haven, CT: Yale University Press, 2002.

Murphy Selinger, Eric. "Love in the Time of Melancholia." In *Mina Loy: Woman and Poet*, edited by Maeera Shreiber and Keith Tuma, 19-43. Orono, ME: National Poetry Foundation, 1998.

Nadis, Fred. *Wonder Shows: Performing Science, Magic, and Religion in America.* New Brunswick, NJ: Rutgers University Press, 2005.

Oxford English Dictionary. www.oed.com.

Paret, Paul. "Sculpture and Its Negative: The Photographs of Constantin Brancusi." In *Sculpture and Photography: Envisioning the Third Dimension*, edited by Geraldine A. Johnson, 101-115. Cambridge: Cambridge University Press, 1998.

"PARIS WEEK BY WEEK: FAMOUS CABARET CLOSES DOWN." *Observer*, October 31, 1937.

Parmar, Sandeep. "Not an Apology: Mina Loy's Geniuses." *The Wolf* 17 (2008): 77-85.

Parsons, Deborah L. *Streetwalking the Metropolis: Women, the City and Modernity.* Oxford: Oxford University Press, 2000.

Pomerance, Murray. "Tinker Bell, the Fairy of Electricity." In *Second Star to the Right: Peter Pan in the Popular Imagination*, edited by Allison B. Kavey and Lester D. Friedman, 13-49. New Brunswick, NJ: Rutgers University Press, 2009.

Potter, Rachel. *Modernism and Democracy: Literary Culture, 1900-1930.* Oxford: Oxford University Press, 2006.

Potter, Rachel, and Suzanne Hobson. *The Salt Companion to Mina Loy.* London: Salt Publishing, 2010.

Pound, Ezra. "Brancusi." *The Little Review: A Quarterly Journal of Art and Letters* 8, no. 1 (1921): 3-7.

Powell, Jim. "Basil Bunting and Mina Loy." *Chicago Review* 37, no. 1 (1990): 6-25.

Prescott, Tara. *Poetic Salvage: Reading Mina Loy.* Lewisburg, PA: Bucknell University Press, 2017.

Pryor, Sean. *Poetry, Modernism, and an Imperfect World.* Cambridge: Cambridge University Press, 2017.

Rainey, Lawrence, Christine Poggi, and Laura Wittman, eds. *Futurism: An Anthology.* New Haven, CT: Yale University Press, 2009.

Re, Lucia. "Mina Loy and the Quest for a Futurist Feminist Woman." *European Legacy* 14, no. 7 (2009): 799-819.

Roberts, Andrew Michael. "'How to Be Happy in Paris': Mina Loy and the Transvaluation of the Body." *Cambridge Quarterly* 27, no. 2 (1998): 129-147.

Rosenbaum, Susan. "Paris 1923: Lunar Baedeker." In *Mina Loy: Navigating the Avant-Garde*, edited by Suzanne W. Churchill, Linda A. Kinnahan, and Susan Rosen-

baum. University of Georgia, 2020. https://mina-loy.com/chapters/surreal-scene
/1-surreal-scene-paris-1923-36/.

Schmid, Julie. "Mina Loy's Futurist Theatre." *Performing Arts Journal* 18, no. 1
(1996): 1-7.

Scuriatti, Laura. *Mina Loy's Critical Modernism.* Gainesville, FL: University Press of
Florida, 2019.

Scuriatti, Laura. "Negotiating Boundaries: The Economics of Space and Gender in
Mina Loy's Early Poems." *Feminismo/s* 1, no. 5 (2005): 71-84.

Sharpe, William Chapman. *New York Nocturne: The City After Dark in Literature,
Painting, and Photography, 1850-1950.* Princeton, NJ: Princeton University
Press, 2008.

Shreiber, Maeera. "'Love is a lyric/Of bodies': The Negative Asthetics of Mina Loy's
Love Songs to Joannes." In *Mina Loy: Woman and Poet,* edited by Maeera Shreiber
and Keith Tuma, 87-109. Orono, ME: National Poetry Foundation, 1998.

Shreiber, Maeera, and Keith Tuma. *Mina Loy: Woman and Poet.* Orono, ME:
National Poetry Foundation, 1998.

Tabart, Marielle, and Isabelle Monod-Fontaine. *Brancusi photographe.* Paris: Musée
National d'Art Moderne Centre Georges Pompidou, 1979.

University of Glasgow History of Art and HATII. "Mariette Mills." Mapping the
Practice and Profession of Sculpture in Britain and Ireland 1851-1951. 2011.
https://sculpture.gla.ac.uk/mapping/public/view/person.php?id=msib2
_1205880348&search=mariette%20mills.

Wharton, Edith. *The House of Mirth.* Oxford: Oxford University Press, 1936.

Wharton, Edith, and Ogden Codman Jr. *The Decoration of Houses.* London: Bats-
ford, 1898.

Wood, Jamie. "'On or about December 1910': F. T. Marinetti's Onslaught on
London and Recursive Structures in Modernism." *Modernist Cultures* 10, no. 2
(2015): 135-158.

Wood, Jon. "Brancusi's White Studio." In *The Studio Reader: On the Space of Artists,*
edited by Mary Jane Jacob and Michelle Grabner, 269-284. Chicago: University
of Chicago Press, 2010.

Woolman Chase, Edna. "Decorating: Interior Decoration for Limited Incomes."
Vogue, April 15, 1916.

Wosk, Julie. *Women and the Machine: Representations from the Spinning Wheel to
the Electronic Age.* Baltimore, MD: Johns Hopkins University Press, 2003.

Chapter 4. Bringing Down the Stars

Agee, William C. *Modern Art in America, 1908-68.* London and New York: Phaidon,
2017.

Ahearn, Barry. *William Carlos Williams and Alterity: The Early Poetry*. Cambridge: Cambridge University Press, 1995.

Asciuto, Nicoletta. "A Half-Watt Light for Photography in Ezra Pound's 'Medallion' (1920)." *Notes and Queries* 68, no. 3 (2021): 347-351.

Baker Jr., Houston A. *Afro-American Poetics: Revisions of Harlem and the Black Aesthetic*. Madison, WI: University of Wisconsin Press, 1988.

Barson, Tanya. "O'Keeffe's Century." In *Georgia O'Keeffe*, edited by Tanya Barson, 8-21. New York: Abrams, 2016.

Bazin, Victoria. *Modernism Edited: Marianne Moore and the* Dial *Magazine*. Edinburgh, UK: Edinburgh University Press, 2019.

Beeston, Alix. *In and Out of Sight: Modernist Writing and the Photographic Unseen*. Oxford: Oxford University Press, 2017.

Bennett, Gwendolyn Bennetta. *Heroine of the Harlem Renaissance and Beyond: Gwendolyn Bennett's Selected Writings*. Edited by Belinda Wheeler and Louis J. Parascandola. University Park, PA: Penn State University Press, 2018.

Bennett, Gwendolyn Bennetta. "Street Lamps in Early Spring." *Opportunity: Journal of Negro Life* 4, no. 41 (May 1926): 152.

Berke, Nancy. "'Electric Currents of Life': Lola Ridge's Immigrant Flaneuserie." *American Studies* 51, no. 1-2 (2010): 27-47.

Berke, Nancy. *Women Poets on the Left: Lola Ridge, Genevieve Taggard, Margaret Walker*. Gainesville, FL: University Press of Florida, 2001.

Berman, Avis. "City Lights: Urban Perceptions of Night." In *Night Vision: Nocturnes in American Art, 1860-1960*, edited by Joachim Homann, 33-44. Munich: Delmonico Books, 2015.

Brevda, William. *Signs of the Signs: The Literary Lights of Incandescence and Neon*. Lewisburg, PA: Bucknell University Press, 2011.

Brooker, Peter. "Growth through Disagreement: *S4N* (1919-25)." In *The Oxford Critical and Cultural History of Modernist Magazines: Volume II, North America 1894-1960*, edited by Peter Brooker and Andrew Thacker, 655-675. Oxford: Oxford University Press, 2012.

Buhler Lynes, Barbara. "The Language of Criticism: Its Effect on Georgia O'Keeffe's Art in the 1920s." In *From the Faraway Nearby: Georgia O'Keeffe as Icon*, edited by Christopher Merrill and Ellen Bradbury, 43-54. Reading, MA: Addison-Wesley Publishing, 1992.

Buhler Lynes, Barbara. *O'Keeffe, Stieglitz and the Critics, 1916-1929*. Ann Arbor, MI: UMI Research Press, 1989.

Burke, Carolyn. *Foursome: Alfred Stieglitz, Georgia O'Keeffe, Paul Strand, Rebecca Salsbury*. New York: Vintage Books, 2020.

Burrows, Edwin G., and Mike Wallace. *Gotham: A History of New York City to 1898*. Oxford: Oxford University Press, 1998.

Campbell, Joseph. *Mearing Stones: Leaves from My Note-Book on Tramp in Donegal, with Sixteen Pencil Drawings by the Author.* Dublin: Maunsel and Company, 1911.

Chave, Anna C. "O'Keeffe and the Masculine Gaze." In *From the Faraway Nearby: Georgia O'Keeffe as Icon*, edited by Christopher Merrill and Ellen Bradbury, 29–42. Reading, MA: Addison-Wesley Publishing, 1992.

Chave, Anna C. "'Who Will Paint New York?': 'The World's New Art Center' and the Skyscraper Paintings of Georgia O'Keeffe." In *From the Faraway Nearby: Georgia O'Keeffe as Icon*, edited by Christopher Merrill and Ellen Bradbury, 65–82. Reading, MA: Addison-Wesley Publishing, 1992.

Cheng, Anne Anlin. *Second Skin: Josephine Baker & the Modern Surface.* Oxford: Oxford University Press, 2013.

Churchill, Suzanne W. "An Introduction to *Others: A Magazine of the New Verse*." Modernist Journals Project. https://modjourn.org/an-introduction-to-others-a-magazine-of-the-new-verse/.

Cirasa, Robert J. *The Lost Works of William Carlos Williams: The Volumes of Collected Poetry as Lyrical Sequences.* Madison, NJ: Fairleigh Dickinson University Press, 1995.

Crawford, T. Hugh. *Modernism, Medicine, & William Carlos Williams.* Norman, OK: University of Oklahoma Press, 1993.

Cummings, Edward Estlin. *Complete Poems 1904–1962.* Edited by George J. Firmage. New York: Liveright Publishing Corporation, 2016.

Cummings, Edward Estlin. *A Miscellany Revised.* Edited by George J. Firmage. New York: October House Inc., 1967.

Davis, Keith F. *Night Light: A Survey of 20th Century Night Photography.* Kansas City, MO: Hallmark Cards, Inc., 1989.

Demuth, Charles. *Letters of Charles Demuth: American Artist, 1883–1935.* Edited by Bruce Kellner. Philadelphia: Temple University Press, 2000.

Diggory, Terence. "William Carlos Williams' Early 'References to Freud.'" *William Carlos Williams Review* 22, no. 2 (1996): 3–17.

Dijkstra, Bram. "America and Georgia O'Keeffe." In *Georgia O'Keeffe: The New York Years*, edited by Doris Bry and Nicholas Callaway, 105–130. New York: Alfred A. Knopf, 1991.

Dijkstra, Bram. *The Hieroglyphics of a New Speech: Cubism, Stieglitz, and the Early Poetry of William Carlos Williams.* Princeton, NJ: Princeton University Press, 1969.

Dijkstra, Bram. *O'Keeffe and the Eros of Place.* Princeton, NJ: Princeton University Press, 1998.

Douglas, Ann. *Terrible Honesty: Mongrel Manhattan in the 1920s.* New York: Farrar, Straus and Giroux, 1996.

Doyle, Charles. *William Carlos Williams and the American Poem*. Basingstoke, UK: Macmillan, 1982.

Dunbar, Paul Laurence. *Collected Poetry*. Edited by Joanne M. Braxton. Charlottesville, VA: University Press of Virginia, 1993.

Dyer, Richard. *White: Essays on Race and Culture: Twentieth Anniversary Edition*. London and New York: Routledge, 2017.

Elcott, Noam Milgrom. *Artificial Darkness: An Obscure History of Modern Art and Media*. Chicago: University of Chicago Press, 2016.

Elkin, Lauren. *Flâneuse: Women Walk the City in Paris, New York, Tokyo, Venice and London*. London: Chatto and Windus, 2016.

Ellison, Ralph. *Invisible Man*. London: Penguin, 2001.

Fairclough, Mary. *Literature, Electricity and Politics 1740–1840: Electrick Communication Every Where*. London: Palgrave Macmillan, 2017.

Fitts, Norman. Letter to Jean Toomer, dated Good Friday 1923. MSS 1, box 3, folder 79. Jean Toomer Papers, Beinecke Rare Book and Manuscript Library, Yale University.

Foley, Barbara. *Jean Toomer: Race, Repression, and Revolution*. Urbana-Champaign, IL: University of Illinois Press, 2014.

Goody, Alex. "Poetry and Technology." In *A History of Twentieth-Century American Women's Poetry*, edited by Linda A. Kinnahan, 359–374. Cambridge: Cambridge University Press, 2016.

Green Fryd, Vivien. "Georgia O'Keeffe's *Radiator Building*: Gender, Sexuality, Modernism, and Urban Imagery." *Winterthur Portfolio* 35, no. 4 (2000): 269–289.

Greenough, Sarah. "Touching the Centre: Georgia O'Keeffe and Alfred Stieglitz's Artistic Dialogue." In *Georgia O'Keeffe*, edited by Tanya Barson, 50–97. New York: Abrams, 2016.

Halter, Peter. *The Revolution in the Visual Arts and the Poetry of William Carlos Williams*. Cambridge: Cambridge University Press, 1994.

Haskins, Jim. *James Van DerZee: The Picture-Takin' Man, Illustrated with Van DerZee Photographs*. New York: Dodd, Mead and Company, 1979.

Hughes, Langston. *The Collected Poems of Langston Hughes*. Edited by Arnold Rampersad and David Roessel. New York: Vintage Books, 1994.

Hughes, Langston. *The Collected Works of Langston Hughes: Volume 9: Essays on Art, Race, Politics, and World Affairs*. Edited by Christopher C. De Santis. Columbia, MO, and London: University of Missouri Press, 2002.

Ingold, Niklaus. *Lichtduschen: Geschichte einer Gesundheitstechnik, 1890–1975*. Zürich: Chronos Verlag, 2015.

Jackson Ford, Karen. *Split-Gut Song: Jean Toomer and the Poetics of Modernity*. Tuscaloosa, AL: University of Alabama Press, 2005.

Jakle, John Allais. *City Lights: Illuminating the American Night.* Baltimore, MD: Johns Hopkins University Press, 2001.

Jameson, Frederic. *Signatures of the Visible.* New York and London: Routledge, 1990.

Johnson, Helene. *This Waiting for Love: Poet of the Harlem Renaissance.* Edited by Verner D. Mitchell. Amherst and Boston: University of Massachusetts Press, 2000.

Jones, Henry Lewis. *Medical Electricity: A Practical Handbook for Students and Practitioners.* London: H. K. Lewis and Co. Ltd., 1920.

JRG. "Out Out the 'Great White Way.'" *New York Times*, October 1, 1907.

Kennedy, Richard S. *Dreams in the Mirror: A Biography of E. E. Cummings.* New York: Liveright, 1980.

Koprince, Susan. "Moon Imagery in *The Ways of White Folks.*" *The Langston Hughes Review* 1, no. 1 (1982): 14-17.

Kreymborg, Alfred. *Troubadour: An Autobiography.* New York: Liveright, 1925.

Latimer Norman, Winifred, and Lily Patterson. *Lewis Latimer.* New York: Chelsea House Publishers, 1994.

Leeds, Valerie Ann. *Dreams and Dramas: Moonlight and Twilight in American Art.* New York: Hollis Taggart Galleries, 2003.

Lemke, Sieglinde. *Primitivist Modernism: Black Culture and the Origins of Transatlantic Modernism.* New York: Oxford University Press, 1998.

"Liberty's Torch Lighted: The Beacon on Bedlow's Island a Success: An Illumination Aided by a Brilliant Exhibition of Fireworks That Was Seen by Thousands on Shore and on the Water." *New York Times*, November 2, 1886.

Marcus, Laura. *Dreams of Modernity: Psychoanalysis, Literature, Cinema.* Cambridge: Cambridge University Press, 2014.

Marcus, Laura. *The Tenth Muse: Writing about Cinema in the Modernist Period.* Oxford: Oxford University Press, 2007.

Mariani, Paul. *William Carlos Williams: A New World Naked.* New York: McGraw-Hill Book Company, 1981.

Marinetti, Filippo Tommaso. "Futurism." Translated by Norman Fitts. *S4N*, May-August 1923.

Marling, William. *William Carlos Williams and the Painters, 1909-1923.* Athens, OH: Ohio University Press, 1982.

Marston, Glenn. "ELECTRIC SIGNS Have Given 'The Great White Way' Its Name." *New York Times*, July 20, 1910.

Maun, Caroline. *Mosaic of Fire: The Work of Lola Ridge, Evelyn Scott, Charlotte Wilder, and Kay Boyle.* Columbia, SC: University of South Carolina Press, 2012.

Mayakovsky, Vladimir. *My Discovery of America.* Translated by Neil Cornwell. London: Hesperus Press, 2005.

Mayakovsky, Vladimir. *"Vladimir Mayakovsky" & Other Poems*. Translated and edited by James Womack. Manchester, UK: FyfieldBooks/Carcanet, 2016.

Mayakovsky, Vladimir. *Собрание сочинений в двенадцати томах* [Collected Works in Twelve Volumes]. Moscow: Pravda, 1978.

McCabe, Susan. *Cinematic Modernism: Modernist Poetry and Film*. Cambridge: Cambridge University Press, 2005.

McKay, Claude. *Complete Poems*. Edited by William Maxwell. Champaign, IL: University of Illinois Press, 2004.

McLuhan, Marshall. *Understanding Media: The Extensions of Man*. New York: McGraw-Hill Book Company, 1964.

McSorley's Old Ale House. "History of McSorley's." https://mcsorleysoldalehouse .nyc/history/.

Miller, Nina. *Making Love Modern: The Intimate Public Worlds of New York's Literary Women*. Oxford: Oxford University Press, 1999.

Mitchell, Joseph. "The Old House at Home." *New Yorker*, April 14, 1940. https:// www.newyorker.com/magazine/1940/04/13/the-old-house-at-home.

Moody, A. David. *Ezra Pound: Poet: A Portrait of the Man and His Work, Volume I: The Young Genius, 1885-1920*. Oxford: Oxford University Press, 2007.

Moreno, María Paz. "Gypsy Moon over Harlem: The Intertwined Voices of Langston Hughes and Federico García Lorca." *Langston Hughes Review* 20 (2006): 17-33.

Müller, Richard W. *Baldness: Its Causes, Its Treatments and Its Prevention*. New York: E. P. Dutton and Company, 1917.

Müller, Richard W. "The Nagelschmidt Modification of the Kromayer Quartz Lamp in the Treatment of Diseases of the Hair and Scalp." *Medical Record* 87, no. 19 (1915): 773-775.

Mumford, Lewis. *Sketches of Life: The Autobiography of Lewis Mumford, The Early Years*. New York: Dial Press, 1982.

Norman, Charles. *E. E. Cummings: The Magic-Maker*. Indianapolis: The Bobbs-Merrill Company, 1972.

Norman, Dorothy. *Alfred Stieglitz: An American Seer*. New York: Aperture, 1990.

North, Michael. *The Dialect of Modernism: Race, Language, and Twentieth-Century Literature*. Oxford: Oxford University Press, 1994.

Nye, David E. *American Technological Sublime*. Cambridge, MA: MIT Press, 1999.

Nye, David E. *Electrifying America: Social Meanings of a New Technology, 1880-1940*. Cambridge, MA: MIT Press, 1992.

O'Keeffe, Georgia. *Georgia O'Keeffe*. New York: Viking Press, 1976.

Orange, Tom. "William Carlos Williams between Image and Object." In *William Carlos Williams and the Language of Poetry*, edited by Burton Hatlen and Demetres Tryphonopolous, 127-156. Orono, ME: National Poetry Foundation, 2002.

Otter, Chris. *The Victorian Eye: A Political History of Light and Vision in Britain, 1800-1910*. Chicago: University of Chicago Press, 2008.

Oxford English Dictionary. www.oed.com.

Panadero, Laura. "James Van Der Zee's Retouched Portraits." National Gallery of Art. https://www.nga.gov/blog/james-van-der-zee-retouched-portraits.html.

Parsons, Deborah L. *Streetwalking the Metropolis: Women, the City, and Modernity*. Oxford: Oxford University Press, 2000.

Patterson, Anita. *Race, American Literature and Transnational Modernisms*. Cambridge: Cambridge University Press, 2011.

Perfume Intelligence: The Encyclopaedia of Perfume. "Perfume Houses, Volume Q, R, Page 5." https://www.perfumeintelligence.co.uk/library/perfume/q/q7/q7p5.htm.

Perloff, Marjorie. "'To Give a Design': Williams and the Visualization of Poetry." In *William Carlos Williams: Man and Poet*, edited by Carroll F. Terrell, 159-186. Orono, ME: National Poetry Foundation, 1983.

Perlow, Seth. "Description as Chance Operation: Stein, Williams, and After." In *Criticism* 62, no. 4 (2020): 573-598.

Pierce, R. F. "The Quartz Lamp." *Illuminating Engineer* 6, no. 3 (1911): 133-137.

Pollock, Griselda. "Seeing O'Keeffe Seeing." In *Georgia O'Keeffe*, edited by Tanya Barson, 102-137. New York: Abrams, 2016.

Pound, Ezra. "Books Current—The New Poetry." *Future* 2, no. 7 (1918): 188-190. In *Ezra Pound's Poetry and Prose: Contributions to Periodicals, Volume III: 1918-1919*, edited by Lea Baechler, A. Walton Litz, and James Longenbach, 115-117. New York: Garland Publishing, 1991.

Pound, Ezra. *Patria Mia and the Treatise on Harmony*. London: Peter Owen Limited, 1962.

Pound, Omar, and Robert Spoo. *Ezra Pound and Margaret Cravens: A Tragic Friendship, 1910-1912*. Durham, NC: Duke University Press, 1988.

Quagliano, Tony. "Tony Quagliano Presents Reuel Denney and 'McSorley's Bar.'" *Spring: The Journal of the E. E. Cummings Society* 7 (1998): 146-147.

Ridge, Lola. "Diaries 1940-1941." Lola Ridge Papers, SSC-MS-00131, Sophia Smith Collection of Women's History. Smith College Special Collections, Northampton, Massachusetts.

Ridge, Lola. *To the Many: Collected Early Works*. Edited by Daniel Tobin. Manchester, UK: Little Island Press, 2018.

Robinson, Peter. "'I like the Spanish title': William Carlos Williams's *Al Que Quiere!*" In *Modernism and Non-Translation*, edited by Jason Harding and John Nash, 86-103. Oxford: Oxford University Press, 2019.

Sawyer-Lauçanno, Christopher. *E. E. Cummings: A Biography*. London: Methuen, 2005.

Schorb, E. M. "A Tall One." *Spring: The Journal of the E. E. Cummings Society* 19 (2012): 132-133.

Schwarz, Daniel R. "Painting Williams, Reading Demuth: 'The Great Figure' and *I Saw the Figure 5 in Gold*." *William Carlos Williams Review* 32, nos. 1-2 (2015): 17-32.

Scruggs, Charles. "The Photographic Print, the Literary Negative: Alfred Stieglitz and Jean Toomer." *Arizona Quarterly: A Journal of American Literature, Culture, and Theory* 53, no. 1 (1997): 61-89.

Seshagiri, Urmila. *Race and the Modernist Imagination.* Ithaca, NY: Cornell University Press, 2010.

Sharpe, William Chapman. *New York Nocturne: The City After Dark in Literature, Painting, and Photography, 1850-1950.* Princeton, NJ: Princeton University Press, 2008.

Siddons, Louise. "African Past or American Present?: The Visual Eloquence of James VanDerZee's *Identical Twins*." *African American Review* 46, no. 2/3 (2013): 439-459.

Slater, Avery. "Technology and the Rise of the Vernacular Object in William Carlos Williams's *Spring and All*." *William Carlos Williams Review* 33, no. 1-2 (2016): 189-205.

Spector, Herman. *Bastard in the Ragged Suit: Writings of, with Drawings by, Herman Spector.* Edited by Bud Johns and Judith S. Clancy. San Francisco: Synergistic Press, 1977.

"The Statue of Liberty." *Harper's Weekly* 30 (1886): 714.

Stein, Gertrude. *Tender Buttons: The Corrected Centennial Edition.* Edited by Seth Perlow. San Francisco: City Lights Books, 2014.

Svoboda, Terese. *Anything That Burns You: A Portrait of Lola Ridge, Radical Poet.* Tucson, AZ: Schaffner Press, 2016.

Svoboda, Terese. "Lola Ridge and the Literary Soirée." *American Poetry Review* 45, no. 1 (2016): 9-12.

Tante, Dilly, ed. *Living Authors: A Book of Biographies.* New York: H. W. Wilson Company, 1935.

Tobin, Daniel. "An Unfinished Tower: On the Early Poems of Lola Ridge." *Hopkins Review* 11, no. 1 (2018): 69-85.

Toomer, Jean. *Cane: Authoritative Text.* New York: Liveright, 2011.

Toomer, Jean. *The Collected Poems of Jean Toomer.* Edited by Robert B. Jones and Margery Toomer Latimer. Chapel Hill, NC: University of North Carolina Press, 1988.

Toomer, Jean. *The Wayward and the Seeking: A Collection of Writings.* Edited by Darwin T. Turner. Washington, DC: Howard University Press, 1980.

Trotter, David. *Cinema and Modernism.* Oxford: Blackwell, 2007.

Trotter, David. *Literature in the First Media Age.* Cambridge, MA: Harvard University Press, 2013.

Troyen, Carol. "Common Ground: The Romance of the Place for O'Keeffe and Artists of the Stieglitz Circle." In *Georgia O'Keeffe*, edited by Barbara Buhler Lynes, 35-50. Milan: Skira, 2011.

Valance, Hélène. *Nocturne: Night in American Art, 1890-1917.* Translated by Jane Marie Todd. New Haven, CT: Yale University Press, 2018.

Weaver, Mike. *William Carlos Williams: The American Background.* Cambridge: Cambridge University Press, 1971.

Weld Grimké, Angelina, *Selected Works.* Edited by Carolivia Herron. New York: Oxford University Press, 1991.

Whalan, Mark. "Jean Toomer, Technology, and Race." In *Journal of American Studies* 36, no. 3 (2002): 459-472.

Wharton, Edith, and Ogden Codman Jr. *The Decoration of Houses.* New York: Charles Scribner's Sons, 1898.

Whitaker Peters, Sarah. *Becoming O'Keeffe: The Early Years.* New York: Abbeville Press Publishers, 2001.

Widdemer, Margaret. *A Tree with a Bird in It: A Symposium of Contemporary American Poets on Being Shown a Pear-Tree On Which Sat a Grackle, With Illustrations by William Saphier.* New York: Harcourt, Brace, and Company, 1922.

Williams, William Carlos. *The Autobiography of William Carlos Williams.* New York: New Directions, 1967.

Williams, William Carlos. *The Collected Poems of William Carlos Williams: Volume I 1909-1939.* Edited by A. Walton Litz and Christopher MacGowan. Manchester, UK: Carcanet, 2000.

Williams, William Carlos. *The Collected Poems of William Carlos Williams: Volume II 1939-1962.* Edited by Christopher MacGowan. Manchester, UK: Carcanet, 2000.

Williams, William Carlos. "Good . . . For What?" *Dial*, March 1929.

Williams, William Carlos. *I Wanted to Write a Poem: The Autobiography of the Works of a Poet.* Edited by Edith Neal. New York: New Directions, 1978.

Williams, William Carlos. Letter to Marianne Moore, January 14, 1926. YCAL MSS 34, series I, box 8, folder 283. The Dial/Scofield Papers, Beinecke Rare Book and Manuscript Library, Yale University.

Williams, William Carlos. "A Note on the Art of Poetry." *Blues: A Magazine of New Rhythms*, January-February 1929.

Williams, William Carlos. *A Recognizable Image: William Carlos Williams on Art and Artists.* Edited by Bram Dijkstra. New York: New Directions, 1978.

Williams, William Carlos. *Selected Essays.* New York: Random House, 1954.

Williams, William Carlos. *The Selected Letters of William Carlos Williams.* Edited by John C. Thirlwall. New York: McDowell, Obolensky Inc., 1957.

Willis-Braithwaite, Deborah. "They Knew Their Names." In *VanDerZee Photographer, 1886-1983*, edited by Deborah Willis-Braithwaite, 8-25. New York: Harry N. Abrams Publishers and the National Portrait Gallery, 1993.

Wintz, Cary D. *Black Culture and the Harlem Renaissance.* College Station, TX: Texas A&M University Press, 1996.

Wong, Hannah W. "Powering Portraiture: Francis Picabia's *291* Mechanomorphs Revived." *American Art* 29, no. 3 (2015): 118-131.

Woroszylski, Wiktor. *The Life of Mayakovsky.* Translated by Boleslaw Taborski. London: Victor Gollancz Ltd, 1972.

Conclusion

Allen, Edward. "Nocturne: J. H. Prynne Among the Stars." In *Forms of Late Modernist Lyric*, edited by Edward Allen, 243-278. Liverpool, UK: Liverpool University Press, 2021.

Andree, Courtney. "Cripping the Pastoral: Rural Modernisms in Sylvia Townsend Warner's *The True Heart*." *Modern Fiction Studies* 65, no. 1 (2019): 12-34.

Bluemel, Kristin, and Michael McCluskey, eds. *Rural Modernity in Britain: A Critical Intervention.* Edinburgh, UK: Edinburgh University Press, 2018.

Bowen, Elizabeth. *People, Places, Things: Essays by Elizabeth Bowen.* Edited by Allan Hepburn. Edinburgh, UK: Edinburgh University Press, 2008.

City Lights Bookstore and Publishers. "A Short History of City Lights." https://citylights.com/our-story/a-short-history-of-city-lights/.

Ferlinghetti, Lawrence. *A Coney Island of the Mind: Poems.* New York: New Directions, 1958.

Ferlinghetti, Lawrence. *Poetry as Insurgent Art.* New York: New Directions, 2007.

Gunning, Tom. "Light, Motion, Cinema!: The Heritage of Loïe Fuller and Germaine Dulac." *Framework* 46, no. 1 (2005), 106-129.

Gunning, Tom. "Loïe Fuller and the Art of Motion: Body, Light, Electricity, and the Origins of Cinema." In *Camera Obscura, Camera Lucida: Essays in Honor of Annette Michelson*, edited by Richard Allen and Malcolm Turvey, 75-90. Amsterdam: Amsterdam University Press, 2003.

Jeffers, Robinson. *Selected Poetry.* New York: Random House, 1959.

Loy, Mina. *The Lost Lunar Baedeker.* Edited by Roger L. Conover. Manchester, UK: Carcanet, 1997.

Morgan, Bill. "Bookstore Tour." City Lights Bookstore and Publishers. https://citylights.com/our-story/bookstore-tour/.

Pešánek, Zdeněk. *Kineticism.* Translated by Ivan Gutierrez. Prague: Academy of Performing Arts and Kunsthalle Praha, 2021.

Pound, Ezra. *Patria Mia and the Treatise on Harmony.* London: Peter Owen Limited, 1962.

Ridge, Lola. *To the Many: Collected Early Poems*. Edited by Daniel Tobin. Stroud, UK: Little Island Press, 2020.

Ronetti, Alessandra. "'Chromo-culture': Les danses de la nature de Loïe Fuller et la force énergétique de la lumière." *Romantisme* 3, no. 193 (2021): 72-83.

Toomer, Jean. *The Collected Poems of Jean Toomer*. Edited by Robert B. Jones and Margery Toomer Latimer. Chapel Hill, NC: University of North Carolina Press, 1988.

Williams, William Carlos. *The Collected Poems of William Carlos Williams: Volume I 1909-1939*. Edited by A. Walton Litz and Christopher MacGowan. Manchester, UK: Carcanet, 2000.

Willis, Artemis. "'What the Moon is Like': Technology, Modernity, and Experience in a Late-Nineteenth-Century Astronomical Entertainment." *Early Popular Visual Culture* 15, no. 2 (2017): 175-203.

Index

Page locators in *italics* indicate figures.

Abbott, Berenice, 111-113, *112*, 169, *170*
Adorno, Theodor, 22
Altomare, Libero, 30, 90-91
Anderson, Margaret, 111-113
Apollinaire, Guillaume, 37
arc light: Balla and, 88; dislike of, 131-132; history of, 4-8, 27; Loy as, 130; in Loy's plays, 130-131; Marinetti and, 21, 72, 75-76, 86; in Milan, 83-85, 90; in Paris, 36-37; in Ridge, 184, 188
Atget, Eugène, 43, *46*, 46-47, *47*

Bachelard, Gaston, 24-25, 50
baldness, 108, 163-164, *165*, 167, 169, 246n32
Balla, Giacomo, 30, 87-89, 181
Barrie, J. M., 133
Baudelaire, Charles: and Eliot, 30, 33-36, 40-41, 50, 53; and Futurism, 79-80, 91, 102, 105-106; and Loy, 119, 122; and Stieglitz, 174
Beardsley, Aubrey, 10-12, *11*, *12*, 30, 61-66, *63*, *64*, 101
Beaton, Baba, 3
Beaton, Cecil, 1-3; *Miss Nancy Beaton as a Shooting Star*, *2*
Beaton, Nancy, 1, *2*, 3
Benjamin, Walter, 20
Bennett, Gwendolyn B., 29, 31, 205; "Street Lamps in Early Spring," 197-198
blackness/race, 31, 160, 191-199, 205, 252n120

body, 130-131; and blackness, 193-198, 205; men's, 135; of light, 161; of the city, 174, 178, 180, 182; women's, 1-2, 81-82, 121-122, 128, 197-198
Book of Home Building and Decoration (1912), 142, *143*
Bowen, Elizabeth, 200-202
Brancusi, Constantin, 31, 111-117, *112*, *115*, *116*
brilliance, 3-4, 18-20, 24; instances of, 97, 151, 156, 160, 177, 181, 184, 193-195, 201, 203-206
Brown, Henry Collins (*Book of Home Building and Decoration*), 142, *143*
Brown Lyman, Clara, 142-143
Buzzi, Paolo, 30, 89-90

cabarets, 119-123, 150, 197, 239n34
Caledoniensis, 6-7
calla lily (lamp and art), 144-145, *146*, 147, 148, *149*
Campbell, Joseph, 155
Carli, Mario, 30, 101-104
Clair de lune, 10, 13, 33-36, 75, 93, 124, 178, 219n4; "Tuons le clair de lune!!," 21, 67, 75-77, 80-83, 130. *See also* moon
Coney Island, 155, 157
Content, Marjorie, 148
Corbière, Tristan, 10, 33, 56
Cornell, Joseph, 31, 153
Corra, Bruno, 94
Covarrubias, Miguel, 148